Advanced Praise for *Sources of Light*

"*Sources of Light* does more than celebrate the breadth and particularity of the Spirit's work in local congregations. It provides a tool box for robust practices of congregational discernment. The book is an invaluable resource for preachers who want to invite congregations past insular theological cul-de-sacs and into the broad expanse of God's faithful witness. Listening and responding to that witness is the challenge and joy of our Baptist inheritance."

—Jerusha Matsen Neal, assistant professor of
Homiletics, Duke Divinity School

"For those of us who believe that local congregations are uniquely equipped by the Holy Spirit and empowered by the Risen Jesus to offer a compelling witness to God's love in this broken world, and who also know that individual congregations deeply need community with the global church in order to flourish through participation in the life of the Triune God, *Sources of Light* provides both a powerful challenge and significant resources. By inviting congregations and their leaders to a much more substantial theological practice through listening to voices and testimonies from all across Christ's church, Amy Chilton and Steve Harmon have offered us a way to see difference not as an occasion for fear, but instead an opportunity for discernment, love, and greater faithfulness."

—Paul Baxley, executive coordinator,
Cooperative Baptist Fellowship

"This book provides a stimulating introduction to a whole range of theological lenses, offering multiple starting points for an in-depth exploration as well as providing an overall 'map' of the diversity within Christ's body. It offers models of healthy theological engagement from a Baptist perspective and will be of help to anyone engaged in guiding theological practice. Every reader (and community of readers) is bound to be surprised and challenged by some unexpected source of light presented here."

—Lina Toth (Andronoviene), assistant principal
and lecturer in Practical Theology, Scottish
Baptist College, University of the West of Scotland

"This well-organized, well-focused study brings together a diverse group of scholars who address Christian and Baptist identity as a guide for congregations and individuals. These insightful essays cover a wide range of topics and issues confronting the twenty-first-century church…a timely contribution to Christian communities."

—Bill J. Leonard, founding dean and professor of Divinity emeritus,
Wake Forest University Divinity School

"The diverse voices in this book come together wonderfully to illuminate the value of taking specific communities of faith seriously as subjects of theology, even while challenging them to look beyond themselves to communities—both past and present—who both shed light and cast shadows on what it means to practice theology. The book is a splendid gift of love from Baptists to all those who care about the church, regardless of confessional leanings."

—Nancy E. Bedford, Georgia Harkness Professor of Theology,
Garrett-Evangelical Theological Seminary

PERSPECTIVES ON BAPTIST IDENTITIES

The National Association of Baptist Professors of Religion is proud to join with Mercer University Press in the creation of a new academic series. *Perspectives on Baptist Identities* will explore the rapidly evolving questions of identity that press upon those who call themselves Baptist in the twenty-first century: What does it mean to be Baptist? What does the future hold for Baptists? How does the Baptist tradition relate to the global Church and other ecclesial traditions? How does Baptist identity impact Scripture reading and Christian practice? The series hopes to generate significant scholarly research and engender fruitful and lively conver-sation among various types of Baptists and non-Baptists.

SERIES EDITORS

Dr. Adam C. English
Professor of Theology and Philosophy
Department of Christian Studies, Campbell University

Dr. Alicia Myers
Associate Professor of New Testament and Greek
Divinity School, Campbell University

PUBLISHED TITLES

Ryan Andrew Newson, *Inhabiting the World: Identity, Politics, and Theology in Radical Baptist Perspective* (2018)

Mikeal C. Parsons, *Crawford Howell Toy: The Man, the Scholar, the Teacher* (2019)

SOURCES OF LIGHT

Resources for Baptist Churches
Practicing Theology

Amy L. Chilton and Steven R. Harmon, editors

FOREWORD BY

MOLLY T. MARSHALL

For Ben,

In appreciation for much support
and encouragement in my work.

Steve Harmon

Eastertide 2020

MERCER UNIVERSITY PRESS
Macon, Georgia

MUP/ P610

© 2020 by Mercer University Press
Published by Mercer University Press
1501 Mercer University Drive
Macon, Georgia 31207
All rights reserved

30 29 28 27 26 25 24 23 22 21   9 8 7 6 5 4 3 2 1

Books published by Mercer University Press are printed on acid-free paper that
meets the requirements of the American National Standard for Information
Sciences—Permanence of Paper for Printed Library Materials.

Printed and bound in the United States.

This book is set in Adobe Garamond Pro.

Cover/jacket design by Burt&Burt

ISBN   978-0-88146-771-0
Cataloging-in-Publication Data is available from the Library of Congress

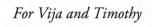

For Vija and Timothy

Contents

Part II
LIGHT FROM OUR LIFE-IN-COMMUNITY

Acknowledgments

Theology practiced in, with, and for the church is necessarily a communal endeavor—a truth that our work on this book has reinforced. In addition to the community of theological colleagues who have contributed chapters to this book, to whom we acknowledge our deep gratitude, many other people have provided illumination for our labors through their advice, encouragement, and support. We are grateful to the National Association of Baptist Professors of Religion for its publishing program that includes the Perspectives on Baptist Identities series in which this volume appears. Series editors Adam C. English and Alicia D. Myers recognized the merits of this project and provided wise guidance that transformed our original proposal into a much better book. Mercer University Press Director Marc Jolley and his staff have helpfully answered our occasional questions and assisted us in many other ways at various stages in the publication process. Inspired by a Facebook post in which former NABPR President Eileen Campbell-Reed observed that "commentary on the Bible written by white males...often skews the interpretations uncritically from the perspective of the powerful, privileged, dominant culture" and that therefore "we need to read with others from various margins (their centers and not our own) in order to see more," we issued a social media crowdsourcing appeal to our colleagues to suggest commentary resources for reading Scripture along with others from various social locations. Dalen Jackson did us the favor of collating their numerous and helpful responses, which have been incorporated into a commentary bibliography at the conclusion of our final chapter. Discussions with our students at Fuller Theological Seminary, Azusa Pacific University, Wingate University, and Gardner-Webb University School of Divinity during the time of our work on this project have sharpened the focus and application of our work. Students in two Christian Theology courses at Gardner-Webb read drafts of our introductory chapter and provided useful feedback from the perspective of our intended readership in sessions of classes taught by Steve in which Amy delivered guest lectures.

I (Amy) am thankful for Steve (colleague, friend, and fellow adoptive parent), who proposed this book to me at just the right time and for his patience as life has intervened on numerous occasions—including my move from coast to coast and transition to teaching in the Department of Religion and Philosophy at Wingate University. His initial vision for this book and interest in sharing its journey with me gave me space to see the hope and passion that our many friends and colleagues, whose work is represented in these pages, have for the church. During this complex season in our nation, our seminaries, and our churches, this was no small gift. I hope the many faith communities in which I have "done" theology might see themselves in my portions of this work. Grace Baptist Church in Tacoma, Washington, where I served as an associate pastor alongside Rev. Cathy Kernen from 2005 through 2010, opened their lives and pulpit to me as a seminary student seeking her prophetic voice and helped navigate my transition into motherhood and academic ministry. My mentors at Fuller Theological Seminary, Veli-Matti Kärkkäinen and Nancey Murphy, as well as my many theology and ethics colleagues (most notably Rebecca Horner Shenton, Ryan Andrew Newson, and Andrew C. Wright), contributed in numerous ways to my theological journey of unraveling a bit more of the knot between our embodied ways of faith life together and the words we use to name and speak of God. Finally, my gratitude goes to my family, who has celebrated and suffered the theologian life alongside me. My mother, Mary Chilton, has journeyed up and down the West Coast and across the country to keep my home fires burning—even driving a hybrid through Los Angeles traffic!—so I could conference, teach, and write, while my father, Stan Chilton, kept their home fires burning in her absence. My journey to theology was a journey of dreaming dreams, prophesying, and trusting that Pentecost's fires had fallen even on me, a journey that has become in no small part also about making space for my own daughter's dreams and prophetic utterances. Vija, who traveled across oceans with me and whose elementary years were spent in seminary student housing supping with my theology professors (most notably Charlie and Pam Scalise) and playing leapfrog with Glen Stassen on the Fuller lawn, shines her own brilliant light on the church. My greatest prayer for this work, and all work to which I set my hand, is that my labors may help create a wider space in which Pentecost's promise might fall on her and in which her own voice might bravely and freely join this symphony we call church.

I (Steve) want to express my gratitude to Amy for her willingness to be my co-editor and co-author. It is primarily because of her contributions that this is an infinitely better project than the one I began imagining shortly after the publication of my book *Baptist Identity and the Ecumenical Future* in 2016. My own written contributions to it are greatly improved because of her keen editorial instincts for clear communication (thanks to which my tendency to write sentences of "Pauline" length and complexity has been remedied!). A "Writing Across the Curriculum" retreat sponsored by the Center for Excellence in Teaching and Learning at Gardner-Webb University provided a weekend in the beautiful North Carolina mountains with time for writing an early draft of chapter 24 and an opportunity to discuss our book-in-progress with fellow retreat participants. A "mini-sabbatical" course load reduction during the Spring 2019 semester awarded by the Gardner-Webb University Faculty Development and Improvement of Instruction Committee, with the support of Provost Ben Leslie, my School of Divinity Dean Robert Canoy, and my Associate Dean Gerald Keown, provided time for attention to the final stages of editorial work on this book amidst other writing projects. My local church community, the First Baptist Church of Forest City, North Carolina, is my specific community of reference for doing theology in, with, and for the church, and in that connection my church family has shaped this book in significant ways. One of its ministers, my wife Kheresa—who read drafts of some of the chapters of this book during its development over the past two years—is my daily theological conversation partner. Her weekly work in both a congregational setting and an institution of theological education means that our conversations frequently involve the intersection of the church and the theological academy that serves it. My own intentions for this book are inseparable from this aspect of our shared life. Kheresa and my son Timothy are daily reminders to me that theology matters in relation to what matters most in life, and their love sustains my own theological work. Our mutual love forms a transracial adoptive family, and this dimension of our family life in particular convinces me that the theology expressed in the pages of this book matters.

We dedicate this book to Amy's daughter Vija and Steve's son Timothy, who were born in the same year (in India and South Korea, respectively) and coincidentally were adopted through the same American international adoption agency. They have made our lives necessarily inter-contextual, and their own voices have shaped us. May these faithful contributions help form a more faithful church where their voices and the voices of the communities that birthed them might be heard as part of the church's global symphony, that the world they will inhabit might be transformed through the reconciling love of God.

Charlotte, North Carolina and Boiling Springs, North Carolina
Easter 2019

MERCER UNIVERSITY PRESS

Endowed by

TOM WATSON BROWN
and
THE WATSON-BROWN FOUNDATION, INC.

Foreword

Molly T. Marshall

This is truly a remarkable book. Refracted through many lenses, *Sources of Light* offers a luminous vision of how the church can more fully practice its faith under the rule of Christ, guided by the Spirit. It is forthright in its awakening to the limitation and provisionality of many of the apertures employed when Baptist communities gather, and it seeks to correct this myopia as it contends for full participation in the communion of the Triune God. The goal is to provide resources for Baptist churches practicing theology, and the book's contributions are expansive and generative.

The imprint of key Baptist thinkers is palpable in these chapters. James Wm. McClendon, Jr. and Paul Fiddes, in particular, have shaped the next generation of theologians, as have wider ecumenical conversations. Clearly, these writers, "lit from within," as Rilke puts it, know both their heritage and long for deeper immersion in the larger stream of faithful Christian witness, the true catholicity of the church.

Nothing less than a reformation is occurring in these learned essays as scholar-practitioners draw Baptists toward a more traditional identity within the larger Body of Christ. Eager to engage sources that a simple biblicism ignores, the authors provide illumination that will strengthen the exercise of Baptist freedom in thoughtful appropriation of the larger intellectual and liturgical heritage of the Church. Acknowledging that separatism, individualism, and insularity have characterized much of Baptist identity, the writers draw from the deep well of Scripture, tradition, saints of yore, confessional statements, ecumenism, interreligious dialogue, and experimental communities to offer a collaborative theology that is tested in its discrete contexts. Social location is a key interpretive framework, as these scholars confess.

Light breaks through the interstices between gender, sexuality, race, class, and diasporic experience, and representatives of varied wings of the Baptist family seek to add their enlightening perspectives about what God is beckoning in our time. One sees clearly the generational shifts as fresh voices articulate a more inclusive, less white, non-patriarchal understanding of the intersectionality of all interpreters of the faith. This book refuses to shutter light from neglected sources. Welcoming queer voices, persons of differing abilities, and even the ways creation speaks comprises a more holistic theological vision for our time.

According to the editors, Amy Chilton and Steven Harmon, the 2016 U.S. election was an inflection point for the meaning of Christian identity. The preponderance of conservative Christians elected a person whose policies trounce key virtues of caring for vulnerable people and the vulnerable earth. How had churches failed to form these voters toward a more compassionate and humble theological vision? How had churches (many of them Baptist) moved away from being under the rule of Christ to being blinded by a vision of white supremacy, nationalism, American exceptionalism, and incivility? Clearly, congregations require a deeper grounding that comes from intentional teaching and reflection on the practice of theology.

Readers will find clear guidance and imaginative possibilities as they tune the voices, practice "converted listening" (in the words of Chilton and Harmon), and filter the inbreaking light found in this collection. Regarding the church as the contextualized theologizing community requires humility and trust. Too often theologians pontificate about ecclesial matters as an abstraction; however, one senses the deep engagement of these writers in their local communities and their appreciation of the promise of theological thinking that can occur.

I commend this venture in constructive theology. Whether a seminarian, working pastor, or theological educator, *Sources of Light* will assist you in dispelling shadows of unexamined assumptions and finding pathways that bring you toward the brightness of God's vision of participation in the perichoretic movement of the divine life.

1

Introduction:
Imagining Radical Baptist Practices
of Local Church Theology

Steven R. Harmon and Amy L. Chilton

From 2011 through the end of 2014, I (Steve) worked on writing a book published in 2016 under the title *Baptist Identity and the Ecumenical Future: Story, Tradition, and the Recovery of Community*.[1] One chapter of that book described the local practice of theology by Baptist communities as an exercise of "Free Church magisterium."[2] I argued that in addition to the Roman Catholic magisterium (its authoritative teaching office) and its functional equivalents in Eastern Orthodoxy and Magisterial Protestantism, there is a Free Church practice of magisterium which localizes teaching authority in the gathered congregation that gives attention to doctrine in the sense of "a church teaching as she must teach if she is to be the church here and now."[3] I envisioned this Free Church magisterium as a minister-facilitated practice of theology by the members of local church communities seeking the guidance of the Spirit in their efforts to imagine what it will look like to follow Christ in their context. In facilitating this local practice of theology, pastors help the congregation to hear discerningly voices from elsewhere in the whole church that provide resources for bringing congregational life more fully under the rule of Christ, which I identified in terms of this nine-fold typology: (1) ancient creeds that stem from the early church's rule of faith; (2) historic Reformation confessions and catechisms, along with more recent confessional statements from various denominations; (3) the confessions of the Baptist tradition; (4) Catholic magisterial teaching; (5) the liturgical texts of other traditions; (6) the reports and agreed statements of bilateral and multilateral ecumenical dialogues, at both the national and international levels; (7) the contextual theologies that emerge from social loca-

---

[1] Harmon, *Baptist Identity and the Ecumenical Future*.

[2] Harmon, *Baptist Identity and the Ecumenical Future*, chapter 7, "Receiving the Gift of Magisterium," 165-88. This proposal was influenced by the ecumenical paradigm of "receptive ecumenism" that will receive attention in chapter 23 of the present book.

[3] McClendon, *Systematic Theology*, vol. 2, *Doctrine*, 23-24.

tions other than the context of the local Baptist church engaged in this practice of theology;[4] (8) ecclesial resolutions on ethical issues adopted by diverse church bodies; and (9) the lived Christian lives of the saints.[5]

Meanwhile I (Amy) had been engaged with constructing an account of theology as a living practice of the church as a first step in trying to move evangelicals beyond their experience-aversion and toward an inter-contextual practice of theology involving the discernment of one's own local theology in dialogue with other locally discerned theologies. This account drew on Baptist theologian James Wm. McClendon, Jr.'s imagining of theology as the hospitable space in which people from diverse "localities" humanely engage one another in mutually informative dialogue and Catholic liberation theologian Jon Sobrino's concept of "christopraxis" as a means of locating Christology within communities that follow Christ. I developed this perspective on the practice of inter-contextual theological dialogue in a doctoral dissertation on "Practiced Theological Diversity" and in a series of journal articles.[6] In May 2016 I served as a member of a panel of theologians and historians of Christianity affiliated with the National Association of Baptist Professors of Religion and the Baptist History and Heritage Society who presented responses to Steve's book *Baptist Identity and the Ecumenical Future* during joint annual meetings of the two organizations at Baylor University in Waco, Texas.[7] During the panel session Courtney Pace (a contributor of one of the chapters in

---

[4] Regarding these I wrote: "It is especially important that these theologies be heard and not silenced, for they are a necessary check on the blind spots that may come from the social location of our own community when it is not intentionally interdependent with the global church. For Baptist communities in North America and Europe, this might mean deliberately seeking out and reading the theologies of liberation that emerge not only in Latin America but in many other contexts where oppression is a reality the practices of the church must address; black theology in its American and African developments; the various efforts by Asian theologians to contextualize the faith in non-Western cultures; feminist, womanist, and *mujerista* theologies; and the growing body of theological literature by Christians whose sexual orientations likewise represent differing social locations within which they seek to bring their life under the lordship of Christ. These voices from other social locations must also be weighed, but unless a community hears them and refrains from silencing them, its capacity for weighing its own voices will be diminished" (Harmon, *Baptist Identity and the Ecumenical Future*, 186).

[5] Harmon, *Baptist Identity and the Ecumenical Future*, 180-88.

[6] Chilton, "Practiced Theological Diversity"; idem, "Transformed by the Spirit"; idem, "Unsettling Conversations"; idem, "How Do I Speak of God from This Place?"

[7] Revised versions of these responses were published along with Harmon's response to the panel in a book symposium issue of the *Pacific Journal of Baptist Research* (11, no. 2 [November 2016]) edited by Adam C. English: Wilhite, "Baptists, Catholicity, and Visible Unity"; Chilton, "Response to Steven R. Harmon's *Baptist Identity and the Ecumenical Future*"; Pace, "Baptists, Catholicity, and Missing Voices"; Smith, "Description, Prescription, and the Ecumenical Possibilities of Baptist Identity"; Harmon, "Locating the Unity of Christ's Rule."

the present book) and I both proposed possibilities for expanding the range of resources in Steve's typology of the sources of light from the whole church that can help Baptist churches bring their congregational life more fully under the rule of Christ in their local practice of theology.[8]

We (Steve and Amy) are convinced that embedded in the congregational ecclesiology of the Baptist tradition are unexplored openings to resources distributed throughout the whole church that can equip local Baptist churches for the theological task of discerning what it means to bring their life together under the rule of Christ in their own contexts. Rooted in an ecumenical perspective on Baptist identity and employing the methodology of inter-contextual theological dialogue, and thus representing the confluence of complementary dimensions of our individual areas of expertise and interests as theologians, this book is a collaborative attempt to imagine how Baptist communities might draw more intentionally on the resources of the whole church in our congregational practice of theology.

1. Theology as a Baptist Local Church Practice

Baptist communities have engaged in theology as a local church practice since the 1609 foundation by John Smyth and Thomas Helwys in Amsterdam of the first Baptist congregation, for its members would "confer upon" the sense of the biblical text read and proclaimed in their gatherings.[9] Baptist theologians have offered various accounts of the theological work that local Baptist churches do when they come together to discern the mind of Christ regarding how they might bring their life together more fully under Christ's rule in a core practice of their "gathering church" ecclesiology rooted biblically in Matt. 18:20 ("For where two or three are gathered in my name, I am there among them").[10] British Baptist theologian Paul Fiddes envisions the local "church meeting" as a search for the mind of Christ about what it means to embody the way of Jesus in a particular time and place:

---

[8] Pace, "Baptists, Catholicity, and Missing Voices"; Chilton, "Response to Steven R. Harmon's *Baptist Identity and the Ecumenical Future*."

[9] A description of worship in the Smyth-Helwys congregation in Amsterdam in 1609 is provided by a letter from two of its members, Hugh and Anne Broadheade, quoted in Burrage, *Early English Dissenters in the Light of Recent Research*, 2:176-77: "The order of the worship and government of our church is [this]: we begin with a prayer, [and] after reading some one or two chapters of the Bible give the sense thereof, and confer upon the same; that done we lay aside our books, and after a solemn prayer [is] made by the speaker, he propounds some text out of the Scripture, and prophecies out of the same, by the space of one hour, or three-quarters of an hour" [spelling and punctuation modernized].

[10] All Scripture quotations in this book are from the New Revised Standard Version Bible, © 1989 by Division of Christian Education of the National Council of the Churches of Christ in the United States of America. Used by permission. All rights reserved.

Upon the whole people in covenant there lies the responsibility of finding a common mind, of coming to an agreement about the way of Christ for them in life, worship and mission. But they cannot do so unless they use the resources that God has given them, and among those resources are the pastor, the deacons and (if they have them) the elders....The aim is to search for consent about the mind of Christ, and so people should be sensitive to the voices behind the votes, listening to them according to the weight of their experience and insight.[11]

Several British Baptist theologians including Fiddes have explored this "search for consent about the mind of Christ" in terms of a practice of "congregational hermeneutics" in a series of consultations on "Baptists Doing Theology in Context" and in ensuing publications.[12] Fiddes applies this local church practice of theology also to the interdependence of local congregations with translocal associations of Baptist churches and with ecumenical councils and commissions, insisting that "[s]ince the same rule of Christ can be experienced in assemblies of churches together, there is also the basis here for Baptist associational life, and indeed for participating in ecumenical clusters."[13]

2. Encountering the Spirit's Illumination

This book draws its main title *Sources of Light* from an image employed by another characterization of the local practice of theology by Baptist churches. In 1997 a group of six Baptist theologians in the United States that included James Wm. McClendon, Jr. proposed a re-envisioning of Baptist identity beyond its modern American polarized distortions of freedom, inviting their fellow Baptists to join them in "resisting all destructive ideologies that subvert the gospel." The first of their five affirmations regarding the nature of freedom, faithfulness, and community was this:

> We affirm Bible Study in reading communities rather than relying on private interpretation or supposed 'scientific' objectivity....We thus affirm an open and orderly process whereby faithful communities deliberate together over the Scriptures with sisters and brothers of the faith, excluding no light from any source. When all exercise their gifts and callings, when every voice is heard and weighed, when no one is silenced or privileged, the Spirit leads

---

[11] Fiddes, *Tracks and Traces*, 86.

[12] Fiddes, Haymes, Kidd, and Quicke, *Doing Theology in a Baptist Way*; Fiddes, ed., *Under the Rule of Christ*.

[13] Fiddes, *Tracks and Traces*, 6.

communities to read wisely and to practice faithfully the direction of the gospel.[14]

In this account of the local practice of theology, Baptist churches are "reading communities" seeking pneumatological guidance in their reading and performance of the Scriptures. The framers of "Re-Envisioning Baptist Identity" employ two images for the mediation of this guidance: *voices* through which the Spirit helps us *hear* and *sources of light* through which the Spirit helps us *see*.

We find both the aural and visual images helpful and make use of both in this book. It could be objected that "voices" which are "heard" can imply passivity on the part of the hearing community rather than active engagement in dialogue and can suggest a patronizing stance of an "insider" community that invites the perspectives of "others" as a means of enriching the discourse of a community to which the "others" nevertheless remain "outsiders" (though this is not the intent behind the use of the image in "Re-Envisioning Baptist Identity"). While recognizing that the visual image also has limitations in that it can suggest an emphasis on active practices that sometimes resist a stance of humble receptivity,[15] we have chosen "sources of light" as a core metaphor for the mediation by the whole church of the illuminating work of the Spirit that helps the local church see the way it must walk as a community of fellow travelers on the way of Jesus Christ, whose rule among them draws them ever more deeply to participate in the communion of the Triune God so that they may offer the gift of this Trinitarian communion to a fractured world.[16] This metaphor also has historic connections with the much-quoted words attributed to English Separatist John Robinson (1575/76-1625) regarding "fresh light that may yet break forth from the Word."[17] The concluding

---

[14] Broadway, Freeman, Harvey, McClendon, Newman, and Thompson, "Re-Envisioning Baptist Identity." It should be noted that this account of Baptist identity is contested by some who inhabit the same Baptist context as the authors of "Re-Envisioning Baptist Identity"; see, e.g., Shurden, "The Baptist Identity and the Baptist Manifesto," in idem, *Not an Easy Journey*, 23-47. It should be noted that not all contributors to this book would identify with "Re-Envisioning Baptist Identity" as an expression of their sense of Baptist identity, and that embracing it is by no means necessary for taking up the proposals of this book.

[15] Cf. Newson, *Inhabiting the World*, 19-26.

[16] Cf. World Council of Churches, *The Church*, § 1 (p. 5): "The Church, as the body of Christ, acts by the power of the Holy Spirit to continue his life-giving mission in prophetic and compassionate ministry and so participates in God's work of healing a broken world. Communion, whose source is the very life of the Holy Trinity, is both the gift by which the Church lives and, at the same time, the gift that God calls the Church to offer to a wounded and divided humanity in hope of reconciliation and healing."

[17] Robinson's address was recounted by Edward Winslow (1595-1655) in *Hypocrisie Unmasked*. As scholarship on Robinson has noted, however, the quotation in question may be apocryphal; so, e.g., George, *John Robinson and the English Separatist Tradition*, vii.

chapter will return to the aural image and connect it to the visual image by exploring the practice of listening as a means by which the Spirit helps us not only to hear what the Spirit is saying to us but also to see what the Spirit is showing us. The second stanza of the hymn "Open My Eyes, That I May See" by nineteenth-century Baptist hymn writer Clara H. Scott makes a similar connection between the aural and visual images associated with this work of the Spirit: "Open my ears, illumine me, Spirit divine!"[18]

3. Resources for Churches Practicing Theology: Ecclesial Life-in-Context

This book urges local Baptist communities in their practice of theology to take on the discipline of being formed by the faith witness of others through seeking out diverse sources of this "fresh light that may yet break forth from the Word"—not merely as a preface to the practice of theology, but as a theological practice. Some of these sources of light are distinctively shaped by the contexts in which the church and its members seek to live under Christ's rule.[19] Part One: Light from Our Life-in-Context introduces these, beginning with my (Amy's) exploration in chapter 2 of the resources found in contexts in which a struggle for the liberation of the oppressed is taking place. I will illustrate these resources by giving particular attention to the liberation theology of Jon Sobrino, in whose work may be recognized theological tools that are already present in the Baptist tradition and whose contextual concern for the liberation of the oppressed serves as an introduction to recurrent themes in some of the contextual theologies treated in subsequent chapters of this portion of the book.

The next chapters in Part One treat various contextually-rooted resources for the local practice of inter-contextual theology. Some of these resources are rooted in contexts of ethnic identity. Noel Leo Erskine (chapter 3) introduces notable expressions of black theology and their contributions to Baptist communities practicing theology. Nora O. Lozano (chapter 4) surveys the resources offered by Hispanic/Latina theologies, giving particular attention to the emerging theologies that attend to the experiences of Latina women in differing particular social and ecclesial locations. Atola Longkumer (chapter 5) introduces the varied efforts of Asian theologians to contextualize the faith in non-Western cultures, highlighting along

---

[18] Clara H. Scott, "Open My Eyes, That I May See" (1895).

[19] Cf. Karl Barth's insistence on receiving "the confession of others…who are beside [us] in the church" as a precondition for the practice of theology (*Church Dogmatics*, I/2:589), a practice Barth envisioned as the responsibility of the whole church, including "congregation members" who "are co-responsible to see to it that the theology of the professors and pastors be a good one and not a bad one (idem, *God in Action*, 56-57).

the way the light that women's increasingly prominent participation in local Christianities offers to the church in those contexts and elsewhere. Mikael N. Broadway (chapter 6) offers a critical and autobiographical account of "whiteness" as a social location that, while a fiction as a racial classification of people, represents a standpoint for doing theology that has all too often been blind to its own Euro-American social locatedness while treating other self-consciously socially located theologies in terms of their difference from a supposedly neutral theology thought to transcend social location.[20] What Broadway describes as an "awakening" from these fictions of whiteness in theology is a necessary dimension of theology as an intentionally inter-contextual practice.[21]

Other chapters in Part One relate to the contextual locations of gender and sexual orientation. Courtney Pace (chapter 7) explores how the lived religious experiences of women from the sixteenth-century Reformation through the present may serve as resources from the whole church to be welcomed into local church conversations about the faith and practice of the community. Susan M. Shaw (chapter 8) not only calls attention to the resources offered by feminist theologies, both from the larger church and from within the Baptist tradition, for the local practice of theology; she also makes a compelling case for their coherence with historic Baptist emphases. Khalia J. Williams (chapter 9) explores more fully a theological resource introduced in chapter 3 in relation to black theologies and in chapter 8 in relation to feminist theologies: womanist theology, which gives voice to the distinctive theological insights of black women, many of whom have been Baptist theologians themselves. Cody J. Sanders (chapter 10) turns to LGBTQ+ voices in the church as sources of light that must not be excluded by the church seeking to bring its life together under the rule of Christ. Many Baptist congregations, associations, and

---

[20] In an interview conducted by Kristopher Norris, the ethicist Stanley Hauerwas "suggested that the reason one of his former white students, Mikael Broadway, is able to write about race and even teach in a historically black seminary is because of his long-time commitment to a black congregation" (Norris, "Witnessing Whiteness in the Ethics of Hauerwas," 120, citing Hauerwas, "Interview with Kristopher Norris").

[21] As the editors of this book, we acknowledge our white identity and that we are hosting this conversation by means of the publishing program of the National Association of Baptist Professors of Religion, historically a predominantly white academic organization. Baptist communities in North America and beyond, however, represent a diversity of predominating ethnic identities. Without Broadway's contribution of chapter 6, our commendation of a diachronic engagement of resources in the Christian tradition could suggest the false notion of a "neutral" theology that transcends social locatedness. Furthermore, apart from Broadway's chapter, our insistence that we pay heed synchronically to such "other" socially located sources of light as black, Asian, and Latin@ theologies could reinforce an insider/outsider discourse in which the "outsider" voices serve to enrich a supposedly neutral theology articulated by white voices and received as normative by predominantly white congregations.

unions have engaged in theological conversations *about* LGBTQ+ people and the extent of their inclusion in the life of the church, but LGBTQ+ *voices* have not often been heard without being silenced in these discussions. Sanders therefore encourages Baptist churches to welcome to the conversation both the faith stories of LGBTQ+ people and the growing body of theological literature by Christians whose gender identities and sexual orientations represent distinctive social locations of Christian faith and practice.

Yet other chapters in Part One address contextual circumstances in which Christians in a variety of contexts live beyond the contexts explored in the previous chapters. The nature of global Christianity is increasingly shaped by Christian participation in the phenomenon of diaspora, as refugees and as immigrants who form and contribute to church communities in their new places of residence. May May Latt (chapter 11) explores the contributions that refugees and immigrants offer to local church conversations about what embodying the biblical story in their time and place entails, illustrated through a diasporic reading of passages in the book of Esther. Jason D. Whitt (chapter 12) gives attention to the ways that people with disabilities often serve as sources of light for Baptist congregations in and through their disabilities as they worship and serve, helping Baptist communities to expand aspects of their soteriology and ecclesiology in the process.

The global church exists in a world of religious plurality. The chapters of this book described thus far focus on resources for the practice of theology by local Baptist communities that are ecumenical in the sense of intra-Christian dialogue with the theological diversity of the global church, but interreligious dialogue also offers voices to be heard and weighed and not silenced if no light is to be excluded from any source. Raimundo C. Barreto, Jr. (chapter 13) explores the relevance of dialogue with adherents of non-Christian religious traditions, who inhabit along with Christians the world God hopes to reconcile and heal, for the efforts of local Baptist churches to bring their life together and their life toward their world under the rule of Christ.

While the focus of this book is on what local churches can learn about the mind of Christ through the voices of people created in the image of God, Scripture portrays creation itself as having a voice, "telling the glory of God" (Ps. 19:1-4). Yet impacted by the actions of sinful humanity, creation also speaks with another voice, "groaning in labor pains" in expectation of a liberation and redemption wrought by the Spirit (Rom. 8:19-23). Rebecca Horner Shenton (chapter 14) imagines what it might mean for congregations to attend not only to this voice but also to voices of eco-theologians, the scientific community, and the environmental movement as sources of light, suggesting practices by which they may respond to the current ecological crisis and the light the Spirit shines upon it by participating in the Spirit's creation-healing work.

4. Resources for Churches Practicing Theology:
Ecclesial Life-in-Community

The chapters in Part Two: Light from Our Life-in-Community explore as sources of light various expressions of the church's efforts to bring its life *together* under the rule of Christ. Some of the communal voices engaged in these ongoing ecclesial efforts are contemporary, while others speak from the Christian past. Baptists have had reservations about privileging the confessions of others who preceded them in the church[22] in the form of creeds and confessions employed as exclusionary tests of faith. Yet Curtis W. Freeman (chapter 15) contends that when the ancient creeds are freely confessed by un-coerced consciences as an expression of Baptist freedom to follow the leadership of the Spirit in bringing their ecclesial life under the rule of Christ, they can form Baptist congregations in the church's faith in the Triune God and in the church's practices of worship, work, and witness that embed and enact this faith. While women have significantly shaped the church's historical journey in the "Great Tradition" that included these ancient confessions, the narration of this history has tended to feature male protagonists and subplots involving ecclesial institutions and movements led by men, with the contributions of women sometimes mentioned as an afterthought. Yet the confession of others before us in the pre-Reformation church included significant women's voices, from Thecla in the second century to Catherine of Genoa in the fifteenth. Kate Hanch (chapter 16) contemplates the contributions made by these voices, using the English late medieval mystic Julian of Norwich as a test case for how they might enlighten Baptist efforts to read the Bible and practice theology together.

Some Baptist confessions of faith from the seventeenth century reflect a hearing and weighing not only of confessional voices of the ancient ecumenical creeds but also of the confessions of the Baptists' Mennonite, Reformed, and Anglican ecclesial neighbors, echoing and even incorporating passages from them. Rady Roldán-Figeroa (chapter 17) shows how contemporary Baptist communities might learn from the efforts of other churches in the Magisterial Protestant traditions to teach what they must teach to be the church here and now in our own practice of theology: in particular, how we might confess the faith against populist authoritarianism. Because the pilgrim character of Baptist communities makes them reluctant to regard even their own confessions of faith as definitive, they have felt themselves free to issue new confessions with comparatively great frequency. Stephen R. Holmes (chapter 18) explores how knowing what their own confessional voices

---

[22] Echoing Barth, *Church Dogmatics*, I/2: 589, who regarded the hearing of "the confession of others who were before me in the Church" as a precondition for the practice of theology along with the hearing of "the confession of others…who are beside [us] in the church."

have said will enable Baptist congregations not only to confess their faith afresh but also to listen to voices beyond the Baptist tradition with discerning openness.

Coleman Fannin (chapter 19) contends that the communally crafted proposals of Catholic magisterial teaching that include the *Catechism of the Catholic Church*, the documents of Vatican II, papal encyclicals, and letters and statements issued by conferences of bishops such as the United States Conference of Catholic Bishops have the capacity for transcending the subjectivity of the theological constructions and moral judgments of individual theologians and ethicists, and ought to be weighed accordingly by Baptists—even if such weighing results in heavily qualified reception. The same might be said of various types of ecclesial resolutions on ethical issues that are issued by Christian world communions, national denominational organizations, and regional conferences as expressions of ecclesial community that are seeking to bring their churches under the rule of Christ. Myles Werntz (chapter 20) engages these potential sources of light for ecclesial moral discernment in a manner consistent with Baptist ecclesiology: by attending first to the congregational patterns and practices of moral deliberation that constitute distinctively Baptist resources for navigating moral disagreement.

This book's identification of voices to be heard and weighed and not silenced in the theological work of local churches is perhaps disproportionately weighted toward texts. But the local church that practices theology in dialogue with the whole church is comprised primarily of people who seek to embody the way of Jesus Christ rather than the theological texts that very few of them produce or read. Derek C. Hatch (chapter 21) engages the church's practices of identifying saintly examples of the Christian life and explores their significance for the theological work of local Baptist communities.

Some of the most enduringly formative sources of guidance for the church in bringing its faith and practice under the rule of Christ are the patterns and practices of worship that have formed the Christian identities of the faithful. As Baptists exercise their freedom as a communion without a mandated liturgy to enrich their worship by incorporating faith-forming patterns and practices of worship from other traditions into their own liturgical life, they can receive much helpful guidance from the churches that have engaged in communal deliberation about the liturgies that will best serve their communions, shaped by the "Liturgical Movement" that began in the mid-twentieth century. Philip E. Thompson (chapter 22) engages the fruit of the Liturgical Movement as valuable resources to be heard and weighed by Baptist congregations in light of the liturgical insights that belong to the Baptist tradition as we seek the Spirit's guidance in the ordering of our worship of the God made known in Jesus Christ. The liturgical freedom of Baptist communities also means that our liturgical renewal may be facilitated not only through reception of patterns and practices of worship from churches with institutionally traditioned forms of worship, but also through openness to new forms of liturgical experimentation explored by Jennifer W. Davidson (chapter 23).

A joint commission of the delegations to a bilateral or multilateral ecumenical dialogue possesses ecclesiality as a community of persons who represent their churches in collaboratively seeking to bring what their churches teach under the Lordship of Christ. In chapter 24 I (Steve) suggest how the developments of ecumenical convergence in faith and order may serve as resources for Baptist churches in discerning the mind of Christ regarding what they teach internally as Christian faith and faithfulness and how they should relate to other expressions of church, locally and globally.

In the concluding chapter we (Amy and Steve) make concrete recommendations for drawing these resources rooted in diverse contexts into constructive conversation with one another in the context of the local congregation, so that its members exclude no light from any of these sources, hearing and weighing and not silencing these voices as they do the theological work necessary to their formation as a community under Christ's rule, participating in the communion of the Triune God and offering the gift of this communion to the world.

5. Practicing Theology with the Whole Church for the Sake of the Whole World

This book began to take shape in the aftermath of the 2016 U.S. presidential election, which arguably revealed an American church not fully under the rule of Christ, diminished in its participation in Trinitarian communion and thereby diminished in its capacity for offering this communion as a gift to the world.[23] What it revealed was not primarily any contribution that various American expressions of the church may have made to the outcome of the election. Rather, the 2016 election cycle and its aftermath exposed the churches' longstanding failures in forming their members into communities capable of Christ-following cruciform practices of caring for vulnerable people and a vulnerable earth in resistance to the spirit of the age, of offering the Triune God's gift of communion to a fractured world. Baptist theologian and ethicist Myles Werntz, a contributor to this volume, offered this nonpartisan assessment of what the election was revealing about the church a month prior to Election Day:

> We have been shown to be far more susceptible to promises of power and influence than we hoped. We have been shown to be more informed by party lines, which grind the meat of the gospel down to gristle and fat, than by

---

[23] Echoing again the language of World Council of Churches, *The Church*, § 1 (p. 5) quoted in a previous note.

a gospel that is comprehensive in nature and is not contained in full by any platform. We have been shown we are a people far more interested in our self-interests than in our neighbors. And we have been shown we are willing to divide ourselves en masse from other Christians for the sake of donkeys and elephants who never will love us back.[24]

Another Baptist theologian, Barry Harvey, underscores the urgency of congregational formation in the midst of such circumstances in his book drawing on the thought of Dietrich Bonhoeffer as a resource that can help the church meet its current challenges. Harvey contrasts the tragedy of Bonhoeffer's association with the failed conspiracy to assassinate Hitler, lacking the strength of a church community sufficiently formed in deeply Christian convictions and practices to be able to offer other forms of resistance, with the response of deeply formed members of the Reformed congregation in Le Chambon-sur-Lignon to pastor André Trocmé's charge to resist the Nazi regime in Vichy France by hiding Jews and other refugees sought by the authorities, ultimately saving between 2,500 and 5,000 lives. This resistance "grew out of a distinctive pattern of life together that had been formed by the common life and language of a community over several generations."[25]

There have been Baptists who likewise have been sufficiently formed in the convictions and practices of Trinitarian communion that mark life under Christ's rule to have the capacity for engaging in cruciform acts of solidarity with and ministry to those on the margins, such as the American Baptist home missionaries who joined the Japanese Americans they served in the internment camps created by Executive Order 9066 in 1942[26] and the Baptist peacemakers throughout Baptist history profiled by Baptist historian Paul Dekar.[27] The goal of this book is to encourage the formation of more Baptists in the convictions and practices that will help them do likewise through pointing Baptist ministers and theological students, as well as their theological educators, to the sources of light found in the whole church through which Baptists congregations may receive the illumination of the Spirit necessary for this urgently needed formation.

---

[24] Werntz, "The Revelatory Election for U.S. Churches."

[25] Harvey, *Taking Hold of the Real*, 289. Harvey treats the stories of Bonhoeffer and Trocmé in relation to one another in chapter 9, "A Tale of Two Pastors," 269-302.

[26] Allen, "American Baptist Leaders Recall 'Other Side' of Pearl Harbor."

[27] Dekar, *For the Healing of the Nations: Baptist Peacemakers.*

Part I

LIGHT FROM OUR LIFE-IN-CONTEXT

2

Light from Liberation Theologies

Amy L. Chilton

My first introduction to liberation theology was at the direction of a seminary theology professor. Although not on the faculty of a Baptist seminary, he is a Baptist, and I was early in my "seminary conversion" to the American Baptist Churches (although I had always been a "baptist," having been initially called, educated, and ordained in the Stone-Campbell movement).[1] With some trepidation, I embarked on what would become for me an ongoing journey: for while the communism scare was before my time of cognizance, I was well aware that the liberation theologians were accused of being Marxists by many of my classmates. What I found, however, was much different than a political ideology that would bring about the end of the world as we know it. Rather, it was a theology critical of status quo power inequalities and committed to the value and theological voice of each person—particularly those who had been marginalized by the church and polis (more often than not in cahoots with one another). I recognized in Latin American liberation theologies, as I would with feminist theologies the following semester, values closely aligned to those of Baptists: the reality and power of the Spirit's presence outside the control of church and ministerial institutions; the recognition that the "least of these" have important and necessary contributions to make to the church's witness; the critical recognition that reading Scripture is a community affair that can only adequately be done in the *entire* community of saints; and the confession and insistence that conversion and salvation is a whole-life experience—Jesus came to conform, reform, and transform us in our entirety—body and soul, person and community, present and future.

Yet, the question still remained: is liberation theology Marxist, and if so, should it be rejected? Undoubtedly late twentieth-century Latin American liberation theology drew on Marxist social theory as means of getting out from under oppressive economic paradigms, but in doing so the liberation theologians were

---

[1] McClendon, *Systematic Theology*, vol. 1, *Ethics*, rev ed., 19. McClendon, a Baptist, uses lower-case-"b" "baptist" to refer collectively to the heirs of the radical reformation—including Baptists.

critical users of Marxist social theory rather than "orthodox" Marxists (a difference I will explore below). Despite the frequently voiced concerns of many of my own seminary students, liberation theology indeed warrants a hearing by us Baptists, for we share concerns with liberation theology—both as a movement of the 1960s and as an ongoing collection of theologies concerned with the voices of the marginalized and the holistic nature of salvation. We Baptists, with our own contesting practices and histories, can easily identify with the protestations of liberation theologians against social, economic, and ecclesial abuses and the bringing into the spotlight of the breadth and depth of the church's voices. This chapter will provide a brief overview of the theological phenomenon called "liberation theology" as well as a more in-depth analysis of one Latin American liberation theologian who offers a particularly robust Christology, Jon Sobrino.

1. Liberation Theology in Historical and Global Context

Although the very brief overview offered below is of the socio-political and ecclesial birthing of liberation theologies in Latin America that are commonly known as "liberation theology," this should not obscure the reality that liberation theology (in name and content) is much wider than post-Vatican II developments in Catholic Latin American theology. More broadly, liberation theology also includes an extensive collection of theologies with shared themes arising in the second half of the twentieth century. This "collection" includes (amongst others): (1) the black liberation theology that began in North America with James Cone's groundbreaking *Black Theology of Liberation*; (2) Latina Roman Catholic *Mujerista* theologies; (3) Latina *Evangélica* theology; (4) white feminist theologies; (5) black Womanist theologies; (6) the liberation theologies of post-Apartheid South Africa; and, (7) various Asian theologies vitally concerned with religious pluralism and interfaith dialogue.[2]

Additionally, liberation theologies include what in a North American seminary catalogue could be categorized as biblical studies, church history, missiology, practical theology, philosophy, ethics, and systematic theology. Within this broad collection there are shared emphases: the contextualized nature of interpreting Scripture and "doing" theology (divine revelation requires recipients—and recipients are contextually located); the mutually informative nature of orthopraxis and orthodoxy (right knowledge of God begins with the right practice of faith); the hermeneutical priority of the poor and oppressed (in Catholic thought this is the

---

[2] These theologies are exemplified by the following works: Cone, *A Black Theology of Liberation*; Isasi-Díaz, *Mujerista Theology*; Martell-Otero, Maldonado Pérez, and Conde-Frazier, *Latina Evangélicas*; Schüssler Fiorenza, *Discipleship of Equals*; Grant, *White Women's Christ and Black Women's Jesus*; Martey, *African Theology*; and Phan, ed., *Christianities in Asia*.

"preferential option for the poor"); and, most importantly, that Christ came to liberate the oppressed from crushing poverty (spiritual, material, religious, ecclesial, cultural, and/or social).

An overview of the historical development and theological content of each of these areas of liberation theology is certainly interesting, and if provided would show myriad connections between socio-political pressures and colonialisms and ecclesial-theological responses leading to related theological outcomes—namely that Christian salvation must liberate whole persons and that true theology must be done in the voices of those who have been oppressed (for example, James Cone's black liberation theology arose in response to the Jim Crow south and the deficits he saw in Western understandings of Christ—thus, his concept of the "black Jesus"). However, as some of my colleagues' chapters in this book address in detail many of these liberation theologies,[3] this chapter will look at liberation theology through the lens of Latin American liberation *Christology*—for liberation theologies have consistently focused on Christ—which argues for understandings of Christ in his whole, historical person and in relation to the whole, historical persons who follow him. One excellent example of this comes from the work of Jon Sobrino, Jesuit priest and theologian at the University of Central America in San Salvador, El Salvador. In Latin America what came to carry the moniker of "liberation theology" was the outcome of both the political destabilization of the region and the urging of the church toward stronger responses to poverty by Pope John Paul II and the preceding Second Vatican Council (in which the future Pope John Paul II participated as Bishop Karol Wojtyla).

Beginning with the Cuban revolution in 1953, the entire Central American region began to destabilize, and with the Nicaraguan revolution in 1979, the stage was set for the twelve-year Salvadoran Civil War (1979-1992)—which is the direct context in which Jon Sobrino wrote. The United Nations estimates that El Salvador's Civil War resulted in at least 75,000 murders, untold disappearances, and the displacement of one-sixth of the population, with the majority of the burden born by the poorest Salvadorans. The ravages of this war followed on the heels of the previous decades of regional unrest—with 300,000 Salvadorans already living as refugees in neighboring Honduras.[4] Prior to and throughout the war, numerous popular organizations rose up advocating for the rights of the poor, resulting (unfortunately) in an increase of the repressions they sought to lift—including a num-

---

[3] Some of these theologies are explored more fully in chapters 3 (black theologies), 4 (Hispanic/Lantin@ theologies), 5 (Asian theologies), 8 (feminist theologies), and 9 (womanist theologies).

[4] Prendes, "Political Radicalization and Popular Pastoral Practices in El Salvador, 1969-1985," 107. Prendes lays out in great detail the political machinations of this era of Salvadoran history.

ber of massacres (May Day in 1977, El Sumpul in 1980, and El Mozote in 1981), with the institutional church playing an ambivalent role.

In the midst of this regional destabilization, Vatican II (1962-65) included the publication of the Council's "Pastoral Constitution on the Church in the Modern World" (*Gaudium et Spes*). Herein, great emphasis is placed upon the fractured nature of a world divided by wealth and poverty: "Never has the human race enjoyed such an abundance of wealth, resources and economic power, and yet a huge proportion of the world's citizens are still tormented by hunger and poverty, while countless numbers suffer from total illiteracy."[5] Beyond recognition of global injustice, *Gaudium et Spes* also prophetically calls Church participants to recognize in all people the image of God, particularly in partnerships between men and women, the whole person (body and soul), and in persons as necessarily dignified and free. *Gaudium et Spes* issued a call that might be considered "socialist," for "every group must take into account the needs and legitimate aspirations of every other group, and even those of the human family as a whole."[6] At the close of Vatican II forty bishops, including many from Brazil and Latin America, gathered in the Domitilla Catacombs outside Rome and voluntarily committed to "evangelical poverty" in solidarity with the poor in what came to be known as the "The Pact of the Catacombs."[7] This renewed emphasis on poverty by the Catholic Church was then taken up by the Latin American Bishops at their 1968 gathering in Medellín, Colombia, where they expanded the definition of poverty to include spiritual poverty and poverty of lack of commitment and called those present to solidarity with the poor.[8] It was from this increasing commitment within the church to the alleviation of all forms of poverty that the earliest Latin American liberation theologies arose.

While Latin American liberation theology is primarily Catholic in origin, it is not exclusively so. Latin America has produced some Protestant liberation theologians and theological organizations with similar concerns to their Catholic counterparts. One example of this is the Congreso Latinoamericano de Evangelización, formed in 1969 by young leaders who, like their Catholic colleagues, wanted the church to respond to the issues of injustice raised by the liberation theologians. Participants included René Padilla, an Ecuadorian Evangelical; Orlando Costas, an Hispanic Baptist; and Samuel Escobar, a Peruvian Baptist. José Míguez Bonino, who as a Methodist was one of the first Protestant liberation theologians and served as President of the World Council of Churches from 1975 through 1983, declared

---

[5] Vatican II, "Pastoral Constitution on Church in the Modern World (*Gaudium et Spes*)," § 4.

[6] Vatican II, "Pastoral Constitution on Church in the Modern World (*Gaudium et Spes*)," § 26.

[7] Bingemer, *Latin American Theology*, 49-53.

[8] Bingemer, *Latin American Theology*, 19-20.

Catholic liberation theology to be a step toward ecumenism because of its core conviction: equality of persons.[9] While Protestant liberation theology has not gathered nearly as much attention, it continues to expand. One notable example of this is the recent publication of *Latina Evangélicas,* in which the contextualized faith of Latina Protestants in the context of their multiform oppression is brought to bear on theology in such a way that the incarnation of the Spirit is re-visioned in particularly life-giving ways.[10]

2. Jon Sobrino's Contextual Method

Sobrino (b. 1938) was ordained a Jesuit priest and moved from his native country, Spain, to El Salvador in 1956, where he has since spent the majority of his career teaching theology at the Universidad Centroamericana José Simeón Cañas (UCA), where he narrowly escaped being murdered in 1989 along with his Jesuit co-workers.[11] Reflecting back, Sobrino described himself at the time of his move as "the typical 'missionary,' full of good will and Eurocentricity—and blind to reality."[12] His self-described "awakening" from his reality-blindness was an awakening to the unfolding brutality and oppression in El Salvador, which ultimately caused him to argue that theology must develop greater honesty with historical realities, an emphasis shaped in large part by his colleague Ignacio Ellacuría (one of his murdered Jesuits colleagues). At a retreat held in San Salvador the year after Medellín, Ellacuría helped lead the UCA priests through the Ignatian spiritual exercises, the result of which was a large-scale "turn to the poor" amongst the UCA Jesuits.[13]

Sobrino and his colleagues were faced with the reality that theology had been shaped and used to support the political and ecclesial status quo of a violent and tumultuous era: their "continent [had] been subjected to centuries of inhuman and anti-Christian oppression, without Christology giving any sign of having noticed this."[14] In response to this disconnect, Sobrino turned to Ellacuría's concept of *realidad histórica*, which argued that God's revelation could only be known in the whole of the reality; thus, the poor could not be ignored if theology was to speak truthfully of God. Ellacuría crafted *realidad histórica* in order to overcome various

---

[9] E.g., Bonino, *Doing Theology in a Revolutionary Situation.*

[10] Martell-Otero, Maldonado Pérez, and Conde-Frazier, eds., *Latina Evangélicas.*

[11] For Sobrino's reflections on the murders of his colleagues, see Sobrino and Ellacuría, *Companions of Jesus,* 45. Sobrino escaped death because he was in Thailand teaching a course on Christology, and the priest who had slept in Sobrino's room that evening was murdered in his place.

[12] Sobrino, "Awakening from the Sleep of Inhumanity," 364.

[13] Lessalle-Klein, *Blood and Ink,* 32-52.

[14] Sobrino, *Jesus the Liberator,* 3.

philosophical systems that had rendered only part of reality meaningful and meaning making. He concluded that just as the "material" world is a meaningful part of reality and theology, so too is the "secular" world meaningful in the face of the sacred. According to Ellacuría, and then Sobrino, the secular and sacred worlds only have meaning together and when given meaning by what is ultimately meaning-making: God's own history. God's own history itself is only knowable "in the concrete space where one is located": a space that is spatial, temporal, and biological.[15] One can only know God in the entirety of spaces where God is at work. Thus, to ignore the darkest parts of history (poverty and injustice) is to ignore parts of God's own history and thus to fail in fully knowing God. Sobrino, following in Ellacuría's footsteps, argues that God is actively present in theology, thus to know God is not to retreat from the world or into the Spirit or the prayer closet (although there are certainly roles for these contemplative practices), for when participating in God "one does not abandon the human, does not abandon real history, but rather deepens one's roots, making more present and effective what was already effectively present."[16] Theology takes place in life, all of life, even the broken places of the world. For Sobrino, this means the poor and oppressed of El Salvador, those who were literally crushed under the weight of the world, have necessary and important theological contributions to make, yet the dominant economic paradigm in play during the development of liberation theology could not support this.

The inability of dominant economic paradigms to make the poor and injustice of poverty visible is what caused liberation theologians to incorporate Marxist theory—critically—into their work. Although concern for the poor had long been a stated goal of Catholic and Protestant churches, liberation theology was subsequently highly criticized for using Marxist social analysis to bring to light the socio-economic injustices that perpetuated poverty. The Vatican's own Congregation for the Doctrine of the Faith (CDF) denounced liberation theology's use of Marxism, arguing that Marxism is inappropriate for Christian theology because "atheism and the denial of the human person, his liberty and rights, are at the core of the Marxist theory."[17] Critiques specific to Sobrino and his use of Marxist thought were then raised by Cardinal Ratzinger (subsequently Pope Benedict XVI) as well as by numerous other Catholic and Protestant theologians.[18] Ellacuría himself argued, in response to Cardinal Ratzinger's critiques, that Marxism is "absolutely marginal" in

---

[15] Burke, *The Ground Beneath the Cross*, 64.

[16] Ellacuría, "The Historicity of Christian Salvation," 255.

[17] Congregation for the Doctrine of the Faith, "Instruction on Certain Aspects of the 'Theology of Liberation'."

[18] For Cardinal Ratzinger's personal critique, see Ratzinger, "Vi Spiego La Teologia Della Liberazione," 48-55.

Sobrino's thought.[19] The reality is that Sobrino *was* indirectly influenced by Marxism because he draws on theologians who were admittedly influenced by it, most notably Ellacuría and Jürgen Moltmann.

Enrique Dussel, a first-generation liberation theologian and early importer of Marxism, argues that liberation theology's new move was adopting and using the social sciences *at all*, with Marxism being just one aspect. In the "development" economic model in play at the time, poor persons and countries only have identity as not-yet-arrived-at developed persons and countries. The model itself did/could not account for the economic and social injustices that oppress the poor because it simply could not recognize the failures of the *system*.[20] Additionally, Dussel points to the ways that Christian theology has historically drawn widely from various "secular" philosophies, and that Marxism is but one in a long lineup (most notably, the philosophies of Aristotle and Descartes). He also argues that liberation theologians have very rarely accepted Marxism as a whole, but instead have used "a *certain* Marxism in a *certain* way."[21] For Sobrino, unlike orthodox Marxists, participating in and transforming history always has as its goal making God's reign present in history because it is God's reign that is meaning-making for the *realidad histórica*. Thus, while it must be recognized that Sobrino, and Latin American liberation theology as a whole, did engage Marxist thought (albeit indirectly), he did not incorporate it as a ruling motif but rather as tool for the actualization of the reign of God.

3. Sobrino's Theological Contributions

What then are the substantive theological contributions that Sobrino arrives at both *for* the poor and *from* the poor themselves? His chief contribution is the way in which he links the Jesus of/in history with persons living in the *realidad histórica* who follow Jesus in discipleship: i.e., his *christopraxic method*. Unlike the historical Jesus work of the nineteenth and twentieth centuries, which sought to find the real Jesus *behind* the biblical texts, Sobrino defines the historical Jesus holistically as "the person, teaching, attitudes, and deeds of Jesus of Nazareth insofar as they are accessible, in a more or less general way, to historical and exegetical investigation."[22] Christopraxis is his correction to the Christology that is disconnected from the poor, a Christology in which "Christ has been reduced to a sublime abstraction" and that does not reflect Jesus' history or hold any ethical imperatives for the

---

[19] Ellacuría, "Historicity of Christian Salvation," 280.

[20] Lessalle-Klein, *Blood and Ink*. In chapter 1, Lessalle-Klein traces the development of the use by liberation theologians of *liberation* in place of *development*.

[21] Dussel, "Theology of Liberation and Marxism," 92. Italics in original.

[22] Sobrino, *Christology at the Crossroads*, 3.

church's involvement in reality.[23] Rather, he argues, we must root theology in the Jesus who is present in history (his own history and the ongoing history of the world) and in the practices of the church that follows Jesus. He argues that Christology is only possible if the theologian or theologizing community begins with the actual history of Jesus as remembered in the New Testament (which is the method that the New Testament itself shows) and if they do so from their particular place in history as disciples of Jesus. Using this method, he critiques any Christology that separates the divine and human natures of Christ and leaves the historical Jesus behind altogether.[24] He argues that the church of the poor contributes an important theological truth by reminding the rest of the church that the historical Jesus is essential to Christology. Doctrinal Christology is important, but only insofar as it does not forget the reality of the historical Jesus or the necessity of following Jesus in history.

The historical Jesus is primarily known by the church as it follows the practice of Jesus, for "the most historical element in the historical Jesus is his practice...his activity brought to bear upon the reality around him in order to transform it in a determinate, selected direction, the direction of the kingdom of God."[25] Sobrino shows that Jesus' most meaning-making practices are found in his relationship with the poor of his day: his healing, feeding, loving, and forgiving the poor and oppressed. By paying attention to what Jesus actually did (particularly for the poor), the church can understand who he is in his person: "We have better access to the inner life of Jesus (his mind in history) from his outward practice (his making of history) than vice versa."[26] The historical Jesus reveals how humanity can correspond to God in the midst of historical reality; Jesus' life is the full example of this correspondence, and by following these examples the correspondences of the faithful are possible and meaningful (what Sobrino calls the *isomorphic* relationship between Jesus and the poor).[27] The historical Jesus judges between true and false practices and holds theology accountable without dismissing the absolute necessity of human participation in discipleship, which "means doing, *in terms of the present,* what Jesus did, and doing it in the way that he did it."[28]

This sounds rather general, but recall that Sobrino, and Latin American liberation theology as a whole, is focused on righting injustices perpetuated on the poor, and his christopraxic method is focused on the theological contributions made by the broad base of the church that *is* the poor. He defines the "poor" them-

---

[23] Sobrino, *Christology at the Crossroads*, xv.

[24] Sobrino, "Systematic Christology."

[25] Sobrino, *Christology at the Crossroads*, 66.

[26] Sobrino, *Jesus the Liberator*, 54.

[27] Sobrino, *Christology at the Crossroads*, xxiv.

[28] Sobrino, "Systematic Christology," 451 (emphasis added).

selves as systemically oppressed and impoverished in many ways: materially, socially, culturally, and even ecclesially. Over the course of his writings, Sobrino expands his definition of the poor beyond merely that of material impoverishment in order to include "victims" and "martyrs": ultimately arguing that "poverty means death to the poor."[29] Yet, the poor are not merely victims; they are also theological contributors. They contribute from their place of poverty by the mere fact that they have hope and faith when they should, on the basis of their situations, have none. However, the poor are essential to theology not only because they make up the majority of the *realidad histórica* and the church itself, but also because it is to them that the gospel is addressed and made real in the life of Jesus. Because the poor have hope in seemingly hopeless situations, they bring the gospel out of the realm of ideas, making it concrete in the midst of historic reality.

Sobrino also defines the "church of the poor" as the church as a whole that is confronted by the reality of poverty and centered on the concerns of the poor, thus making theological space for communities that are not actually poor. The actual poor "confront the Church both with its basic theological problem and with the direction in which the solution to the problem is to be found"; they uncover the *realidad histórica* in all of its broken reality.[30] The actual poor also make the ethical demand that the church exist in solidarity with them, and the methodological demand that the church de-ideologize itself by aligning itself with them rather than with idols of power. This is what Sobrino calls the "irruption" of the poor, their coming into visibility, or busting onto the stage, that questions the theological status quo that would present a sublime Christ apart from the life and practices of Jesus of Galilee.

4. Conclusion: Hearing Liberating Voices

I am certainly thankful that my seminary professor encouraged me to pick up and read that first liberation theology text and for the subsequent discovery of shared values between Catholic liberation and Baptist theologies. Sobrino and his colleagues gave me language to translate theologies of a high view of Scripture and the priesthood of all believers in light of a world beset by various death-dealing injustices. How might a local faith community read Scripture in light of Latin American liberation theology? Certainly, the call to participating in Jesus' own practices as a means of theological accountability is always timely, as well as a necessary reminder that knowledge is community- and practice-shaped. We will be shaped by what we

---

[29] Sobrino, "Poverty Means Death to the Poor," 267-76.
[30] Sobrino, *The True Church and the Poor*, 93. See also Sobrino's discussion on the theological significance of the martyrs in idem, "Los mártires y la teología de la liberación."

do together, be that shaped into the likeness of Christ or not. Beyond that, liberation theology can help us see how the life of Christ calls the church into prophetic acts, be they speaking truth from the underside of history or repenting of perpetuating a history that has undersides. Perhaps that call to repentance is really what caused many to reject liberation theology.

5. For Further Reading

Bingemer, Maria Clara. *Latin American Theology: Roots and Branches*. Maryknoll, NY: Orbis Books, 2016.

De La Torre, Miguel A. *Liberation Theology for Armchair Theologians*. Louisville, KY: Westminster John Knox, 2013.

Lessalle-Klein, Robert. *Blood and Ink: Ignacio Ellacuría, Jon Sobrino, and the Jesuit Martyrs of the University of Central America*. Maryknoll, NY: Orbis Books, 2014.

Sobrino, Jon. *Jesus the Liberator: A Historical-Theological View*. Translated by Paul Burns and Francis McDonagh. Maryknoll, NY: Orbis Books, 1993.

_____. *The True Church and the Poor*. Translated by Matthew J. O'Connell. Maryknoll, NY: Orbis Books, 1984.

3

Light from Black Theologies

Noel Leo Erskine

"Black theology" is not monolithic, and while in its origins black theology was dominated by male theological voices, that is happily no longer the case. Therefore, this chapter seeks to investigate the evolution and interrelationship between black and womanist theologies, noting points at which they converge and diverge, and to gesture toward the light they may provide for Baptist congregations in their practice of theology. I offer these observations as a black Baptist theologian and ethicist born in Jamaica who, though male, has been deeply influenced by womanist theology as well as black theology. (Chapter 9 will explore the contributions of womanist theologies more fully on their own terms.)

Black theology is the elder sibling of these two approaches to doing theology, as it came on the academic scene as early as 1969 through the writing of James Cone. Cone contends that an impetus and inspiration for the crafting and articulation of black theology came from Malcolm X and Martin Luther King, Jr., both African Americans, who sought through their prophetic words and action to change the face of America in the area of race relations. The publication of Professor Cone's first book was a year after King's assassination and four years after the assassination of Malcolm X.[1] The civil rights and black power movements led by Martin Luther King, Jr. and Malcolm X were of utmost importance for the evolution of black theology. During the first decade of its development, all black theologians were men, and it did not seem to occur to these black male theologians that the perspectives of women, particularly black women, were not given consideration.

James Cone acknowledged that one reason for the articulation of this new theology was the exclusion of black people by white religionists. Black theologians were careful not to adopt the exclusionary approach of white theologians and were intentional to include them both in the exposition and analysis of its major themes and arguments. A cursory look at the index of James Cone's first book *Black Theol-*

---

[1] Cone, *Black Theology and Black Power*. Pioneering texts in womanist thinking are Cannon, *Black Womanist Ethics* and Grant, *White Women's Christ and Black Women's Jesus*.

ogy and Black Power indicates black theology's commitment to white ways of talking about God, humanity, and the world. Cone engages white thinkers as diverse as Emil Brunner, Rudolf Bultmann, Dietrich Bonhoeffer, Billy Graham, Karl Barth, and Richard Niebuhr. Cone was introduced to white theologians in seminary and graduate school and wrote his doctoral dissertation on Karl Barth's anthropology. I find it instructive for ecclesial practice and pedagogy that black theologians refused to pattern God-talk after the model of exclusion of black people by white theologians, insisting that if theology is to be in the service of creating a compassionate and diverse community, then the stranger must be embraced both in the academy, church, and wider society.

1. Highlighting the Situation of Faith

Taking my cue from black theologians, it is appropriate to ask: what does it mean for the academy and the church to include the stranger—the person of a different race, ethnicity, religion, and culture? What is troubling and revealing is that black theologians in embracing the stranger—white theologians—nevertheless excluded the person of the same race, ethnicity, religion, and culture. Black women were excluded. Could it be that because black women were of the same race, culture, and in many instances religion, they were excluded? Was sameness a problem? Did black theologians fail to note that sameness does not mean identical? While black theologians saw white men as different and understood difference in terms of transcendence, they understood black women in terms of the familiar and overlooked issues of transcendence.

In his articulation of black theology within a framework of reconciliation and liberation, Baptist theologian J. Deotis Roberts highlights the importance of the academy and church providing a context for the embrace of history and culture that are indigenous to the black community. Roberts questions whether the space that black persons inhabit within the academy allows for the discovery of their identity and voice that the black church has made possible. Should theology within the academy allow for testimonies and stories of resistance and adventure as does the black church? In a move that would anticipate the emergence of womanist theology, Roberts posits that theology needs to be holistic in thought and faith and that the entire family should be embraced. In his essay "Liberating Theological Education: Can Our Seminaries be Saved?"[2] Roberts points out that theological education must do more than ask about continuities between the academy and the church. Theology must address the cries that exude from the oppressed in our societies and be insistent that theology is for liberation and reconciliation. It is interest-

---

[2] Roberts, "Liberating Theological Education," 98, 113-16.

ing to note that in 1983 when this article was published, Roberts served as president of the Interdenominational Theological Center in Atlanta. He emphasized that the theological task must be framed within the context of liberation and reconciliation for God's children. Yet he did not speak with specificity to the invisibility of black women in the academy and their absence as contributors to black theology. Roberts frames the issue this way:

> When Blacks excavate their African roots, they participate in a holistic view of reality. When we are at home with ourselves and our culture, and not trying to be like someone else, we are holistic in thought and faith. We are never liberated until we make this discovery. What this means is that we Blacks have a real contribution to make to theology and the Christian movement—if we can be set free. Thus, the first item on our agenda may be the psychological freedom to think and believe out of our own culture and history.[3]

Roberts reminds us that black theology may properly be defined as theology of the black experience. For him black history, culture and black faith provide the primary data for God-talk which must become black-talk. As it was for Cone, so it was for Roberts and other black theologians that during the first decade of black theology sexism, the marginalization of women, had not yet come within the purview of their attempt to relate God-talk to the black religious experience. The central theological problem for both Roberts and Cone was racism in the form of white supremacy or the privilege that skin color gave the white majority. Roberts pleads for a holistic world view that brackets the subordination and marginalization of the black race. Cone and Roberts remind us that the defining symbol of black inferiority as articulated by the majority culture was color, the color of one's skin. Color determined where black people lived, where they went to church or school, and whom they married and thus became a central category in the development of black theology. For black theologians, blackness is at once descriptive and normative. Both Roberts and Cone remind us that blackness is descriptive because it gives sociological concreteness to the brokenness and tragic in black life. In the preface to the fortieth anniversary edition of *A Black Theology of Liberation,* Cone points out that the tragic in black life—segregation, racism, plantation slavery—are prerequisites for understanding black theology. Although white people may read black theology, it is clear they will not understand unless they are willing to become black. It is at this point that Cone leaves a crack in the door for dialogue between black and white theologians, if they can enter into solidarity with oppressed blacks

---

[3] Roberts, "Liberating Theological Education," 115.

of the land. Roberts couches the language of solidarity in terms of liberation and reconciliation between black and white people.

2. Black Theology and 'the Stranger'

One may find it intriguing that hidden within black theology in its formative years was an openness to the stranger—the person of a different race, culture, ethos—but not yet to the friend, the sister, the mother. Cone states the issue succinctly:

> The most glaring limitation of *A Black Theology of Liberation* was my failure to be receptive to the problem of sexism in the black community and society as a whole. I have become so embarrassed by that failure that I could not re-issue this volume without making a note of it and without exchanging the exclusive language of the 1970 edition to inclusive language. I know that this is hardly enough to rectify my failure, because sexism cannot be eliminated (any more than racism) simply by changing words. But it is an important symbol of what we must do, because our language is a reflection of the reality we create. Sexism dehumanizes and kills, and it must be fought on every front.[4]

Cone was emphatic that black theologians and black preachers needed to take the marginalization of women in academy and church seriously and not relegate this to the purview of white women. According to Cone, many black preachers understand sexism to be a problem highlighted by white women and assume that black women who placed the family at the forefront in church and the wider community did not have a problem with male leadership as evidenced in the black church where women are in the majority:

> Any black male theologian or preacher who ignores sexism as a central problem in our society and church (as important as racism, because they are interconnected), is just as guilty of distorting the gospel as is a white theologian who does the same with racism. If we black male theologians do not take seriously the need to incorporate into our theology a critique of our sexist practices in the black community, then we have no right to complain when white theologians snub black theology.[5]

During the formative years of black theology, and certainly during its first decade, black theologians contended that the primary truth was truth about the black community, the recounting of their stories, and the affirmation of their heritage. J. Deotis Roberts would join the quarrel with James Cone as to whether or

---

[4] Cone, *A Black Theology of Liberation*, 40th anniversary ed., xx.
[5] Cone, *Black Theology of Liberation*, xx.

not the hermeneutical key was liberation or reconciliation, but they were agreed that the central theological problem was racism. According to black theologians, to identify the problem was to begin to press for liberation or reconciliation. The theological task was to free the people with truth gleaned from the gospel of Christ and the situation of faith. The theological method that emerged was a dialectical relationship between the good news about black existence as enshrined in the gospel of Christ, on the one hand, and the truth concerning black existence gleaned from the sociological perspective of black people, on the other hand. Central here is that as far as black theologians were concerned, whether they listened to the gospel of Christ or to the cries of the oppressed, the word that came through was the word of freedom. These theologians sought to free their people with truth as they engaged those within the academy, church, or wider society who had compromised their humanity. Theology had to be in service of creating and fashioning a compassionate and diverse community, one in which the neighbor as stranger and critic had to be embraced.

3. The Influence of Martin Luther King, Jr.

Because black theology is Christian theology and affirms the church as the home of theology, it begins to make sense that with the influence of the black church in the background and often in the foreground, the church's reference to the biblical injunction to be hospitable to strangers (Heb. 13:1-2) would be taken seriously. In his book *God of the Oppressed*, James Cone informs us that he was licensed to preach at age sixteen.[6] I would not be surprised if this invitation to be hospitable to strangers would have been an aspect of the culture in Macedonia African Methodist Episcopal Church in which he was reared in Bearden, Arkansas. There was always an air of expectancy in black churches that God would treat us the way we treated strangers. Perhaps because of this ethos of hospitality there was not any expectation within black churches of reverse discrimination. No one illustrates this better than Martin Luther King, Jr. Cone points to the role of the civil rights movement in the United States under the leadership of King as indispensable for the visioning and articulation of black theology.[7]

King indicates that the black church's understanding of what it means to be human in church and in the wider society is an outgrowth of the church's understanding of God. Because God is love, a God who is generous to all God's children and does not privilege one group of children over another, all God's children have

---

[6] Cone, *God of the Oppressed*, rev. ed.
[7] Cone, *Martin & Malcolm & America*.

virtue and inherent worth, even if some of God's children advocate segregation and racism.

King would insist that every human being by virtue of being human has inherent worth, and no person, society or culture has the right to deny his/her dignity. The bottom line for King was that racism was sin against God. Love for God meant working to dismantle the very fabric of racism. But in spite of the human condition soiled by racism, every human being may claim access to the tree of life because of God's love: "The worth of an individual does not lie in the measure of his intellect, racial origin, or social position. Human worth lies in relatedness to God. An individual has value because he has value to God."[8]

God's love is the basis for of the worth of human beings, it means that all persons are of equal worth. There is no theological or biblical basis for regarding white people as superior to black people. Here King echoes the black church's perspective:

> Our Hebraic-Christian tradition refers to this inherent dignity of man in the Biblical term the image of God. The innate worth referred to in the phrase the image of God is universally shared in equal portions by all men. There is no graded scale of essential worth: there is no divine right of one race which differs from that of another. Every human being has etched in his personality the indelible stamp of the creator.[9]

It is of first importance to note that Cone and Roberts, like their mentor King, would insist on a relationship of love for the critic and neighbor who sought to render black people invisible and, in some instances, to render harm. For these theologians there was an indissoluble relationship between love and justice. These theologians learned this in the black church. King was able to give this claim theological and sociological concreteness in a dissertation for Boston University on the thought of Henry Nelson Wieman and Paul Tillich.[10]

From Tillich, King learned that any responsible attempt to practice love in church, society, or the academy had to take seriously the interrelatedness of love, power, and justice. King would often remind his listeners that love without power was anemic and power without love was calculated. Students of the civil rights movement will remember that King was forced to engage in this analysis because of the leaders of Student Non-violent Coordinating Committee, who pointed out to King that in his constant plea for black people to confront white brutality with nonviolent resistance—to turn the other cheek—he was calling on black people to

---

[8] King, "The Ethical Demands for Integration," in *A Testament of Hope*, 122.

[9] King, "Ethical Demands for Integration," 118-19.

[10] King, "A Comparison of the Conceptions of God in the Thinking of Paul Tillich and Henry Nelson Wieman."

love white people without demanding that black people practice justice toward themselves by learning to love themselves. The students contended that there was nothing that hurt the oppressed community as too much love for others, especially when the intent of others was the destruction of black lives. This was an important lesson for King and black theologians: loving self last was a danger, for last frequently meant not at all, as often one never got around to finding time or space to love self. The students taught this to King, and Cone and Roberts insisted in their attempt to reach out to the stranger that love as it engages power must insist on justice. These theologians understood justice as the essence of love. But the error they made was seeing justice primarily in terms of the analysis of the structures of alienation and oppression.

Although intellectually King, Cone, and Roberts understood that an examination of relations of love, power, and justice must begin with justice, these theologians did not practice love toward and accord justice to women in the civil rights movement and as active participants in the evolution of black theology in its formative years. This was why in the case of King women were often not affirmed in leadership positions in the running of the civil rights movement. Although women were the most vulnerable, they were often invisible when opportunities for leadership in the movement presented itself, and when given an opportunity to lead they were not affirmed. It stands to reason then that there were no women among black theologians in the first decade of the development of black theology.[11] Further, the names of women who were active in the civil rights movement do not come as readily to mind as do the names of men who were identified with King. Students of the civil rights movement are familiar with the names of Jesse Jackson, Ralph David Abernathy, John Lewis, Andrew Young, and C. T. Vivian. But if asked to name women who identified with the movement, they stop at Coretta Scott King, the wife of the slain civil rights leader. There is a sense in which black women were invisible. But this was not because they were not there, for Rosa Parks started the trail that led to the movement. As someone has said, "She sat down so that Martin Luther King, Jr. could stand up." Further, it was the Women's Political Council at

---

[11] The career of womanist theologian Prathia Hall illustrates the invisibility of influential women at this stage of the movement, even while her subsequent career as an academic theologian is a link between earlier expressions of black theology and the emergence of womanist theology. As a civil rights activist Hall led a SNCC-sponsored meeting in the aftermath of the burning of the church building of a black congregation in 1962 at which she prayed a prayer that included the repeated phrase "I have a dream!" King reportedly attended the meeting, and his use of the phrase in his speech at the Lincoln Memorial on August 28, 1963 has been attributed to Hall's use in prayer of that memorable refrain. Hall went on to earn the M.Div., Th.M., and Ph.D. degrees from Princeton Theological Seminary and later held the Martin Luther King, Jr. Chair of Social Ethics at Boston University School of Theology. See Pace, *Freedom Faith*.

Alabama State College led by Jo Ann Robinson that got the leaflets out to advertise the bus boycott. Besides, both the jails and freedom rides were crowded with women. Women who had leadership roles in the movement included Dorothy Cotton, the director of the Citizenship Education Program (CEP), and Ella Baker, who organized the Southern Christian Leadership Conference (SCLC) and served as its acting director for a short while. Commenting on Baker's tenure as acting director, Cone states:

> Although she served as its "acting director," most of the male preachers were uneasy with her presence because she did not exhibit the "right attitude" (read "submissiveness'?) which they expected from women, an expectation no doubt shaped by the role of women in their churches. Ella Baker's tenure with SCLC was relatively brief (though longer than she expected), largely because of her conflicts with King and others regarding their attitude toward women and their leadership style built around the charisma of one person—Martin Luther King, Jr. Baker preferred the group-centered leadership developed by SNCC, whose founding she initiated.[12]

4. Black Women in Black Theology?

In embracing the stranger, the person of a different race, King and later Cone and Roberts as theologians rendered invisible the most vulnerable among them, the black woman. This seems to be the assessment of womanist theologian Jacquelyn Grant in her important article "Black Theology and the Black Woman." Grant begins by pointing out the importance of theological analysis that honors the interrelationship of racism, sexism, and classism. According to Grant, to highlight any one of these foci apart from the others is to fail to press for authentic liberation. Professor Grant inquires:

> Where are black women in Black theology? They are in fact invisible....In examining Black theology it is necessary to make one or two assumptions: (1) Either Black women have no place in the enterprise, or (2) Black men are capable of speaking for us. Both of these assumptions are false and need to be discarded. They arise out of a male-dominated culture which restricts women to certain areas of society. In such a culture men are given the warrant to speak for women.[13]

According to Grant, one word gets to the reason for the invisibility of black women in black theology: patriarchy. Patriarchy is the subordination of women to

---

[12] Cone, *Martin & Malcolm & America,* 278.
[13] Grant, "Black Theology and the Black Woman," in *Black Theology,* vol. 1, *1966-1979,* ed. Cone and Wilmore, 420.

a male-oriented worldview. It is also the attempt of men to act and speak for women. Patriarchy manifests itself in the notion that men are superior to women because women are given to emotionality and intuition while men are given to reason and intellect. Grant observes:

> Just as White women formerly had no place in White theology—except as receptors of White men's theological interpretations....Black women have had no place in the development of Black theology. By self- appointment, or by the sinecure of a male dominated society, Black men have deemed it proper to speak for the entire Black community, male and female.[14]

Womanist theologian Kelly Brown Douglas agrees with Grant that womanist theology in contradistinction to black theology must focus on "the woman question and the race question." Douglas states the issue succinctly: "The image of a Black God gave me a new sense of pride in my own Blackness....But as I developed an awareness of what it meant to be a woman in a sexist society I saw the limitation of the Black God and the Black Christ."[15]

If black theology helped her identify and deal with racism in church, academy, and society, womanist theology provided a critique of patriarchy within society, and church as it helped her name the discrimination she experienced at the hands of black men. "It was sexism. I became painfully aware that sexism was not just a 'White woman's thing.' It also pervaded the Black church and community. This meant that if the entire Black community was to be free, both racism and sexism, at the very least had to be eradicated.[16]

Douglas gets to the heart of the matter as she points out why black theology is inadequate as a tool for the liberation of the oppressed. According to both Douglas and Grant, black theology is one-dimensional. It does an important service in taking on racism in American society and does this in a powerful way in that speaks out of the Black Power and civil rights milieu. However, the major problem was that the experience of black women was omitted. Black theology was incapable of addressing the multiple social burdens engendered by classism, sexism, racism, and heterosexism that plague the black community. This meant that the liberation project was limited to the disempowerment of racism, while the evils of classism, sexism, and heterosexism were left unattended. One wonders to what extent this myopic way of being in the world reflected in Black theology's neglect of gender, and class issues, is a carryover from the black church experience. It is widely acknowl-

---

[14] Grant, "Black Theology and the Black Woman," 420.
[15] Douglas, "Womanist Theology," in *Black Theology,* vol. 2, *1980-1992,* ed. Cone and Wilmore, 291.
[16] Douglas, "Womanist Theology," 291.

edged that in many black churches in the United States of America, women are not encouraged to share in leadership positions throughout the church and seldom make it beyond being minister of music or an associate pastor. There are not many black churches that call women as senior pastors. The responsibilities of women in the area of church leadership do not correspond with women comprising the majority population in most of these churches. The question being raised is, to what extent is the myopia exhibited in relation to black theology's neglect of black women's experience a carryover of the black church ethos?

Grant and Douglas affirm that the starting point for black theology—the black religious experience—does not include black women's experience. The starting point for womanist theology is black women's struggle for survival and the conviction that God participates in the struggle to defeat the many forms of oppression that assail the black family.

5. Learning from the Outsider Within

It was highlighted earlier that the womanist theologian has to deal with the woman question and the race question. Historically, womanist thinking has been interested in both questions, and it is this twoness, so to speak, that allows the womanist theologian to both identify with and differentiate herself from the white woman and the black man. The black woman is both insider and outsider. She is an outsider who because of the reality of gender is able to relate to the white woman and in her capacity as "Mammy" functions as insider in white homes. Because of her race she is an insider in black homes and community, and there in home and community she is often oppressed because of gender. Patricia Hill Collins in her important essay "Learning from the Outsider Within" argues that African American women have functioned as insiders in relation to white families for many years: "Countless numbers of Black women have ridden buses to their white 'families,' where they not only cooked, cleaned, and executed other domestic duties, but where they also nurtured their 'other' children, shrewdly offered guidance to their employers, and frequently became honorary members of their white 'families.'"[17]

It is critical to remember that the black woman who lives in the nexus between black and white and male and female worlds and inhabits an insider status in both worlds remains an outsider. In spite of her insider status she is forced to view reality from within the tension of her racial and sexual identity and is often torn in either direction. The black woman is forced to be bifocal, relating to both worlds and not being fully accepted in either.

---

[17] See Collins, "Learning from the Outsider Within," 35.

Black women live with double warrants at the same time. They are black and female and experience a sense of alienation in both. According to womanist scholars, one problem that they have in relation to white feminists is that the feminists' narrow focus on patriarchy make them uninterested in the survival issues of black women. Primary issues for black women include survival with dignity, racial discrimination, and the black family. Further, womanist scholars point out that white women could not deny that in their drive to join white men in the private sector, black women were called on to take care of their children and run their homes. To expect white women to become passionate in the fight against racism was often to expect too much. If white women were unresponsive to the unique needs of black women, there was hardly any more hope from black men. Douglas explains:

> What was Black women's status in the freedom struggle? Many of the African American women involved in this struggle soon discovered that the civil rights/Black power movement was as sexist as the women's movement was racist. Although Black women helped found some of the freedom fighting organizations, spearheaded local protest activities, and risked their lives for the Black community's freedom, they were rarely afforded the opportunity to hold national leadership roles or to have decision-making responsibilities within various organizations.[18]

The way forward was clear for womanist theologians. Black women's experience of struggle and survival with dignity had to become the point of departure for a methodology that engaged racism, sexism, classism and heterosexism in its quest for wholeness for the black family and community. "Black women were searching for the politics of 'wholeness.' They needed a political strategy that would insure Black people, men and women, rights to live as whole, that is, free, human beings and that would keep the Black community whole, that is unified, struggling together to survive and be free in relationships of mutuality."[19]

For womanist theologians, it was clear that they were working for the liberation of the entire community—women and men. Womanist theology appeals to the justice and judgement of God to challenge obstacles in the community that thwart human flourishing. Because the focus is on the liberation of the entire community, there is no attempt to save women and condemn men. The goal is salvation through liberation for the entire family and community. Patriarchal systems are a problem and create an obstacle for the salvation of the entire community. One implication of this emergent methodology is that black women become the key for the liberation of both women and men, indeed the entire family. On the

---

[18] Douglas, "Womanist Theology," 294-95.
[19] Douglas, "Womanist Theology," 295.

other hand, the evil of patriarchy gets in the way and blinds men from seeing the ways in which they privilege their own experience and thereby thwart the flourishing of the entire community. Biblical bases for these claims include 1 Cor. 11:3 ("But I want you to understand that Christ is the head of every man, and the husband is the head of his wife, and God is the head of Christ") and Eph. 5:22-23 ("Wives, be subject to your husbands as you are to the Lord. For the husband is the head of the wife just as Christ is the head of the church, the body of which he is the Savior"). Christian interpretation of these texts often valorizes the Christian ecclesial tradition in which men are valued over women and the male experience is normative for women's ways of being in the world.

The challenge is to dismantle patriarchy and posit a different starting point for dreaming a new world and a new church. The womanist vision is for women and men to be with the most vulnerable among us, black women, and to allow their ways of being in the world as a servant community to provide a conceptually refreshing frame of reference for how we navigate reality, from the bottom up and not from the top down. This approach asks what would community look like, what would the church become, if the point of departure for talk of hope for humanity is not some notion of man lording it over woman, but a new egalitarianism with women's ways of being and knowing constructing our dreams for a new social reality? At his best St. Paul came close to this ideal of community when in 2 Cor. 5:17 he states: "So if anyone is in Christ, there is a new creation: everything old has passed away; see, everything has become new!" It is clear that for Paul being in Christ was his way of talking about a new social reality in which old ways of understanding the world were dated, and the challenge was to evidence new reality, new ways of being human in the world.

Black and womanist theologies hold out new possibilities and an invitation to envision a new church and world. In black and womanist theologies, those who for so long have been excluded take their rightful place as servant leaders, and through language that suggests new ways of being in the world they begin to shape reality differently. For Baptists, theology at its best is always an invitation to know, and to love God through the neighbor—those who are different. Black and womanist theologies challenge us to see afresh our Lord's identification with the least of these, "for I was hungry and you gave me food, I was thirsty and you gave me something to drink. I was a stranger and you welcomed me" (Matt. 25:35). The way forward is clear. Like Jesus, we are called to solidarity with the least of these.

6. For Further Reading

Cannon, Katie. *Black Womanist Ethics*. Atlanta: Scholars Press, 1988.
Cone, James H. *A Black Theology of Liberation*. 40th anniversary ed. Maryknoll, NY: Orbis Books, 2010.

Cone, James H. and Gayraud S. Wilmore, eds. *Black Theology: A Documentary History*. 2 vols. Maryknoll, NY: Orbis Books, 1979-93.

Grant, Jacquelyn. *White Women's Christ and Black Women's Jesus*. American Academy of Religion Academy Series, no. 64. Atlanta: Scholars Press, 1989.

Hopkins, Dwight N. and Edward P. Antonio, eds. *The Cambridge Companion to Black Theology*. Cambridge Companions to Religion. Cambridge: Cambridge University Press, 2012.

4

Light from Hispanic/Latin@ Theologies

Nora O. Lozano

Hispanic/Latin@[1] theologies emerged as a way to provide a voice to the particular theological perspective and concerns of Hispanics/Latin@s in the United States. As contextual theologies, they take into consideration the particular history, identity, and issues of this community, as well as the way in which this community approaches and lives Christianity (spirituality, worship, hermeneutics, and theological insights). These theologies and theologians are like a kaleidoscope of the Hispanic/Latin@ community. This kaleidoscope, with its different shapes and colors, can function as a conduit that shows Baptist churches the richness of this community, helps them understand their struggles, and invites them to minister with and to Hispanics/Latin@s in ways that honor God's plans of shalom and justice for this community and the world.

1. One Diverse Community

Even though there have been attempts to define this group as a single, homogenous one (Hispanics),[2] this community is extremely diverse. Some of the major Hispanic/Latino@ groups—Mexicans, Puerto Ricans, and Cubans—have in common a history of Spanish conquest and colonization that led them to have Catholic religious roots; a biological, cultural, and social *mestizaje/mulatez* (mixture between Spaniards, Indigenous, and African people); a linguistic connection to Spanish; and the unfortunate experience of racism and marginalization in the U.S. Yet they are very different.

---

[1] This chapter employs "Latin@" as a gender-inclusive alternative to "Latino/Latina" (the asperand symbol @ resembles both the Spanish masculine noun ending -o and the feminine noun ending -a).

[2] Joanne Rodríguez-Olmedo explains that the term Hispanic was coined by the government in the 1970's to group together all of the people from Latin American countries with linguistic and cultural ties to Spain. It is also used to include people from Brazil and Spain. Rodríguez-Olmedo, "The U.S. Hispanic/Latino Landscape," in *Handbook of Latina/o Theologies*, ed. Aponte and De La Torre, 12

People of Mexican descent form the largest group of Hispanic/Latin@s in the United States. Many of them became part of the U.S. due the annexation of large portions of Mexican territory. Suddenly these Mexicans became Mexican Americans, learning to live in a new country that would consider them the inferior "other." Through this process, they experienced a new mixture, what Mexican American theologian Virgilio Elizondo calls the second *mestizaje*. These Mexicans were forced again to mix, but now with the Anglo-Saxon culture of the U.S. Due to the common border between the U.S. and Mexico and various political, economic, and social events, throughout the years many more Mexicans have migrated to the U.S., with and without immigration documents.[3]

Puerto Ricans have their own history, too. After centuries of Spanish colonization, Puerto Rico became a U.S. colony. In 1898, Spain and the U.S. became engaged in the Spanish-American war. Spain lost and ceded Puerto Rico to the U.S. Since that time, Puerto Ricans have held different legal standings. At the beginning, their status was indeterminate. In 1917, when the U.S. needed young men to fight in the First World War, Puerto Ricans were given citizenship. Throughout the years, Puerto Ricans have continued to live in an ambiguous political situation. In 1952, Puerto Rico received the status of Commonwealth. However, Puerto Rico continues to live in a neocolonial state permeated with ambiguity. Puerto Ricans living in the continental U.S. can vote in federal elections, but this right is denied to Puerto Ricans living on the island. Even though Puerto Ricans are citizens of the U.S., they continue to be treated as the inferior other. These detrimental racial dynamics affect the self-image, value, and agency of Puerto Ricans and may explain why many of them live at the poverty level and why months after Hurricane Maria major sectors of the population in Puerto Rico were still without electricity. This history of colonization colors Puerto Rican theology.[4]

Cubans also have their own story and issues. Before the 1959 Cuban revolution, there was moderate migration from Cuba to the U.S. After the revolution, many Cubans came to the U.S. looking for freedom. They thought they were coming for a brief season until Fidel Castro was overthrown. But this did not happen, and they had to stay indefinitely in the U.S. Unlike Mexicans and Puerto Ricans, Cubans were not allowed to travel freely back and forth between the U.S. and their original land, and thus Cubans learned to live as exiled people. In light of this, the topic of exile has become a very important one in their theological articulations. They identify with the people of Israel who had to survive in exile in Babylon, al-

---

[3] Lozano, "Mexicano/a Descent," in *Handbook of Latina/o Theologies*, ed. Aponte and De La Torre, 136-37.

[4] Isasi-Díaz, *En la lucha*, 13; Ortiz, *The Hispanic Challenge*, 48-51.

ways maintaining the hope of returning to their original land.[5] In the same way, other Hispanics/Latin@s who have a heritage from other countries have their own history, concerns, and identity.

While this diversity is enriching, it also poses a problem related to the issue of naming the members of this group. While some of them like to be called Hispanic, others dislike this name because it was assigned by the government as a way to put together, in one box, all of the different groups. Due to this, some prefer to be called Latinas and Latinos, or Latin@s, and still others have adopted names with more political overtones such as "Chicanos/as" and most recently "Latinx". Still, some reject all of these names and prefer to be called according to their country of origin, "Mexicans," "Cubans," "Puerto Ricans," or "Salvadorans." Others prefer to attach also the word "American" to their identity, thus they call themselves "Mexican-Americans" or "Cuban-Americans." It is wise to ask members of these groups what they prefer to be called.

This diversity in naming is reflected also in the way that the theology articulated by these groups is called. While some prefer to call it Hispanic theology, others prefer to use Latino/a or Latin@ theology, and still others prefer to be more specific and use their own particular background such as a Mexican American theology or Puerto Rican theology. I will use the term Hispanic and Latin@ theologies to refer to the theological articulations coming from this diverse group, while respecting the way particular authors have named their theological articulations.

2. Hispanic/Latin@ Theologies

Hispanic/Latin@ theologies are one expression of the theologies of liberation. While it is true that theologies of liberation have their foundation on the biblical themes and impetus of liberation,[6] they owe a great deal to Latin American liberation theology. Hispanic/Latin@ theologies are connected with liberation theology in their objectives of providing a voice for the oppressed people, as well as promoting justice and liberation for them. While liberation theology has defined oppression primarily through a social analysis based on political, social, and economic issues, Hispanic/Latin@ theologies have also included a social analysis that attends to racial and cultural marginalization and exclusion.[7]

---

[5] Suárez, "Cubanas/os," in *Handbook of Latina/o Theologies*, ed. Aponte and De La Torre, 152-54, 158-59.

[6] Martell-Otero, "Liberation Theology," in *Hispanic American Religious Cultures*, ed. De La Torre, 671.

[7] Hernández-Díaz, "Latino/a Theology," in *Hispanic American Religious Cultures*, ed. De La Torre, 657.

A trait common to most of these theologies is a communal perspective. Since the beginning, Hispanic/Latin@ theology has been regarded as a communal enterprise because it represents the voices and insights of the community. It comes from the community and it is for the community.[8] José David Rodríguez identifies this theology as a *teología en conjunto* (a collaborative theology) defined as "the contribution of intellectuals organically rooted in their communities and working in collegiality with other Hispanic theologians in their efforts to bring meaning and public hearing to the faith of their community."[9] As such, one of the goals of this theology is the improvement of the community.

In addition to this collaborative approach, Hispanic/Latin@ theologies are characterized by a rereading of the Bible, history, tradition, and theological articulations from the perspective of the Hispanic/Latin@ community.[10] Due to the oppression and marginalization that this community has suffered, the methodological foundations for this theology, in concurrence with liberation theology, are social location, a preferential option for the poor that includes cultural and social oppression and marginalization, and a liberating praxis that confronts all oppressions.[11]

Hispanic/Latin@ theologies had their origins in the 1970's with pioneers such as theologians Virgilio Elizondo, Orlando Costas, and Justo L. González. Elizondo (1935-2016) was a native of San Antonio, Texas and a well-known Mexican American Catholic priest, leader, and theologian. One of his major contributions is his identification of Jesus as a cultural *mestizo* from Galilee and Mexican Americans as *mestizos,* too. Both are despised by people, but God has a special place and mission for them in the history of salvation. This theme of *mestizaje* has become a major one in Hispanic/Latin@ theologies and later was expanded to include the terms *mulatez*[12] and *sato/a*.[13] Puerto Rican American Baptist pastor and theologian Costas (1942-1987) challenged Christians to proclaim Christ holistically, starting from the perspective of the poor and oppressed and following Jesus' model of movement

---

[8] González, *Mañana*, 28-30.

[9] Rodríguez, "On Doing Hispanic Theology," in *Teología en Conjunto*, ed. Rodríguez and Martell-Otero, 12, 20 n. 6.

[10] Aponte, "Theological and Cultural Competence in Conjunto," in *Handbook of Latina/o Theologies*, ed. Aponte and De La Torre, 6.

[11] Hernández-Díaz, "Latino/a Theology," in *Hispanic American Religious Cultures*, ed. De La Torre, 660.

[12] Hernández-Díaz, "Latino/a Theology," in *Hispanic American Religious Cultures*, ed. De La Torre, 662. Mulatez refers to the mixing of people of African and European roots.

[13] Martell-Otero, "Encuentro con el Jesús Sato," in *Jesus in the Hispanic Community*, ed. Recinos and Magallanes, 74-91. In this essay, Martell-Otero describes a "sato/a" as an impure, worthless, rejected, non-person in Puerto Rico.

toward the oppressed people at the margins of society.[14] Cuban American historian, theologian, and ordained Methodist minister González (1937-) has made significant contributions to the theology and Christian history in general as well as to
Hispanic theology, hermeneutics, homiletics, and liturgical studies, serving also as a
leader in theological education by mentoring and supporting theological students
through the formation of organizations that have been key in increasing the number of Latin@ theological educators in the U.S. In the 1980's Ada Maria Isasi-Díaz
and Yolanda Tarango brought a fresh perspective to Hispanic theologies by giving
expression to the voices and concerns of women in the form of Latina theology.

3. The Development of Latina Theologies

Latina theologies have not grown in a vacuum. They have differing relationships
with traditional theologies, Hispanic theologies, and feminist theologies. Latina
theologies have blossomed in a particular time and space, producing new theological voices and perspectives. This section situates Latina theologies within the history of feminist theologies, discusses the different Latina Feminist theologies, and
explores some of the major topics in these theologies.

Rosemary Radford Ruether argues that even though the major emergence of
feminist theology was in the late 1960's, there were earlier women's voices that
articulated "a critique and reconstruction of sexist paradigms in religion."[15] After
these early voices, the history of feminist theologies has been categorized in three
waves. The first wave (1840-1920s) brought some liberation to women in the U.S.
and England.[16] These theologies recognized the absence of women's perspectives in
Christian theology, which presented only a particular male perspective, that of Eu-
ropean/Euro-American, middle-class, well-educated men.[17]

The second wave of feminist theology dates to the 1960s in the context of the
civil rights and anti-war movements on the one hand and new access for women to
theological education and ministerial opportunities on the other. This period witnessed the emergence of feminist theologians such as Mary Daly, Rosemary Radford Ruether, Elisabeth Schüssler Fiorenza, and Letty Russell who were white
women with formal theological education. They became models and mentors to a
new generation of feminist theologians, and "by the late 1970s and the early 1980s

---

[14] *The Westminster Dictionary of Theologians*, ed. González, s.v. "Orlando Costas" by David
Traverzo Galarza (99).
[15] Ruether, "The Emergence of Christian Feminist Theology," 4-5.
[16] Ruether, "The Emergence of Christian Feminist Theology," 6.
[17] Clifford, *Introducing Feminist Theology*, 29.

feminist theology became an established discourse of American theological schools."[18]

The third wave of feminist theology witnessed a diversification of women's theological voices as ethnic women started to attend theological schools and to reflect from their own context. In the same way that earlier feminist theologians had regarded traditional theology as exclusive, representing only a male voice, ethnic women regarded feminist theology as a white women's theology, representing the voice of only one group of women (white, well-educated, middle-class women). These ethnic women theologians criticized white feminists' universalization of women's experience as well as the omission of ethnic women's experiences, which were affected not only by gender but also by race and class. African American theologians adopted the designation "womanist" theologians and began to reflect from their own experience by following specific theological methods that could address their particular situation. Asian theologians began to reflect also from their own perspective. Likewise, Latina women started to emerge as theologians articulating methods and theologies appropriate to their own reality.[19]

4. Latina Women's Theologies

The diversity in Latina theologies is a reflection of the diversity that exists within the Latin@ population in terms of cultural, historical, and denominational backgrounds. In light of this, there is literature that supports at least three different ways of articulating the theological task from a Latina perspective.[20] The first one is *mujerista* theology, represented by Catholic theologians such as Cuban Ada María Isasi-Díaz (1943-2012) and Mexican American Yolanda Tarango.

Mujerista theology is a liberative praxis—reflective action that has as its goal the liberation of Hispanic women. *Mujerista* theology reflects upon and articulates the religious understandings and practices of Hispanic women. *Mujerista* theology is a communal theological praxis that endeavors to enable Hispanic women to be agents of our own history, to enhance our moral agency, and to design and participate in actions that are effective in our daily struggle for survival.[21]

This theology is concerned primarily with the liberation of Hispanic women and deals with issues of justice and well-being for them and their communities. The primary location of this theology is the U.S., but it is in dialogue with other theologies from around the world. This theology deems inappropriate the term

---

[18] Ruether, "The emergence of Christian feminist theology," 7-10.

[19] Ruether, "The emergence of Christian feminist theology," 10-11; Clifford, *Introducing Feminist Theology*, 25-28.

[20] María Pilar Aquino, "Latina Feminist Theology: Central Features," 133-139.

[21] Isasi-Díaz, "Mujerista Theology's Method," 177.

Hispanic feminism because while it is true that Hispanic women are concerned with sexism, they are equally concerned with issues of race and class, and due to this they have been marginalized within the Anglo feminist community.[22] This term is also problematic because, according to Isasi-Díaz, many Hispanics consider feminism an Anglo concern.[23] Isasi-Díaz suggests the use of the term "*mujerista*" to identify Hispanic women who seek liberation and "*mujerista* theology" for the theological movement that articulates these women's perspectives.[24] Even though *mujerista* theology places itself in discontinuity with the feminist movement, it still maintains a dialogue with feminist and women's theologies around the world. In terms of method, *mujerista* theology regards the "lived-experience" of Hispanic women as its starting point as well as its main theological source. The primary way in which the lived experience of these women is captured is through ethnographic interviews.[25] Regarding the issue of authority, Isasi-Díaz and Tarango affirm that while "both Scripture and Christian tradition are dealt with insofar as they inform and are part of the Hispanic Women's experience and contribute to their liberation," *mujerista* theology considers authoritative "the experience of the Hispanic Women's community."[26]

A second way of doing theology among Latina women is identified as Latina feminist theology. Mexican Catholic Latina feminist theologian María Pilar Aquino (1956-) provides a description of this approach:

> [Latina feminist theology] adopts the understandings and orientations of Latina/Chicana feminism. This theology explicitly acknowledges the feminist struggles of the Latina community. It is internally connected with the history, the legacy, and the current developments of the feminist sociopolitical and ecclesial subjects and movements on both sides of the border. [It takes] seriously the basic premise of all liberation theologies, according to which theological thought emerges from the actual political actors and social movements for social transformation.[27]

Aquino describes the particular commitment and vision of this theology as a new society that is free from patriarchal injustice and violence. Thus, it affirms and

---

[22] Isasi-Díaz, *En la Lucha*, 1-4.

[23] Isasi-Díaz, *En la Lucha*, 4; idem, *Mujerista Theology*, 60-61.

[24] Isasi-Díaz, *En la Lucha*, 4.

[25] Isasi-Díaz, "Mujerista Theology's Method," 177-186; Isasi-Díaz and Tarango, *Hispanic Women: Prophetic Voice in the Church*, xiii.

[26] Isasi-Díaz and Tarango, *Hispanic Women: Prophetic Voice in the Church*, xiv.

[27] Aquino, "Latina Feminist Theology," 138.

promotes new ways of relating that "fully sustain dignity and the integrity of crea-tion."[28]

This theology, unlike *mujerista* theology, is perceived in direct continuity with Latina/Chicana feminist theories and movements. Aquino affirms that femi-nism has a specific Latina/Chicana basis which is not Anglo-oriented, and notes that many Hispanic women identify themselves as feminists. For this reason, the terms "Latina feminist" and "Latina feminist theology" are appropriate for Latina women who seek liberation and the theological movement that supports these women. This theology contrasts with *mujerista* theology in that it extends beyond the U.S., connecting with feminist movements on both sides of the border. Thus, as a feminist theology of the Americas, it is deeply influenced by liberation theolo-gy and Latin American feminist liberation theologies. Latina feminist theology, like *mujerista* theology, seeks the liberation of Latina women by dealing with issues of justice, equality, and integrity for all.[29] It is rooted in the daily lived experiences of grassroots, oppressed Latina, who suffer exploitation and dehumanization. On the other hand, Latina feminist theology contrasts with *mujerista* theology in emphasiz-ing more explicitly the central place of the Bible in the identity of Latina women.[30]

As a way to materialize this dialogue between Latina feminist theology and Latina American feminist theology, María Pilar Aquino organized a symposium in 2004 in Mexico City, where Latina women theologians from both sides of the bor-der gathered to articulate a feminist intercultural theology. This theology, accord-ing to Aquino, is an invitation to a true dialogue that recognizes, but also trans-cends, Latina identities from different contexts (religious, geographic, and racial), in order to challenge "kyriarchal" relations of domination and power, with the goal of joining forces to bring a radical transformation, full of justice, to women's par-ticular environments and the world in general.[31]

The third way of approaching the theological task from Latina women's per-spective is identified as Latina evangélica theology, represented by Loida I. Martell-Otero, an American Baptist theologian from Puerto Rico. She defines this theology as "a collaborative, incarnational, and constructive theological reflection done for the particular perspective of Latina Protestant women."[32] For Martell-Otero, Lati-nas evangélicas are:

---

[28] Aquino, "Latina Feminist Theology," 139.

[29] Aquino, "Latina Feminist Theology," 135-39.

[30] Aquino, "Latina Feminist Theology," 139, 150-53.

[31] Mena-López and Aquino, "Feminist Intercultural Theology," in *Feminist Intercultural Theology*, ed. Aquino and Rosado-Nunes, xxv-xxvii.

[32] Martell-Otero. "Latina Evangélica Theology," in *Hispanic American Religious Cultures*, ed. De La Torre, 327.

[W]omen who, conscious of their religious and cultural roots, construct new theological paradigms that contribute to the transformation of their communities and the liberation of Latinas and other oppressed women....They maintain a vital tension between affirming the life-giving aspects of evangélica beliefs and offering a prophetic critique of the traditions that contribute to the injustice against women in particular, and to oppressed communities in general.[33]

Furthermore, Latina evangélicas are grounded in the life of the grassroots church, in the power of the Holy Spirit, the centrality of the Bible, and a holistic notion of salvation that is manifested in daily life and beyond.[34]

This movement, unlike *mujerista* theology but together with Latina feminist theology, affirms the importance of the Bible for Latina women. Furthermore, it affirms that the Bible must be interpreted under the guidance of the Holy Spirit and that it is authoritative in matters of faith and order.[35] Like *mujerista* and Latina feminist theologies, it is also rooted in the lives of grassroots Hispanic women and seeks their liberation, but unlike them, it is grounded in a particular ecclesiastical belief and practice that has allowed for Latina Protestants a wider participation in church ministries and leadership.[36]

Although there are clear differences among these three approaches, there are also some evident commonalities:

All of them are seeking to liberate women from the social, economic, and political oppressions from which we suffer. Hispanic/Latina women recognize that our community suffers from survival issues: racism, unemployment, staggering health care problems and poverty, crime and domestic violence. We recognize that the liberation of women means that the theological and traditional biblical presuppositions of the community must be reexamined. We recognize that the liberation of women...must reach the home

---

[33] Martell-Otero. "Latina Evangélica Theology," in *Hispanic American Religious Cultures*, ed. De La Torre, 328.

[34] Martell-Otero. "Latina Evangélica Theology," in *Hispanic American Religious Cultures*, ed. De La Torre, 328-29.

[35] Martell-Otero, "Women Doing Theology," 76-78.

[36] Martell-Otero, "Women Doing Theology," 73-75, 82-84. According to Martell-Otero there is a contrast between the way in which Catholic Hispanic women and *evangélicas* relate to their churches because Hispanic Protestant churches have given women more access to positions of power and leadership than their Catholic counterparts. This moderate openness within the churches has influenced the way in which evangélicas articulate their theology.

and the daily reality of our women. It needs to look at, not only how others see and treat women, but also how women see and treat themselves.[37]

5. Latina Theological Themes

5.1. Lo Cotidiano. Lo cotidiano—everyday/daily life—is perceived in Latina feminist theology "as the center of history, invading all aspects of life."[38] María Pilar Aquino argues that traditional theology many times is articulated in the abstract, or it reaches only to the public sphere of life, but in Latina feminist theology daily life is where "the real existence of people is carried out. Daily life is where real transformations take place. Daily life has to do with the totality of life."[39] If this is so, daily life encompasses the whole of life, both the public and the private, and all the relationships that happen within these realms; thus this importance of this category in Latina feminist theology. Although Aquino acknowledges the oppression that *is* produced in the public arena, she insists that daily life is where we find real oppressive structures for women as well as the opportunity to generate a transformation of societal relationships.[40]

Lo cotidiano is also very important in *mujerista* theology. For Isasi-Díaz *lo cotidiano* functions as a descriptive category that elucidates the ways in which Hispanic women go about their daily practices—ways of speaking, relating, and existing. *Lo cotidiano* represents also a hermeneutical category because it not only describes the daily life of Hispanic women but also involves the way this daily life is interpreted and lived according to the discourse, norms, and social roles of Hispanic women themselves. Furthermore, *lo cotidiano* is also an epistemological tool for understanding women's reality—why Hispanic women do what they do and are who they are. It helps in perceiving what is oppressive in their lives and points to a hopeful transformation of this reality. Finally, it helps in differentiating between Latina women's experiences and those of other women in the world. The use of this category is an act of subversion because it challenges the normativity of traditional theologies that have perceived Hispanic women as objects instead of subjects. For all these reasons, *lo cotidiano* functions as a starting point and key theological source for the articulation of a pertinent theology for Hispanic women.[41] *Lo cotidiano* is crucial, too, for Latina evangélica theology. According to Martell-Otero: "Jesus' life and ministry and the Spirit's outpouring save in very concrete ways *en lo*

---

[37] Martell-Otero, "Women Doing Theology," 74.
[38] Aquino, *Our Cry from Life*, 39.
[39] Aquino, "The Collective 'Dis-covery' of Our Own Power," 256.
[40] Aquino, "The Collective 'Dis-covery' of Our Own Power," 256-57.
[41] Isasi-Díaz, *Mujerista Theology*, 66-73.

cotidano (in the spaces of the everyday)." This salvation thus includes "the holistic humanization of the oppressed and disenfranchised."[42]

5.2. Spirituality. Catholic theologian Anita de Luna connects *lo cotidiano* with religious experiences in writing about popular religiosity, spirituality, and faith formation. According to her, "Hispanic women are the transmitters of faith within the culture."[43] Since these women experience all of life through the eyes of faith, they are able to teach and model for the younger generations a devoted and strong faith. Often, these women do this by drawing from their daily religious experiences which constitute a popular religiosity that "is the expression of uncomplicated and profound belief in God,"[44] and is "lived in community in struggle, hope...accessible through simple and direct ways."[45]

Catholic theologian Jeanette Rodríguez researches the relationship between spirituality and activisim in the lives of Latina women by exploring the topic of Latina leadership. It is in the expression of leadership that spirituality becomes embodied, concrete, and present in the world. With other Latina theologians, she affirms the importance of *lo cotidiano* as the context where Latina women experience oppression, but also where they perceive some hopeful seeds of transformation. "Daily life then becomes the point of departure, and women's spirituality and leadership are work done with the body, the heart, the hands, and the head."[46] For Rodríguez, spirituality and leadership are holistic and reflect a desire for life because they are expressed in everything that Latina women do that sustains life. It is this spirituality, expressed in activism and leadership, that empowers and encourages women as they struggle against injustices.[47]

On the Protestant side, *evangélica* theologian Elizabeth Conde-Frazier also affirms the importance of *lo cotidiano* in her insistence that the spirituality of Hispanic women is conditioned by their stories as well as their sexuality. This means that spirituality is grounded in women's concrete lives in a particular culture, time, and space. Regarding sexuality, Conde-Frazier maintains that women's bodies are intrinsic to how women understand and experience God. Since women, whether

---

[42] Martell-Otero, "From Satas to Santas," in *Latina Evangélicas*, ed. Martell-Otero, Pérez, and Conde-Frazier, 35.

[43] De Luna, *Faith Formation and Popular Religion*, 171.

[44] De Luna, *Faith Formation and Popular Religion*, 168.

[45] De Luna, *Faith Formation and Popular Religion*, 40.

[46] Rodríguez, "Latina Activists," in *A Reader in Latina Feminist Theology*, ed. Aquino, Machado, and Rodríguez, 122.

[47] Rodríguez, "Latina Activists," in *A Reader in Latina Feminist Theology*, ed. Aquino, Machado, and Rodríguez, 125–128.

they are biological mothers or not, give and nurture life in all of its expressions (physical, spiritual, emotional), they perceive God as creator and sustainer of life.[48]

Conde-Frazier argues that Hispanic women's spirituality is characterized by attentiveness and waiting that leads women to take time to discern wisely how to speak or be silent, act or refrain from acting. But spirituality is also characterized by a relational connectedness that leads women to connect with God and each other through prayers and powerful testimonies that help them find their own voice as they seek God's will for their lives. These intimate and intense moments lead women to a passionate compassion that is translated in support for each other and the community through words and acts of encouragement and struggle.[49]

5.3. Reinterpretations of Hispanic Female Symbols of Womanhood. Latina theologians have been interested in the historical roots and developments of these Hispanic female symbols of womanhood as well as concerned with the effects that they have had upon Latina women. For these reasons, some Latina theologians have engaged in research that analyzes these symbols and provides new alternative readings that are more liberating for Latina women

Traditionally, the Virgin Mary/Virgin of Guadalupe has been seen as an oppressive figure for women because she seems to provide an example of purity, patience, obedience, submission, and long-suffering for women.[50] However, some people see her in a different way. Latina theologian Jeanette Rodríguez perceives the Virgin as a liberating figure for women. For her, the encounter between the Virgin of Guadalupe and Juan Diego is liberating because after this encounter Juan Diego was able to relate differently to God and the world around him. She affirms that this liberating moment happens again every time Mexican American Catholic women encounter the Lady of Guadalupe: it is a liberating experience for them. Rodríguez stresses that Mexican American Catholic women need to know more about the Guadalupe event in order to find in it more options for liberation and empowerment.[51]

While Catholic Hispanic people usually interpret this event through the eyes of faith,[52] I contend that this is impossible for Protestants because of their lack of faith in the Virgin of Guadalupe. In addition, they have actively been taught to ignore her (both the biblical Virgin Mary and her representation in the Virgin of

---

[48] Conde-Frazier, "Hispanic Protestant Spirituality," in *Teologia in Conjunto,* ed. Rodríguez and Martell-Otero, 138-40.

[49] Conde-Frazier, "Hispanic Protestant Spirituality," in *Teologia in Conjunto,* ed. Rodríguez and Martell-Otero, 140-42.

[50] Lozano-Díaz, "Ignored Virgin or Unaware Women," 209-11.

[51] Rodríguez, *Our Lady of Guadalupe,* 159-65.

[52] Elizondo, *La Morenita,* 79, 86. Rodríguez also affirms this in *Our Lady of Guadalupe,* 6-17, 159.

Guadalupe). However, ignoring her is not easy because long ago the Virgin of Guadalupe became much more than a Catholic devotional figure; she became a part of the Mexican culture. Thus, I suggest that Protestants, but especially Protestant women, deal with the Virgin of Guadalupe as a cultural symbol that has affected the meaning of womanhood in this patriarchal culture. By questioning and challenging the traditional view of the Virgin and providing feminist liberating reinterpretations of the biblical Virgin Mary, Hispanic Protestant women will find new roads toward liberation and wholeness.[53]

Another female symbol that has been used to define Latina womanhood is that of La Malinche. La Malinche's story is one of betrayal, as she was sold by her family as a slave and later given to the Spanish conqueror Hernan Cortez. She became his translator, lover, and eventually mother of one of his sons. Traditionally, La Malinche has been perceived as the opposite of the Virgen of Guadalupe. If the Virgin is seen as the pure, idealized woman, La Malinche has been perceived as the Mexican Eve who is a traitor, temptress, and sexual object. Aware of the problems of identity that La Malinche presents for Latina women, Nancy Pineda-Madrid has reinterpreted her by providing an alternative reading presenting her as a woman who was a visionary because she was able to foresee what Cortez or Moctezuma could not: the creation of a new race. In the process of this creation, Pineda-Madrid stresses that La Malinche acted as an agent who was knowledgeable of her historical circumstances, made her own decisions, and was in charge of her sexuality.[54]

A third female symbol that has determined to a certain extent the meaning of womanhood in Latina culture is Sor Juana Inés de la Cruz, a Mexican nun from the seventeenth century. Since her childhood, Sor Juana displayed an amazing intellect that led her to be one of the most prolific scholars of her time and the first woman theologian of the Americas. Since she was a woman, she became the victim of discrimination and abuse by both society and the church. By studying and reinterpreting her life, Michelle Gonzalez recovers a marginalized voice in the history of the Christian tradition that has much to teach about beauty, goodness and truth and reclaims a foremother as a model that challenges and encourages Latina women to think, to do intellectual work, and to be theologians and scholars.[55]

5.4. Nepantla. According to Gloria Anzaldúa, "Nepantla is the Nahuatl word for an in-between state, that uncertain terrain one crosses when moving from one

---

[53] Lozano-Díaz, "Ignored Virgin or Unaware Women," 204-16.
[54] Pineda-Madrid, "Notes Toward a Chicana Feminist Epistemology," 257-260.
[55] Gonzalez, *Sor Juana.*

place to another."[56] Nepantla can mean a physical or emotional crossing of borders that sometimes can produce a sense of disorientation. This disorientation is a reality for people who live in the borderlands.[57] "To exist in Nepantla is to live on the border, on the boundaries of cultures and social structures, where life is in constant motion."[58] These in-between spaces can be confusing and debilitating, until a person recognizes and understands the forces of colonization and domination in them. Once this level of awareness is reached, living in Nepantla may turn into a rich, powerful, meaningful, and transformative space.[59] For Latina theologians "entering Nepantla means...that we are willing to engage in new explorations about God and ourselves from the creative 'border' locations."[60]

6. Conclusion

Hispanic/Latin@ theologies offer rich contributions to Baptist practices of theology in terms of method and content. They give expression to new voices offering perspectives that display Hispanic/Latino@ diversity and strengthen the theological dialogue around the academic world. But these contributions go beyond the academy as these theologies empower grassroots Latin@s in their struggle to find liberation and a better existence. If ministers who lead Baptist churches attend to the work of listening to them, they will be able to help the members of their churches to walk along pathways that become more fully visible when viewed through the kaleidoscope of Hispanic/Latin@ theologies, learning about the struggles and needs of the Hispanic/Latino@ community and finding the most appropriate ways to minister with and to this community.

7. For Further Reading

Aquino, María Pilar, Daisy L. Machado, and Jeanette Rodríguez, eds. *A Reader in Latin Feminist Theology: Religion and Justice.* Austin: University of Texas Press, 2002.

Elizondo, Virgilio. *Galilean Journey: The Mexican-American Promise.* Maryknoll, NY: Orbis Books, 2005.

González, Justo L. *Mañana: Christian Theology from a Hispanic Perspective.* Nashville: Abingdon Press, 1990.

---

[56] Anzaldúa, "Chicana Artists: Exploring Nepantla, el Lugar de la Frontera," 165. The Nahuatls were indigenous people from central Mexico.

[57] Anzaldúa, "Chicana Artists: Exploring Nepantla, el Lugar de la Frontera," 166.

[58] Medina, "Nepantla," in *Hispanic American Religious Cultures*, ed. De La Torre, 406.

[59] Medina, "Nepantla," in *Hispanic American Religious Cultures*, ed. De La Torre, 405.

[60] Aquino. "Latina Feminist Theology," 149.

Isasi-Díaz, Ada María. *Mujerista Theology.* Maryknoll, NY: Orbis Books, 1996.
Martell-Otero, Loida I., Zaida Maldonado Pérez, and Elizabeth Conde-Frazier. *Latina Evangélicas: A Theological Survey from the Margins.* Eugene, OR: Cascade Books, 2013.

5

Light from Asian Theologies

Atola Longkumer

Asian Christianity presents many new prospects and hope for global Christianity, especially through its encounter with the ancient religious traditions of the continent. (Felix Wilfred)[1]

The continent of Asia is diverse with a myriad of cultures, languages, and religious traditions. The plurality of socio-cultural ways also engenders intricate complexities and multiple identities across Asian societies. The aspect of immense diversity in Asia is also evident in Christianity and its expressions in many forms of Christianities observable in Asia.[2] While the Bible remains the fundamental foundation for theological discourse and local Christian spiritualities, Asian theologies have attended to the contextual realities of the communities. A region home to many ancient civilizations, Asia straddles both traditions of antiquity and a modern period marked by globalization and its many cognates. Asian theologies, therefore, emerge from Asian Christianities that attempt to dialogue with the complexities of Asia. The illumination, understanding, and witness to the goodness of the gospel become real in engaging the challenges inherent in Asian contexts.

Sources of light from Asian theologies emit from the lived struggles and hopes of the people as they respond to the good news in Christ. Inspired by the challenges of the contexts, distinctively Asian theologies have developed that interpret and contextualize the Christian faith in Asian contexts: theologies forged through interreligious dialogue, feminist theology, and people's theologies such as Minjung, Dalit, tribal, and indigenous theologies. The position and participation of women remains a critical topic that needs to be seen as transversing all the theologies articulated in Asia. The chapter will underscore women's active participation in local Christianities despite ecclesiastical discriminations as a shining source of light from Asian theologies that is Christ-centered and transformational. It begins with a brief description of Asia and clarification of such terms as contextual, inculturation, and

---

[1] Wilfred, ed., *Oxford Handbook of Christianity in Asia*, 2.
[2] Phan, ed., *Christianities in Asia*. For a concise summary of Asian theology see Evers, "Asian Theology." See also Kim, ed., *Christian Theology in Asia*.

indigenous, and concludes by highlighting some distinct aspects of Asian Christianities that could be considered as gifts to global Christianity in the shared commitment to witness to Christ, the light of the world.

1. Asian Diversity

Peter C. Phan begins with two questions, "Which Asia?" and "Which Christianity?", to introduce the continent of "extreme contrasts."[3] "Asia is not one but many,"[4] and one or more representative contexts or articulations cannot comprehensively portray Asia with all its heterogeneity. The idea of the continent of Asia is more a convenient term tracing back to antiquity and solidified during medieval times as the then-known earth was divided into three parts: the continents of Asia, Europe and Africa.[5] Such plurality and heterogeneity of Asia have enormous implications in efforts to define and articulate Asian theologies. Asia is more than the geographical designation; as the largest and most populous continent, it also has a complex web of socio-cultural identities and disparate economies.[6] Theological articulations in every historical period are invariably inspired by and rooted in the contexts,[7] and therefore, theological enunciations from Asia emerge from the contexts of the "promises and crises"[8] of the rapidly transforming Asia.

Drawing from the contextual realities and critical analyses of the historical experiences of Christian mission, Asian theologians have developed critical theologies. These critical and contextual theologies engage robustly the Euro-centric theology.[9] While contextually rooted, Asian theological articulations also acknowledge the historical fact of Asia as the cradle of Christianity, which ironically has encoun-

---

[3] Phan, ed., *Christianities in Asia*, 2.

[4] Elwood, "Asian Christian Theology in the Making," 23-39.

[5] Reichert, *Das Bild der Welt im Mittelalter*, 9-42.

[6] Among the many resources that define, describe, and delineate Asia in its diverse regions, see Johnson and Ross, eds., *Atlas of Global Christianity 1910-2010*, 134-53; Moffett, *A History of Christianity in Asia*; Wilfred, ed., *Oxford Handbook of Christianity in Asia*; Kim, ed., *Christian Theology in Asia*.

[7] Morimoto, "Asian Theology in the Ablative Case," 201-15. See also Song, *Theology from the Womb of Asia*.

[8] Kwok, *Introducing Asian Feminist Theology*.

[9] Elwood, ed., *Asian Christian Theology*. For a helpful bibliography of Asian Christian theologies in three volumes, see England, *Asian Christian Theologies*. The critical theological articulations from Asian contexts are recognized by, e.g., Stephen B. Bevans, who states, "Asian Christians are engaged in some of the most exciting and creative theologizing in the world today" (Bevans, *An Introduction to Theology in Global Perspective*, 311).

tered the most vehement resistance from other ancient civilizations.[10] Hence, Asian theologies include critical awareness of the tremendous impact of Christianity in Asian cultures and societies. As Felix Wilfred writes, "[t]he impact of Christianity in Asia cannot be overestimated; it led to intellectual revolutions, religio-cultural confrontations, and social conflicts but also to fundamental transformation of Asian societies."[11] By the same token, the encounter of Christianity with Asian cultures also occasioned critical theological questions often manifested in theological controversies as well as the expansion of theological perspectives, transforming Christianity in the process.[12] The heterogeneity of Asian contexts thus includes the conditions encapsulated by the following terms among others: "diversity of cultures," "ancient," "plurality of religions," "Christianity," "poverty," "indigenous peoples," "new economic era," "social hierarchy," "development," "environment," "youth," "women," "migrants," "sexuality," "religious freedom," "violence," and "repressions."

2. Theologies in Asia: Contextual, Inculturated, Indigenous

"And if the church cannot speak to issues of authentic human life, what does it have to say?"[13] In this statement, the Taiwanese theologian C. S. Song captures the fundamental *raison d'etre* for Asian theologies. The church as harbinger of the good news of Christ is relevant only when it becomes aware of the immediate lived realities, identifies itself with the struggles of the contexts, critically engages the destructive, life-denying structures, and translates the good news into lived ways for the flourishing of all.

The need to "speak to the issues of authentic human life" has underpinned the many theological articulations that have emerged from contexts in Asia. Speaking to the issues, engaging the contextual realities, and sharing in the hope of transformation and freedom are defining marks of the theologies developed in Asia.

Local theology generally is framed and informed by terms such as "contextual," "inculturation," and "indigenous," and specific terms related to the contexts such as Dalit, Minjung, tribal, and Adivasi. While the different terms share a common objective of articulating theological concepts that engage particularly the socio-economic and religio-cultural terrains, the different terms might also indicate

---

[10] Wilfred, *Oxford Handbook of Asian Christianity*, 2. For a Catholic perspective, see, Evers, *The Churches in Asia*, xx-xxi.

[11] Wilfred, *Oxford Handbook of Asian Christianity*, 2.

[12] Wilfred, *Oxford Handbook of Asian Christianity*, 2. Cf. Worcester, "Chinese Rites Controversy," 165; Bays, *A New History of Christianity in China*; Ward, *Women Religious Leaders in Japan's Christian Century, 1549–1650*.

[13] Song, *Tracing the Footsteps of God*, 116.

diversities of historical periods, church traditions, and for some, political positions—as is the case with "indigenous theology."[14]

The encounter and embrace of the Christian faith cannot be understood in isolation from the particular context and its socio-cultural realities. In other words, espousal and expression of faith in Christ is always anchored in the individual's existential conditions. For instance, the narratives of conversion to Christianity in Asia describe the events ingrained in the intricacies of socio-cultural and political locations.[15] The term "contextual" became prominent in relation to the shaping of theological education and its curricula into a more context-related approach as proposed and developed by C. S. Song. Contextual theology then was further developed in other contexts, interpreting the good news of the gospel in cognizance of such realities as poverty and plurality of faiths.[16]

"Inculturation" is another term associated with theology that arises from the engagement of local religio-cultural realities. The term is long associated with the modes of introducing the gospel by employing local terms and ritual practices and often identifying with the local elite cultures, particularly in the evangelization by the Jesuits.[17] Articulation of local responses and interpretation of the good news has also popularized another term, "indigenous," which underlines the agency of the native and the accommodation of the local cultures in expressions of Christianity.[18]

"World Christianity" is another term that has gained prominence in exploring local experiences and expressions of Christianity. The emergence of World Christianity takes into account the growth and impact of Christianity in cultures of the Global South, making Christianity a world religion.[19] World Christianity's defining objective is locating under-represented, marginalized, and supplanted voices and narratives in the cultures and communities wherein Christianity has taken root and initiated transformation.

These above mentioned terms provide a rubric for the articulations of Asian theologies in Asian contexts and their embrace of the good news, characterized by intense and often contested and negotiated appropriation of the existing religio-

---

[14] Stanley, "Inculturation: Historical Background, Theological Foundations and Contemporary Questions," 22; Costa, ed., *One Faith, Many Cultures*.

[15] For discussions on this theme, see Viswanathan, *Outside the Fold*; Sharkey, *Cultural Conversions*; Kwok, *Chinese Women and Christianity 1860-1927*; Hayami, *Between Hills and Plains*.

[16] Schreiner, "Contextual Theology."

[17] The term "inculturation" gained usage in reference to the mission history of the Jesuits. See Pieris, *An Asian Theology of Liberation*, 52.

[18] See Bhakiaraj, "Forms of Asian Indigenous Christianities."

[19] Kim and Kim, eds., *Christianity as a World Religion*; Robert, *Christian Mission*; Sanneh, *Whose Religion Is Christianity?*; Tan and Tran, eds., *World Christianity*.

cultural templates, which in turn result in transformation of the social matrices.[20] Sources of light from Asian theologies therefore emit from the processes of reception, appropriation, and interpretation of the gospel.

3. Interreligious Theology in Asia

Asia is generally described as a continent of religions, where most of the world religions have their historical roots of origin. Indic religions (Hinduism, Jainism, Sikhism), Buddhism (and the many local interpretations and experiences such as Zen Buddhism and Tibetan Buddhism), Zoroastrianism, Daoism, Shinto, Confucianism, Islam, and many indigenous people's religiosities are active religions in Asia. These religions actively influence and direct the ways of living for both individuals and the communities of Asia. While Christianity took shape as a religion in its interactions and responses to challenges and questions in West Asia, the form, beliefs, and practices that most of Asia encountered was Christianity as shaped and interpreted by the western cultures. Although there were earlier encounters with Christianity in Asia, the Christianity that left the most vibrant impact on the continent was introduced concurrent to the rise of the West and its imperial conquests. These historical realities had implications for Christian witness.[21]

Asia with its plurality of religions has provided vibrant examples of interreligious dialogue. The new forms and the innovative interpretations of the received religious teachings observed in the history of religious developments in Asia are evidence of the fecund interactions between religious truth claims and local appropriations. For instance, the intense devotional spiritual path—known as bhakti in Hindu tradition—has been influenced by the Islamic *sufi* tradition, and the Tibetan Buddhism that incorporates both the teachings of Buddha and existing local traditions such as the *bon* (spirits) produced a distinct Buddhism with Lama (teacher) as a central figure.[22]

While there are also records of contests and conflicts among Asia's plurality of religions, the interreligious interactions and cross-fertilizations have inspired later Christian theological articulations to develop dialogical conversations between Asian religions and Christianity.[23] Springing from these dialogical conversations,

---

[20] Brian Stanley argues that "Inculturation is arguably the most far-reaching of the three concepts, for it implies that the whole body of the Christian message, not just its external wrapping, needs to take flesh, become incarnate, in the patterns of thought, language, and symbols of a particular culture." Stanley, "Inculturation," 22.

[21] See Stanley, *The Bible and the Flag*; Etherington, *Mission and Empire*; Ward, "Christianity, Colonialism and Missions."

[22] Hawley, *Three Bhakti Voices*; Lopez, ed., *Religions of Tibet in Practice*.

[23] Phan, *Being Religious Interreligiously*; Samartha, *One Christ Many Religions*.

sources of light from Asian theologies include Christian faithful witness amidst a plurality of religions in Asia, marked by its intentional posture of being a respectful conversation partner in seeking a vision that includes the flourishing of all creation.

4. Minjung Theology

Minjung theology is a theology that is rooted and developed in Asia in the late twentieth century in the Republic of Korea. The term "minjung" is a Korean term, which gained coinage as a term to describe the nameless, vulnerable people who were exploited, discriminated against, and powerless in a socio-economic system dominated by a capitalistic neo-liberal society.[24] Minjung theology was developed in the 1970s as Korea was rapidly pursuing neo-liberal economic policies at the expense of people's dignity and well-being. Minjung theology emerged as a people's theology as workers began protest movements voicing their discontent against exploitations of labor.

A poignant event on November 13, 1970 serves as a defining moment of the minjung movement. As workers staged protests against labor exploitations, a young worker named Chun Tae Il immolated himself. In respond to this sacrifice, masses of young people were mobilized to demand labor rights and further the democratization movement. Ahn Byung Mu, Suh Nam Dong, Hyun Young Hak, Kim Yong Bock, and Chung Hyun Kyung are the theologians who provided the earliest articulations of Minjung theology.[25] Minjung theology is marked by the passionate struggle to interpret the gospel of Christ in the context of a people striving for dignity and recognition in a socio-economic structure that valued profit more than the dignity of the people.

5. Dalit Theology in India

Like the Minjung Theology of Korea, Dalit Theology is a theology in the vein of the people's liberation movement. Dalit theology arises from the socio-cultural background of India.

The earliest proponents of Dalit theology have defined the term "dalit," derived from Sanskrit, as "broken" or "crushed."[26] As a critique of contextual theology in India that sourced itself from the Hindu traditions, Dalit theology was developed to resist and to articulate the experience of oppression of a group of people in India through the social practice of caste violence. The Hindu religious traditions derived from the Vedas—the sacred scripture of the Brahminical traditions—

---

[24] Chung, Kärkkäinen, and Kim, eds., *Asian Contextual Theology for the Third Millennium.*
[25] Kuster, *A Protestant Theology of Passion.*
[26] Nirmal, "Toward a Christian Dalit Theology"; Webster, *Dalit Christians.*

categorized and classified their members according to socially rigid caste groups.[27] Based on this social stratification, the people who were classified as Dalits are suppressed and violated to inhuman levels.[28] They are dehumanized, landless, bonded laborers, branded as impure, and they comprise the mass of poverty in India. According to the Vedas, the Dalits are prohibited to read the Hindu sacred scriptures, prohibited to co-inhabit village spaces, and are not allowed to enter the temples.

In the development of an inculturated and indigenous Indian Christian theology, aspects of Hinduism were uncritically appropriated, in that a Brahminical understanding of society was privileged as the conversation partner in the so-called Indian Christian theology. Dalit theology, therefore, was developed with dual objectives: on one hand, to critique the Indian Christian theology that privileged a Brahminical aspect of the religion,[29] and on the other hand, to give voice to the experience of dehumanization of the Dalits and to claim freedom and dignity.[30]

6. Indigenous/Tribal/*Adivasi* Theology

Asia is home to many indigenous peoples, although Asia's indigenous peoples are often ignored or subsumed within the larger religio-cultural traditions. According to statistics, there are about 260 million indigenous peoples in Asia, making it the most culturally diverse region in the world.[31] Different terms are used, often local terms such as *adivasi* (first dwellers in Sanskrit) in India; however, the broad rubric term "indigenous" encompasses these local variations to identify the cultures that are distinct from the dominant traditions. Shared features include the experience of invasion and subjugation by dominant groups, consciousness of the natural environment, the centrality of land, oral-based knowledge, the lack of canonized sacred texts, and a social structure often based on rigid social kinship.

As minorities, the indigenous peoples experience marginalization and discrimination, often compounded by policies of exclusion that threaten the obliteration of their cultural heritage and land rights. Indigenous theology asserts the voice and identity of the indigenous peoples by highlighting the central features of the com-

---

[27] Significant studies on the reification of the caste structures in relation to colonial period is another perspective; e.g., Dirks, *Castes of Mind*.

[28] Gidla, *Ants among Elephants*.

[29] Modern Hinduism and its reification as a religion cannot be isolated from the modern Christian movement. See Oddie, *Imagined Hinduism*, and King, *Orientalism and Religion*.

[30] Clarke, Manchala, and Peacock, eds., *Dalit Theology in the Twenty-First Century*.

[31] International Work Group for Indigenous Affairs, online www.iwgia.org/regions/asia (downloaded February 27, 2019). For a discussion on the term "indigenous" and its international usage, see Erni, ed., *The Concept of Indigenous Peoples in Asia*.

munity and reclaiming their narratives as repositories of wisdom.[32] Indigenous theology is affirmed by the Federation of Asian Bishops Conference (FABC), which
states that "much of the indigenous peoples' world view and ethos is compatible
with the Christian faith," and therefore the "traditional beliefs, rites, myths and
symbols of indigenous peoples provide material for developing indigenous theologies and liturgical ceremonies."[33]

7. Feminist Theology and the Participation of
Women in Local Asian Christianities

Kwok Pui-Lan rightly cautioned against a "generalized, monolithic and ahistorical"
image of Asian women.[34] Despite variations, Asian societies are fundamentally patriarchal with male-centric attitudes that render women marginalized and excluded
in many ways. The intersection of religious restrictions, socio-cultural expectations,
and economic policies produces social realities that often restrain women from participation in the society as well as ecclesiastical spaces. While women's movements
toward the transformation of patriarchal cultures to more inclusive communities
are taking place, often spearheaded by feminist theological proposals, across the
diverse sectors and social classes women in Asia continue to face discrimination,
violence, and victimization.

Asian feminist theology includes the diversity of socio-economic, religio-
cultural, political, and ecclesial contexts, as well as a plurality of experiences: not
only of being victims, poor, and marginalized, but also of being capable and active
agents in their contexts. Asian women occupy multiple identities—modern, post-
modern, liberated, and creative, together with being excluded, exploited, and vulnerable.[35] Herein lies the strength of Asian feminist movements and theologies.
Amidst rigid patriarchal attitudes, women in Asian Christianities have participated
in nurturing the community of faith, often from peripheral locations. Asian wom-
en exhibit courage and wisdom in voicing their discontent. Being relegated to marginal locations has not suppressed Asian women in employing their gifts. Examples

---

[32] Fung, "Postcolonial Encounters with Indigenous Religions for Peace and Ecological
Harmony," 4; Minz, "Religion, Culture, and Education in the Context of Tribal Aspirations in
India,"; Longchar, *Tribal Theology*.

[33] Federation of Asian Bishops Conferences, *The Spirit at Work in Asia Today*, 23.

[34] Kwok, *Introducing Asian Feminist Theology*.

[35] Fabella and Park, eds., *We Dare to Dream*; Kang, "Re-constructing Asian Feminist Theology"; Kim, "Cutting Edges." Among the many Asian scholars and theologians who have provided critical commentary on the term Asian and cautioned against homogeneity are idem, "The
'Indigestible' Asian"; idem, "Which Postcolonialism?" 23-35; Ching, "Negotiating for a Postcolonial Identity of 'the Poor Women' in Asia."

abound: the Japanese *Kirishitan* women martyrs, Myanmar Karen Baptist women refugees, Filipina Christian maids, the many Bible women who were often the first evangelists in many communities, and Korean women theologians. Asian feminist theology is therefore marked by dual emphases: to name and challenge the oppressive attitudes against women, often rooted in the religious practices legitimized by the sacred texts, and to recover, highlight, and bring to the fore the active embrace of the Gospel and active participation in its witness.

8. Asian Theologies as Sources of Light for the Global Church

As the world becomes more interconnected and interdependent, Christian witness is a common witness. With the diversities of historical experiences, contextual realities, and local expressions, Christians share a common foundation and a common call to witness to the good news in Christ. The shared identity as members of the one body of Christ with a common vision to witness to the joy of the gospel was reiterated at the Edinburgh 2010 centenary celebration of the World Missionary Conference, in the following words:

> Recalling Christ, the host at the banquet, and committed to that unity for which he lived and prayed, we are called to ongoing co-operation, to deal with controversial issues and to work towards a common vision. We are challenged to welcome one another in our diversity, affirm our membership through baptism in the One Body of Christ, and recognize our need for mutuality, partnership, collaboration, and networking in mission, so that the world might believe.[36]

The call for mutual learning and witness invites openness and hospitality to the diversities of contexts. Asian theologies have emerged that are rooted in and defined by the historical contexts of suffering, exploitation, discrimination, and marginalization, wherein the good news of the gospel holds the promise of reconciliation, compassion, and flourishing of life for the whole creation.

The contextual inspirations that feed Asian theologies entail for the global church the challenge to translate, interpret, and live the good news, providing answers to "immediate authentic issues of life." As minority communities with inherent complexities and ambiguities, Asian theologies represent rays of light that are hopeful in their commitment to the flourishing of all.

While Asian Christianity has its own critical challenges to continuing to be a faithful witness, in its struggle to live as minorities amidst ancient and dominant civilizations compounded by culture of growing materialism as a consequence of

---

[36] Edinburgh 2010 Conference, *Edinburgh 2010 Common Call.*

economic globalization, Asian Christianity offers an example to the global church of the transformation possible in the gospel.

9. Conclusion

With broad strokes of the brush, this chapter has attempted to present a complex portrait of Asia and its Christianities, with a history of critical engagement with the cultures and the questions they raise for bearing faithful witness to the gospel. Christianity in Asia, despite its minority status, demonstrates its commitment to the freedom and flourishing of God's creation. The emergence of Asian theologies is therefore inspired by the compassionate God, revealed in Jesus Christ, and empowered by the Holy Spirit. In their expression of theologies that call for just society, these Asian theologies have been enlightened by the light of the gospel, while the socio-economic and political contexts have posed a challenge for interpreting the good news in light of the immediate questions and issues. Writing on World Christianity and its prospects for continuing the early church ethos, Andrew F. Walls affirms that "[o]nce more, there is a church across the world, across the continents, across cultures, across languages and once more there is just the glimmering hope of a world Christian consciousness, a recognition that we belong together."[37]

The global Christian community shares in a common hope and joy in the gospel. The task remains for forging partnerships towards a common witness undergirded by mutual learning and deep conversations, for the Triune God intends the flourishing of all creation and invites the global church to participate in God's desire for creation.

10. For Further Reading

Brazal, Agnes M. A *Theology of Southeast Asia: Liberation Postcolonial Ethics in the Philippines*. Maryknoll, NY: Orbis Books, 2019.

Elwood, Douglas J., ed. *Asian Christian Theology: Emerging Themes*. Philadelphia: Westminster Press, 1980.

Kim, Sebastian C. H. *Christian Theology in Asia*. Cambridge: Cambridge University Press, 2008.

Kyung, Chung Hyun. *Struggling to be the Sun Again: Introducing Asian Women's Theology*. Maryknoll, NY: Orbis Books, 1990.

Orevillo-Montenegro, Murial. *The Jesus of Asian Women: Women from the Margins*. Maryknoll, NY: Orbis Books, 2006.

Pieris, Aloysius. *An Asian Theology of Liberation*. Maryknoll, NY: Orbis Books, 1988.

---

[37] Walls, *Crossing Cultural Frontiers*, 16.

6

Mistaking White for Light:
Awakening to a Truthful Search for the Light

Mikael N. Broadway

The work of theology originates in crisis and struggle. This acknowledgment is one of the first things my divinity students learn from James Wm. McClendon, Jr., as they read from his introduction to the practice of theology.[1] It is not hard for them to relate to the identity-forming nature of theological convictions and the dislocation that comes from encountering God revealed in Jesus Christ through the power of the Holy Spirit. In their introductory theology course, they grapple with the historical moment of crisis when followers of Jesus found their hopes destroyed by his execution as an enemy of the empire and its client regime. Yet only days later, the same friends were hearing or even seeing for themselves that the one who had died was alive and explaining to them so many things they had not understood.

The crisis of the resurrection was an awakening for the people around Jesus. It became a fruitful growing space for the creation of concepts and language to describe this unique work of God that would anchor and center the church's understanding of what God had done from eternity—through creation, the election of Israel, the exile and restoration, and now the incarnation, the calling of the church, and the coming of the Spirit. What they *had not* thought and understood was becoming the very convictional center of a new world with a new way of living as God's people. It did not happen immediately. It took some time to make the transition from one version of monotheistic faith which saw Jesus' words as implicating him in blasphemy to a new version which could encompass the inward relationality of the One God now understood as eternal Trinity.

In the early twenty-first century, another era of awakening is taking place. While we don't need a repeat of the incarnation and resurrection, we do need to awaken to the distorted theological frame in which we see God and the world in this age. The current awakening comes out of a long-enduring crisis: the invention of a stratified human world based on the false doctrines of race. The rise of modern

---

[1] McClendon, *Systematic Theology*, vol. 1, *Ethics*, rev. ed., 17.

European world domination was accompanied by a theoretical shaping of a racialized world. Through the invention of race, political and economic structures of domination gained justification by ranking people according to the characteristics of their bodies—most importantly the lightness and darkness of their skin. This was, above all, the invention of whiteness as an idea and categorical standard by which to judge all humanity and culture.

Whiteness is a fiction. People designated as "white" as well as other racialized groups in fact have a wide polychromatic range. Skin color and other bodily features do tell us some history of a person's ancestors' geographical location and might provide significant information about a person's cultural heritage, but there is no essential relationship between these body features and a person's character, abilities, and limitations.

1. Awakening to See Whiteness and Its Regulatory Power

To say that whiteness is a fiction is not to say that people who have come to know themselves as "white" do not have a heritage worth acknowledging and preserving. However, the lumping together of an immense and complex variety of people from different language, ethnic, and national groups tends to obscure the actual heritage and traditions passed on by these people's ancestors. Instead, whiteness overlooks these particularities and seeks to replace them with an invented commonality of Euro-American solidarity. This idea grew into prominence in the modern age, the era marked by the expansion of European power to other continents, aided by asserting the Doctrine of Discovery.[2] Ultimately, the racial stratification from white to black became a regulatory structure to organize bodies in a budding global society, marking some bodies for power, opportunity, and life while marking other bodies for subordination, marginalization, and death.[3]

The impediment of whiteness is its merging of Christianity with the ways of the dominant Euro-American colonizing powers. Many have recounted the historical record that led to our current crisis.[4] Papal decrees granted Europeans the right to claim lands occupied by people who had not yet received the gospel. Casuistic theological arguments justified the enslavement of inhabitants of the Americas and

---

[2] For Christians interested in learning about the Doctrine of Discovery from the perspective of a theological reflection and critique, I recommend the work of Mark Charles available via his web site *Wirelesshogan*, online https://wirelesshogan.com/category/doctrine-of-discovery/. See also Charles and Rah, *Unsettling Truths*.

[3] Carter, *Race*, 66-68, 249-50.

[4] One of the better condensed histories of the rise of white supremacy, especially in the American colonies and the U.S., is Douglas, *Stand Your Ground*.

Africa.[5] British colonial church law determined that baptism cannot change a person's condition of freedom or servitude. Laws declared skin color a permanent marker for freedom or enslavement. Almost all churches of European colonial powers accommodated this racialized structuring of the world; thus, people who had received faith in Christ through families and communities who had passed it down through generations came to accept a theology in which whites were favored by God for political rule over the bodies of darker-skinned people.

Baptist history runs closely parallel to the rise of the modern age and its reorganization of the world according to race. The seventeenth century during which Baptists originated among English expatriates and in England itself also marks the rapid rise of British imperial power and the early stages of colonization of North America. The eighteenth-century Great Awakening in New England, and its later spread to the southern colonies, corresponds to an era of Anglo-American national identity formation. In both cases, Baptists came into being as a distinct confessional group in times when racialized political and economic structures played crucial roles in establishing their contexts of existence. Baptists have sometimes found themselves resisting elements of the Anglo-American cultural context, but they have also been encompassed by its besetting sins.

2. Awakening from Whiteness—A Personal Account

Having grown up happily as the son of a Southern Baptist pastor, I was a willing recipient of the narrative of Southern Baptist rise. We began among rebels who chose to read the Bible for themselves, to live and worship as their consciences guided them, to endure persecution and ridicule, to rise up from common stock as farmers and laborers, to struggle and win the revolution for religious liberty, and to accept the divine calling to bring the gospel to all nations. Thinking ourselves too radical to fit the label Protestant, we yet carried the banner of the Reformation as the sole remnant against all deficient forms of Christian faith, ready to evangelize both Italy and China where millions did not know Jesus as we did. Of course, there were elements of the self-description that even the initiated could reasonably question. Equivocation about the past became strikingly evident when Baptist minister Martin Luther King, Jr. and many other Baptist colleagues pressed for change in church and society in the name of following Jesus out of the wilderness of racist beliefs and social structures. A decade later, the growing partisan politics among Baptist pastors embraced a nationalistic faith allied with American power and wealth at the cost of diminishing rights and quality of life in many parts of the

---

[5] The early centuries of theological entanglement with racism receive outstanding treatment in Rivera-Pagán, *A Violent Evangelism*.

world.[6] Rampant individualism that undermined most U.S. churches was regularly embraced as the genius of Baptist theology, ignoring the Bible's calling to community.[7] The story was not uniformly triumphal, but I clung to its overall vision of a people leading the way to advance the work of God. Even while accepting some limits to our uniqueness and ascendancy, I embarked on a path toward ministry and leadership in the cause.

As a graduate student, I set out to find resources in the Baptist story from a purer age that was less individualistic, less nationalistic, and less allied to white supremacy. I turned to the seventeenth-century Baptist writers in England and New England in hopes of seeing a more coherent articulation of the faith. I hoped to encounter Baptists untainted by the emerging era of European world domination, the rise of nation-states and perpetual warfare, and the economic system based on enslavement, displacement of peoples, and expropriation of lands to create wealth for the newly dominant powers. What I found was both more rich and complex than I had anticipated. Those who became known as Baptists came to their theology through a variety of routes. Their priorities for change were not always identical. Some did not advocate what twentieth-century Baptists assumed to be the core beliefs that all Baptists must hold. They disagreed with one another and sometimes parted ways. Eighteenth-century colonial era Baptists sometimes showed critical capacity for challenging the status quo.[8] On the other hand, they also often embraced cultural norms, such as enslaving Africans, that seemed to defy some of the important theological ideas that had defined the Baptist movement, such as freedom in Christ. In both eras, they were not necessarily concerned with the same kinds of problems that I was bringing to my study. In fact, on matters on which I hoped to find them helpful, they often were not asking any questions at all. Chastened from my presuppositions, I did my best to learn what I could learn from them, which turns out to have been a great deal, if not exactly what I had sought.

But none of those studies were adequate preparation for the crisis of identity faced in the congregation to which I belonged in the mid-1990s. We were an aging, urban, moderate, nominally integrated church, predominantly white with several black families and a few additional black children and youth who attended because they were friends of church members. This pattern of membership had continued across more than two decades under the leadership of two pastors, the

---

[6] A helpful summary of the growth of partisan nationalism in Baptist churches in the U.S. is found in Bean, *The Politics of Evangelical Identity*, 30-34.

[7] A few examples can be found in Freeman, "Can Baptist Theology Be Revisioned?" 281-83.

[8] A classic account of Baptists resisting and organizing against religious establishment in the era of constitutional construction can be found in Butterfield, "Elder John Leland, Jeffersonian Itinerant."

latter of whom had been leading the church for most of that time. I had served as Sunday School Superintendent, men's fellowship leader, deacon, and choir member. When the long-time pastor left to serve another church, the tenuous peace he had helped to knot together began to unravel. An older generation began to express openly their hope to return the church to its earlier days of glory, and for them this meant returning to being an all-white congregation. I quickly became identified as a leader who did not want to see this change happen. The battles were mostly fought in coded language about church buses and unsupervised children, but few would doubt that it was a fight over race. Despite a conflict resolution process, the congregation could not ultimately arrive at an acceptable level of trust among leaders and agreement on the nature of the gospel for our times.

My wife and I found ourselves unable to face explaining to our children that we would stay in that church, for some of their African American friends no longer felt welcome because of painful arguments among the adults. A dear friend encouraged me to come to his historically African American church, where our family eventually became members. Slowly we worked on our healing and reorientation to a similar, yet significantly different, way of being Baptist. My job as a professor then and now has been at the oldest historically black university in the South, and thus I found myself immersed in a context of African American ecclesial and intellectual life as my primary social location. Within a few years, my teaching assignment shifted to seminary education in the Baptist divinity school of this HBCU. Worshiping, teaching, and preaching among African American Baptists, I found myself constantly engaged in the re-evaluation of my faith and living. A different cultural context challenged the assumptions of my previous immersion in white communities. To be white predisposes one to overlook one's particularities and context, simply assuming oneself to be a part of the norm. To step out of that space meant I received a vantage point from which to challenge that normativity.

After a few years of this immersion among people whose upbringing and life experiences were quite different from my own, I began to experience an awakening. I began to recognize the truth of being white. I began to grapple more deeply with what it means to be of European descent. I began to recognize that I have been formed in whiteness, participate in white privilege, and benefit from the assumption of white supremacy. I was not merely noticing my skin color, which is actually more beige and pink than white. What I was learning about was my intellectual perspective, my cultural formation, and my place in the racialized positioning of human bodies in the body politic. In church, this meant that I was learning to read Scripture again through sharing a pew with black bodies.[9] This reading with new

_____

[9] For an extended account of the influence of reading scripture with people across racial lines, see Broadway, "Racialized Ecclesiology, Oneness, and Catholicity."

brothers and sisters awakened me to previously hidden worlds in which some people find themselves marked for mistreatment by police and courts, school systems and employers. I found myself seeing anew Jesus' associating and conversing with those his society marked as outcasts and despised. Sharing communion regularly with those whose ancestors faced genocidal violence and generational oppression forced me to rethink stock interpretations of Old Testament stories of victory in warfare and destruction of neighboring communities.

I came to understand that in my own education in Predominantly White Institutions, the challenges that came from black, Latin American liberation, feminist, and womanist theologies had largely been deflected as those institutions assumed the normativity of the received tradition of European theologies. Some PWIs have simply seen black theology as misdirected or wrong. Others have read black theologies with interest, even accepting some of the criticisms, but they have also positioned black theology in a way that makes it tangential to the larger scheme and task of theology. Some see black theology as a passing phase—it offered a needed critique which, when complete, will no longer be necessary. Others treat it as a boutique theology, a fascinating little shop full of knickknacks, but not adequate to furnish a home. Still others see it as one among many multicultural flags to display as ornaments upon normative theology structured around mainstream European tradition.

By situating black theology as contextual, specialized, perspectival, partial, or derivative, in comparison with Euro-American theologies judged to be universal, general, circumspect, complete, and original, whiteness continues to deny its own positioning. In doing so, theologians do not recognize that all theologies are human productions emerging from the practices of particular communities in particular times and places. Assuming that one theology, which originated on one continent and was transported by means of imperialistic domination onto other continents, is *normative* exemplifies white supremacy in theology. My own learning of the difference came largely from the shared presence of Baptists with different relationships to our heritage, whose ancestors of recent memory received a gospel of freedom while being denied freedom by the very same church people who loved their own freedom.

Their churches existed underground, for they stole away to secret places beyond the ears of white Christian people to meet God in prayer, praise, and proclamation. Denied access to literacy, they learned to depend on the Holy Spirit to guide the church, in contrast to the rationalistic biblicism that performed interpretive gymnastics to justify perpetual slavery of dark-skinned people. White Baptist use of the Bible to justify the terrorism of slavery is a textbook example of a particularistic and contextual theology. Awakening to whiteness means that our Euro-American traditions of theology need to recognize this as exemplifying the shaping of our theology by a world structured around racial hierarchy and systems of global domination. White Baptists in the mid-twentieth-century South have theologians such as T. B. Maston, Henlee Barnette, Clarence Jordan, Martin Luther King, Jr., and leaders of the Woman's Missionary Union[10] to thank for helping them awaken to the distorted, racialized biblical interpretations and theological claims about the doctrine of creation and the doctrine of humanity. Other theologians have challenged Christological and soteriological assumptions of theologies shaped by white supremacy. It is likely that white supremacy, an ideology which has pervasively shaped the modern world order, affects and infects every doctrine of the churches that have coexisted with that social order. Attending to the task of this critique and reform requires an awakening.

3. Beyond Whiteness to a Particular Ecclesial Heritage

Whiteness attempts to sum up difference into sameness by claiming for itself the ultimate standard of universal normativity, behaving as if it has set aside its particularities and distinctiveness and shed those impurities for the sake of distilling the universals. In actuality, all so-called white people have particular and often varied provenance and heritage. The history of whites demonstrates this in that Irish, Italian, Greek, Polish, Jewish, and many other immigrants to the U.S. were initially treated as lower forms of humanity,[11] polluted or lesser versions of the pure whiteness of Teutonic or Anglo-Saxon races. They were treated as social, cultural, and religious outsiders by the Protestant Anglo-Saxon hegemonic culture. Over time, they became absorbed fully into whiteness because of the power of skin color to shape thought, along with their willingness to suppress ethnic differences for the sake of membership in white Anglo-Saxon hegemony. Moreover, they pursued relentlessly the effort to align themselves with whites against darker-skinned peoples. Most current observers would only recognize the residue of this whitenizing process in the continued suspicion toward the Jews because they maintain their historical distinctiveness. Looking back only a few decades, one can also see how purifying a world for the sake of the white race was embraced as an immediate goal by the National Socialists of the Third Reich, who sought to eliminate lower races and impurely white communities from society.

By awakening to the lie of whiteness and white normativity, people of European descent and Christians of various ethnicities and ethnic denominational traditions find reason to search their own heritage for its contributions to the broad

---

[10] On the influence of women in pushing Southern Baptists toward racial reform, see Maxwell, "'Christ the Answer to Racial Tension'," in *A Marginal Majority: Women, Gender, and a Reimagining of Southern Baptists*, ed. Flowers and Seat, forthcoming.

[11] One helpful source for learning about this process of assimilation into whiteness is Roediger, *Working Toward Whiteness*, 8-9.

traditions of the Christian faith. Moreover, they can become receptive to the idea that Christianity cannot be traced in a linear fashion through a unicultural European history. Rather, many streams of Christian faith, including new springs breaking forth in subsequent centuries, are tributaries to the great river of faith that the church has been and is becoming.

The light that Baptist theology needs in this *kairos* moment cannot be found in the whiteness that blinds us to the true light. But we should be able to glimpse light in the specific path of our heritage that traces through our struggles and victories back to the originating conditions of our movement. Baptist theology has been grounded in the calling of Jesus to "follow me," the hearts burning within the disciples on the road to Emmaus, the impulse of Peter and his colleagues to answer the high priest with the commitment to "obey God rather than any human authority," and the conviction of Paul that all of the congregation can prophesy one by one so that all may learn and be encouraged. Without denying our proximate origins among Anabaptist and Baptist communities in the sixteenth, seventeenth, and eighteenth centuries, we can also discover Baptist roots in a mix of first-century cultures spanning three adjacent continents near the eastern end of the Mediterranean.

Acknowledging our deep origins in the earliest days of the Jesus movement that became the church does not allow us to jump over the centuries and claim to be a pristine new birth of the church unconnected to all that changed and grew through a millennium of historical developments. We must recognize the impossibility entailed in our impulse to leap over the past to find pure, unblemished Baptists in contrast to medieval or imperial aspects of the church's past that we disdain.

There is no need to repeat arguments made by others in this volume about the complex interconnections between the Baptist heritage and the great traditions of the church. Finding resources in the European and American origins of Baptist movements means examining the turning points of Baptist theology in context. For instance, examining the appearance of Baptist congregations *in England and among expatriate English communities* in the first half of the seventeenth century can provide resources for theology. More than a century of turmoil in the English church of the fifteenth and sixteenth centuries helped to shape the emergence of these new groups. The royal family's frustrations with the power of a dominating Catholic church bear some similarities to core concerns of the Baptist movement in relation to the Church of England. Much early English Baptist writing includes rejection of distant, centralized ecclesiastical authority. Unlike Tudor rulers, however, they did not see having the English monarch as Head of the Church as an improvement, thus rejecting the Anglican hierarchical system as well. The turmoil of church politics in England had seen a back-and-forth conflict between parties who sided with either Rome or the Protestant movements. In either case, the parties sought to leverage the power of the monarch and Parliament to impose uniformity upon the churches across the realm. In this context, clergy often functioned as partisans in the power struggle, sometimes becoming its victims through imprisonment, exile, or execution. Chaos and constant conflict between theological and ecclesiastical systems no doubt influenced early Baptists to reject such use of power against local congregations. The ecclesiological concern with forming local covenant communities without a clerical hierarchy reflects an effort to reconcile the biblical calling to be a community united like the parts of a body without accepting a system of battling parties trying to enforce their point of view through structures of domination.

The seventeenth century was an era of revolution in England, and the emerging Baptists reflected aspects of the cultural milieu. One of the earliest congregations in England identifiable as Baptist appeared in Gainsborough in the first decade of the century. While they continued the process of clarifying their theological perspectives, they fled to Amsterdam in order to avoid persecution that was increasing under James I. There, they encountered other English Separatist expatriates as well as Dutch Mennonites, both of whose understandings of the church shared strong similarities with theirs. Leaders John Smyth, Thomas Helwys, Leonard Busher, and John Murton all later wrote treatises describing and defending the views of the congregation that adopted and began practicing believer's baptism while in Amsterdam.

Smyth found himself drawn more toward the continental version of "baptist" theology encountered among the Mennonites, rejecting the Reformed tradition's embrace of civil government as a divinely sanctioned mediator of God's will. In contrast, Helwys rejected the Mennonite challenges to the use of force and violence by magistrates, adopting aspects of the Magisterial Protestant theology of the state. He, Busher, and Murton, along with most of the congregation, returned to England hoping to influence church reform in their homeland, publishing writings on the church and religious liberty in the form of calls for the king to reform the church. All three died in prison, having been arrested for failing to conform to the Church of England. The ambiguity of this early English congregation's vision of the church and civil society has emerged repeatedly in the history of Baptist and "baptist" theological struggle.

4. From Captivation by Whiteness to Freedom as Outsiders

The era of these early English Baptists' creative response of faithfulness to the gospel also included the construction of a theology to support European world domination, which ultimately grounds itself in a theory of race rooted in white supremacy. Not long before the English Baptists sojourned in Amsterdam, English colonists made their first permanent settlement in North America at Jamestown. A few years later, in 1619, the first African slaves were sold to the Jamestown colonists as indentured servants by Dutch traders. The concept of race-based slavery soon emerged in the island colonies of the British empire, and the imaginative construct of racial difference was already widespread. By 1640, a Virginia colonial court declared that being a "negro" was justification for lifetime enslavement.[12] According to church rulings and colonial laws adopted in the 1660s, a child of a black mother was born a slave, and baptism had no effect on one's status as a slave.[13]

Luis Rivera-Pagán,[14] a Baptist theologian from Puerto Rico, describes a long and painful history of debate among Catholic theologians and bishops, especially in Spain, over the status of indigenous peoples. Having been granted sovereignty over lands discovered in the New World by papal authority, Spanish and Portuguese colonial powers had met the resistance of indigenous peoples in the Caribbean and the Americas with wars of conquest followed by enslavement of resistant populations they defeated in war. Some theologians questioned the justice of appropriating occupied lands and demanding subservience from their inhabitants. Eventually the practices that produced wealth gained the upper hand over scruples about how to treat people who rejected European domination. Even when Spain finally made it illegal to enslave the Native Americans, systems of forced labor continued under another name. As the island-born populations of forced laborers declined, the church justified enslaving Africans on the assumption that they all could be considered *Saracens*, enemies of the church in the wars of the Crusades. By international law, a prisoner of war can be enslaved as an act of mercy. Protestants eagerly followed suit.

These tortuous arguments provided a casuistic legal framework that allowed European colonial powers to justify practices of forced labor and extract wealth from the lands of their conquest. They were the pretext through which the mercantile interests of European powers became the driving force in reshaping the history and landscape of the globe. But fine legalities receded to the background once the ideology became so widespread that it established the assumptions on which society was understood and organized.

While many white Baptists in the southern U.S. were not prosperous enough to own slaves, the cultural acceptance of enslaving dark-skinned people of African descent became widely accepted among white people of almost all Christian sects. There were exceptions among Baptists who challenged the worldview that allowed conquest and enslavement as an entitlement of European Christian empires. Roger Williams, who spent some time as a Baptist in the Massachusetts and Rhode Island colonies in the early seventeenth century, advocated a policy of diplomatic relations

---

[12] Donoghue, "'Out of the Land of Bondage'," 3-6.

[13] Jordan, *Slavery and the American South*, 72.

[14] Rivera-Pagan, *A Violent Evangelism*, passim.

with the native peoples that included payment of a fair price for lands occupied by European immigrants.[15] A little over a century later John Leland, an itinerant Baptist evangelist in Virginia, helped encourage Baptists to advocate the end of slavery with the legislature in the 1790s. It was a short-lived resolve that within a few years was overcome by widespread sentiment favoring black slavery and white supremacy.[16]

Learning from our own heritage is complicated. Learning is often impeded in the U.S., where the economic structures and constitutional system have necessitated and accommodated enslaving Africans and displacing and eliminating Native Americans. Letting the gospel speak in the midst of these circumstances requires people of European descent and other immigrants to grapple with the powerful cultural force of white supremacy. Awakening to the intermingling of theological reflection with doctrines of white supremacy is prerequisite for taking on the work of appreciative and critical inquiry about our past and theological heritage. We can analyze the ways white Baptists have addressed various doctrines and bring a level of suspicion that some insights have been pushed to the background by our forebears because they might threaten cherished practices of the slavocracy and its residual Jim Crow society. We can question with Michael Emerson and Christian Smith why black and white Christians in the same denominations have such different views of the causes of poverty and whether the struggle for justice is a matter for the church's concern.[17] We can recognize that Baptist movements come from various cultures, even though our own is primarily Anglo-American. Rather than classifying all those cultural heritages as paganism, we can become open to the ways that the Holy Spirit has irrupted in various places among various peoples to bring about movements for the reign of God.

Baptist theologian Willie Jennings has helped to clarify this struggle in which we find ourselves during this season of awakening to the reality of whiteness in theology. He writes about the heritage of the modern age of European imperialism, its general unwillingness to see the presence of God as active in other parts of the world, and its colonizing impulse to replant Europe on every continent, even at the cost of destroying peoples, cultures, and ecological systems. Jennings describes this not only in geopolitical terms, but also in terms of the distorting of the human within the European heritage of theology. God has made us to desire relationships with one another so that love might be fulfilled in this world which the Triune God created in God's own image of eternal loving relationship. Somehow, this

---

[15] Morgan, *Roger Williams*, 27.

[16] Semple, *History of the Rise and Progress of Baptists in Virginia*, 77, 79, 116, 134; also Mathews, *Religion in the Old South*, 79.

[17] Emerson and Smith, *Divided by Faith*, 93ff.

desire became truncated through the entry of greed and ambition, lust for power, and fear of difference. Europeans developed a theology of whiteness that limited the image of God to those of their so-called race; the desire to love one another therefore stopped at the racial division.[18]

Disordered and distorted desire is the socially formed heart dynamic of white supremacy that continues to this day to make people of European descent thoroughly comfortable without significant relationships across racial lines. Recent studies show that the average white adult in the U.S. has at most one black friend.[19] The situation is quite different from the other side of the divide, according to Jennings, because it is necessary that blacks learn all about white people's ways of thinking and living in order to survive in a world where they cannot avoid being surrounded by whites. For both groups, real friendships across racial lines remain difficult to sustain.

One theological bombshell of Jennings's argument is the recognition that all of us who are Gentiles are outsiders. In contrast to the misguided belief that America is the new chosen people, the New Testament does not teach any doctrine of supersession.[20] Israel remains the chosen people of God, and a biblical understanding of Jesus recognizes that he has come to fulfill the calling of God's servant Israel, not to destroy or replace God's people. For Jews and those who are Gentiles alike, the path to understanding this *convergence* of our destinies which mostly *looks like divergence* remains to be discerned. One thing that should seem clear to us who are Gentiles is that we are all invited into the life of the God of Israel, who was not our God but has welcomed us through Jesus. We are the branches grafted into the vine. Through sharing in his life, death, and resurrection, we are made a people who were not a people. The far off have been brought near, and the dividing wall of hostility has been broken down. In our captivity by whiteness, we keep trying to rebuild the wall that Jesus has broken. The gospel that Jesus brought offers us a better way to make use of the wall's rubble, these living stones destined to be a temple not made by hands.

5. For Further Reading

Carter, J. Kameron. *Race: A Theological Account*. New York: Oxford University Press, 2008.

---

[18] Jennings, *The Christian Imagination*, 20ff, 58ff, 172ff, 240ff.

[19] Ingraham, "Three quarters of whites don't have any non-white friends."

[20] Along with Jennings, other theologians make important contributions to reflection on the problematic doctrine of supersessionism, none more significant than Carter, *Race*, 30ff, 239ff, 309, 346; see also Jennings, *The Christian Imagination*, 32ff.

Douglas, Kelly Brown. *Stand Your Ground: Black Bodies and the Justice of God.* Maryknoll, NY: Orbis Books, 2015.

Jennings, Willie James. *The Christian Imagination: Theology and the Origins of Race.* New Haven: Yale University Press, 2010.

Roedinger, David R. *Working Toward Whiteness: How America's Immigrants Became White. The Strange Journey from Ellis Island to the Suburbs.* Boston: Basic Books, 2006.

7

Light from Modern and Contemporary
Women's Religious Experiences

Courtney Pace

This chapter chronicles modern and contemporary Christian history through the lived religious experiences of women. While many histories of Christianity focus on men, treating women as occasional exceptions to the normativity of male leadership, this chapter tells the story from the perspectives of women, particularly how they practiced their faith. As Baptists interested in welcoming voices from the whole church to better understand Christ, we must be particularly attuned to the voices of women for what they can teach us about the nature of God, how God is at work in the world, and how we can be faithful hands and feet of Christ.

In modern and contemporary history, women have both affected and been affected by religious developments, particularly through new ideas regarding marriage, church leadership, missions, social justice, collective responsibility, and denominational identity.[1] This chapter examines the lived religious experiences of women from the early modern period through the twenty-first century, focusing both on the ways women have affected religion as agents and on the ways that religious developments have affected women's experiences and practices. Their experiences have much to teach the contemporary church, global and local, about the meaning of Christ-following in the present day.[2]

---

[1] The modern era spans the Renaissance through the middle of the twentieth century and is typically divided into the early modern era (ca. 1500-1800) and the late modern period (ca. 1800-1945). The contemporary period refers to history from 1945 to the present.

[2] Most of this chapter emerged from a regular course offering, "Subversive Sisters and High-Heeled Holiness: Women in Christian Tradition," at Memphis Theological Seminary. I have cited unique sources where applicable, but otherwise, the content of this chapter represents material from my course or my original historical analysis. In the course, I regularly draw material from Malone, *Women & Christianity*, 3 vols.; Moore, *Women in Christian Traditions*; MacKenzie, *Not Without a Struggle*; Clark and Richardson, eds., *Women and Religion*; Riggs, *Can I Get A Witness?*; and Lerner, *Women and History*, 2 vols.

1. Women in the Early Modern Period

During the early modern period, Protestant ideas of marriage created new roles for women, ultimately limited by the persistence of patriarchal theology. (Patriarchy, as I use it here, refers to the exploitation of power to oppress others based on race, gender, economic class, sexual orientation, and ability.) In continuity with the past, women led religious communities, even countries, created new monastic orders, and challenged patriarchy in the church and home. Some women also utilized patriarchy as a mechanism of gaining influence.

The Reformations introduced new theological ideas with the potential to reverse patriarchal dominance in the church. Martin Luther's insistence that every believer had direct access to God effectively made every believer part of the priesthood. Unmediated access to God leveled the clerical playing field, decentralizing devotion from the church hierarchy and toward the laity. This moment had the potential to embrace medieval mystic visions of God in female language and symbolism, to welcome women into the actual priesthood, and to reverse patriarchal dominance in the church, home, and society. While the Reformations expanded the kinds of roles women played, they perpetuated patriarchal dominance through new theologies.

In a marked turn from the Catholic celibacy ideal, Protestants welcomed marriage as a noble civil union. Rooted in the theological understanding that humans were created for community, Protestants honored women's contributions to communities and families, respected women's rights in marriage, and made possible the new status of "pastor's wife." Some women, like Katherine Von Bora, a nun who later married Martin Luther, managed their households like ministry centers, caring for refugees and orphans, visiting the sick, and creating new liturgies. Puritans honored the spiritual relationship between spouses as more important than the sexual bond, such that John Milton argued that marriage is a love relationship for sharing joy and mutual help and that a loveless bond is anti-marital. Protestant marriage continued patriarchal household codes rooted in the Augustinian tradition of women as a cure for male lust, the prehistoric tradition of the commodified exchange of women and subsequent naming of women by their husbands, and Aristotelian expectations of women's obedience to their husbands due to women's irrationality and inferiority. Catholic women with the economic means to enter convents had opportunities for study, leadership, and status, all lost within Protestant marriage.

Within Protestantism, some women led religious communities. Lollard women led communion in their homes and helped forge a vernacular English liturgy. Elizabeth I, as Queen of England, created a via media to unify a theologically divided nation under one Protestant church and liturgy. Catholic recusant women in

Protestant countries organized underground networks for Catholic worship and hiding priests. Moravians boasted gender equality in community and leadership, as did Quakers. Puritan women gathered in each other's homes after Sunday worship regularly to discuss the week's sermon and encourage each other's piety; some home group leaders, like Sarah Edwards, had as much spiritual influence over the community as the parish minister.

While responding to the Protestant Reformations preoccupied the Catholic hierarchy for much of the sixteenth and seventeenth centuries, Catholic women created new monastic orders to serve the needs of the people. Angela Merici founded the Ursulines as an order of laywomen to teach poor women outside the convent. Louise de Marillac created the Daughters of Charity to organize young rural women to minister to the urban poor. Mary Ward established the Institute of the Blessed Virgin Mary, essentially Jesuitesses, to win Protestants back to Catholicism through education. In every case, these women had to fight the Catholic Church for permission to organize and serve their communities, and once they were successful, they were stripped of their power and placed under male supervision.

Patriarchal society isolated women to the private sphere (home) and, in turn, men to the public sphere, but women's religious work moved some into public leadership, challenging gender roles in the church and home. Sor Juana Ines de la Cruz, a self-taught scholar, argued that women and men should study the sciences widely in order to understand theology, explicitly challenging the exclusion of women from higher education. Others, like Massachusetts Bay colonist Anne Hutchinson, offered an implicit challenge by defying conventional women's behavior norms. The church forced de la Cruz to divest of her library (she donated them instead), after which she died while volunteering as a nurse during an epidemic. Hutchinson was excommunicated from her colony and was later killed by Native Americans. Other women who defied gender norms, particularly those with financial independence or land, were persecuted or executed for witchcraft. Violence toward women and other forms of misogyny correlated with women's surges of increasing influence, as an explicit patriarchal attempt to subvert women's impact.

The eighteenth-century Enlightenment ushered expanded opportunities for affluent women to access education, Bible study, and writing. The Reformations increased access to religious education regardless of class, though boys received more thorough education than girls, and girls' education reinforced submission as orthodoxy. Unless women belonged to a convent or were financially independent, either by their own wealth or dependence on a supportive male, they had to choose between education or marriage because society considered intellectualism incompatible with motherhood, the spiritual zenith for women. Puritan Anne Bradstreet wrote extensive devotional poetry, Anglican Mary Wollenstonecraft and mystic Catholic Anna Maria von Schurman wrote defenses of the rights of women in education and society, and Quaker Margaret Fell wrote in defense of women speaking and preaching publicly. Anglican Mary Astell organized multiple self-supported women's communities to increase women's access to education and, consequently, to social power. Methodist Hannah More strongly advocated for women's education and aided the Sunday School movement to offer educational access to the poor through public education.

Whatever potential the Reformations had for correcting gender inequality, these advances were undermined by a renewed Catholic effort to cloister women's orders away from the public and under male authority and by Protestant elevation of maternal destiny and demonization of women's intellectualism. In spite of women's demonstrated excellence in ministry, public leadership, communal organizing, education, devotion, and spiritual formation, the Catholic hierarchy and Protestant denominations reinforced patriarchal dominance.

2. Women in the Nineteenth Century

In America and parts of Europe, the nineteenth century ushered in a new wave of Spirit-filled proclaimers who worked both through and around the institutional church to pursue their callings. The revivalism of the Second Great Awakening widened the path of those sensing call, and in combination with the cult of domesticity, launched a multitude of lay women into benevolence and social ministries. Women organized through denominational and social clubs, building national and international infrastructures for missions, education, and social activism. Those unable to find support for their work within the church embraced entrepreneurial ministry leadership through itineracy and founding new religious movements.

Catholicism wavered between the extreme of Gallicanism, or local authority over the church, and ultramontanism, or papal supremacy, ultimately affirming the latter. In response to the highly rational Enlightenment, Catholic devotion embraced the emotional, particularly Marian devotion. Rosaries, commonly carried by women, armed Catholics against Protestant aggression. The First Vatican Council canonized the Immaculate Conception of Mary, which affirmed the protection of Mary from original sin in her conception. Catherine Laboure of Paris and Bernadette Soubiroux of Lourdes reported Marian apparitions, similar to medieval mysticism, and women pilgrimaged to the sites where these visions happened. Such devotional practices rejected industrialization and modernity, favoring domesticity and anti-scientific sentiment. In many ways, nineteenth century Catholicism transformed Mary from female to the Roman ideal of female nature, which is, arguably, the utilization of Mary to repress women.

Revivalism in the nineteenth century prioritized the Bible and Holy Spirit over tradition, creating new opportunities for women's religious leadership and devotion. The Second Great Awakening inspired intense personal experiences with God, emotional worship, and greater desire for personal and societal holiness. Anglican Susanna Wesley encouraged her son John to welcome lay preachers, including women. The Holiness Movement from Methodism opened the door wider for women preachers and evangelists, such as Phoebe Palmer. Spiritualism gathered lower-class women in small groups and networks where they cultivated new ways of describing their religious experiences, visions, and theology. African Methodist Episcopal Jarena Lee pioneered women's itinerant ministry, focused on sanctification. Rebecca Cox Jackson, an African Methodist Episcopal laywoman, transitioned into ministry leadership through "prayer band" small groups and eventually founded a black Shaker community.

The nineteenth century cult of domesticity celebrated private women focused on their families. On the one hand, the cult of domesticity created a theological dilemma for women in which sacrificial love became a new kind of martyrdom. Women wore modest clothing to protect the male gaze from temptation. Mothers gave their daughters baby dolls to nurture their maternal instincts. As women denied their own needs and interest in service to others, they perceived themselves to be more spiritually mature; as women prioritized domestic service over self-actualization, they believed they were also fulfilling their female destiny.

On the other hand, Spirit-filled revivalism amid women's domesticity led women into public spaces as leaders of benevolence and social ministries. Women's concern for other women and families around the world inspired abolitionism and anti-vice activism, including temperance and anti-prostitution. Anglican Josephine Butler established homes to rescue sex workers, and she rallied the Church of England to lobby against health laws harmful to women. Methodist Frances Willard and the Women's Christian Temperance Union lobbied against the alcohol industry to protect women from men's financial irresponsibility and violence. Catherine Mumford Booth co-founded the Salvation Army as a Protestant order for social service.

Women organized locally and nationally through denominational and social clubs, focused on education, missions, and care for women and children. Initially working through male-led mission groups, women created their own female-led bodies for missionary work. Methodist Isabella Thoburn worked to expand education to women in India, while Methodist Clara Swain established women's hospitals throughout India. Presbyterian Maria Fearing raised her own money to travel to the Congo to care for orphaned and kidnapped girls, and she started a home for girls in Luebo. Catholic and Orthodox women established schools and missionary centers throughout Canada and the West. More women than ever had access to education, and some even went to medical school to ensure that they could provide medical care to women.

Concern for families directed many women to abolitionism, recognizing the irreconcilability between slavery—brutality, rape, and dehumanization—and Christian love. As women's abolitionism increased, so did misogynistic critiques of women's emotional state and rational capabilities. Some women hid copies of Harriet Beecher Stowe's *Uncle Tom's Cabin* in their sewing baskets so their husbands would not know they supported abolitionism, while others, like Quaker Lucretia Mott, Congregationalist Rev. Antionette Brown Blackwell, and Methodists-turned-Quakers Angelina and Sarah Grimké, became public activists against slavery. Women activists encountered resistance to their public speaking, necessitating their public advocacy for women's rights. Sarah Grimké wrote *Letters on Equality of the Sexes*, the first major feminist book by an American, in direct response to criticism of her lecture tour. Methodist Sojourner Truth spoke nationally and published both for abolitionism and women's rights. Truth and Anna Julia Cooper both offered black women's exegesis in their public work. Elizabeth Cady Stanton's *The Woman's Bible* offered feminist biblical criticism, though failing to cite previous women's work or express anti-racism as a necessary component of feminism. As women's rights work shifted focus to suffrage, many white women's rights activists betrayed black women to pursue white women's right to vote, a betrayal that continues to challenge the ability of American women to unite against patriarchy.

A number of women birthed new religious movements, aiming to purify Christianity, honor the motherhood of God, and restore older gifts to religious practice. Ann Lee led Shakers in total abstinence for pure living in anticipation of Christ's return. Mary Baker Eddy founded the Christian Scientists, teaching God as infinite love and the source of healing and restoration. Following visionary revelations, Ellen G. White co-founded the Seventh-Day Adventists, a rigorous practice toward obedience to the Bible against traditional religion. Lucy Farrow, a pioneer of speaking in tongues, co-led the Azusa Street Revival in 1906 and essentially co-founded Pentecostalism alongside Charles Parham and William Seymour. Aimee Semple McPherson created a Pentecostal empire with the Four Square Church and her global ministry.

The tides of revivalism empowered women to exercise agency within traditional structures and theologically equipped them to circumvent those structures as needed in order to follow their callings. Patriarchal structures tried to impede women's organizing and proclamations, but by the end of the nineteenth century, women had built too strong of a momentum to be deterred. Women recognized their collective economic, political, and social power. Denied a voice within most Christian traditions, women exercised theological creativity through art, poetry, and other writing. Spirit-filled women, independent of the institutional church, charted new paths for and pioneered new practices of spirituality, embracing their feminine identity as revelatory of the divine.

3. Women in the Twentieth Century

The twentieth century dawned amid tremendous population migrations and industrial exploitation of vulnerable laborers. As the world exploded in war, neither Catholic nor Protestant churches dealt with the suffering and injustice of the wars. The twentieth century intensified women's commitments to social causes, though splintering this cause in numerous directions. As women gained political, social, religious, and economic power, they used this public influence both to advance and deter progressive notions of womanhood and church leadership. Race, gender, class, nationality, and sexual orientation both divided and united women across fault lines, generating new theologies, socio-political movements, and models of ministry.

Women's international missions increased in the twentieth century, offering Protestant women opportunities for lay service through local churches and missions organizations. This expanded women's literacy about the world and simultaneously created avenues within patriarchal institutions for women to develop skills in leadership, organizing, fundraising, and communications. The Woman's Auxiliary to the National Baptist Convention, Inc. particularly exemplified this, as leader Nannie Helen Burroughs had opportunities to address her denominational assembly, influence denominational priorities, and found and maintain control of the Nannie Helen Burroughs School for Girls and Women. In many cases, missions organizing launched women into advocacy for women's ordination. In the Southern Baptist Convention, for example, many leaders of the Women's Missionary Union became leaders or supporters of Baptist Women in Ministry.

Even with the reforms of Popes Leo XIII and John XXIII, Catholic women's religious experiences did not improve in the twentieth century. Though the language of Vatican II in many ways empowered laity to take a greater role in the church, the exclusively male priesthood continued the disenfranchisement of Catholic women. Private Catholic schools isolated many Catholic families from the larger community.[3] The Church's opposition to birth control and abortion limited women's options for family planning and health care. Catholic Dorothy Day's concern not only for meeting the needs of the poor but also for changing systems which caused and perpetuated poverty inspired her to publish *The Catholic Worker* magazine and open Dorothy Day Houses for those in need of shelter. Mary Daly, a Catholic seminary student at the time of Vatican II, was so disillusioned by her exclusion from Vatican II meetings and Catholic leadership positions that she ultimately left the church, convinced its misogyny was irreparable. Many Catholic

---

[3]For more on this, see McDannell, *The Spirit of Vatican II*.

women, however, volunteered within Catholic social care, benevolence, and even political organizations, emulating monastic women's historic legacy of service within patriarchal structures. Because the Catholic Church condemned women's ordination and non-heterosexuality, a number of para-Catholic denominations emerged in the twentieth century offering the liturgical experience of traditional Catholicism with progressive, inclusive theology. For example, the organization DignityUSA offers "LGBTQ+" Catholics opportunity to worship in a traditional Catholic setting and style while affirming their sexual and gender identities, and the Association of Roman Catholic Women Priests describes itself as a renewal movement within the Catholic Church, aimed at preparing women and men for justice-oriented ministry in the church.

The Civil Rights Movement (1954-1968) depended on the leadership and volunteerism of women. Episcopal priest Pauli Murray organized churches in support of civil and women's rights and was the first black woman ordained an Episcopal priest. Baptist Marjorie Penney mentored young activists in Philadelphia, including then-seminarian Martin Luther King, Jr. Baptist Ella Baker also advised King and advocated for student activists to have organizational independence. Baptist Prathia Hall, a movement leader in Southwest Georgia, Selma, and Atlanta, functioned as a spiritual mentor to hundreds and later became an influential clergywoman. The music of the movement drew upon spirituals and hymns, and churches housed mass meetings and demonstration recoveries. In every local community where people moved for equality, there were women leading and volunteering in the effort, convinced that their activism was spiritual practice.

The Civil Rights Movement and anti-colonialism internationally sparked feminist consciousness in many women, and a renewed movement for women's rights soon followed. In many countries, women gained the right to vote, property, and legal recourse. Economic gains provided more opportunities for women to access education, including higher education. Health care advances improved quality of life and allowed women to plan maternity, and thus, to pursue their personal and career goals. Women's expanded opportunities to work consequently enabled women to make choices for their lives, like professional child care or divorce from dysfunctional or dangerous marriages. Women slowly gained more ground in political offices and public and private leadership, though still significantly underrepresented in both.

Utilizing intellectual tools from secular disciplines, women developed feminist theologies and hermeneutics, which they argued were critical to orthodoxy. These feminist methodologies reclaimed the significance of women in the biblical text, challenged patriarchy within the text and ecclesial structures, and embraced divine feminine language and imagery. Phyllis Trible's *Texts of Terror* addressed texts historically used to justify violence against women.[4] Rosemary Radford Ruether pioneered feminist liberation theology. Jann Aldredge-Clanton offered feminine images of God, particularly the Christ Sophia.

Because feminism prioritized the concerns of white women, womanism emerged in the 1980s and 1990s as a liberation theology of black women, committed to addressing race, gender, class, and any other layered oppression.[5] Fiction authors like Zora Neale Hurston and Alice Walker proclaimed womanist messages long before the theological discipline took shape, and many womanists drew upon Hurston and Walker as foremothers. Presbyterian Katie Cannon, a biblical scholar turned ethicist, engaged black women's lived experiences as revelatory of God. Prathia Hall, a civil rights activist and Progressive National Baptist preacher, decried sexism and homophobia in black churches and nurtured a generation of aspiring black clergywomen. Presbyterian theologian Delores Williams challenged crucicentric atonement theory as death-dealing for black women since such could be used to justify and even glorify suffering and to condemn those seeking escape from suffering; she instead affirmed Jesus's redemption of humanity through his life and ministry. Williams was the first to use the term "womanist" to describe her theological method. Other notable womanists include African Methodist Episcopal theologian Jacquelyn Grant, nondenominational theologian Marcia Riggs, American Baptist theologian Emilie Townes, and National Baptist theologian Angela Sims.

Similarly, a spectrum of feminisms (in addition to womanist theology) emerged honoring the experiences of a variety of women. *Mujerista* theology, most notably developed through the work of Catholic Ada Maria Isasi-Diaz, explored poverty and particularly the lives of Latinas. Chung Hyun Kyung elucidated Asian women's theological and practical wisdom as revelatory of the divine for global Christianity. Evangelical Methodist Marcella Althaus-Reid of Argentina challenged feminism and liberation theology for patriarchal views of gender and Christology. Feminist and liberation theologies blossomed into ever-widening trajectories of theological inquiry and demarginalization.[6]

The rise of militant fundamentalism in the 1970s came on the heels of movements for racial, gender, and sexual equality. Promoting a white, affluent, Southern, heteronormative family structure, fundamentalism merged misogynist theology with institutional and political power, particularly in its takeover of the

---

[4] Trible, *Texts of Terror*.

[5] African Methodist Episcopal theologian James Cone introduced black liberation theology with his *Black Theology and Black Power*, and womanism emerged as both a critique of Cone's failure to address sexism and feminism's failure to address racism and classism. These movements are treated in chapters 3 and 9 of the present book.

[6] See chapters 4, 5, 8, and 9 of this book for explorations of these theologies.

Southern Baptist Convention in 1979 and its unofficial alliance with the Republican Party. Shamed to privatizing their white supremacy, religious conservatives turned to gender roles as a new public litmus test, insisting on male headship in churches, seminaries, and homes. Conservative women endorsed female submission to patriarchy as biblical necessity, and women's ministries in local churches transitioned from missions organizing to individualistic piety.[7] Beth Moore's 1990s rise to fame for women's devotional materials exemplified women's investment in themselves, and away from collective organizing and global awareness. Even the popularization of the internet and the resultant emergence of Christian women bloggers did not deter the inward focus of conservative women's ministries.

The major ecclesial debates of the twentieth century centered around sacramental traditions and sexuality—including gender, sexual identity, and marriage—and were rooted in women's issues. Baptism, linked to birth; communion, linked to feeding families; and ministry, linked to healing and caretaking, were affirmed as holy sacraments, yet women's bodies were anything but holy. Capitalism and technology pioneered new ways to objectify and commodify women's bodies and insecurities, compounded by religious battles over the same. The church's failure to affirm women's bodies as part of God's revelation fundamentally undermined whatever attempts it made to oppose systemic injustices elsewhere in society.

By the end of the twentieth century, women were a formidable force of economic, political, social, and religious power. A numerical majority of the global population, church membership, and even university enrollment, women used their influence according to their religious convictions. Some organized for justice and liberation, while others organized for women's submission to male authority, but women on all sides of the issue felt increasing urgency for their beliefs. Women with privilege could opt in or out of activism, while women without privilege had to navigate patriarchal structures for survival. Technology and increased access to education and travel let women connect with each other as never before possible, yet women were more divided than ever over race, class, ability, gender roles, and theology.

4. The Twenty-First Century Dawns

At the dawn of the twenty-first century, the resurgence of white supremacy in the public sphere divided white and non-white women from collaboration, masking racism and classism as religious concern, particularly concerning abortion and child-drearing. The GOP-evangelical alliance utilized language of family values to institute death-dealing fiscal, health care, immigration, and civil policies against wom-

---

[7] Flowers, *Into the Pulpit.*

en, racial minorities, people with disabilities, LGBTQ+ people, and the poor. The successful 2008 presidential campaign of Barack Obama galvanized the GOP-evangelical alliance, enabling and kindling the openly white supremacist, misogynistic, homophobic, and classist 2016 campaign of Donald Trump. In spite of Trump's history of sexual assault and pedophilia, conservative women rallied around him because he opposed abortion, and, in many cases, because of their internalized misogyny.

There are as many kinds of Baptists as there are Baptists, and the twenty-first century has expanded the ways Baptists divide themselves. The ends of the spectrum have intensified, and fewer occupy the middle. The heightened rhetoric around race, gender, class, sexual orientation, and nationality in the twenty-first century has challenged Baptists to take a side, which challenges the core Baptist commitment to local church autonomy. Individually, Baptists have always taken sides, but Baptist denominations and organizations have begun to issue public statements in light of current events in unprecedented ways, on all sides of the issues. Conservatives have reiterated their homophobia, toxic masculinity, complicity with exploitative economic structures, and white supremacy. Liberals have galvanized around care for the poor, welcome to refugees and immigrants, health care as a human right, interfaith association, women's rights, LGBTQ+ rights, and anti-racism. And others, like the Black Lives Matter movement, have formed by religious people dismayed at churches' inaction in light of traumatic disparity, creating new spaces of spiritual practice disconnected from institutional or local churches.

The single most influential theological challenge to Baptists, and to the global church, has been liberation theology. Originating in South America through Gustavo Gutiérrez's theology of God's concern for the poor and the oppressed, liberation theology has blossomed into a multi-faceted, eye-opening, prophetic proclamation of God's concern for all oppressed peoples and of how the identities and experiences of those on the margins reveal God. Baptists must listen to the Bible through third-world eyes. Baptists must consider God as female, as Rosemary Radford Ruether has challenged. Baptists must challenge any hermeneutic which dehumanizes or demonizes another based on one's race or sexual orientation, as Delores Williams, Katie Cannon, Prathia Hall, and Marcella Althaus-Reid have proclaimed. Liberation theologies disorient power structures by turning toward the outer rims rather than the centers. They decentralize authority and empower the priesthood of the people, which is a very Baptist notion indeed.

Baptists could learn from the voices and examples of women who refused to let denominational battles deter them from ministry. Our Catholic sisters, amid theological debates, turned their energies instead to serving the people. Women of all denominations lobbied against slavery, prostitution, domestic abuse, and substance abuse. Locally, nationally, and internationally, Protestant women have organized to support missions and ministries, including health care, education, and job training, to serve people neglected by institutional churches.

Baptists of all stripes must listen to the voices of the global church and the global population if they wish to call themselves the hands and feet of Christ. Baptists clinging to historical distinctives may inadvertently enable inaction in the face of gross injustice, such as those who refuse to speak against white supremacy because of local church autonomy. Baptists clinging to biblical inerrancy abuse the Bible as a weapon against people rather than as a proclamation of love for people; this brand of Baptist life has empowered a few men to rule the rest of us. Baptists devoted to denominational ties must be willing to evaluate their denomination in light of present circumstances. The voices of women have called us to follow God, over and against the institutional church if necessary, bequeathing us a treasure of dissent. May we have the courage to hear their voices that we might be found faithful to God.

5. For Further Reading

Clark, Elizabeth A. and Herbert Richardson, eds. *Women and Religion: The Original Sourcebook of Women and Christian Thought.* Rev. and updated ed. San Francisco: HarperSanFrancisco, 1997.

Lerner, Gerda. *Women and History.* 2 vols. Oxford: Oxford University Press, 1986-1994.

Malone, Mary T. *Women & Christianity.* Vol. 3, *From the Reformation to the 21st Century.* Maryknoll, NY: Orbis Books, 2003.

Moore, Rebecca. *Women in Christian Traditions.* New York: NYU Press, 2015.

Riggs, Marcia. *Can I Get A Witness? Prophetic Religious Voices of African American Women. An Anthology.* Maryknoll, NY: Orbis Books, 1997.

8

Light from Feminist Theologies

Susan M. Shaw

I came to feminism through my Baptist faith. As a child growing up in a funda-mentalist Southern Baptist church in Georgia in the 1960s and 1970s, I did not hear explicitly feminist messages. In fact, in light of the burgeoning Women's Movement I was watching on TV, what I did hear were overtly anti-feminist mes-sages, and what I experienced was the sexism of a church that treated girls and women differently and subordinated us to the men in our homes and churches. Nonetheless, I also heard "You can be anything God calls you to be." "All people are equal at the foot of the cross." "God speaks directly to each of us without need for a mediator." "You can read the Bible for yourself."

These deeply Baptist beliefs, rather than the sexist beliefs of my Baptist con-gregation, created a space for me where feminism both addressed my experiences of sexism in church and society and felt like a natural extension of Baptist beliefs about the priesthood of the believer, soul competency, and ontological equality. Feminism provided a way for me to make sense of my growing awareness of the gap between words and practice about women in my Baptist congregation and to challenge and expand my Baptist faith, particularly as I discovered feminist theolo-gies.

1. What Are Feminist Theologies?

Feminist theologies begin in women's diverse experiences of oppression across in-tersecting forms of difference, such as race/ethnicity, sexual identity, social class, ability, age, and nation of origin. On one hand, feminist theologies offer challenge to the dominant patriarchal order that structures women's subordination within and across social institutions such as family, government, education, healthcare, media, and religion. On the other, feminist theologies propose innovative theologi-cal possibilities by moving diverse women's experiences to the center of theological reflection. As a form of liberation theology, feminist theologies understand women as an oppressed class (with whom God sides) and call for the liberation of all wom-en across their differences. Feminist theologies confront the traditional formula-tions of Christian doctrine that position women as inferior, subordinate, and responsible for evil and reclaim women's important and equal roles in the church. Feminist theologies suggest directions toward liberation for all people and demand ethical relationships and practices that affirm dignity and freedom for all women. Feminist theologies recognize that traditional ecclesiologies have functioned to maintain male power through exclusion of women from ordination, preaching, pastoring, and administering the ordinances.[1] In contrast to women's exclusion, feminist ecclesiologies move women to the center of our thinking about church. So, for example, feminist ecclesiologies question the discrepancies between the church's embrace of a ritual that commemorates the body and blood of Christ even as the church degrades the bodies and blood of women. Natalie K. Watson asks, "How can a meal, symbolic or actual, be a symbol of empowering and celebrating women's bodies and sexualities if society and the church itself send out such conflicting messages?"[2]

Another example comes from feminist Christologies, which call attention to the myriad ways traditional understandings of the suffering of Christ have harmed women by encouraging them toward self-sacrifice and self-abnegation without attending to women's suffering and subordination. In traditional theologies of the cross, patriarchal power protects itself by presenting the suffering of women as inevitable and possibly even positive and redemptive. Feminist theologies, on the other hand, reformulate understandings of Christ's suffering to recognize Christ as a co-sufferer, one who suffers with women. These feminist theologies are complicated by attention to differences among women. In African feminist theologies, Christ becomes the one who heals suffering caused by patriarchy and colonialism. For womanist theologians, Christ transforms suffering by naming it as evil. For Latin American feminist theologians, Christ is the co-revolutionary in their struggle against colonial and patriarchal power (even when it is embodied in male liberation theologies).[3]

Feminist theologies are a necessary corrective to the hegemony of traditional theologies that assume the experiences of white, heterosexual, Western, able-bodied, and educated men as the norm for theological reflection and church practice. While Baptists were born dissenting, the subversive elements of Baptist theologies that might have challenged hegemonic patriarchal theologies and practices in Baptist life were subordinated to cultural heteronormative and masculinist norms that ensured the second-class status of women and their marginalization in church practice.

---

[1] Watson, *Introducing Feminist Ecclesiology*, 78.
[2] Watson, *Introducing Feminist Ecclesiology*, 90.
[3] Shaw, *Reflective Faith*, 117.

In 1984, the Convention passed a resolution that excluded women from ordination because "the woman was first in the Edenic fall."[4] The 2000 Baptist Faith and Message included a new section on the family that mandated a wife's gracious submission to her husband.[5] Local Baptist associations disfellowshipped churches that called women as pastors, and the six Southern Baptist seminaries systematically removed progressive women and men who supported women in ministry from their faculties. Additionally, the Convention continued to vilify LGBTQ+ people through its resolution and its eventual 1993 constitution change that excluded congregations that expressed any kind of support for LGBTQ+ people. The Cooperative Baptist Fellowship formed from the exodus of moderates from the SBC, and, while it embraced women in ministry, it avoided taking a stance on LGBTQ+ issues, only developing a hiring policy that excludes non-celibate lesbians and gay men.[6]

While these resolutions and policies reflect the most overt expressions of patriarchal religion, more subtle practices in Baptist churches reinforce gender hierarchies and maintain the dominance of men over women in Baptist life, even in churches that profess an egalitarian theology. Many churches express support for women in ministry, but very few ever actually call women as senior pastors. Among American Baptists, women make up half of all ABCUSA seminary students but hold less than 10% of senior pastor positions in the denomination.[7] Volunteer tasks in churches are deeply gendered—mostly men serve as deacons and ushers; women work in the nursery and prepare Wednesday night fellowship meals. In some weddings, fathers still "give" their daughters away, and women promise to obey their husbands. Curriculum materials show boys and girls engaged in traditionally gendered activities—boys play sports, and girls play with dolls. Many churches still teach young women that they are responsible for the sexual desires and behaviors of young men, and clergy sexual misconduct continues to allow predatory men to exert dominance over the women, girls, and boys in their care.

---

[4] Southern Baptist Convention, "Resolution on Ordination and the Role of Women in Ministry."

[5] Southern Baptist Convention, "The Baptist Faith and Message (2000)."

[6] The organization entered a lengthy dialogue over sexuality with the Illumination Project in 2016. The report issued by the Illumination Project Committee included the recommendation of a new hiring policy, approved by the CBF General Board on February 9, 2018, that does not mention sexuality as a criterion for hiring; an "implementation procedure" outlined in the report, however, continued to restrict LGBTQ+ persons from serving in some key positions even while opening up the possibility that they would be considered for employment in other positions in the organization (Allen, "CBF Relaxes Policy on Hiring LGBTQ+ Staff, but Maintains Some Restrictions."

[7] American Baptist Churches USA, "Mission Table 2015: Case Statement on Women in Ministry."

Within traditional patriarchal theologies, these behaviors reinforce male dominance and buttress gendered stereotypes, roles, and behaviors that maintain women's subordination in church and home. Notions of the maleness of God, the responsibility of women for the Fall, the maleness of Jesus, the centrality of suffering and death, hierarchy, and sin and the invisibility or marginalizing of women's issues within the church underline women's supposed inferiority and shore up the institutions, beliefs, and behaviors that preserve patriarchy within the church.[8] Feminist theologies offer critiques of these traditional theologies that sustain patriarchy and provide perspectives and possibilities for theologies that center women, across their differences, in both theologizing and in the practices of church.

1.1 Feminist Critiques of Traditional Theologies. Traditional theologies are rooted in men's experiences and set up false hierarchical binaries that assume men's experiences as normative. In a groundbreaking essay, Valerie Saiving pointed out that our tendency to read the sin of the garden as one of pride is rooted in men's experiences. Women, she noted, rarely struggle with pride as a primary issue and, in fact, are more likely to fall into the sins of self-abnegation and erasure than pride.[9] Traditional theologies also rely almost exclusively on male God-language that reinforces the falsehood that men are somehow more like God than women. So important is this commitment to male God language that the Southern Baptist Convention passed a resolution in 1992 affirming "that the revelation of God as Father is central and essential to Trinitarian faith."[10]

Feminist theologies also note the many ways traditional theologies have relegated women to second class status—from excluding women from ordained ministry to demanding women be submissive in the home to devaluing women's contributions and pursuits. These exclusions and marginalizations are justified by stereotypes and stories the church creates and maintains—women are weak; they are seductresses; their primary role is child-bearing; they are associated with the body, and the body is associated with the material world which is less important than the spiritual one. Furthermore, feminist theologies recognize the ways traditional theologies have ignored the perspectives of multiply marginalized people. The theological mythical norm has been not only male, but also white, heterosexual, able-bodied, Western, educated, financially well off, not too old and not too young. Feminist theologies also draw attention to the ways traditional theologies have ignored how power is deployed in biblical and theological texts and in the

---

[8] For example, conservative evangelical theologian Wayne Grudem argues for male headship and female submission, even going so far as to argue that women's submission was part of God's original design for human relationships before the Fall in *Countering the Claims of Evangelical Feminism*, 21.

[9] Saiving, "The Human Situation."

[10] Southern Baptist Convention, "Resolution on God the Father."

church. In other words, traditional theologies rarely acknowledge their own social location and the ways that power in the church accrue to those who most closely approximate the mythical norm.

1.2 Tasks of Feminist Theologies. Feminist theologies use gender (along with the intersecting axes of race, sexuality, ability, class, and other forms of social difference) as a primary lens for doing theology. This process begins in awareness of how one's own gender affects how one does theology. So, for example, African women's theologies are inextricably linked with their experiences within the kinship networks and family relationships characteristic of many African women's lives. Marriage and child-bearing then become central theological issues in African women's theologizing.[11] White feminists must be especially attuned to the ways whiteness intersects with gender so from their position of relative privilege as white women they do not reinforce racist norms against women of color in their theological analysis or assume they can speak for all women or that all women share common issues and problems. Feminist theologies are attentive to issues of intersectionality and work to avoid paying attention only to gender as if women are a monolithic group.

Given the church's long history of masculinist language, feminist theologies seek to challenge the traditional language of the church and offer alternative words, images, and ways of thinking that are inclusive of all genders. For example, Sallie McFague encourages us to think of God as Mother and the earth as God's body.[12] Recent theologies by transgender people challenge us to imagine a transgender God.[13] Feminist theologies also challenge the dehumanizing myths of the church that situate women as primarily sexual beings, as temptresses, as morally and intellectually weak inferiors, or as rebellious children. Furthermore, feminist theologies challenge the ideologies that institutionalize the subjugation of women—systemic beliefs that as lesser beings women need protection, guidance, discipline, and leadership from men—and demand the rereading of the Bible in a way the center and empowers women. They call for a reclaiming of women's history as active agents within the biblical text and the history of the church beginning in the Jesus movement. Feminist theologies also insist on women's equal access and participation in church, home, and society rooted in a belief in women's ontological equality.

Feminist theologies seek to disrupt the hegemony of masculinist theologies that have dominated Christian thought for most of the church's history. By challenging traditional theologies and offering alternative ways of doing theology, fem-

---

[11] Oduyoye, *Introducing African Women's Theology*, 25.

[12] McFague, *Models of God*.

[13] B. K. Hipsher, "God is a Many Gendered Thing," in *Trans/Formations*, ed. Althaus-Reid and Isherwood, 97.

inist theologies center women across their differences to expand our understandings of God and to create a more inclusive and just church. In particular, feminist theologies offer focused attention to intersections of difference and encourage us to think about theological experiences with greater complexity and nuance.

1.3 Intersectionality and Feminist Theologies. Grace Ji-Sun Kim and I have called for all theologies to become intersectional. By this, we mean that all theologians should give attention to the ways their own particular social locations influence their theologies. Rather than seeking to create a systematic theology that states some universal truth, we call for a recognition of "the impossibility of universalizing theologies, and an embrace of multiple theological perspectives as necessary and desirable in moving toward more inclusive theologies that capture the breadth and diversity of human encounter with the Divine."[14] We define intersectionality in this way:

> Intersectionality is a tool for analysis that takes into account the simultaneously experienced multiple social locations, identities, and institutions that shape individual and collective experience within hierarchically structured systems of power and privilege. It is a praxis—an ongoing loop of action-reflection-action—that integrates social justice-oriented theory with activism toward social justice on the ground so that theory informs practice and practice informs theory.[15]

In theology, by making room for multiple and competing theologies arising from our various social locations and experiences of advantage and disadvantage based on the intersections of identities within interlocking systems of oppression, we expand the possibilities of theology and recognize the significant contribution of each person to the theological task. Thus the contributions of womanist,[16] *mujerista,*[17] *minjung,*[18] and African feminist theologies[19] along with lesbian, gay, trans, and queer theologies and postcolonial theologies,[20] are intersectionally relevant for discerning the liberative light offered by feminist theologies. Like feminist theologies, intersectionality theory is biased toward justice.[21]

---

[14] Kim and Shaw, *Intersectional Theology: An Introductory Guide,* 41.

[15] Kim and Shaw, *Intersectional Theology: An Introductory Guide,* 2.

[16] Williams, "Womanist Theology," in *Feminist Theology from the Third World,* ed. King.

[17] Isasi-Díaz, *Mujerista Theology.*

[18] Kwok, *Introducing Asian Feminist Theology.*

[19] Oduyoye, *Introducing African Women's Theology;* Dube, ed., *Other Ways of Reading.*

[20] Dube, *Postcolonial Feminist Interpretation of the Bible;* Kwok, *Postcolonial Imagination and Feminist Theology.*

[21] May, *Pursuing Intersectionality, Unsettling Dominant Imaginaries,* 28.

1.4 Baptist Feminist Theologies. A great deal of the work done by Baptist feminists has focused on issues of women in ministry. In the 1970s, as the Women's Movement led women to leadership positions in businesses, higher education, and government, increasing numbers of women enrolled in Baptist seminaries in answer to a call to ministry. At the same time, conservative forces among Southern Baptists amplified their opposition to women's ordination, and so Baptist women began to develop feminist readings of the Bible and feminist theologies to articulate their calling to ministry and right to equal access to ordination. Citing Eileen Campbell-Reed, Molly Marshall notes, "We cannot understand Baptist identity over the past several decades without paying attention to 'women's entry into leadership and ministry.'"[22] Like many Baptist women, Marshall traces her roots in feminism to her Christian faith: "I became a feminist not by reading Betty Friedan and Gloria Steinem but by reading the Apostle Paul, who offered the magna carta of Christian freedom: '...there is no longer male nor female; for all of you are one in Christ Jesus' (Gal. 3:28). He did not mean, obviously, that we cease to be gendered humans; rather, he meant that religious privilege in patriarchal structures was coming to an end."[23] She finds Baptists' opposition to women in ministry puzzling given their beliefs in the priesthood of the believer and local church autonomy. In the last decade, a number of former Southern Baptist scholars have provided a wealth of research on Southern Baptist women in ministry from feminist perspectives, all of which recognize the obstacles to women in Southern Baptist life and the resiliency of women who claimed their calling in the face of bitter opposition.[24] These women developed feminist theologies of personhood and ministry deeply and profoundly rooted in the Baptist belief in soul competency. They understood themselves as equal children of God with equal access to God and equal opportunity to respond to God's call to ordained ministry. So powerful were these convictions that the Southern Baptist Convention's pronouncements had no impact on their sense of calling. Most of them simply left Southern Baptist life to live out their callings elsewhere.

American Baptists, on the other hand, affirmed women in ministry, issuing a statement in 1985 on "Women and Men as Partners in Church and Society" that called for equal opportunity and equal compensation for women in all positions in the churches.[25] National Baptists have taken no official stand on women's ordination and leave the decision to local churches. Progressive National Baptists wel-

---

[22] Marshall, "Is Feminist a Baptist Word?"

[23] Marshall, "Is Feminist a Baptist Word?"

[24] Campbell-Reed, *Anatomy of a Schism*; Bledsoe Bailey, *Strength for the Journey*; Flowers, *Into the Pulpit*; Shaw, *God Speaks to Us, Too.*

[25] American Baptist Churches USA, "American Baptist Policy Statement on Women and Men as Partners in Church and Society (1985)."

come and support women in ministry. Free Will Baptists have historically ordained women, but the trend in the denomination is moving away from women's ordination. Not surprisingly, across other Baptist groups, women's ordination remains a controversial issue, and the level of support varies from group to group and often from church to church.

Baptist feminist thinkers have further developed theologies that called for understandings of women's ontological and theological equality. Molly Marshall argues that the subordination of women is a "result of human fallenness" rather than "God's ordained pattern for relationships."[26] In her theology of the Spirit, she goes on to add that the work of the Spirit "labors toward the liberation of all oppressed."[27] Emilie Townes, a black, lesbian American Baptist theologian and ethicist sits at the center of these many intersections of feminist theologies and Baptist life. A pioneering womanist theologian, Townes identifies the way evil has been constructed so that black women are seen as inherently morally depraved and calls for people of faith to live in justice and love, even in the face of evil.[28] From her social location as a womanist and lesbian, she interweaves an analysis of gender, race, and class toward the survival of black people through "hope, salvation, and transformation."[29] Jann Aldredge-Clanton identifies Christ-Sophia as a central liberating metaphor who is inclusive of both women and men in ontological equality. She argues then that a radical egalitarianism in the church flows from the ecclesiology of Christ-Sophia.[30] Loida Martell-Otero points to the power of both the theologies handed down by the abuelas and the possibilities of the Spirit to create anew. She recognizes that some of the theologies handed down have been colonized and require a reassessment from the perspectives of those at the margins who offer a needed and valuable voice.[31] Phyllis Trible's groundbreaking work in feminist readings of the Hebrew Bible opened doors for re-inscribing women's presence and agency in the Bible and understanding gendered violence in the Bible as "texts of terror" and also made room for later lesbian, gay, and queer readings of the text— as Baptist developments, perhaps even more challenging than feminist theologies.[32]

---

[26] Marshall, *What It Means to Be Human*, 80.

[27] Marshall, *Joining the Dance*, 128.

[28] Townes, *Womanist Ethics and the Cultural Production of Evil*.

[29] Townes, *Embracing the Spirit*.

[30] Aldredge-Clanton, *In Search of the Christ-Sophia*, 101.

[31] Martell-Otero, "Introduction," in *Latina Evangélicas*, ed. Martell-Otero, Pérez, and Conde-Frazier, 1-3.

[32] Trible, *God and the Rhetoric of Sexuality*; idem, *Texts of Terror*.

2. Feminist Theologies in Baptist Churches

Baptist churches have often had an ambivalent relationship with feminism. While Baptists define themselves in relation to a doctrine of the priesthood of believers that rests on a belief in ontological equality before God, they have sometimes struggled to embody that equality in other church beliefs and practices. Feminist theologies are disruptive. They challenge norms about gender and intersecting forms of difference, and they issue a prophetic call to churches to embody the radical egalitarianism at the heart of Jesus' life and ministry. Feminist theologies have much to offer Baptist churches, as ways both to critique present practice and to imagine a transformed equal, inclusive, and just future of the church as the "discipleship of equals," "a site of emancipatory struggles for transforming societal and religious institutions."[33]

2.1 Identifying and Addressing Historic Discrimination. Feminist theologies offer Baptist churches a powerful tool for examining beliefs and practices, both those meant to subordinate women and those whose unintended consequence is the relegation of women to second class status in the church. Some discrimination is so deeply embedded in the history of church belief and practice that it may not even been recognized as such. Feminist theologies can help Baptist churches root out deep misogyny and bias by asking difficult questions of gender and by demanding justice for women as a standard of Christian belief and practice. On one level, feminist theologies demand we examine our theological beliefs about women in light of the Bible's call for equality and justice. Is the subordination of women somehow rooted in our beliefs about humanity, sin, and redemption? How do these beliefs get embodied in practice? Do we exclude women from leadership positions? If we accept women in leadership, have we actually ever elected women as deacons or called women as pastors? Have we encouraged men to work in the nursery and prepare meals for fellowship dinners? Have we called all people to their full human potential? Or have we continued to reinforce gender stereotypes that maintain patriarchal power?

2.2 Gender as a Lens for Examining Practice. The question of feminist theologies for Baptist churches is not, "Is gender at work here?" but rather "How is gender at work here?" In recent years, more and more women have come forward to talk about how men interrupt them when they talk, how men co-opt their ideas, how men "mansplain" them as if women do not understand the most basic of ideas. How are these gendered behaviors at work in Baptist churches? How do they reinforce women's subordinate status and negate the full valuing of women as equal children of God? How is gender at work when we vote for deacons or call a pastor

---

[33] Schüssler Fiorenza, *Discipleship of Equal*, 369.

or recruit Sunday school teachers or select the hymns we sing or the translation of the Bible we use? What gendered language appears in our prayers, readings, litanies, and sermons? How do we talk about God?

We can also ask how our assumptions about gender inform the ways we think about sexuality. How is gender at work when we exclude LGBTQ+ people from our churches or deny them access to our pastors and sanctuaries for marriage? How is gender at work when we reject transgender people as full children of God and part of our faith communities? Feminist theologies can help Baptist churches deepen and complicate their examination of how gender works and how it may make people feel unwelcome, marginalized, and excluded.

Feminist theologies can also help Baptist churches imagine justice for women and LGBTQ+ people. Feminist theologies provide ways forward in developing beliefs and practices that underscore equality and treat people with openness and equality. Feminist theologies can help Baptist churches ask what liberation for women looks like and how Baptist churches can play a role in moving the world toward that liberation. Additionally, feminist theologies can help Baptist churches imagine a healthy and whole masculinity that does not rely on women's subordination for a feeling of manliness. Feminist theologies can also help Baptist churches grapple with the full inclusion of LGBTQ+ people in the life of the church that affirms their full humanity and God's complete love for them.

2.3 The Centrality of Intersectionality. Feminist theologies can also remind Baptist churches that as they imagine futures of justice for women, they must always keep in mind differences among women. No monolithic "Woman" exists. No "women's experience" encompasses the totality of gender. Rather, race, ethnicity, sexuality, social class, nation, ability, and age always complicate gender and one another in people's lived experience. Feminist theologies can help Baptist churches keep intersectionality at the center of their thinking and practicing. Intersectionality will remind Baptist churches that the work they do in communities must attend to social differences across and within groups as they seek to solve problems and improve lives. Feminist theologies will also remind Baptist churches that all people, especially across their differences, have important perspectives and experiences to contribute to the totality of Christian understandings and faith practices. Intersectionality reminds us to be multiple in our thinking, to make room for contradictions and challenges, and to welcome difference as adding to the fullness of our relationships with God and with one another.

2.4 New Directions for Baptist Ecclesiology. For women, church has been both a place of meaning and a place of suffering.[34] In Baptist churches, women have

---

[34] Watson, *Introducing Feminist Ecclesiology*, in *Feminist Theology from the Third World*, ed. King, 2-3.

been both affirmed as children of God and denied leadership based on gender. They have been expected to prepare the Lord's Supper but not serve it, to be baptized but not to baptize. They have been blamed for the Fall, held liable for sexual temptation, reduced to their sexuality, and marginalized to the peripheries of leadership, even as they made up the majority of congregants and ensured the work of the church continued to be done. They have been betrayed by sexual predators in the church and disbelieved when they have spoken out about their abuse.[35] Moving forward, Baptist churches must take into account both sides of these experiences as they transform themselves into fully welcoming and inclusive places that fulfill the gospel's call for welcome, affirmation, and justice.

Furthermore, feminist theologies suggest that Baptist ecclesiologies must reform themselves with questions of difference and intersectionality at the center of their understandings and practices of church. As Natalie K. Watson asks, what does it mean for women to be part of the 'body of Christ,' when their own bodies are excluded from some of the church's most significant moments?[36] Delores Williams reminds us that how our liturgies portray blackness/darkness, women, and economic justice shape the church as well.[37] Mercy Amba Oduyoye argues that the experiences of African women are often no different within the church than outside the church, and, in fact, African women may experience more recognition of their full humanity outside the church than within.[38] These struggles of diverse women call Baptist churches to accountability. Who will the church be in light of the presence of women across their differences? How will ecclesiologies account for diverse women and ensure just practices toward all women? If they heed the lessons of intersectional feminist theologies, will Baptist churches continue to be silos on Sunday morning where people look and think mostly alike, or will they create transformed multiracial, multicultural, open and affirming congregations that reflect the diverse humanity of God's creation? Will practices of baptism and the Lord's Supper reflect inclusion or exclusion—welcome or segregation? How will Baptist churches address ordination of women and LGBTQ+ people? How will they respond to the world's other religions? How will Baptist churches locate their mission in relation to the gospel's central call to social, political, and economic, as well as religious, justice?

---

[35] Miller, *Enlarging Boston's SPOTLIGHT*.

[36] Watson, *Introducing Feminist Ecclesiology*, 12.

[37] Williams, "Womanist Theology," in *Feminist Theology from the Third World*, ed. King, 84.

[38] Oduyoye, *African Women's Theology*, 81.

3. Conclusion.

Feminist theologies can be an important source of light for Baptist churches. Rather than being in opposition to Baptist theology, feminist theologies are deeply compatible with Baptist notions of soul competency, the priesthood of believers, and local church autonomy. Feminist theologies underline the value of individuals within community and their agency in the world as actors in concert with God's love. By raising awareness of the workings of gender and the importance of intersectionality, feminist theologies can help Baptist churches ask important questions of theology and church practices and can inspire transformation toward inclusion, equity, and justice across Baptist life.

4. For Further Reading

Clifford, Anne M. *Introducing Feminist Theology*. Maryknoll, NY: Orbis Books, 2000.

Dube, Musa W. *Postcolonial Feminist Interpretation of the Bible*. Atlanta: Chalice Press, 2000.

Kim, Grace Ji-Sun and Susan M. Shaw. *Intersectional Theology: An Introductory Guide*. Minneapolis: Fortress Press, 2018.

Kwok, Pui-lan. *Postcolonial Imagination and Feminist Theology*. Louisville: Westminster John Knox, 2005.

Shaw, Susan M. and Janet Lee, eds. *Gendered Voices, Feminist Visions: Classic and Contemporary Readings*. 7th ed. New York: Oxford University Press, 2019.

9

Light from Womanist Theologies

Khalia J. Williams

As an African American woman scholar, deeply rooted in Black Christian expressions of faith, I find my academic home in womanist theology. I discovered this home during my first semester as a student at Columbia Theological Seminary in Decatur, Georgia, where Marcia Riggs[1] delivered a guest lecture in my Old Testament class to introduce womanist scholarship and methodology to a group of zealous first-year seminarians. While trying to reconcile my lived experiences and scholarly interests, this idea of womanism helped me articulate the intersections of myself as a dancer, ordained minister, and scholar, raising questions of women's embodied experiences within the black Christian church in the United States. Given these varying, yet deeply connected, aspects of my life and faith journey, womanist theology provides the foundational support and creative methodology for both academic scholarship and practical ministry.

My faith and artistic journey in a black female body causes me to gravitate to womanist theology as a hermeneutical tool and liberative praxis. While my body has been an agent of creativity and imaginative inspiration through dance, it has also been demonized, ostracized, sexualized, and overlooked because I am an African American woman. These experiences have brought about several questions about my own experience of God, who I believe is at the center of life, worship, and artistic creativity. These questions inspire my study of worship in the black church as I seek to understand the struggle endured by black female bodies in both secular and sacred spaces. Therefore, when I engage in researching and practicing worship in the black church, I do so from a womanist position, which enables me to participate in the struggle for the survival and wholeness of my community.

This chapter will investigate the broad evolution of womanist theologies and point toward the light womanist theologies offer for Baptist congregations in their practice of theology. This chapter will proceed in three movements. First, we will explore the task of womanist theologies, building from a foundational exploration

---

[1] Marcia Riggs is the J. Erskine Love Professor of Christian Ethics at Columbia Theological Seminary in Decatur, Georgia.

of the term *womanist* and proceeding to a discussion of methodology and of the relation of womanism to feminism. From there, we will move to an examination of the primary scholars in the origination of womanist theology in the United States and look at the development of perspectives across the successive waves of womanist theology. This will lead us to deal in a final section with the necessity of womanist theology, concluding with thoughts on what womanist theologies can offer Baptist congregations.

I write as one who is situated in both the Baptist church and the academy in the United States; therefore, my discussion of womanist theology is primarily based on womanism in the United States. I make this specification because there are African womanist scholars who have developed a line of scholarship that employs womanist methodology in the context of the specific experiences of African women, which may not necessarily be identical to the ideas put forth in this chapter. In addition, exploring theologies from a womanist particularity does not ignore or negate the reality of the multiplicity of experiences across the variances of gender, race, class, and sex/sexuality throughout the world. Also, this womanist particularity does not make a generalization that all African American women's experiences are the same, or that all African American women are womanists; nor does it does not assume that all black women's religious experiences are Christian.

1. The Evolution of Womanist Theologies

Womanist theologies are born of the lived experiences of black women. I use the term "lived experiences" to speak of the personal knowledge about the world gained through the direct, first-hand accounts of living as a member of a minority group. These experiences are not generic or universally shared experiences; rather, they are unique and particular to marginalized individuals. Within religious scholarship, Alice Walker's expression of womanism is most often called upon to define the ideas and reflections by and about black women. Walker initially uses the term "womanist" in her 1979 short story, "Coming Apart," and offers a deeper explanation of womanist in her 1981 article, "Gifts of Power: The Writings of Rebecca Jackson." However, it is in her 1983 collection of prose, *In Search of Our Mother's Garden*, that Walker provides a nuanced and poetic expression of womanism that has become the foundation for many womanist scholars' understanding of how they name themselves and shape the work they are doing. In this expression, Walker offers a four-part definition of "womanist":

> *1. From womanish.* (Opp. of "girlish," i.e. frivolous, irresponsible, not serious.) A black feminist or feminist of color. From the black folk expression of mothers to female children, "You acting womanish," i.e., like a woman. Usually referring to outrageous, audacious, courageous or *willful* behavior. Wanting to know more in greater depth than is considered "good" for one.

101

Interested in grown-up doings. Acting grown up. Being grown up. Interchangeable with another black folk expression: "You trying to be grown." Responsible. In charge. *Serious*.

2. *Also:* A woman who loves other women, sexually and/or nonsexually. Appreciate and prefers women's culture, women's emotional flexibility (values tears as natural counterbalance of laughter), and women's strength. Sometimes loves individual men, sexually and/or nonsexually. Committed to the survival and wholeness of entire people, male *and* female. Not a separatist, except periodically, for health. Traditionally universalist, as in: "Mama, why are we brown, pink, and yellow, and our cousins are white, beige, and black?" Ans.: "Well you know the colored race is just like the flower garden with every color flower represented." Traditionally capable, as in: "Mama, I'm walking to Canada and I'm taking you and a bunch of other slaves with me." Reply: "It wouldn't be the first time."

3. *Loves music.* Loves dance. Loves the moon. *Loves* the Spirit. Loves love and food and roundness. Loves struggle. *Loves* the Folk. Loves herself. *Regardless*.

4. *Womanist is to feminist as purple is to lavender.*[2]

As seen in her definition, community is an important component of womanist ideals and presents an ethic of survival that emphasizes the self and the body. While Walker coined the term womanist, black women's religious scholarship is what made (and continues to make) womanism a movement that unites theological reflection and social transformation. As black women's religious scholarship blossomed in the 1980s, womanist theologies began to present an epistemology that focused on the historical and social experiences of black women, essentially giving "hermeneutical privilege to black-embodied-being-in-the-world, specifically that of black women."[3] Womanist theologies first consider the experiences of black women's bodies that have suffered under multiple lines of oppression that intersect upon them in the extreme, stripping them of their humanity and relegating them to objects.

Ultimately grounded in and accountable to the religious reality of black women's bodies, womanist theologies maintain a commitment to reflecting on the social, cultural, and religious experiences of black women. The roots of modern womanist theologies developed out of—and as a critique of—both black liberation theology (James H. Cone) and feminist theologies. While rooted in black liberation theology, as explored in chapter 3 of this book, womanist theologies added the

---

[2] Walker, *In Search of Our Mother's Garden*, xi-xii.
[3] Copeland, *Enfleshing Freedom*, 25.

goals of survival, quality of life, and wholeness to black theology's goals of liberation and justice, particularly in light of black women's experiences. Womanist theologies expanded black theology to include the concerns of black women in the
United States while maintaining a commitment to the survival of the whole community—men and women. Womanist theologians analyze the oppressive aspects of
society that prevent black women from having the quality of life and wholeness
that God desires for them and for all creation.[4]

Womanist theologies also associate with and depart from feminist theologies,
as expressed in Walker's fourth definition of womanist: "womanist is to feminist as
purple is to lavender."[5] With a wide array of critiques from womanist scholars,
womanism essentially pushed against the racist and classist implications of the
"white and middle-class" positionality of white feminist perspectives and critiqued
the privileging of gender issues that seemingly minimized the totality of oppressions that black women experience. Feminist theologies had lacked attention to the
everyday realities of black women, so womanist theologies called for theological
perspectives that made these lived experiences a point of departure, while also holding the unity of the black community as a priority. It was these tensions between
black women and white women surrounding black women's tridimensional oppression that led to Alice Walker's suggestion that the experience of being a black
woman was so different from that of white women that it called for another word
that would more adequately describe the liberative efforts of black women.

2. The "Waves" of Womanist Theologies

Womanist theologies interpret a multiplicity of concepts within the Christian tradition in light of the experiences of black women. Womanist theologians connect
biblical witnesses to Jesus with the experiences of contemporary black women to
discuss God's transformative role in their lives.[6] This school of religious thought
has emerged and expanded in what has been named as "waves." The first wave of
womanist theologians includes those identified as the matriarchs of womanism:
Jacquelyn Grant, Delores Williams, and Katie Geneva Cannon. These women are
the first to engage the term womanist in relationship to the development of their
own theologies and theological ethics. Jacquelyn Grant was the first theologian to
articulate a womanist theology centered in her writings on Jesus Christ, in which
she pushed the point that understandings of Jesus must address the core problems
of black women as they experience "triple jeopardy"[7]—racism, sexism, and

---

[4] Coleman, *Making a Way Out of No Way*, 11.
[5] Walker, *In Search of Our Mother's Garden*, xii.
[6] Coleman, *Making a Way Out of No Way*, 12.
[7] Hoover, "Black Women and the Churches: Triple Jeopardy."

classism. For Grant, black women identify with the suffering Jesus who embraced the outcast and subverted oppressive systems. Grant was the first to theologian to state that the savior can be seen as a black woman, and she presented a Christology that focused more on redemptive activity than the maleness of Jesus. This identification with a liberating Jesus invites black women to be full participants in church and society.[8]

Delores Williams introduced a womanist theology that focused on the role of survival and quality of life in the pursuit of liberation. She also offered a clear methodology for doing womanist theology, which insisted on a womanist hermeneutic of wholeness as an interpretive procedure that requires theologians to begin with the African American community and its understanding of God's historic relation to the black female life,[9] without prohibiting the wholeness of others. Williams constructs a womanist theological method that engages four categories: (1) a multidialogical intent, (2) a liturgical intent, (3) a didactic intent, and (4) a commitment both to reason and to vitality of female imagery and metaphorical language in the construction of theological statements.[10] While many (if not all) womanist theologians employ theologies with an implicit understanding of African American women's connections to and experiences within the black church, Williams is the first to articulate the necessity of engaging a liturgical perspective in order to be relevant within the thought, worship, and action of the black church. In doing this, Williams called for a womanist theology that consciously impacts the foundations of liturgy and shapes liturgy based upon justice principles.

Katie Geneva Cannon, a womanist theological ethicist, brought into religious scholarship her own experience as a girl processing the relationship between faith and ethics as she witnessed her grandmother navigating a racially segregated society. This motivation, accounted for in her book *Black Womanist Ethics*, sparked her journey toward womanist theological ethics and reflects an experience out of which many womanist theologies are born—lived experiences meeting individual wrestlings with faith. While an ethicist, Cannon belongs among these matriarchs of womanist theologies because she contributes to womanist theologies through her naming of black women's dissonance between life situations and the professed values of mainstream Christian faith. Cannon demonstrated the differences that black women's experiences create through a reconsideration of history and the construction of basic theological and ethical frameworks for moral values and judgments. Cannon, Williams, and Grant (as well as others that are not named here) created a shift within religious scholarship by centering and naming black women's experi-

---

[8] Grant, *White Women's Christ and Black Women's Jesus*.
[9] Williams, *Sisters in the Wilderness*, 3.
[10] Williams, "Womanist Theology," in *Black Theology*, ed. Cone and Wilmore, 266.

ences as viable and valuable sites for theological reflection and by rendering different theological conclusions than their black male and white feminist counterparts.

The second wave of womanist theological scholarship builds on the work of these matriarchs and digs deeper into theological reflection based on black women's experience. As a result, among second-wave womanist scholarship we see more reflections on Christology, most notable in the work of Kelly Brown Douglas, who centered investigations of Jesus Christ on the experiences of black women. In her book *The Black Christ*, Douglas identifies the sources of black women's oppressions in terms similar to those used by Grant, considering racism, sexism, and classism as key challenges for theologians to consider. However, she also adds the dimension of heterosexism to the conversation. She clearly states, "Womanist scholars must make clear that homophobia in any form is unacceptable, and that heterosexism must be eradicated as it is a part of the same interlocking system of race, gender, and class oppression."[11] The primary goal of Douglas' theology is wholeness for black women and the black community, which is the vision that centers her theology on the experiences of black women's bodies and their relationship to the black church.

Douglas's work is a representation of the deeper explorations found among second-wave womanist theologies, which are grounded in first-wave womanist theologies and begin to establish a normative womanist discourse. As a result, this second wave is marked by the development of deeper womanist Christologies (as noted above), soteriologies, doctrines of the Trinity, and other themes in constructive theology. However, there is room for this strand of womanist theologies to continue to expand, even with the surfacing of a third wave of womanist theologies, which is in both a descriptive and constructive phase of development. This third wave of womanist theologies is distinct in that it is slowly moving beyond the the necessity that its practitioners be black women engaging in theology as black women thinking theologically about black women to become more focused on the ideologies shaped by womanist methodology. This is to say that not all third-wave womanist theologians are black women and that this scholarship is beginning to push beyond the binary racial and gender codes of the United States. As a full movement within religious scholarship, womanist theologies are groundbreaking and fruitful not only for theological study, but also for the Christian church itself.

3. Womanist Theologies in Baptist Churches

Womanism has been deemed a movement, or a revolution of sorts. Womanist theologies have brought a new and liberating perspective to theological studies. The

---

[11] Douglas, *The Black Christ*, 101.

paradigm shift introduced through womanist theologies has given black women their liberation and brought value to experiences that have been minimized and even invisible for centuries. Womanist theologies have presented new methods for doing theology that includes the most marginalized in communities by modeling this work through privileging the experiences of black women in religious thought. By taking seriously the everyday experiences of black women, womanist theologies have shown that lived experience and spirituality are central to the interpretation of and participation in Christian faith. This is necessary work, not only for black religious thought or for black communities; it is necessary work for all communities. Womanist theologies construct theological conversations that unmask the experiences of those on the margins and realize them as sites of divine revelation and theological reflection. In doing this, womanist theologies create a space that allows constructive theologies to present possibilities of achieving alternative and creative ways of knowing and understanding God that are just and include the entire community.

So, what do womanist theologies offer Baptist congregations? First, the methodology of particularity employed by womanist theologies offers Baptist congregations the freedom to walk boldly in the doctrinal tradition of Baptist churches, understanding that there is no "one way" to theologize. This freedom to engage in Baptist autonomy provides the space for attending to cultural particularities and can help Baptist congregations shape ministry practices that are true to, and nurturing for, each individual congregation. With that being said, womanist theologies also hold this freedom to a standard of privileging the voices of the most marginalized of the community. For womanist theologies, this voice is black women; but it can be a different voice depending on the demographic makeup of a congregation. Therefore, the methodology of giving voice to the experiences of the marginalized may manifest itself differently from one congregation to another, but the premise is the same. When we are able to move beyond oppressive structures of religion and religious thought and begin to value the lived experiences of the congregation, we are able to engage in theological conversation and practice that is wholistic and interconnected. The interconnection is both personal and communal, as our spirituality, faith, and lived experiences all happen to us as individuals and as persons within a community.

In addition, womanist theologies provide tools for examining beliefs and practices. When we identify the ways in which dominant structures and religion have been oppressive, and when congregations can name their own participation or complicity within these oppressive structures, we are able to use a new set of tools for beginning to imagine and practice a liberating faith. Womanist theologies cause us to reconsider the traditions, practices, and biblical interpretation of our congregations, and they call for revision in these areas where we find dominance and oppression. This requirement from womanist theologies completely decenters patriarchal systems and provides new directions for Baptist ecclesiology. Womanist theologies offer new possibilities for reimagining the church. When those who have been oppressed and marginalized have a position of leadership and can see themselves reflected in the practices of the church, we are able to see a new church. This reinvigorates the church and brings a level of relevancy that many are fearful has been lost.

Finally, womanist theologies offer the gift of embodied awareness. At the center of womanist theologies are the bodies of African American women and their relationship to the church. This privileging of marginalized, and historically dehumanized, physical bodies incites an awareness of how bodies experience God in congregational spaces and how we give and take away power through the very presence of bodies. This awareness is a gift—one to which we are invited daily as we live as the body of Christ on earth. As the church, we are called to be about God's business here on earth. May we embark upon this call with hearts that are attuned to the nature of our liberating Christ, with minds that are aware of those who are marginalized among us, and with spirits that will not rest until we subvert the oppressive systems at work in our churches and communities. This is womanist work.

4. For Further Reading

Cannon, Katie Geneva, Emilie M. Townes, and Angela D. Sims, eds. *Womanist Theological Ethics: A Reader*. Louisville: Westminster John Knox Press, 2011.

Coleman, Monica A., ed. *Ain't I a Womanist, Too? Third-Wave Womanist Religious Thought*. Minneapolis: Fortress Press, 2013.

Floyd-Thomas, Stacey M. *Deeper Shades of Purple: Womanism in Religion and Society*. Religion, Race, and Ethnicity. New York: New York University Press, 2006.

Grant, Jacquelyn. *White Women's Christ and Black Women's Jesus*. American Academy of Religion Academy Series, no. 64. Atlanta: Scholars Press, 1989.

Mitchem, Stephanie Y. *Introducing Womanist Theology*. Maryknoll, NY: Orbis Books, 2002.

Williams, Delores. *Sisters in the Wilderness: The Challenge of Womanist God-Talk*. 20th anniversary ed. Maryknoll, NY: Orbis Books, 2013.

10

Light from LGBTQ+ Lives

Cody J. Sanders

No one after lighting a lamp puts it under the bushel basket, but on the lampstand, and it gives light to all in the house. (Matt. 5:15)

A pall of ecclesial shadows shrouds LGBTQ+[1] lives as potential sources of light for churches. Our queer lives have become veritable lamps hid under a bushel. Not bushels of our own making, mind you, but bushels of shame cast upon us, of rejection from our families, of excommunication from our communities of faith, bushels heaved upon us through assaults performed on our bodies, and violence perpetrated against our souls. Churches more often attempt to snuff out the light of our queer lives rather than invite them to shine.

Yet, churches can learn a great deal from the lives and experiences and examples of LGBTQ+ people—instructive and inspiring lessons of faithfulness, love, intimacy, community, justice, and the embodied nature of our spiritual lives.[2] Though for churches to learn *any* lessons from the light shining through queer lives requires a substantive shift in our epistemological approach to the knowledge bound up in LGBTQ+ experience.

1. Loving the Light More than the Darkness: Epistemological Shifts

And this is the judgment, that the light has come into the world, and people loved darkness rather than light because their deeds were evil. (John 3:19)

Inviting the light of LGBTQ+ lives to shine on churches, illumining our pathways toward the rule and reign of Christ in all our lives, requires critical epistemological shifts in our theological approach to queer souls. For most of history, churches have not sought the light of queer lives as valued sources of wisdom. Instead, the position of our theological knowing regarding LGBTQ+ people has been a coloni-

---

[1] *LGBTQ* stands for lesbian, gay, bisexual, transgender, queer and the + for numerous other letters that can be added to the acronym like "I" for intersex or "A" for asexual. At times, I use the term *queer* as a shorthand term for all whose lives are encompassed by this acronym.

[2] See Sanders, *Queer Lessons for Churches on the Straight and Narrow.*

alizing *knowing-about*, rather than a compassionately curious *learning-from*. Our theological "knowledge" about LGBTQ+ people positions queer souls as objects of suspicion and scrutiny, producing scads of sermons, articles, and books that bolster churches' heteronormative epistemology—that is, a position of knowing about ourselves as sexual and gendered beings only from the perspectives of those who identify as heterosexual. This epistemology situates LGBTQ+ people as objects of suspicion rather than sources of wisdom.

If Baptist churches desire to bring life more fully under the rule of Christ, churches must repent from the ways that we have denied the image of Christ shining through LGBTQ+ lives, lest we cut off from ecclesial community sacred lives that belong to the *kin*-dom of God, subverting Christ's expansive, communal reign through our own prejudices.[3] Moreover, our repentance must include the deep and contrite acknowledgment of the ways we've crucified Christ myriad times over in the lives of LGBTQ+ people who have been murdered through hate crime violence, left to die of HIV/AIDS through government inattention and collective willful ignorance, abandoned to freeze on the streets by family and community, and bullied, shamed, and rejected to the point of suicide—all with the consent of the Christian theological status quo. Our communities of faith must contritely acknowledge—to God *and* to our queer neighbors—the ways we have "loved the darkness rather than the light" through our evil destruction of the light of Christ shining through our queer siblings' lives.

Only through repentance of our collective derision of queer souls will we experience the *metanoia* necessary for spiritual conversion from our heteronormative and transphobic theological epistemology to look with renewed eyes at the lives of LGBTQ+ people with compassion and gratitude for the wisdom they offer to congregations, Baptist and otherwise. Within the church's sacred task of *metanoia*, a movement toward the numinous and the luminous wisdom of queer lives offers the potential to learn expansive lessons on the formation of resilient Christian community during a time of the church's institutional decline in North America, lessons in tenacious Christian faithfulness in an era of flagging Christian identification, and the nature of Christian practices of care in a social setting of continued prejudice and violence against minority groups in the U.S.

---

[3] "Kin-dom" is an alternative term to "kingdom" introduced by feminist theologians that eschews the patriarchal, hierarchical dominance inherent in the language of "*king*dom," instead pointing to a relational connection within the realm of God, bespeaking the kind and quality of beloved community Jesus envisioned. For example, "I do not call you servants [Gk. *slaves*] any longer, because the servant does not know what the master is doing; but I have called you friends because I had made know to you everything that I have heard from my Father" (John 15:15), or "See what love the Father has given us, that we should be called children of God; and that is what we are" (1 John 3:1).

2. Lessons of Christian Community

...and I by my works will show you my faith. (James 2:18)

It will be news to many to learn that the first building ever owned by a gay organization wasn't a community center or a recreation complex, an office building for lobbyists or a facility for activists. It was a *church*. The first building ever owned by a gay organization was the permanent sanctuary built by the Metropolitan Community Church (MCC) in the early 1970s. What's more, the MCC quickly grew to become the largest LGBT grassroots organization in history![4] For a group that has been on the receiving end of ecclesial disdain for supposedly sinful activity, putting us outside of the boundaries of good standing in Christian community, this fact should open eyes to the possibilities of learning important lessons on the nature of Christian community! Even prior to MCC's founding, however, there are stories of Christian community that defy the seemingly possible.

Historian Heather Rachelle White tells one of the most compelling narratives of early Christian community in LGBTQ+ religious liberation movements in the U.S. There were about a half-dozen gay members of a Catholic parish who approached the altar week after week to partake in those ancient symbols of the kindom of God: bread and cup. But the priest who had heard their private confessions refused to serve the sacramental elements to gay members of the parish and denied them participation in the Eucharist week after week, leaving them standing at the altar rail, cut off from Table of the Lord. But they showed up, uninvited and unwelcomed by the brokers of the Divine gifts, again and again, refusing to silently submit to their own exclusion.

This was not the first time that queer Christians were barred from receiving the elements of communion and the sustenance of community by guardians of the ecclesial status quo. But this time the excluded mounted an audacious response, *long before* high heels went flying on Christopher Street outside the Stonewall Inn in what is typically thought of as the riot sparking the gay rights movement in 1969.

Renting space in a hotel lounge with a makeshift altar constructed from cocktail tables, a small group of faithful formed a new congregation under the pastoral leadership of George Hyde. They eventually took the name the "Eucharistic Catholic Church"—a reminder of the sacrament once, but never again, denied them. And if you imagine this taking place in the 1960s in New York or San Francisco, you'd be dead wrong. This story—the founding of the *first* congregation by lesbian and gay Christians in faithful defiance of those intent upon their perpetual exclusion—took place in 1946 in Atlanta, Georgia, the heart of the American

---

[4] Chauncey, *Why Marriage?*, 91-92.

South.[5] In the 1940s, the Eucharistic Catholic Church not only provided the first explicitly welcoming religious space for LGBTQ+ worshippers, but they also broke with many other exclusionary social norms of that era, forming a *racially integrated* community of both *LGBTQ+ and straight* members who *transcended denominational divisions*.[6]

Decades later, another gay minister with a history of anguished soul searching and, at times, outright despair (a spiritual experience reminiscent of so many saints in the Christian tradition), came to understand his call not to *divorce* his sexuality from his Christian faith but to *vocation* as an openly gay pastor, ministering with gays and lesbians marginalized by their own faith communities. Troy Perry, a Pentecostal minister, gathered twelve people in the living room of his Los Angeles home on October 6, 1968 for the first service of worship for what would grow to become the Metropolitan Community Church.[7] As mentioned above, the MCC—founded months before the famed Stonewall Riots that sparked so much queer activism—would grow to become the largest grassroots movement in LGBT history. While the majority of early MCC members came from mainline Protestant churches, a quarter were Roman Catholic in heritage, some joined MCC from the Church of Jesus Christ of Latter-day Saints, and still others joined as "friends"—a category of membership that included Jews, agnostics, atheists, and Buddhists who could not align themselves with historic tenets of Christian faith, but who were woven into the fabric of this expansive community.[8]

Yet another group began to work from *within* their tradition to open space for the LGBTQ+ faithful to worship more freely. As MCC became the largest LGBT grassroots organization, Dignity emerged as the first effort of queer organizing within any particular tradition: the Roman Catholic Church.[9] Dignity groups met on Saturdays instead of Sundays so that members could continue worshipping in their local parishes[10] while benefiting from the combination of theological discussion, group therapy, and Mass offered at Dignity gatherings. Its founder, Father Patrick X. Nidorf—an Augustinian priest and counselor concerned for the wellbeing of gay Catholics—was eventually barred by his superiors from continuing his ministry with gay Catholics, turning leadership of the organization over to its many lay members.[11]

---

[5] White, "Proclaiming Liberation," 103-4.
[6] Jordan, *Recruiting Young Love*, 70.
[7] Jordan, *Recruiting Young Love*, 119.
[8] White, "Proclaiming Liberation," 109.
[9] Jordan, *Recruiting Young Love*, 113.
[10] Jordan, *Recruiting Young Love*, 121.
[11] White, "Proclaiming Liberation," 111.

In a cultural climate that makes nominal identification with the Christian faith fairly easy, what can we learn from those who have had no easy time maintaining connection to Christian faith communities? Catholic theologian M. Shawn Copeland writes in her book *Enfleshing Freedom*:

> If my sister or brother is not at the table, we are not the flesh of Christ. If my sister's mark of sexuality must be obscured, if my brother's mark of race must be disguised, if my sister's mark of culture must be repressed, then we are not the flesh of Christ. For, it is through and in Christ's own flesh that the "other" is my sister, is my brother; indeed, the "other" is me.[12]

According to this theology of the body of Christ, members of the church have clearly marred the flesh of Christ by exclusion of LGBTQ+ people from the table of grace in Christian community. Yet, LGBTQ+ Christians have not been waiting around in docile hope for an official proclamation of their acceptability before joining in the worship and work of faith communities. Refusing to divorce their faith and their sexual and gender identities, LGBTQ+ people forge Christian community at the margins of Christian community. They serve churches in every capacity imaginable, even when sometimes that means having to hide important parts of their lives to escape the scorn of their fellow church members, and they have taken to heart the admonition of James to allow our works to demonstrate our faith (James 2:18-26). Allow that nurturing light of community to shine upon the churches of the twenty-first century United States.

3. Lessons in Christian Faithfulness

...work out your own salvation with fear and trembling." (Phil. 2:12)

Our Baptist faith tradition instills a strong commitment to the historic Baptist distinctive of "soul freedom." Other terms employed to capture the meaning of "soul freedom" include "the competency of the soul before God" and "soul liberty."[13] Baptist historian Walter Shurden claims that soul freedom "affirms the sacredness of individual choice" as an "inalienable right and responsibility of every person to deal with God without the imposition of creed, the interference of clergy, or the intervention of civil government"[14]—to work out one's "own salvation with fear and trembling" (Phil. 2:12).

Rooted in the theological notion of the *imago dei* instilled in human beings at creation, the Baptist notion of soul freedom affirms the ultimate dignity and integ-

---

[12] Copeland, *Enfleshing Freedom*, 82.
[13] Shurden, *The Baptist Identity*, 23.
[14] Shurden, *The Baptist Identity*, 23.

rity of the singular, individual life hewn in the divine image. This Baptist distinctive of every person's competence to make moral, spiritual, and religious decisions without privileging institutionally or sacramentally mediating authorities held many implications for Baptist forbearers in the early seventeenth century. For John Smyth and Thomas Helwys in England as for Roger Williams in the colonies, it was the primary theological impetus for preserving "freedom of the human spirit" from state-enforced religion.[15] This led Smyth and Helwys to flee to Amsterdam from the rule of King James I of England and sent Roger Williams into exile from the Massachusetts Bay Colony. So strongly did these early Baptists hold to their conviction of soul freedom that Williams called the violation of this freedom "Soule rape,"[16] and Thomas Helwys wrote a lengthy tract to the King on the matter, which eventuated in his arrest and death in prison.[17]

Our Baptist tenacity in clinging to the ideal of soul freedom despite virulent opposition through the centuries should raise our curiosity about what we, of all people of faith, can learn from the tenacious practice of soul freedom by LGBTQ+ people. In my doctoral research, I interviewed LGBTQ+ people from Christian faith traditions who experienced suicide attempts, often amid punishing cruelty and rejection from faith communities. Aside from the primary inquiries of my investigating, I witnessed in their stories contemporary portraits of soul freedom with the potential to teach churches lessons in Christian faithfulness.

Thomas is a forty-eight-year-old white, cisgender, gay man who grew up in a conservative Christian environment where he heard consistent condemnatory messages about same-sex sexuality. Thomas explains the effects his experience, saying,

> I very gradually got the impression that most of what was inside me should be kept separate from everybody, from the world—my attraction to men, my confusion about women...The most horrible violence is that the message that comes through the word itself [i.e., the Bible] is a message of hope and the feeling that you get from the people who are saying the words is a message of violence. And you're a child. A message of damnation—be clear. The words say a message of hope and the person says a message of damnation or condemnation. And you're a child! You're trying to make sense of that.[18]

Using the language of the soul's sense of coreness, Florence—a thirty-seven-year-old white, cisgender lesbian who attempted suicide at age eighteen—describes

---

[15] Shurden, *The Baptist Identity*, 27.

[16] Williams, "The Bloudy Tenent of Persecution" (1644), in *The Complete Writings of Roger Williams*, vol. 3, ed. Caldwell, chap. 62 (p. 182) and chap. 80 (p. 219).

[17] Helwys, *A Short Declaration of the Mistery of Iniquity*.

[18] Sanders, "Re-Visioning the Care of Souls," 99.

the effects of similar messages she encountered in her own conservative Christian upbringing this way:

> I think when I'm talking about the core, that sort of inner sense—I think that's probably what I would call a soul. And that sense that, you know, as I was trying to own a lesbian identity, the sense that my soul was just sort of rotting was definitely leading up to [my suicide attempt]...like that sense that the thing that was my center, my heart, my, you know, connection to the divine was just rotting away.[19]

Thomas was sixteen years old at the time of his first suicide attempt and age twenty-two at the time of his last attempt. He estimates that he attempted suicide from five to seven times over the course of that span of time. Reflecting back on his suicide experience, Thomas says,

> I don't think people kill themselves because they want to die. I think they kill themselves because the pain is too bad...There was no way to figure it out and it was so early in my life that it was established—like as a boy. You know? It was so early that all my life I just like, "Oh my God, this is awful! What an awful place to be! God loves you and hates you. What the [expletive] is that?"...The feelings of that, "God loves me, God hates me. All this stuff in my life is bad, and all this stuff is good. Oh my God." You don't think that, you just feel it.[20]

These are clear and palpable pictures of souls under attack—narratival evidence of the ultimate dignity and integrity of the singular, individual life hewn in the Divine image disregarded and degraded by their own Christian communities. The tenacity of these queer souls, however, puts on display the capacity of the soul's struggle for freedom in the faithful working out of one's own salvation with fear and trembling. After describing the pain and turmoil that the religious messages of his upbringing caused him leading up to his numerous suicide attempts, Thomas described his journey toward a renewed practice of faith, saying,

> I became calm enough to realize that I would rather jettison the teachings that I'd been given about God, and Christ, and the Holy Spirit, and the Kingdom of God and hold onto my faith in Christ. And if it meant that I never had a community ever again, [expletive] it. I will just take it. Because my faith is more important. My faith is the only thing. I couldn't explain it.[21]

---

[19] Sanders, "Re-Visioning the Care of Souls," 111.
[20] Sanders, "Re-Visioning the Care of Souls," 102.
[21] Sanders, "Re-Visioning the Care of Souls," 128.

Forsaking the faith community—the theological praxis of which he experienced as imposition and interference with the sacredness of his relationship to God—Thomas forged new spiritual pathways in the metaphoric wilderness, evidencing the stalwart commitment to soul freedom that animated so many of our Baptist forbearers like Helwys and Williams.

Likewise, Florence described a period of time after her suicide attempt when she realized that the sense she had of having a "rotten core" was not necessarily the case, saying, "It really started to kind of gradually penetrate me that this wasn't necessarily a conflict [between lesbian sexuality and Christian faith]. Like it didn't have to be a rotten core and a good façade. That it really could be a good core." Florence describes what went into changing this sense she had about herself, describing a season in her university choir during which she had an important solo in a religious song. She continued,

> And after our concert, the director came up to me and said, "I think the reason you're so good at singing this is because you really believe it and it just radiates out from the inside of you when you sing." And that was I think that point I thought there is something in me that's not just rotten—that there is maybe light in there. And it was kind of the affirmation of others that who I was came through in what I was doing—that it wasn't just, it wasn't really a façade and I could really believe that was part of who I was.[22]

And though Florence continues, at times, to deal with the reemergence of LGBTQ+-denigrating spiritual narratives in her own experience, her spiritual practices serve as forms of resistance to violent theological narratives that assail her soul's freedom. She describes their freeing effect saying, "And so coming back to that to remind myself that that connection is there and that story is not my story."

Our Baptist story is a story of soul freedom. Yet, we have too long been complicit in violence enacted upon queer souls, forcing their Christ-light under bushels of shame, rejection, excommunication, bodily assault, and soul violence. It is time now to learn queer lessons about Christian faithfulness from the light of Christ's rule and reign shining through the lives of LGBTQ+ people who have learned more about soul freedom in imposed wildernesses than most will ever know.

These lessons of Christian faithfulness and the soul's freedom under the reign of Christ point toward the transformation of a world in the making. In the words of queer theologian Elizabeth Stuart,

> To be baptized is to be caught up in a kingdom that does not yet fully exist, that is in the process of becoming; it is to be caught up in the redemption of this world. It is not that the baptized are called to live beyond culture, but

---

[22] Sanders, "Re-Visioning the Care of Souls," 138-39.

that they are called to transform culture by living in it in such a way as to testify to the other world being born within it.[23]

For queer souls like Thomas, it is the tenacity of a soul's struggle for freedom against religious imposition of soul-crushing violence toward a world of transformation struggling to be born: "[Expletive] it…Because my faith is more important. My faith is the only thing."

4. Lessons of Christian Care

"I give you a new commandment, that you love one another." John 13:34

In addition to the first-person narratives of those like Florence and Thomas above, historian John D'Emilio describes in broader terms that isolation is a "defining feature of gay experience," pointing to "the fact that almost all gay men and lesbians are neither raised in nor socialized at an early age into a gay community."[24] He goes on to say, "the imprint of those critical years of isolation, especially when compounded by the historic invisibility of homosexuality in everyday social life and in popular culture, creates an insistent need for the alternative—for visibility and the connection that community provides."[25]

Unlike children of many other minoritized groups, LGBTQ+ people are not born into a family and a community network of others who share their embodiment of difference and can prepare them for experiences of injustice and violence. A young girl most likely grows up with a mother, aunts, grandmothers and close female friends who populate her life with examples of adult women who know the experience of life in a male-dominated society and who can teach her important lessons about the difference between loving touch and sexual violence. An African American child most likely grows up with a family and community of others— adults and children—who share the child's racial identity, who will pass on and celebrate important pieces of African American heritage even when they are obfuscated by white-dominated educational institutions, and who will teach the child difficult lessons about navigating life in a racist society. But biological families and community networks rarely operate in this caring way for LGBTQ+ people. For numerous LGBTQ+ people, the family of origin turns very suddenly from a source of support into a source of scorn.

At no time was this more evident than during the AIDS crisis in the 1980s that led queer people to begin forming communities that were *exemplars of mutual care* in the face of widespread familial rejection in a largely uncaring society. For

---

[23] Stuart, "Sacramental Flesh," 68.
[24] D'Emilio, *The World Turned*, 96.
[25] D'Emilio, *The World Turned*, 96.

those not personally faced with the reality of AIDS at the height of the crisis of the 1980s, it may be difficult to imagine the terror and uncertainty induced by the myriad of early unknowns surrounding the disease. Amid government inattention and social apathy to the plight of LGBTQ+ people, the high mortality rates of gay people from a largely mysterious disease demonstrated that the need for community had never been greater. And this cultivation of community at the margins of church, family, and society became part of the very fabric of the LGBTQ+ rights movement.

Urvashi Vaid describes the impact of AIDS on broadening the work of gay and lesbian rights organizations, which "suddenly became engaged in building local gay and lesbian institutions—service organizations that became centers for gay men and lesbians to meet, work, and take care of one another."[26] Historian George Chauncey describes the ground-level communities of care that formed, saying, "In the city's dance clubs, bathhouses, and cruising areas, many men had developed strong friendships with other gay men who rallied around them when they became ill."[27] At a time when government attention toward AIDS was either punitive or altogether lacking and the mainstream press refused to provide serious coverage of the AIDS crisis,[28] LGBTQ+ people formed the communities of mutual support that cared for the sick and dying, planned countless funerals and memorials for loved ones whose biological families had abandoned them, and founded the organizations that would mount the most effective and meaningful response to the disease.

In the midst of such a dismal history of death among LGBTQ+ people, the praxis of mutual care among LGBTQ+ people stands to shed light on the praxis of Christian care more broadly, shaping our imaginations for communal possibilities for care of the most vulnerable in our midst today. As queer theologian Kathy Rudy aptly notes, the focus of Christian care is not exclusive to one's familial relationships but moves ever outwards to encompass a community of care. Rudy says:

> The church has historically attempted to break down the boundaries that exist around primary, particular relationships in favor of relationships and dependencies on a community of believers. Christians throughout the centuries have understood that life in Christ means being responsible to and for many more people than one's spouse and children. Life in Christ, in the most radical sense, demands an openness to other community members.[29]

---

[26] Vaid, *Virtual Equality*, 294.

[27] Chauncey, *Why Marriage?*, 97.

[28] Vaid, *Virtual Equality*, 79.

[29] Rudy, *Sex and the Church*, 72.

LGBTQ+ communities hold a mirror up to churches, reminding them of their heritage of communal care and beckoning them toward greater reflection of this heritage in contemporary iterations of Christian community. Inspired by this reflection, churches may begin to ask how queer expressions of community at the margins of church and society may serve as guides for churches seeking to cultivate communities of mutual care and support for the isolated and those marginalized in society by forces of oppression and violence today. This may include offering sanctuary to the undocumented at risk of deportation amid increasingly punitive immigration policy or solidarity with Muslims targeted for unjust surveillance through "Countering Violent Extremism" programs funded by the U.S. government.[30] Seriously considering what lessons queer communities can teach communities of faith will necessitate an increased focus upon human situations of suffering and injustice—circumstances similar to those encountered by LGBTQ+ communities throughout the last century—and learning from the queer, subversive practices of community that counter the prevailing culture of violence and division.

4. Conclusion

José Esteban Muñoz says, "We may never touch queerness, but we can feel it as the warm illumination of a horizon imbued with potentiality...The future is queerness's domain."[31] My hope is that this chapter begins to open imaginative possibilities for what queer illumination is possible if we begin to remove the bushels under which churches have unduly hid the bright light of LGBTQ+ lives. Through a spiritual practice of *metanoia*, turning from our sinful contentment with the absence of Christ's light shining through LGBTQ+ faces, may our Christian future be oriented toward a warm queer illumination on the horizon of the transformational world of becoming that is the kin-dom of God.

---

[30] See U.S. Department of Homeland Security, "Terrorism Prevention Partnerships."
[31] Muñoz, *Cruising Utopia*, 1.

5. For Further Reading

Jimmerson, Ellin Sterne, ed. *Rainbow in the Word: LGBTQ Christians' Biblical Memoirs*. Eugene, OR: Wipf & Stock, 2017.

Sanders, Cody J. *Queer Lessons for Churches on the Straight and Narrow: What All Churches Can Learn from LGBTQ Lives*. Macon, GA: Faithlab, 2013.

Shore-Goss, Robert E., Thomas Bohache, Patrick S. Cheng, and Mona West, eds. *Queering Christianity: Finding a Place at the Table for LGBTQI Christians*. Santa Barbara, CA: ABC-CLIO, 2013.

11

Light from Refugee and Immigrant Perspectives

May May Latt

This is a new era in which global community is shaped by diverse groups of people, and in which global Christianity is formed not only by indigenous and native Christians but also by immigrants, including refugees and diasporic communities who form the community of the church in the new places of their residency. The global church is embodied by these immigrants, refugees, and diasporic communities, and the Bible comes to be interpreted in new perspectives based on people's experiences of migrating in their new lands. This chapter will explore the light offered to the church by these perspectives through a particular example: how the two queens in the book of Esther are read and interpreted in Burmese immigrant, refugee, and diasporic communities.

On January 27, 2017, the headline of the New York Times read "Full Executive Order Text: Trump's Action Limiting Refugees into the U.S.," under which the newspaper reporter wrote, "President Trump signed an executive order on Friday titled 'Protecting the Nation from Foreign Terrorist Entry into the United States.'"[1] Although President Trump's order puts the two terms "refugees" and "foreign terrorist(s)" into the same category and bans everyone in those categories ostensibly for the purpose of keeping America safe, "refugees" are ones forced to migrate to one place after another until they can settle down in one place permanently, or they can call their host country "home."

In past few years, the U.S. under President Obama had allowed Burmese refugees to settle in the U.S.; in 2015, the Burmese refugee population was 18,386 and in 2016 was 12,347. But in 2017, President Trump allowed only 5,078 Burmese refugees into the U.S.[2] Recently the American Baptist Churches USA (ABCUSA) has published a report of their visit to Burmese diasporic communities in Malaysia, in which, due to the current U.S. administration's policy for immigration and refugee admissions, the United Nations Higher Commissioner for Refugees (UNHCR) is able to consider only 1,700 registered refugees for resettlement

---

[1] Crowley, "Full Executive Order Text."

[2] López, Bialik, and Radford, "Key Findings About U.S. Immigrants."

in the U.S. in 2018. ABCUSA, working together with the leaders of "Coalition of Burma Ethnics in Malaysia" (COBEM), tries to help Burmese refugees, displaced persons, or diasporic communities in Malaysia to give pastoral training, leadership skills, counseling, and opportunities in the area of education.[3] This can be seen as building a global community and a global church, working together without any ethnic and cultural boundaries for refugees, displaced people, and diasporic communities.

Diasporic communities belong not only to the global church that reads the Bible but to the biblical story itself. In reading the book of Esther, the term *diaspora* is usually used for the people of Israel, who are already displaced in a foreign land. Between the two queens mentioned in the book, the focus is usually on Queen Esther rather than on Queen Vashti in a diasporic perspective, that is, Esther lives in a foreign land in order to save her own people. This chapter will address various theories that define diaspora and will argue that not only Queen Esther but Queen Vashti is also exiled in her own country. Narrative criticism will be used to look at the two characters of the queens in the book of Esther. By reading the narrative with the contemporary theory on diaspora, we will see that Queen Vashti represents the community of internally displaced people in their homeland, while Queen Esther constitutes the diasporic community living in a foreign land. This chapter will conclude with a reading of these two queens in Esther 1:10–22 and 8:3–7 from the perspective of Burmese immigrants as an illustration of the manner in which reading the Bible through the eyes of refugees and immigrants may illuminate the church's practices of reading and performing Scripture.

1. The Term "Diaspora"

The term "diaspora" has been defined in several ways. Justo L. González points out that the life of exiles is not the life that someone wishes to live: it is "a life in which one is forced to revolve around a center that is not one's own, and that in many ways one does not wish to own." He continued, "Exile is a dislocation of the center, with all the ambiguities and ambivalence of such dislocation."[4] González does not use the term "diaspora"; he uses the term "exile." However, the meaning of the terms "diaspora" and "exile" are inseparable. Along with González, Ruth Behar, a Cuban-American anthropologist, defines the term "exile," but she compares it with the term "diaspora" used broadly. The term reflects the changing lives of Cubans in

---

[3] American Baptist Churches USA, "ABCUSA Burma Refugee Commission and IM Delegation Visits Burma Diaspora Communities in Malaysia."

[4] González, *Santa Biblica*, 134.

the United States (i.e., their foreign land) and includes Cubans still living in Cuba. She said,

> Cubans outside Cuba are perhaps immigrants, perhaps exiles, perhaps both, perhaps neither, and Cubans inside Cuba are in certain ways perhaps more exiled in their *insile* than the so-called exiles themselves....Diaspora also counters the Cuban tendency toward exceptionalism and the arrogance of insularity, allowing us to place the Cuban counterpoint within a wider framework of twentieth-century unbound nations, borderizations, and deterritorializations.[5]

Behar defines as diasporic communities both Cubans living outside Cuba under any circumstances and those living inside in a form of exile. Behar's definition of diaspora is applicable to my reading of the character of Queen Vashti in Esther 1:10-22. Vashti is considered to be the so-called exile herself in her own country. The term "diaspora" suits Queen Vashti in that she is pushed away from her position and may be dislocated in her own land. Here I would identify the diasporic character of Queen Vashti with the internally displaced people.

William Safran identifies six components of diaspora:

1. They have been dispersed from an original "center" to two or more "peripheral" settings;

2. They preserve a "memory, vision, or myth about their original homeland";

3. They believe that they are not or cannot be fully accepted by their host country;

4. They consider their ancestral home as their ideal home and a place of eventual return, at the appropriate time;

5. They have a sense of commitment to the maintenance and restoration of their homeland;

6. They maintain a relationship to the homeland to the extent that their communal consciousness and solidarity are shaped by it.[6]

A critique of Safran's position, however, is that it fits well only with the first generation of a diasporic community, whose minds are attached to the idea of returning to their homeland. After the first generation, the sense of desire to return home

---

[5] Behar, *The Vulnerable Observer*, 135.
[6] Safran, "Diaspora in Modern Societies," 83-84; Segovia, *Interpreting Beyond Borders*, 161-62.

gradually disappears. Safran's definition of the term "diaspora" can be interchangeably used for the term "refugees," who are living outside of their home countries.

James Clifford provides yet another definition: "Diasporas are caught up with and defined against (1) the norms of nation-states and (2) indigenous, and especially autochthonous, claims by 'tribal' peoples."[7] Clifford draws a clear distinction between a diasporic community and an immigrant community. While immigrants try to assimilate themselves into the host country, diasporic communities resist assimilation. The reasons for difficulties in assimilation are: (1) their attachment to the homeland (or) relocation without their own desire; and (2) their experience of discrimination and expulsion. In this definition, the term "diaspora" can apply beyond the first generation of the diasporic community; in fact, this theory focuses only on how the foreign land has treated the dispersed community. Both Safran and Clifford define the term "diaspora" as the people who live outside their home countries but keep their home identities.

While González's and Behar's theories are applied to the interpretation of Esther 1:10-22, Safran's and Clifford's theories of diaspora can be applied in the reading of Esther 8:3-17. Queen Vashti is deposed from her position and exiled from the royal palace. She is touched by diaspora in her own country, representing the community of internally displaced people in their homeland. Since the book seems to lack any direct knowledge of the situation in Judah and its cultic institutions, Queen Esther is likely not among the first generation of those living in the foreign land. She is identified with the diasporic community in Susa under the Persian Empire, and she exemplifies many diasporic communities in foreign countries. Thus, Vashti and Esther represent the community of internally displaced people and diasporic communities inside and outside of their home country. By reading the book of Esther in conversation with contemporary theories of diaspora, we are able better to understand the characters of queen Vashti and Esther: one internally displaced, and the other a member of a diasporic community.

2. The Diasporic Reading of Esther 1:10-22

This section examines how authors in three different time periods—in the Masoretic Text, Josephus, and rabbinic midrash—treated Queen Vashti. By using the diasporic theories of González and Behar, we may understand that queen Vashti is displaced from her position in Esther 1:10-22. Although the text does not mention her location after she is driven out from the palace, it should be considered that she

---

[7] Clifford, "Diasporas," 307; Segovia, *Interpreting Beyond Borders,* 162.

is exiled from the palace, but with the assumption that she remains in her own country, as Cubans are exiled in Cuba.[8]

The book of Esther begins with the king Ahasuerus, who rules over 127 provinces from India to Ethiopia. In the third year of his reign, he displayed the great wealth of his kingdom to the provinces for six months. He invited to his kingdom the army of Persia and Media, in addition to the nobles and governors of the provinces. When the display was done, he gave a banquet to his whole city of Susa for a week. At the same time, Queen Vashti also gave a banquet for the women in the king's palace. Although both banquets were held in the king's palace, the text does not mention whether they were in the same room or separate rooms. The king held his own banquet, in which alcoholic beverages were served. He also ordered that all the officials of his palace could do whatever they desired. On the seventh day of the banquet, every one (especially the king) was drunk with wine. However, the text does not describe the nature of the queen's banquet. It might be filled with talk and food. According to Persian culture, it was usual for women and men to banquet together; however, when the drinking started, the women would leave the banquet.[9]

The nature of the queen's banquet may include only women. Linda M. Day raises the question whether "the women [are] the recipients of gender discrimination" by not being invited to the king's party or, on the contrary, "they [are] given special treatment, invited both to the king's party and to the queen's special party just for them."[10] In response to Day's question, I suggest that both Queen Vashti and all the women are the victims of gender discrimination when they are segregated in the king's palace, having their own party. Although the Masoretic Text (MT) does not describe who Queen Vashti is in detail, this segregation of the party by the king may be related to the queen's ethnic identity.

According to Josephus, Persian court culture does not allow anyone except the king and his eunuchs to look at the queen and his concubines.[11] Therefore the king violates the cultural norm that Josephus outlines when he desires to show his

---

[8] The idea of "Cubans exiled in Cuba" can apply to the situation in Myanmar. The current situation in Rakhine State is the battle between the Myanmar military and minority Rohingya, who resided in the country for many years and fled to the borderland between Myanmar and Bangladesh. In past years, the situation in Kachin State highlights that the runaway people of war are citizens of Myanmar, and they are in refugee camps in the border area of Kachin State. Both Rohingya and Kachin, so-called Internally Displaced People (IDPs), are exiled and deposed by the battles with the Myanmar military in the country.

[9] Crawford, "Book of Esther," 879-80.

[10] Day, *Esther*, 31.

[11] Crawford, "Book of Esther," 882. Crawford disagrees with Josephus that his information is historically inaccurate, cf. Herodotus 9.110 and Neh 2:6.

queen's beauty in public, so that she may be admired by other men. We should remember that this king liked to show everything that he owned to all his officials to gain honor and praise for himself. Therefore, the king ordered his commanders to bring Queen Vashti before him wearing the royal crown. Although the MT does not mention that the queen wore *only* the royal crown, the Targum (the Aramaic translation of the Hebrew Bible) informs the readers that the king's order entails Vashti's appearance before the king's guests "wearing only her royal crown." Esther Rabbah 3:13 says:

> When the nations of the world eat and drink, they occupy themselves with tasteless words. This one says: Median women are fair! And this one says: Persian women are fair! The fool said to them: The vessel that the man uses is neither Median nor Persian, rather Chaldean. Do you all desire to see her? They said to him: Yes, but only if she is naked. He said to them: Yes and naked.[12]

The king had ordered Queen Vashti, the Babylonian descendant, to appear naked before him and his officials. The queen refuses the king's order out of modesty. The result of her refusal was that Queen Vashti was expelled from the palace.

In rabbinic midrash, Queen Vashti is the great granddaughter of Nebuchadnezzar, the king of Babylon, and the daughter of King Belshazzar, the last monarch of Babylon. During the Persian attack, Belshazzar was killed, and Vashti was kidnapped by King Darius of Persia. Then King Darius ordered his son, Ahasuerus, to marry her.[13] In this narrative, Vashti, the last descendant of a Babylonian monarch, became queen in the Persian palace. The character Queen Vashti is already an internally displaced person, even before becoming a queen. Her Babylonian identity seems to be marginalized and misused under the Persian Empire. The ways she is treated are unusual for Persian culture: (1) the palace held gender-separate banquets (the king and the queen had their own banquets); and (2) the queen was summoned to appear naked in the king's banquet. By adding rabbinic midrash's portrayal of Queen Vashti, we can conclude that Vashti's exile is related to the king's mistreatment of her gender and her Babylonian identity. Applying the diasporic theories of González and Behar to this text, Queen Vashti is deposed from her position and exiled from the royal palace. Certainly, she is displaced from her royal place "with all the ambiguities and ambivalence of such dislocation": she is exiled in her own country. Now the king needs to choose another queen; without the internally displaced queen Vashti, there would be no diasporic Esther.

---

[12] Sefaria Community Translation, trans., "Midrash: Esther Rabbah."
[13] Greenspoon, "The Taming of the Two," 166.

3. The Diasporic Reading of Esther 8:3-17

When the king chooses Esther, she is in Susa, the land of the king Ahasuerus. She is a Judean, but she cannot reveal her identity in the royal palace because of her cousin Mordecai, who sits at the gate of the palace.[14] She has to work wisely within the power structure of the Persian harem system. "She moves from a completely powerless position into the relatively more powerful one of queen."[15]

Hiding Esther's Judean identity became questionable, although Mordecai did not hide his identity when he came to face Haman at the gate. If King Xerxes is identified as King Ahasuerus in Persia from the book of Esther,[16] during the time of Xerxes, Persians made a huge change of social structure in Babylonia; whenever Babylonians rebelled against Persians at that time, Persians dealt with them unmercifully.[17] This may be one of the reasons that people's identities were hidden during the time of King Ahasuerus; Judeans were hiding their identities (Esth. 2:20; 8:17, in which many Judeans unveiled their identities).

The book of Esther was composed among the eastern Judean diaspora in the Persian Empire. The audience of the book is Judean in a foreign land under foreign rulers. They appear to be a minority in Persia and encounter the danger of persecution and oppression. The book focuses on the Persian court and its situation but lacks direct knowledge of the situation in Judah and its cultic institutions.[18] Recall that according to Clifford's theory of diaspora, beyond its first generation, the diasporic community may forget about the situation of their homeland. That might be a reason that the book of Esther does not mention the situation in Judah and its cultic institution. By contrasting immigrants, as Clifford has defined them, the community focuses on how their foreign land of Persia has treated them with the experience of discrimination and expulsion. They try not to assimilate into the host country but survive in the foreign land by hiding their identity. The queen Esther is identified with the Judean diasporic community in Persia.

---

[14] Following Steve Mason's argument on whether "Jews" or "Judean" is the preferred term, I prefer to use "Judean" in this chapter. The term "Judean" is related to geographically dispersed people of Judah, and it indicates the ethnic minority in Babylonia under Persia. Mason, "Jews, Judaeans, Judaizing, Judaism," 457-512.

[15] Crawford, "Esther," in *Women's Bible Commentary,* ed. Newsom and Ringe, 135.

[16] Fox, *Character and Ideology in the Book of Esther,* 13-14, argues that *ahašweroš* in Hebrew and *xšayārša* in Persian can be identified with Xerxes in Greek. Xerxes is the historical figure who reigned from 485 to 465 BCE over India to Nubia and was a son of Darius and a grandson of Cyrus the Great of Persia.

[17] Davies, *Cambridge History of Judaism,* 1:326-58.

[18] Fox, *Character and Ideology in the Book of Esther,* 138; Day, *Esther,* 16.

Esther 8:3-17 opens with Esther speaking to the king in the banquet for the second time. Contrasting Queen Esther with Queen Vashti (whom the king's officials are thought to bring naked into the king's banquet), Esther takes the initiative in talking to the king; she asks the king to bring Haman to the banquet. Most womanist/feminist scholars believe that Esther has found her courage from the example of Vashti. This story expresses that "one injustice can lead to another; one resistance can give rise to another."[19] Esther unveiled her identity and said to the king:

> If I have won your favor and the proposal right to Your Majesty, and if I am pleasing to you—let dispatches be written countermanding those which were written by Haman son of Mammedatha the Agagite, embodying his plot to annihilate the Jews throughout the king's province. For how can I bear to see the calamity that is coming on my people? Or how can I bear to see the destruction of my kindred? (Esth. 8:5-6)

The king commanded Mordecai to send out a new edict, written in the name of the king. Wherever the edict reached, there was gladness, joy, festivals, and a holiday among the Judeans. Finally, many of them confessed that they were Judeans, because in those days, they feared to announce their identity while living in a foreign country and under foreign rulers. One aspect of Safran's theory is particularly relevant (although his theory does not consider those beyond the first generation of exiles to be in a situation of diaspora): "[the diasporic community] believe that they are not or cannot be fully accepted by their host country."[20] If the Judeans were fully accepted in Susa, they would not have the feeling of being afraid to reveal their identity. The members of diasporic community may live in fear when they are outside of their homeland.

4. Reading Queen Vashti and Esther in Myanmar Diasporic Contexts

Using the diasporic theories of González, Behar, Clifford, and Safran in reading Esther 1:10-22 and 8:3-17, we may appropriately suggest that Queen Vashti represents "internally displaced people," and Queen Esther, a "diasporic community." As the last descendant of a Babylonian monarch, Vashti was internally displaced in Babylon even before becoming a queen of Persia. She is marginalized on the basis of her gender and her Babylonian identity. Finally, by using her position to resist injustice, Vashti's actions lead to herself becoming an exile or internally displaced woman in her own country.

---

[19] Florence, "The Woman Who Just Said NO," 37-40.
[20] Safran, "Diaspora in Modern Societies," 83-84.

This reading reflects the community of internally displaced people across the globe, especially in my own country of Burma (Myanmar), in which there is currently ethnic conflict between the Burmese military armed forces and the Arakan Rohingya Salvation Army (ARSA), also an armed force. In between two armed forces, civilian Rohingya, a Muslim minority in Burma, fled from their home of Arakan/Rakhine State, which is in the southwest of Burma, to the area just across the border of Burma and Bangladesh. Since the later twentieth century, nearly one million Rohingya had fled Burma; currently more than 400,000 are internally displaced and refugees in this borderland.[21] In the context of the global church, how do we reflect on this issue when we read about the two queens in Esther? Queen Vashti represents these internally displaced people. Her position is vulnerable. She is the last descendant of Babylonian royalty, and becomes queen of Persia and an internally displaced person, then becomes a forced migrant from her position.

According to the history in Burma, when Portuguese pirates came into Burma in the 1400s, they brought Bengali slaves with them. At that time, Rakhine, the indigenous ethnic group, had a king, and was a small kingdom. Their religion was Buddhism. In the 1700s, the Burmese came into Arakan/Rakhine by way of the Irrawaddy River and destroyed the kingdom. In the early 1900s, the Rakhine became a minority in their own land. Bengali Muslim and Burmese Buddhists became more populous in the land. Burmese nationalism was born in the early 1900s. Since both the Burmese and the Rakhine are tied with Theravada Buddhism, people outside Buddhism became totally strangers for them.[22]

In the late nineteenth and early twentieth centuries, Bengali Muslims were migrating into Rakhine, and millions of others from India arrived in Rakhine by the sea. Then the Japanese invaded Burma in 1942, while the British were still in Burma. The Japanese armed the Buddhist Rakhine, and the British armed the Muslims at that time. Thousands were killed in Buddhist-Muslim ethnic violence. This ethnic conflict has been going on intermittently since 1942. After the war, the leaders of local Muslim communities (who speak a dialect of Bengali) joined with Pakistanis and demanded their own "homeland" within Burma. In the years 1978 to 1990, the whole country was facing a political uprising.[23] Then, in 1988, Burma fell under military dictatorship. Since the 1970s, hundreds of thousands of Muslims have fled from Burma and become refugees in the borderland.

Indigenous, native, or ethnic people in Burma are those who came into the land before British rule in 1824. People who came after struggled to be considered

---

[21] The numbers of refugees cannot be fixed permanently and have been growing continuously: United Nations High Commissioner for Refugees, "Rohingya Emergency."

[22] Thant, "Myanmar's Resurgent Nationalism Shapes New Political Landscape."

[23] Thant, "Myanmar's Resurgent Nationalism Shapes New Political Landscape."

as native or ethnic. Thant Myint-U, a Burmese historian, has explained that according to the 1982 citizenship law, "immigrants and their children may only be 'naturalized' or recognized as 'associate' citizens, with restricted political rights." However, the third generation of any ethnic group, including "the grandchildren of early twentieth century Bengali Muslim migrants," is permitted to have full privileges as citizens. Because of a lack of documentation in immigration, however, it is not clear who are the actual descendants of immigrants who came into the land before 1824. Thant Myint-U says:

> In the 1950s, local Muslim politicians crafted the ethnonym "Rohingya" as a new overarching and indigenous identity for all (Muslims)....Rohingya had become the preferred way for Muslims in northern Rakhine, at least to identify themselves. It is this very claim to be *taing-yin-tha* [indigenous, ethnic, or citizen] that is rejected ferociously by Burmese.[24]

Just as Queen Vashti was a Babylonian internally displaced person in the Persian Empire, the Bengali Muslims, or so-called Rohingya, were already immigrants since they migrated into Burma before and after 1824; but now, because of the battles between the Burmese military and ARSA, some of them are forced to become fully refugees and internally displaced people near the border of Burma and Bangladesh.

There was another conflict in Burma, which was between the Kachin Independence Army (Kachin is one of the major ethnic tribes in Burma) and the Myanmar Army. The conflict was restarted in 2011 and continues intermittently, although ceasefire talks have taken place between the two armies for a long period of time. The results of the conflicts include many deaths of civilians, many villages being destroyed, many thousands of people being internally displaced, and many becoming refugees in foreign countries. The Myanmar Army often attacks the refugee camps and villages and commits "war crimes" such as rape and the murder of civilians. Many women are involved in significant roles in these conflicts, either as victims or combatants, as the Kachin Women's Association Thailand has reported.[25] The victims of the conflict are, like Vashti, internally displaced, exiled from her comfortable place and moved from her center to an unknown place inside the country.

There is a world-renowned woman in Myanmar named Aung San Suu Kyi, a Nobel Peace Prize winner in 1991, who may be compared to Vashti and Esther. Like Vashti she was exiled in her home country for resisting injustice. She stands

---

[24] Thant, "Myanmar's Resurgent Nationalism Shapes New Political Landscape."

[25] Kachin Women's Association Thailand, "Update on the Human Rights Situation in Burma (January—June 2018)."

for civilians, who can identify with an exilic community, that is, internally displaced people in their home country. Clearly, Suu Kyi does not stand for the Myanmar military armed forces; neither does she stand for any violent armed groups. It should be noted that recently she has been criticized by international communities across the globe for failing to respond quickly enough to the Rohingya conflict in Burma. We must point out, however, that between the powers of two violent armed forces, Suu Kyi can do only certain things in a short period of time. She uses a nonviolent approach to end these conflicts. On September 19, 2017, Suu Kyi gave a speech to the whole world in which she condemned "all human rights violations." She has deep concern for the people who are fleeing from Burma to Bangladesh. She said, "the country [i.e., Burma] stood ready to aid the Rohingya returnees."[26] She fights for justice and freedom from fear. Suu Kyi has continued to resist injustice throughout her lifetime so that the country may progress toward democracy.

The character of Esther is identified with the relocated diasporic community in a foreign country. Under the military dictatorship in the past decade, many people in Burma ran away from the country and relocated in foreign countries as refugees, seekers of political asylum, or as immigrants. Although we do not need to hide our Burmese identity in the host countries in this era, unlike the Judean diaspora in Susa, we are never fully embraced by our host countries. We are always defined as Burmese people in their midst. Jeffrey Kah-Jin Kuan says, "we were 'wanted' as long as we could contribute to the economic wellbeing of our host country, and 'unwanted' as soon as problems arose." We cannot expect to be fully embraced by the dominant society of our host countries, but we must learn how to live in harmony with our host countries. It is the nature of our diasporic community. To inscribe our identity, "we remove the power of the dominant society to inscribe us"[27] and engage in the ongoing task of self-definition as "aliens," displaced people, and diasporic communities living in foreign lands.

5. Lessons for a Global Church

Finally, a global church, beyond a local church, must embrace our self-definition and interpretation of the Bible based on our own experience of living in the host countries. Bringing a diasporic perspective to bear on the book of Esther newly illuminates the ways in which Vashti is an internally displaced queen descended from the last Babylonian monarch. Reading the text from the perspectives of refu-

---

[26] Wright, Hunt, and Berlinger, "Aung San Suu Kyi Breaks Silence on Rohingya, Sparks Storm of Criticism."

[27] Kuan, "Diasporic Reading of a Diasporic Text," 167.

gees, immigrants, internally displaced people, and diasporas can facilitate a conversation that allows members of those groups to find our own identities in the midst of communities in which we do not constitute a majority. If the churches of the host countries are fearful of diversity and attempt to assimilate us into their own identity, the "global church" becomes an empty signifier. Yet a global church implies plurality and diversity. The churches should consider that the fear of diversity cannot make their identity more secure, and that acts of exclusion cannot contribute to building the global church. The churches of the host countries will only be strengthened by the inclusion of diverse communities. This is the path toward establishing one global church.

6. For Further Reading

Casal, José Luis. "The Immigrant's Creed." In *Book of Common Worship*, Presbyterian Church (USA), 613-14. Louisville, KY: Westminster John Knox, 2018. Online, Calvin Institute of Christian Worship, https://worship.calvin.edu/resources/resource-library/the-immigrants-creed/ (downloaded November 28, 2018).

Davidson, Steed Varnyl. "Diversity, Difference, and Access to Power in Diaspora: The Case of the Book of Esther." *Word & World* 29, no. 3 (Summer 2009): 280-87.

Hacham, Noah. "3 Maccabees and Esther: Parallels, Intertextuality, and Diaspora Identity." *Journal of Biblical Literature* 126, no. 4 (2007): 765-85.

Humphreys, W. Lee. "A Life-Style for Diaspora: A Study of the Tales of Esther and Daniel." *Journal of Biblical Literature* 92 (1973): 211-23.

Stern, Elsie R. "Esther and the Politics of Diaspora." *The Jewish Quarterly Review* 100, no. 1 (Winter 2010): 25-53.

12

Light from People with Disabilities

Jason D. Whitt

This chapter invites reflection on the lives and theological contributions of people with disabilities. What light might they offer faithful congregations? Unlike many groups to whom this volume gives voice, they do not constitute a common identity. Certainly, no group ever speaks with a single voice. In the case of people with disabilities, however, this is especially true. "Disability" is a construct. It is an umbrella term that attempts to describe as a unified whole what are in reality vastly different impairments. What does the experience of the paraplegic share with the hearing impaired; visual impairment with autism; the soldier who has lost an appendage with the person with Down syndrome? How is Stephen Hawking's experience of disability shared with the experience of the profoundly intellectually disabled child who lacks even the capacity to have a sense of self?

The answer in most cases is nothing. Rather, they share the label "disabled" that relegates their lives as "other." The embodied experience of daily life for each person with a disability is to be named as a deviation from "normalcy."[1] Throughout history, this deviation has caused fear, exclusion, confinement, scorn, and pity.[2] In too many instances, deviation from normalcy has carried the implication that this one is, as a consequence, less than human. The moral status of people with disabilities is a live question: "Are they one of us?" "Do they belong in our community?" "What value could they possibly have in our society?"

These questions are perhaps the one uniting experience that people with various disabilities share. Nevertheless, I would like to suggest in this chapter that people with disabilities of all kinds serve as sources of light for Baptist congregations in and through their disabilities. I will focus particularly on those with intellectual

---

[1] Thomas E. Reynolds describes the "cult of normalcy" as an image that is "cast onto those whose lives disrupt the status quo, manifesting a lack or deficiency of what is construed as standard, ordinary, and familiar" (Reynolds, *Vulnerable Communion*, 33).

[2] For a history of disability, see Braddock and Parish, "Institutional History of Disability," in *Disability at the Dawn of the 21ˢᵗ Century and the State of the States*, ed. Braddock, 11-68; Minnesota Governor's Council on Developmental Disabilities, "Parallels in Time: A History of Developmental Disabilities."

disabilities because they stand at the farthest fringes of those expected to be sources of theological illumination. My aim is to consider two primary avenues by which they offer light. The first focuses on the challenge that their existence offers to expand Baptist understandings of personhood, salvation, and ecclesiology. The second emphasizes the contributions that people with disabilities make to churches through their worship and service.

Before traveling these two avenues, however, I will introduce some matters of prolegomena. First, I will address what is meant by "theology of disability" and why it is needed in contemporary theological discussions. Then I will offer two snapshots—one biblical, one historical—that reveal ways in which those with disabilities have been excluded and also returned to places within the church. Finally, I will suggest how those previously excluded illumine our understanding of humanity, salvation, and the church and help congregations to become more fully who they are called to be in Christ.

1. Theology of Disability

Disability theology is an attempt to engage in theological reflection that takes into account the lived experiences of people with disabilities.[3] For some, such a contextualized approach can be the dominant lens through which the theological enterprise is conducted.[4] One may also understand disability theology, however, as the effort to incorporate disabled voices that have often been omitted from theological conversations, but done within the context of the historic Christian doctrinal tradition.[5] In the latter case, disability is not the perspective that drives all theological reflection. Rather, theological reflection taking account of disability recognizes that because people with disabilities have too often been excluded from the conversation, doctrine and church practices have developed that disadvantage or oppress them. John Swinton points in particular to "the equation of disability with sin or the exclusion of people with intellectual disabilities from the sacraments based on sacramental theologies that emphasize intellect and knowledge."[6]

Disability theology aims at assuring that the lived experiences of people with disabilities are not neglected from theological reflection. Embracing these lives might mean reimagining an account of human being in the image of God that includes the whole range of humans—not just those with well-developed capacities

---

[3] Swinton, "Disability Theology," in *Cambridge Dictionary of Christian Theology*, ed. McFarland et al., 140.

[4] E.g., Eiesland, *The Disabled God: Toward a Liberatory Theology of Disability*.

[5] E.g., Yong, *Theology of Down Syndrome*; Reinders, *Receiving the Gift of Friendship*.

[6] Swinton, "Disability Theology," in *Cambridge Dictionary of Christian Theology*, ed. McFarland et al., 141.

for reason and rational self-willing.[7] Likewise, disability theology might raise questions about a soteriology that excludes the profoundly intellectually disabled because they lack the rational capacity to make a statement of faith. Disability theology may challenge accepted church practices regarding who speaks, what roles are open to different people, and how people with disabilities might have a share in the practices that constitute worship and church life.

2. Disability: Biblical and Historical Snapshots

If such a contextualized approach to theological reflection is the aim of disability theology, what are the biblical and historical conditions that serve as the background for its work? The examples below serve as snapshots. Neither exhausts the fullness of how disability has been understood within the Bible and Christian tradition.[8] Rather, they provide glimpses of both the challenges inherent in each context for addressing disability and the resources present, even if overlooked, within the Christian tradition for incorporating disability voices.

Discussion of disability is prevalent throughout Scripture. In the Old Testament, it appears in legal texts defining the limits of holiness and those who can and cannot serve at the altar (e.g., Lev. 21:17-23). It describes both key figures and minor characters throughout the biblical narrative, offering implicit and explicit commentary on the nature of each and their standing before God (e.g., Jacob, Samson, Mephibosheth). The New Testament most often presents disability in the context of healing narratives. Each case presents its own hermeneutical challenges to determining a "biblical" view of disability.[9]

Each of the Gospels recounts the story of Jesus driving out the money-changers from the Temple (Matt. 21:12-17; Mark 11:15-19; Luke 19:45-48; John 2:13-17). But only Matthew adds the curious note: "The blind and the lame came to him in the temple and he cured them" (v. 14). What seems initially to be merely

---

[7] E.g., Kilner, *Dignity and Destiny*; Mellon, "John Kilner's Understanding of the *Imago Dei* and The Ethical Treatment of Persons with Disabilities."

[8] Yong, *The Bible, Disability, and the Church*; Brock and Swinton, eds., *Disability in the Christian Tradition*.

[9] Hermeneutical principles for reading disability texts must be drawn from the larger context of Scripture about who humans are in relation to God. Asking questions about what is meant by holiness in the Levitical laws and how that understanding is reshaped in light of the Incarnation will inform how scriptural accounts of disability are read. Readers' own presuppositions about the value of a life with disability likewise will significantly shape how they read various accounts in Scripture.

134

a throwaway line reveals a fundamental transformation about how the body of Christ is to receive those with disabilities.[10]

The significance of Matthew's comment about the blind and the lame has its origins in 2 Sam. 5:6-8, the account of David's capture of Jerusalem. As David and his men lay siege to Jerusalem, the Jebusite defenders taunt: "David cannot come in here, even the blind and the lame will turn you back" (v. 6). An unguarded water shaft, however, betrays them. As 2 Samuel reports, the taunt and its failure is the origin of the saying, "The blind and the lame shall not come into the house" (v. 8). David would not forget the mocking of the Jebusites, and so it became the custom that the blind and the lame were not welcome within the Temple. Matthew's seemingly offhand comment that the blind and the lame came to Jesus in the Temple to be healed carries far more weight than first imagined. Tom Wright notes:

> Jesus did with the Temple's traditions what he did with the money-changers' tables: he turned them upside down. The people who had been kept out were now welcomed in. The people who had been scorned were now healed. It was an action full of significance. It summed up everything Jesus had been doing throughout his ministry.[11]

Those with disabilities discover in the Son of David one who welcomes them to the very place from which David had excluded them.

The coming of the blind and the lame to Jesus in the Temple speaks to those with physical disabilities, but does this welcome have implications for those with intellectual disabilities? If this passage is read within the larger context of the life, death, and resurrection of Christ, I believe that it does. In 1 Corinthians, Paul reminds his readers that "the message of the cross is foolishness to those who are perishing" (1:18) and "God's foolishness is wiser than human wisdom, and God's weakness is stronger than human strength" (1:25). He concludes, "God chose what is foolish in the world to shame the wise" (1:27). Amos Yong contends that this passage can be read in light of intellectual disability and so challenges the stigma that prevents their full inclusion within the community of the church. The hubristic knowing of earthly wisdom encounters its limits in divine wisdom that appears as foolishness. For Yong, those with intellectual disabilities, in their seeming foolishness because of intellectual impairment, are those who embody divine wisdom. Those who are outcast from society are those whose very lives in their weakness

---

[10] I am indebted Eric Howell, my pastor at DaySpring Baptist Church in Waco, Texas, for drawing my attention to this passage in a sermon he preached on Palm Sunday, April 9, 2017 (online http://ourdayspring.org/2015-sermons [downloaded March 5, 2018]).

[11] Wright, *Matthew for Everyone: Part 2, Chapters 16-28*, 71.

challenge the power and certainty of a world that cannot comprehend God's wisdom that comes in grace. Most importantly, Christ's crucifixion is the ultimate sign of weakness and foolishness that upends the world's account of power and strength. Jesus' welcome of those with disabilities into the Temple anticipates the divine foolishness of the cross and resurrection that will redeem the intellectually disabled in their disability, not from it. Because of this, "the church is most truly the body of Christ when it is centrally constituted by and honors people with intellectual disability."[12]

Matthew's record of Jesus' actions in the Temple reveals the tension inherent in scriptural accounts of disability. On the one hand, the tradition, embodied in the saying arising from David's capture of Jerusalem and ensconced in purity codes, denies people with disability a place within the worshiping community. They are excluded by virtue of their disabilities, often with the stigma that their condition is revelatory of unrepentant sin or a sign of God's disfavor (exemplified in John 9:2 by the disciples' question to Jesus: "Rabbi, who sinned, this man or his parents, that he was born blind?"). Jesus, however, welcomes those with disabilities into the Temple. But even here tension exists. Is their welcome only on the condition of their healing? If so, what does it mean for those who are not healed? Is the Temple, the worshiping community, still open to their presence? The answers to these questions depend largely on how one understands disability. Is it a burden from which the individual needs to be freed/healed, or is it a way of being that God can use for blessing and good—to the one living with disability and through that one to the church and world?[13]

The second historical snapshot is found in a 1515 painting titled *The Adoration of the Christ Child*, on display in New York's Metropolitan Museum of Art. Attributed to a follower of Jan Joest of Kalkar, the piece depicts the nativity scene with the newborn Christ surrounded by Mary, Joseph, a host of angels, and two shepherds peering through the back window. Flemish artist Jan Joest created an original of this scene on which others in his workshop would model their paintings. Several paintings that match *The Adoration of the Christ Child*—including the characters, their placement, and their clothing—appear in galleries around the world.[14]

The significance of this particular painting of the nativity and its connection to other paintings sharing the same pattern is in what distinguishes it from them.

---

[12] Yong, *The Bible, Disability, and the Church*, 104.

[13] For disability perspectives on the study of Scripture, see Avalos, Melchor, and Schipper, eds., *This Abled Body*; Moss and Schipper, eds., *Disability Studies and Biblical Literature*; Schipper, *Disability Studies and the Hebrew Bible*; Melcher, Parsons, and Yong, eds., *The Bible and Disability*.

[14] Ainsworth and Christiansen, eds., *From Van Eyck to Bruegel*, 244.

The Adoration of the Magi by the unknown
16th-century artist "Follower of Jan Joest of Kalkar."
Courtesy The Metropolitan Museum of Art.

In 2003, two medical researchers, Andrew S. Levitas and Cheryl S. Reid, published an article noting a remarkable feature of the painting unmentioned (and perhaps unnoticed) in previous discussions of the work. After noting the similarities to other works, they describe the striking difference:

> At least one of the angels and one of the earthly admirers have a very similar and distinctive facial appearance. A close examination of the triplet of angels in the foreground shows that the angel next to Mary, whose single visible wing is behind the head, has flattened midface, epicanthal folds, upslanted palpebral fissures, small and upturned nasal tip, and downward curving of the mouth corners.[15]

Noting these clinical features, they conclude that the angel next to Mary had Down syndrome. They also suspect that the shepherd in the background with similar features also shares the condition.

Levitas and Reid believe that this may be the earliest portrayal of Down syndrome in Western art. Other faces in the painting do not have the same telltale markers of Down syndrome, so the depiction is not due to lack of skill. Levitas and Reid argue that the artist must have been sufficiently familiar with a person with Down syndrome to paint the features as he did. This depiction confirms Down syndrome's prevalence since at least the Middle Ages, ending an argument among geneticists as to whether this was a modern condition.[16]

Perhaps more remarkable is that viewers overlooked the obvious features of Down syndrome for so long. Ainsworth and Christiansen make no mention of the features in their discussion of the painting, despite its comparison with the almost identical painting on the following page.[17] It might be enough to wonder at the fact that what seems to be such an obvious feature—at least two faces exhibiting common features of Down syndrome[18]—went unnoticed. The lack of identification of the figures as having Down syndrome in the painting offers evidence of the "otherness" of those with disabilities and the place that they inhabit at the margins of society. Too often, the fate of the figures in the painting—to be seen but not seen—is a metaphor for the experience of people with disabilities in churches.

---

[15] Levitas and Reid, "Angel with Down Syndrome in a Sixteenth Century Flemish Nativity Painting," 401.

[16] Levitas and Reid, "Angel with Down Syndrome in a Sixteenth Century Flemish Nativity Painting," 403.

[17] See Ainsworth and Christiansen, eds., *From Van Eyck to Bruegel*, 244-47.

[18] It appears to me that at least one, though perhaps more, of the smaller angels at the top of the image also displays features of Down syndrome. Cf. Leach, "Down Syndrome Diagnosis at the Adoration of the Christ Child."

But is this all that can be said? The benevolent depiction of the figures in the scene is "inconsistent with other known examples of the artistic practice at the time, where individuals with recognized disabilities tended to be depicted in paintings as symbols of comedy or evil."[19] To account for the positive portrayal, Levitas and Reid suggest that either the artist's model had Down syndrome, that the disabilities were not recognized as such, or that the artist had affection for the model despite his disabilities. Each possibility is a valid answer to the incorporation of Down syndrome into the scene at the manger. Mark Leach astutely recognizes the challenge the artist makes to the prevailing norms of his day (and the present): "The significance of the painting is that it seeks to challenge this segregation and treatment of Down syndrome as 'the other.'"[20]

Leach comments that the shepherd is "shut out of the scene" but looks in the stable through a window. Though remaining outside the stable, "he inserts himself into the scene, adoring nevertheless." One with Down syndrome is, however, on the inside: the angel beside Mary worshiping the Christ-child. For Leach, the painting reveals the struggle, as common in the sixteenth century as the twenty-first, for those with disabilities to break down the walls of exclusion that keep them at the margins. At the manger heaven and earth meet, and in that meeting is the revelation that people with disabilities stand equal before Christ in worship.[21]

Each of these snapshots provides a glimpse into the challenges people with disabilities must overcome to offer their gifts to the community of Christ. The Bible itself has been used to question the goodness of those with disabilities, often tying their impairments to their moral status and serving as the basis of exclusion from the community. Even where Scripture contests oppressive images of people with disabilities, the hermeneutical lenses able-bodied readers employ lead them to miss the message present there.[22] The church's historical record has been little better. The unknown sixteenth-century artist seeks both to reflect the exclusion that defines the world for people with disabilities and to prescribe a new possibility in which welcome and equal recognition mark the coming of Christ's kingdom.

---

[19] Levitas and Reid, "An Angel with Down Syndrome in a Sixteenth Century Flemish Nativity Painting," 403.

[20] Leach, "A Portrayal of Heaven on Earth."

[21] Leach, "A Portrayal of Heaven on Earth."

[22] Cf. Yong, "Zacchaeus."

3. Theology in the Light of Disability

How, then, might people with intellectual disabilities shine light upon Baptist doctrine and church practices? Jason Greig explains,

> People with profound cognitive disabilities cannot write books or papers on what it means to be human or how they understand God or the Bible. Yet they can interrupt overly abstract theologizing by forcing those pursuing moral thinking to pay attention to their very particular and concrete *bodies*, which refuse to be ignored.[23]

Above all, the embodied presence of people with intellectual disability challenges accounts of the image of God in humans that locate the image in the capacity for reason and self-determination. This predominant association of reason with the divine image, however, is curious because of what it implies about who is more and less in God's image. As John Kilner notes, "especially bright atheists" may be more in the image of God than faithful, though less intellectually accomplished, Christians; likewise, "animals with the most developed reasoning abilities become more in God's image than people whose reason is most impaired."[24] The embodied presence of people with intellectual disability in churches should raise questions about Christian articulations of the image of God that seek to locate it in capacities that all humans may or may not share.[25]

People with profound intellectual disabilities also raise soteriological questions for the Baptist commitment to believer's baptism. In practice, the emphasis on personal confession of faith often is expressed as *intellectual* assent to a set of beliefs, thus necessitating reason and self-determination for salvation. This commitment, understood this way, excludes the possibility of salvation for those who lack the capacity for such assent. While the response that God's grace is sufficient for them may be tempting, this approach implicitly calls into question their full humanity by marking them as other than humans with higher cognitive abilities. Likewise, their full membership within the church cannot be established apart from baptism, so they remain throughout life with the status of those who are passive recipients of other Christians' benevolent care. They are never seen as those who have gifts that are necessary for the good of the whole church. Because they are not truly part of the church through baptism, imagining that the spiritual giftedness 1 Corinthians 12 describes includes them is difficult. What would it mean for Baptists to articu-

---

[23] Greig, *Reconsidering Intellectual Disability*, 10.

[24] Kilner, *Dignity and Destiny*, 187.

[25] Cf. Whitt, "In the Image of God"; Reinders, *Receiving the Gift of Friendship*; Haslam, *Constructive Theology of Intellectual Disability*; Yong, *Theology of Down Syndrome*.

late a soteriology that affirmed the lives and place in the church of those with intellectual disabilities?[26]

Even when welcomed, the embodied presence of people with disabilities in
churches can be disconcerting. Including them in worship services can be challenging because they may say and do the unexpected, disrupting the order that is expected from other members of the congregation. "Yet exactly to the extent that
they create the unexpected," Stanley Hauerwas writes, "they remind us that the
God we worship is not easily domesticated":

> For in worship the church is made vulnerable to a God who would rule this
> world not by coercion but through the unpredictability of love. Christians
> thus learn that people with mental handicaps are not among us because we
> need someone to be the object of charity, but because without these broth-
> ers and sisters in Christ we call "retarded," we cannot know what it means
> rightly to worship God.[27]

The worship of people with intellectual disabilities, often jarring and unexpected
for the able-bodied, challenges the comfortable confines into which God is relegated: a god that seems more in the image of "normal" humans than the Triune God
who always remains more than can be known.[28]

The embodied lives of people with intellectual disabilities can also help develop the church's practical theology, expressed through its liturgical practices. For
Hauerwas, what those with intellectual disability offer to the church is "time to be
church."[29] They remind the church that God has given the church all the time it
needs, whether that means allowing the person who does not speak well or quickly
to read Scripture or pray; walking slowly to the communion table with one whose
gait is slow; or creating spaces that are accessible to everyone, not just those who
are able to rush from task to task. The fear is that including people with disabilities
in the life of the church will slow members down. This slowing down, however,
may help speed up the moral formation of the rest of the church.

Christopher Newell, a theologian, Anglican priest, and disability activist, lived
his life making use of a wheelchair for mobility and daily oxygen and respiratory

---

[26] See Whitt, "Baptism and Profound Intellectual Disability"; Taylor, "Include Them
Out?"

[27] Hauerwas, "The Church and Mentally Handicapped Persons," 60.

[28] A growing body of literature supports the inclusion of people with both physical and intellectual disabilities in worship: e.g., Newman, *Accessible Gospel, Inclusive Worship*; Gaventa,
"Preaching Disability"; idem, *Disability and Spirituality*; Newman, "Inclusive Worship." Baptist
Union of Great Britain, *Gathering for Worship*, ed. Ellis and Blyth, 100-106, includes a pattern of
worship for a service for people with intellectual disabilities.

[29] Hauerwas, "The Church and Mentally Handicapped Persons," 60.

therapy treatments for chronic respiratory issues. In an essay on suffering and the paradox of disability, he confesses seeking to present a life of strength and independence while also recognizing that he is very much dependent upon others and biotechnology. He invites his readers to "listen" to his own story and the stories of those with disabilities that challenge cultural narratives—often embraced by Christians—that regard suffering as antithetical to a good life. Disability is associated with suffering perhaps most fundamentally because disability is seen as the antithesis of freedom. As a community formed around the crucified Christ, Newell wishes to question "*how* brokenness will be valued."[30] In contrast to what able-bodied believers imagine to be the greatest source of suffering, Newell points to "spiritual isolation" and "lack of relationship."[31] The lived theology of friendship within the church that embraces those with disability as friends opens the possibility for rightly understanding suffering within every person's life. Newell can finally affirm,

> For me, suffering is crucial to the narration of what it is to be a Christian because, within the broken incarnate God, I find the particular attributes essential for upholding and embracing my life and making sense of my complex journey. In particular, the centrality of the suffering of Jesus—not just in persecution during his life, death, and resurrection but also in his experience of being other—means that I can relate in a very intimate way to a very human God.[32]

This view of suffering can challenge the church's embrace of culturally determined views of technology, the aims of medicine, and how able-bodied believers might understand their own dependence and need for relationship.

Jean Vanier, reflecting on over forty years of living with people with intellectual disabilities in the L'Arche communities, insists that their presence "is helping me discover who I am, what my deepest needs are, and what it means to be human." In this they reveal especially the need of every person for community and that "our vulnerability is a source of communion and unity."[33] The fullness of human being is not independence and autonomy but rather is found in recognizing the need for one another, embodied together in the community of Christ. As Hauerwas concludes, "Only when we learn how to be with those different from us can we learn to accept the love that each of us needs to sustain a community capable of worshiping God."[34]

---

[30] Newell, "On the Importance of Suffering," 174.
[31] Newell, "On the Importance of Suffering," 171 and 175.
[32] Newell, "On the Importance of Suffering," 177-78.
[33] Vanier, "What Have People with Learning Disabilities Taught Me?", 19 and 21.
[34] Hauerwas, "The Church and the Mentally Handicapped," 62.

The embodied presence of people with intellectual disabilities can offer light to the church's account of human being, salvation, and the shape of Christian community. To do so, however, the church must first see them. Too often, congregations keep them at the margins, and so churches do not receive the gifts they offer. As modeled by Jesus, they must be welcomed into the house of worship instead of being excluded. Then, as with the shepherd and angel, they can join their worship to the voices of the congregation before Christ, and with their presence, the church will become more of what it was made to be as it learns to share life with those whose otherness is not as different as imagined.

4. For Further Reading

Brock, Brian, and John Swinton, eds. *Disability in the Christian Tradition: A Reader*. Grand Rapids, MI: Wiliam B. Eerdmans, 2012.

Gaventa, William C. *Disability and Spirituality: Recovering Wholeness*. Waco, TX: Baylor University Press, 2018.

Jacober, Amy E. *Redefining Perfect: The Interplay Between Theology and Disability*. Eugene, OR: Cascade Books, 2017.

Melcher, Sarah J., Mikeal C. Parsons, and Amos Yong, eds. *The Bible and Disability: A Commentary*. Waco, Texas: Baylor University Press, 2017.

Nouwen, Henri J. M. *Adam: God's Beloved*. Maryknoll, NY: Orbis, 1997.

Reinders, Hans S. *Receiving the Gift of Friendship: Profound Disability, Theological Anthropology, and Ethics*. Grand Rapids, MI: William B. Eerdmans, 2008.

Reynolds, Thomas E. *Vulnerable Communion: A Theology of Disability and Hospitality*. Grand Rapids, MI: Brazos Press, 2008.

Yong, Amos. *The Bible, Disability, and the Church: A New Vision of the People of God*. Grand Rapids, MI: William B. Eerdmans, 2011.

_____. *A Theology of Down Syndrome: Reimagining Disability in Late Modernity*. Waco, TX: Baylor University Press, 2007.

13

Light from Interreligious Sources

Raimundo C. Barreto, Jr.

Baptist communities around the world are part of a larger worldwide community, which Martin Luther King, Jr. once called "the great world house."[1] Such broad ecumenical context is uniquely significant for the understanding of our theological task in the current globalized era. In what follows, I locate the conversation about interfaith or interreligious relations and dialogue within the framework of the world-Christian turn, making particular reference to the substantial changes in Christian demographics worldwide in the past half-century and their implications for Christian life and interfaith relations.

1. The World-Christian Turn: Situating the Conversation

If there was ever a time when Christian communities could exist comfortably protected within the nest of Christian hegemony, such an era is definitely gone. In the compressed conditions of a globalized reality, a world consciousness has emerged, along with an increased awareness of the inescapable plurality of life. The demands for peaceful coexistence spark a longing for mutual understanding and dialogue.[2]

Argentinian historian Enrique Dussel dates the start of European modernity to the sixteenth century, making it coincide with the origins of the colonial project.[3] According to Dussel, at the root of modernity is the European "claim to the privilege of supposedly being the sole vehicle for the deployment of human reason capable of transcending the narratives of mythology thus discrediting all the reli-

---

[1] King, Nobel Lecture "The Quest for Peace and Justice" December 11, 1964. This lecture also appears as chapter four of King, *Where Do We Go From Here?*. For a contemporary development of this concept, see Lee, *The Great World House*. Brazilian theologian Leonardo Boff, *Cry of the Earth, Cry of the Poor* uses the term "the Common House" to express a similar concern. Pope Francis has followed that path in his encyclical on the environment, where he uses the term "our common home." See Francis, *Laudato Si'*.

[2] Leonard Swidler has dramatically described this as "a stark choice: death or dialogue!" Swidler, *Dialogue for Interreligious Understanding*, Kindle edition, loc. 342.

[3] Dussel, "Agenda for a South-South Philosophical Dialogue," 5.

gions of the South."[4] European expansionism gave birth to the first world-system in history—prior to that, the world was organized through a combination of different regional systems.[5] The colonial/modern global consciousness that developed in the following centuries spread European philosophy, culture and religion as the norm to be implemented among colonized peoples.[6] Reflections on ecumenical and interreligious relations today cannot overlook the unchecked Eurocentric universalizing pretensions of the modern/colonial project. The twentieth-century ecumenical movement itself was the child of the modern missionary movement, and an expression of its success.[7] It emerged during a time when Europe and the United States were the centers of modern Christianity, and, consequently, of evangelization and mission. In accord with such a framework, the growth of Christianity in the global South was understood as a sub-product of the Western missionary work.

Conversations about Baptist identity in ecumenical and interfaith perspective today must be situated within a theoretical framework that critically examines those modern Eurocentric assumptions and moves beyond them. Such a framework can be found in the paradigm of world Christianity, which emerged in the closing decades of the twentieth century. Scholars such as Andrew F. Walls, Lamin Sanneh, and Kwame Bediako[8] were among the pioneers who drew attention to the broad implications of the demographic and cultural shifts world Christianity experienced in the second half of the twentieth century for contemporary religious and theological studies. Since the 1980s, for the first time in more than a millennium there are more Christians living in Africa, Latin America, and Asia than in the North Atlantic.[9] There is nothing to indicate that such trend will change course in coming decades. Therefore, the world Christianity paradigm needs to be factored in as we reflect about Baptist life in the ecumenical reality of the twenty-first century. The configuration of world Christianity sharply changed after World War II, when the Christianities of the global South became more autonomous and self-aware—a phenomenon that was not unrelated to the political upheavals of an emergent postcolonial era. At that point, Asian-Pacific, African, and Latin American/Caribbean Christians started to see themselves in ways that were not as de-

---

[4] Dussel, "Agenda for a South-South Philosophical Dialogue," 6-7.

[5] Dussel, "Agenda for a South-South Philosophical Dialogue," 7.

[6] Dussel, "Agenda for a South-South Philosophical Dialogue," 6.

[7] See Fey, ed. *A History of the Ecumenical Movement, Volume 2 (1948-1968)*, 51; Mackay, *Ecumenics*. I discussed this topic in Barreto, "Ecumenism in the Era of World Christianity."

[8] Walls, *Cross-Cultural Process in Christian History*; Sanneh, *Whose Religion is Christianity?*; Bediako, *Christianity in Africa*.

[9] Johnson and Ross, eds., *Atlas of Global Christianity, 1910-2010*. See also Granberg-Michaelson, *From Times Square to Timbuktu*, 7.

pendent on Western missionary dominant narratives. Such a "world-Christian turn"[10] began to shed new light on the worldwide, polycentric, and culturally diverse nature of contemporary Christianity.

The rebirth of Christianity as a non-western religion[11]—and the rise of world Christianity as an interdisciplinary field of studies—has profoundly impacted contemporary Christian self-understanding in the past few decades. The paradigm of world Christianity helps us to retell the Christian story in a more inclusive manner, taking into account a variety of narratives, cultural influences, and theological voices.[12] Being constantly in movement, the Christian story can be more fully appreciated when considered from multiple points of view. Princeton historian Afe Adogame, borrowing Chinua Achebe's analogy of the masquerades in the Igbo festivals in Nigeria, offers a snapshot of this polycentric perspective. According to Achebe,

> there's no way you can tell that story in one way and say, this is it. Always there will be someone who can tell it differently depending on where they are standing; the same person telling the story will tell it differently. I think of that masquerade in Igbo festivals that dance in the public arena. The Igbo people say: If you want to see it well, you must not stand in one place. The masquerade is moving through this big arena. Dancing. If you're rooted to a spot, you miss a lot of the grace. So you keep moving, and this is the way I think the world's stories, and the story of Christianity should be told—from many different perspectives.[13]

This colorful and lively image informs Adogame's study of African Christianity. Such powerful image can also contribute to a deeper understanding of the multifaceted phenomenon called world Christianity, and the varied emphases, concerns, forms of worship, and theological insights it comprises. The relocation of theological voices to what used to be the peripheries of Eurocentric modern Christianity not only creates fresh theological agendas but also leads us to consider new ways of

---

[10] This is a turn in the direction of increasing breadth and comprehensiveness in Christian historiography fostering interest particularly "in Christian experiences arising from within long overlooked faith communities and individuals." Cf. Kollman, "Understanding the World-Christian Turn in the History of Christianity and Theology," 168.

[11] The Christian faith, from its inception, was transcultural, moving between multiple cultures and languages, and finding a home in each of them. Although Christianity has remained transcultural throughout history, its Europeanization, particularly as Europe became the self-proclaimed center of the modern world system, led to the subsequent association of Christianity with the West.

[12] Two important resources that brought this discussion to the fore were Irvin, *Hearing Many Voices*, and Shenk, *Enlarging the Story*.

[13] Brooks, "The Art of Fiction No. 139," cited in Adogame, "Mapping African Christianities within Religious Maps of the Universe."

being church.[14] As new theological subjects emerge in different locations across the globe, Christianity is renewed and recreated through heterogenous narratives, with renewed attention to voices from African, Asian, and Latin American Christians.[15]

The stories that emerge in the context of the world-Christian turn tend to give particular prominence to indigenous practices and agency in cultures previously not seen as Christian. Narratives previously ignored now take the center stage. In Latin America, for instance, indigenous peoples and cultures, whose stories and forms of knowledge and knowing were often ignored in theological debates not so long ago, are now telling their own stories and developing their own theologies. Such persistence shows above all that the eclipsing of non-European culture and religion of the modern/colonial age never entirely succeeded.[16] Indigenous peoples and African descendants in Latin America have never given up their agency as moral, cultural, political, and religious subjects.

Enrique Dussel addresses the historical and theological implications of this turn towards local agencies, describing the phenomenon as an "epistemological decolonization of theology."[17] For him, colonial modern Christendom exhibited the contradictory trait of being an imperial religion which legitimized the domination "of oppressed colonies in the name of the Gospel of the Crucified."[18] European Christendom saw itself as "the prototype of human culture," advancing a "fetishized universality" that denied other cultures their truth claims.[19] Such "imperial inversions" in history can be reversed through a return to a Messianic peripheral Christianity that is critical of Empire.

At the same time, Dussel points to theology that cannot be limited to local expressions. In that sense, world Christianity must not be reduced to a code-word that merely refers to a shift in the "epicenter" of Christianity. From an ecumenical perspective, world Christianity means a re-centering of Christian narratives and priorities, which pays attention not only to overlooked centers but also to the dynamic relations within a polycentric *oikoumene*,[20] advancing a relational approach to Christian historiography that focuses on transcontinental links and networks.[21] This intercultural perspective is of even greater value when one considers the impact of mass migration around the globe. Migration connects different worlds, offering new opportunities for intercultural communication and a fuller considera-

---

[14] Aguilar, "Public Theology from the Periphery."
[15] Aguilar, "Public Theology from the Periphery," 325.
[16] Wagua, "Present Consequences of the European Invasion of America," 49.
[17] Dussel, "The Epistemological Decolonization of Theology."
[18] Dussel, "Epistemological Decolonization of Theology," 24.
[19] Dussel, "Epistemological Decolonization of Theology," 25, 28.
[20] See Cabrita, Maxwell, and Wild-Wood, eds., *Relocating World Christianity*.
[21] See Korschorke, "New Maps of the History of World Christianity."

tion of transnational and transcontinental networks in world-Christian perspective.[22]

The world-Christian turn entails also a renewed concern with interreligious relations, which function as a corrective to the arrogance manifest in the imperialistic relations of modern Christianity to non-Western cultures, peoples, and religious traditions. Furthermore, the world-Christian turn sheds light on the fact that most Christians around the world today live in multi-religious contexts, where they interact on a regular basis with neighbors of other faiths. Their religious identity and practices are informed by those relations, as co-existing religions borrow and reinterpret each other's symbols and sacred words.[23] For them, interreligious or interfaith relations[24] are not only unavoidable; they are a constitutive component of their own existence.

2. Interfaith Learning

Baptists living in different parts of the world participate in a number of interreligious relations. In the past several years, Baptists have increasingly become involved in interreligious dialogue. In the United States, for instance, at least one Baptist-Jewish dialogue and three National Baptist-Muslim dialogues have taken place in the course of the last decade.[25] The Baptist World Alliance has created a commission on interfaith relations with members from all continents and has engaged in Baptist-Muslim relations since 2008. In short, Baptists are not strangers to relations and dialogue with adherents of non-Christian faith traditions.

---

[22] See, e.g., Chaves, "Disrespecting Borders for Jesus, Power, and Cash." A revision of a portion of this dissertation will be published as a volume in the same series in which the present book appears: idem, *The Global Mission of the Jim Crow South*.

[23] Baptist scholar La Seng Dingrin, "Is Buddhism Indispensable in the Cross-Cultural Appropriation of Christianity in Burma?" 17, shows how the translation of the Bible in Burma has depended on the canonical language of Burmese Buddhists, making the latter an indispensable for the understanding of some Christian concepts in Burmese Christianity. Filipino scholar Jojo M. Fung, "Emerging Perspectives and Identity Negotiations of the Indigenous Christians," draws attention to the importance for indigenous Christians to include oral indigenous literature in their theological reflections on identity negotiation in intercultural and interfaith contexts.

[24] The more institutional connotation of "interreligious dialogue" is sometimes contrasted with a more interpersonal sense suggested by "interfaith" relations or dialogue. There is a need to put more emphasis on the day-to-day, less formal, more personal, and communal relations among people of different religions, without neglecting the importance of formal and more institutional relations. In this chapter, however, I use both words interchangeably.

[25] Allen, "Third Baptist/Muslim Dialogue Seeks to Build Bridges between Church and Mosque"; Goodman, "Strangers, Neighbors, and Strangers Again."

Interfaith relations are sometimes misunderstood as a luxury for religious scholars or specialized religious leaders. That is a false premise. In fact, an increasing number of people around the world today are exposed, at least to some degree, to people and practices of other faiths on a daily basis. Dialogue is the mechanism that creates a more sustained communication between different faith traditions. But dialogue is not the only way to engage positively neighbors of other faiths. Interfaith relations start at the moment neighbors of different faiths approach one another as fellow human beings and members of a community, neighborhood, school board, classroom, or workplace.

Leornardo Swidler defines dialogue as "a two-way communication between persons who hold significantly differing views on a subject, with the purpose of learning more truth about that subject from the other person."[26] Dialogue implies an understanding that one does not know everything. As Swidler puts it, a basic premise to dialogue is, "Nobody knows everything about anything."[27] Therefore, one must approach dialogue as a learner, not as a master. Those involved in interfaith dialogue avoid making too many assumptions about the other's religion. Instead of making assumptions, dialogue participants are encouraged to ask one another about how they understand themselves, maintaining an open attitude to learn (unlearn and relearn) from that interaction.

Openness to learning in and through dialogue not only encourages learning about the other, but also learning about oneself and one's faith. It is common for people involved in interfaith relations to gain new insights and perspectives about their own faith. During a visit to Yangon, Myanmar, a Baptist pastor and seminary professor offered me a tour to the Shwedagon Zedi Daw, the most sacred Buddhist pagoda in the country. During the tour, he told me that he often brings his seminary students to that pagoda, because for him Burmese Christians cannot fully understand who they are without having a good grasp of Buddhism. This kind of dialogical openness often leads to new depths in self-understanding and in locating one's faith and religious traditions in a religious plural world.

3. From Interfaith Relations to Dialogue

There are different levels of interfaith relations. Experiences on one level may lead to others. Likewise, there are different definitions of interfaith dialogue, some being more elastic than others.[28] However, as a general rule, dialogue involves ideas and words.[29] The open attitude and the ultimate goal of learning in communication

---

[26] Swidler, *Dialogue for Interreligious Understanding*, Kindle loc. 342 and 416-18.

[27] Swidler, *Dialogue for Interreligious Understanding*, Kindle loc. 392.

[28] Swidler, *Dialogue for Interreligious Understanding*, Kindle loc. 536-37.

[29] Swidler, *Dialogue for Interreligious Understanding*, Kindle loc. 536-37.

with someone who is fundamentally different from myself is essential for dialogue to happen. Even more elastic dialogical typologies, like Swidler's dialogue of the head (intellect), the hands (ethics), the heart (affection), and of the holiness (aesthetic/spiritual),[30] do not exhaust all possible interfaith relations. There are forms of relations with people of other faiths that are not necessarily prompted by the openness to learning from the other which characterizes interfaith dialogue.

Multi-faith collaboration, for instance, may involve partners who are not even willing to engage in interfaith dialogue. The International Religious Freedom (IRF) Roundtable in Washington, D.C., of which I was part as a Baptist World Alliance (BWA) representative for several years, is an example of that. The IRF Roundtable describes itself as an informal group of individuals from non-governmental organizations who gather regularly to discuss IRF issues on a non-attribution basis. It is a safe space where participants gather, speak freely in sharing ideas and information, and propose joint advocacy actions to address specific IRF issues and problems.[31]

The IRF Roundtable is not exclusively a religious network. Among its participants, there are individuals and organizations that are not religious or even religiously motivated. Nevertheless, a large number of the individuals participating on the roundtable represent different Jew, Muslim, Hindu, Christian, Baha'i, and other religious organizations. Representatives of Christian denominations include Adventists, Southern Baptists, Mormons—many of which not commonly associated with ecumenical or interfaith relations. They do not gather to talk about their faith. Their goal is not to learn about each other's faith. That safe space is set, instead, around a topic of common interest.

Although dialogue is not the goal of this roundtable, mutual respect and friendships have emerged in the context of its work. People from different faiths at the roundtable often collaborate with one another. They regularly co-sign reports or petitions put forward at the initiative of organizations of other faiths. The work of the IRF Roundtable is based on participant-led initiatives. Any organization or individual can opt in or opt out. Multi-faith delegations created in that setting have traveled together to visit countries and governments advocating religious freedom for all. In all these joint efforts, words such as "dialogue" or "interfaith" are absent. The relationships formed in that context are based on mutual respect among people and organizations who, while not willing to engage the religious other in formal dialogue, acknowledge certain commonalities and are inclined to work together around issues of common concern, forming meaningful relationships in the process that may lead to greater involvement in other sorts of interfaith relations, including interreligious dialogue.

---

[30] Swidler, *Dialogue for Interreligious Understanding*, Kindle loc. 535-37.
[31] International Religious Freedom Roundtable, "Purpose and Overview Statement."

In an autobiographical narrative, Paul Knitter talks about how he moved from functioning with an exclusivist interfaith framework, which handicaps interfaith relations, to embracing an inclusivist view, open to finding some level of truth in other religions that nonetheless remain incomplete and in need of Christianity's enlightenment, but moved further later to adopt a pluralistic perspective, which accepts different religious claims on their own terms, and finally embraced a liberative dialogical standpoint, which combines concern about "the many religions" with a concern for the suffering of "the many poor."[32] The exposure to the humanity of the religious other may gradually lead to dialogical openness as part of an ongoing discernment of how the Spirit of God is moving in the world and how Christians must respond to a world in constant change.

4. Moving Beyond Western Theological Paradigms

According to Lamin Sanneh, "no one culture is so advanced or superior that it claims exclusive access to the truth of God, and none so marginal and remote that it can be excluded."[33] In other words, there is an indigeneity proper to the Christian faith, which makes any culture able to be the vehicle of God's communication. That sociological insight challenges all sorts of theological arrogance, placing priority on the discernment of God's presence, action, and communication in the world—a theological humility that can potentially change attitudes towards different cultures and faiths.

Theologies of world religions have used the paradigms of exclusivism, inclusivism and pluralism—exemplified autobiographically by Knitter—to describe the movement from a self-contained Christianity to one that sees itself in dialogical relationship with other religions. In the Catholic context, the Second Vatican Council (1963-65) represented an important turning point for that conversation, moving the Catholic Church from a position of exclusivism (no salvation outside the church) and monologue to the freedom and openness that "recognized salvific spaces in other religions," giving birth, thus, to an age of dialogue.[34] The rise of many contextual theologies in recent decades—some of which are explored in other

---

[32] Knitter, *One Earth, Many Religions*, 9.

[33] Sanneh, *Disciples of All Nations*, 25.

[34] Casaldaliga, "Foreword," in *Along the Many Paths of God*, ed. Vigil, Tomita, and Barros, 7. This age of dialogue has been advanced particularly through regional agencies such as the Federation of Asian Bishops' Conference and its guiding concern with discerning a new way of being a church for all Asian peoples. See Phan, *In Our Own Tongues*, Kindle edition, loc. 417. Similar regional initiatives can be found on the Protestant end, such as the Christian Conference of Asia. See Ariarajah, "The Challenge of Inter-faith Relations for the Christian Conference of Asia." Equivalent developments are also noticed in Latin America and Africa.

chapters of this book—also points to an increasing openness among many Christians to discerning God's presence and action in different cultural contexts. The welcoming and embracing of this age of dialogue can potentially move Christian communities from a self-contained understanding of revelation and truth to an attitude that acknowledges the sovereignty and *mysterium* of God—one that allows God to be God beyond the confines of modern reason and Christendom.

Yet, as Knitter points out, the openness seen in the Vatican II was still limited. Its inclusivist theology still reflected a Eurocentric cultural and religious superiority that needed to be overcome. In the Vatican II inclusivist perspective, other religions were still perceived as lacking and incomplete. Thus, true dialogue was still handicapped. Christianity was still perceived as the fulfilment of all other religions. For many theologians, particularly in Asia, Vatican II should not be understood as a point of arrival, but instead as a point of departure, which created the conditions for Catholics to participate in their cultural realities, celebrating their discoveries liturgically, and reflecting theologically on those experiences, giving birth to new theological perspectives resulting from deep engagement and dialogue with those realities.[35]

5. Human Suffering and Injustice: The Social Location of Interfaith Relations

Sri Lankan theologian Aloysius Pieris argues that the traditional categories theologians of religions use to describe Christian relations with other religions— exclusivism, inclusivism, and pluralism—do not make sense in the Asian context, where the starting point is not the uniqueness of Christ or of any other religion.[36] In fact, he contends, interreligious dialogue is a non-affordable luxury for many Asian Christians.[37] Writing about the challenge of interfaith relations for the Christian Conference of Asia (CCA), S. Wesley Ariarajah states that although Asia is the cradle of many religions, and religious diversity is the hallmark of most Asian societies, "the CCA has not had a specific inter-faith dialogue department or programme as such over many decades."[38] Why would that be? Because the particular circumstances in which Asian ecumenism has developed are different from those where Western ecumenical structures were formed. By a way of comparison, whereas the post-WWII context was key for the formation of the World Council of

---

[35] E.g., Pieris, *An Asian Theology of Liberation*.
[36] Pieris, "Interreligious Dialogue and Theology of Religions," 108.
[37] Pieris, "Interreligious Dialogue and Theology of Religions," 108.
[38] Ariarajah, "Challenge of Inter-faith Relations for the Christian Conference of Asia," 463.

Churches and the shaping of its priorities, "the post-colonial context—and the priorities of the nations and churches within it—influenced Asian ecumenism."[39]

Most Asian societies lived for a long time under political subjugation. In such context, Christianity enjoyed special privileges as "the religion of the colonizing powers." Although numerically a tiny minority, Christianity controlled many social institutions, exercising a "power disproportionate to its size." Once those nations achieved independence, nation-building became a priority. In such context, what was an advantage in colonial times became a serious disadvantage, as people of other religions began to see Christians as "the vestige of colonialism." As Ariarajah puts it, "This was not a context for Christians to call for dialogue; instead, they needed to find their place in the emerging nations and seek ways to become participants with others in the process of nation-building."[40]

Ariarajah's argument highlights one of the key contributions from world Christianity to interfaith relations. Interfaith relations and dialogue never occur in a social, political, economic or cultural vacuum. Interfaith relations must always attend to experiences of injustice and human suffering. Whereas in Western secularized societies, interfaith dialogue can often be pursued as merely an intellectual luxury, in other parts of the world, interfaith dialogue is always situated within the broader context of living together—of concrete communities where neighbors of different faiths share common daily concerns. In that kind of context, certain Western dialogue typologies may not be as significant.

For many Christians living in postcolonial societies in the second half of the twentieth century, the key theological concern that guided their living, including their interfaith relations, was the search to discern their role as Christians in the nation-building processes and in the social struggles in nations that were in turmoil.[41] The CCA, for example, felt the need to turn its attention to the plight of the peoples of Asia, and consequently to the question of the "Asianness" of Christian identity, the social and cultural location of Asian Christianity. Similar processes—although with distinctions proper to each of the continental realities—also have taken place in Africa and Latin America. Interreligious dialogue is thus placed within broader processes of discerning what means to be a follower of Jesus in a particular place and time.

Aloysius Pieris advances a paradigm that focuses on the acknowledgement of the magisterium of the poor, a common "liberational thrust," and its social location in the Base Human Communities.[42] His Asian liberationist theology of religions

---

[39] Ariarajah, "Challenge of Inter-faith Relations for the Christian Conference of Asia," 463.
[40] Ariarajah, "Challenge of Inter-faith Relations for the Christian Conference of Asia," 464.
[41] Ariarajah, "Challenge of Inter-faith Relations for the Christian Conference of Asia," 465.
[42] Pieris, "Interreligious Dialogue and Theology of Religions," 108.

not only prioritizes the poor (the destitute, the dispossessed, the displaced, and those discriminated against), but also their distinctive religiosity, a "this worldly spirituality," which is not secular but cosmic.[43]

Similarly, Asian Protestant ecumenical organisms, such as the CCA, advance an ecumenical vision that is not ecclesiocentric, focusing instead on how Christian witness takes place in "the social, economic, political, and cultural life of Asian people as a whole."[44] In Africa, similar conversations take into consideration the Africanness of Christianity and the influence of African traditional religions in the formation of both Islam and Christianity.[45] In Latin America, the revitalization of indigenous religions and of the religions of the African diaspora has promoted an important turn, leading to the rise of a Latin American pluralistic theology of liberation.[46] Theological reflection on these new ways of being church and theologizing in religiously plural societies in the global South opens the doors for new possible dialogues, including the dialogue between liberation theologies and the theologies of religion.

These new windows are not restricted to the theologies of the south. North American theologian Paul Knitter acknowledges how pluralistic intercultural encounters have opened new perspectives in his own theological journey.[47] Referring to his encounter with Native Americans, he says,

> More clearly and intensely than ever, I saw that dialogue must include liberation and that liberation must include the Earth, for here was a people who could not talk about the Sacred without talking about the Earth and who could not talk about the horrid sufferings they themselves have endured without talking about the sufferings of Earth and animals. For me, this has become a paradigm for all interreligious encounters.[48]

Under the influence of these intercultural encounters, Knitter was able to move beyond stablished paradigms in his field of study to advance a pluralistic, liberative,

---

[43] Pieris, "Interreligious Dialogue and Theology of Religions," 108-109.

[44] Ariarajah, "Challenge of Inter-faith Relations for the Christian Conference of Asia," 468.

[45] Adogame, "Mapping African Christianities within Religious Maps of the Universe."

[46] See, e.g., Tomita, Barros, and Vigil, *Teologia Latino-Americana Pluralista da Libertação*; Carvalhaes, "Birds, People, Then Religion—An Eco-Liberation Theological and Pedagogical Approach to Interreligious Rituals."

[47] Knitter, *One Earth, Many Religions*, 8. Among the many encounters he cites, Knitter highlights his encounters with Central American students and refugees, with Jon Sobrino and Lutheran Bishop Medardo Gómez, in El Salvador, with the Sanctuary Movement, with Christians for Peace in El Salvador, with the people of India, and with Native Americans as being profoundly transformative for his life and academic work.

[48] Knitter, *One Earth, Many Religions*, 10.

"globally responsible, correlational dialogue among religions."[49] This approach brings together the suffering other and the religious other, focusing on our common humanity and the yearning toward solidarity. Knitter has walked the talk of making the suffering other central to his theology of religions. The global aspirations of his theological discourse are developed in a correlational intercultural/interfaith fashion, avoiding the temptation of imperialistic domination and top-down universalistic approaches.

However, Knitter's discourse still fails to take into full account the shifts that decentralize western Christianity. Aloysius Pieris' placement of interreligious dialogue in the context of human base communities (HBCs), the interfaith version of the Latin American Christian base communities, can serve as a corrective to that limitation. In the Asia context, theologians such as Pieris have moved beyond the classical categories of exclusivism, inclusivism, and pluralism. Pieris uses the word "symbiosis" to describe the experience of the HBCs:

> Each religion, challenged by the other religion's unique approach to the liberationist aspiration of the poor, especially to the sevenfold characteristic of their cosmic religiosity mentioned above, discovers and renames itself in its specificity in response to the other approaches. What I have been describing as Christian uniqueness in the BHC experience reflects both the process and product of a symbiosis. It indicates one's conversion to the common heritage of all religions (beatitudes) and also a conversion to the specificity of one's own religion as dictated by other religionists.[50]

He is aware that the problem of Christian credibility in the non-Western world can only be faced through deep solidarity with non-Christians, which demands full acknowledgement of the other and the uniqueness of their tradition.

Christians in the global South are keenly aware that interreligious dialogue must be situated in the expanded context of living interreligiously. The mutual learning that comes out of living as neighbors with people of other faiths produces transformation, improving relationships among different human beings and between them and other living beings. Such experience can also be noted in new forms of interfaith dialogue taking place in the North Atlantic. In the North American Baptist context, one of the most significant recent experiences of the kind took place in the Third North American Baptist-Muslim dialogue held in 2018 in Green Lake, Wisconsin.[51] Differing from the two previous Baptist-Muslim dialogues in the region, this one focused on one-on-one interactions not among ex-

---

[49] Knitter, *One Earth, Many Religions*, 14.
[50] Pieres, "Interreligious Dialogue and Theology of Religions," 112.
[51] Allen, "Third Baptist/Muslim Dialogue Seeks to Build Bridges between Church and Mosque."

perts, but among local leaders from a same region. The inspiring sharing of experiences aimed, among other things, at humanizing relations in the hope that the mutual learning during a three-day retreat-like interfaith encounter and dialogue would create opportunities for ongoing partnerships. Some statewide or regional groups were formed. A New Jersey Baptist-Muslim small group has already held a follow-up meeting, and local collaborative initiatives are underway.

Above all, it was impressive to see how in the process of learning from each other traditions, individuals and communities that have had the same experience of being minoritized and oppressed due to racial, religious, and/or economic prejudice bonded together in a supra-religious sense of deep solidarity and mutual understanding, reinforcing the comprehensiveness of the recent developments in the theologies of religion discussed above. There is a sense of interconnectedness and intense solidarity that connects an African American Baptist whose ancestors were enslaved and segregated, and who still fights the lasting impact of racism, with a black Muslim who faces the double prejudice of racism and religious discrimination, broadening and deepening their interfaith dialogues on different levels. The same can be said if the Baptist in question is a first or second-generation Latina immigrant who also faces daily xenophobia and racism, thus deeply connecting with the experiences of prejudice and discrimination the Muslim-American community repeatedly experiences. These cases exemplify the growing importance of a liberative dialogue of religions, particularly for the growing Christianities of the global South and their diasporas.

6. Conclusion

Christians in the global South have learned that the interreligious resources for our theologizing need to be situated in the historical, social, economic, political and cultural circumstances of concrete communities engaging one another in dialogue. Consequently, inter-contextual and intercultural aspects of interreligious relations and dialogue, informed by the world-Christian turn, are particularly valuable. Whereas the increasing awareness of religious plurality demands that we learn how to live interreligiously, Christianity itself is more plural than ever before. Intra-religious and interreligious relations are increasingly interconnected. Mounting scholarship demonstrates that the demographics of world Christianity is experiencing the most drastic changes it has seen since its inception two millennia ago. Such changes do not seem to be reversible. Awareness and understanding of the new demographic, cultural, and epistemological configurations of world Christianity is key for both intra-religious and interfaith relations today. The significant shift in the epicenter of world Christianity has profound implications for how one approaches interfaith relations and dialogue. While the old categories Western theologians have used to describe Christianity's relations to other religions seem to be insufficient for the current status of the field, new frameworks are emerging in the global South that deserve greater attention. Placing interreligious dialogue within the broader context of living together interreligiously associates the religious other and the suffering other with interfaith relations and dialogue.

7. For Further Reading

Barreto, Raimundo C. Jr., Ronaldo Cavalcante, and Wanderley Pereira da Rosa, eds. *World Christianity as Public Religion*. Minneapolis: Fortress Press, 2017.

Knitter, Paul. *One Earth, Many Religions: Multifaith Dialogue and Global Responsibility*. Maryknoll, NY: Orbis Books, 1995.

Swidler, Leonard. *Dialogue for Interreligious Understanding: Strategies for the Transformation of Culture-Shaping Institutions*. New York: Palgrave MacMillan, 2014.

Tan, Jonathan Y. and Anh Q. Tran, eds. *World Christianity: Perspectives and Insights*. Maryknoll, NY: Orbis Books, 2016.

Vigil, José M., Luiza Tomita, and Marcello Barros, ed. *Along the Many Paths to God*. Interreligious Studies, vol. 1. Berlin: LIT Verlag, 2008.

14

Light from Ecological Theologies

Rebecca Horner Shenton

We see what we have been trained to see. Often, that is helpful. When the car starts making unusual noises and functioning erratically, the mechanic's knowledge of engines and exhaust systems enables a diagnosis of the problem and recommendations for repair and restoration. The lifetime process of faith formation develops in us moral perception: the ability to see the world around us and the situations we encounter every day through the lenses of the reign of God and our call to live as Jesus' faithful disciples. This awareness is necessary for the development of moral imagination, by which local congregations of believers see the world differently and, guided by the Holy Spirit, envision creative responses to the critical issues of our time and place.

Large-scale environmental issues such as climate change mitigation have been called "wicked problems" because of their complexity and uncertainty.[1] This reveals a need for light from many sources in addressing these problems. It also reminds us that our relationship to creation is itself complex; if we are going to live in ways that reflect our faithfulness to the Lord of all creation, we would benefit from multiple sources of light. In this chapter, I will engage light from four broad sources: the voice of creation itself, voices of Christian eco-theologians, voices from the scientific community and the environmental movement who share wisdom concerning how we might relate to all of creation, and the voices of the marginalized.

1. The Voice of Creation

Creation itself speaks to us, both "telling the glory of God" (Ps. 19:1-4) and "groaning in labor pains" (Rom. 8:19-23). In 2017, creation's groans were deafening. In January, California experienced unusually large amounts of precipitation throughout the state, some locations exceeding normal precipitation by as much as

---

[1] E.g., Summerfield, "Environmental Wicked Problem-Solving."

300%.[2] By the close of the year, the National Interagency Fire Center reported that more than 9.7 million acres had burned in more than 66,000 wildfires.[3] The United States also saw the most expensive hurricane season on record: Hurricanes Harvey, Irma, Maria, and 14 other named storms caused more than $200 billion in damage.[4] Nor were extreme events limited to North America: Peru reported unusually heavy rainfall in the early part of the year, leading to flooding and landslides; western Europe experienced record-breaking heat in early summer, contributing to deadly wildfires; deadly smog from agricultural and garbage burning, industry, power generation, and combustion engines blanketed northern India and Pakistan in November, creating a health hazard for millions of people; and continued droughts in South Africa led to water restrictions in Capetown.[5] Humans have contributed in significant ways to these extreme events. As homes are built closer to wildland areas, smaller fires that once might have been allowed to burn, reducing the amount of combustible material in the forest, must be suppressed to protect lives and property of homeowners—making later fires more dangerous and destructive. Marshland that once served as a buffer absorbing storm surges has been filled and developed into housing tracts or otherwise affected by human development, such as through pollution's effects on native plant species. Creation has lost some of its God-given resilience because of human intervention. It groans under the strain, awaiting redemption.

Humans cry along with it. We have heard the stories and seen the devastation wrought by fire, storm, and flood. Some US victims have insurance to help them rebuild. Others continue to live in their water-damaged homes because they could not afford insurance. For the world's poorest, there is no insurance. If we are not directly affected, we move on, struck by the next disaster or tragedy. We cannot watch for too long; we cannot listen for too long. It is too painful; recovery takes a long time.

We cannot hear the voices of some of those most affected by human impacts on our world. A changing climate may result in higher heating or cooling bills for a middle-class American with central air; for a family farming within Nepal's thin climatic margins, it could mean the difference between a harvest and total crop failure. As the climate changes, plant, animal, and insect species must shift their

---

[2] Di Liberto, "Soaking Rains and Massive Snows Pile up in California in January 2017."

[3] National Centers for Environmental Information, "Wildfires—Annual 2017."

[4] Drye, "2017 Hurricane Season Was the Most Expensive in U.S. History."

[5] Di Liberto reported these events in a series of articles on the NOAA Climate.gov site: "Heavy Summer Rains Flood Peru" (March 10, 2017); "Early Summer Heat Wave in Europe" (July 13, 2017); "Smog Descends on India and Pakistan in Mid-November 2017" (November 15, 2017); "Water Rationing in South Africa's Second-Largest City after Multi-Year Drought" (November 1, 2017); "Mount Agung Erupts in Indonesia" (December 7, 2017).

territories to survive. Some changes they are unable to bear, such as those in the Yangtze River brought about by China's increased shipping traffic, fishing, and industrialization that led to the probable extinction of the river dolphin (baiji) in 2006; scientists report that the baiji suffered "incidental mortality resulting from massive-scale human environmental impacts."[6]

Creation groans—but it sings, too: the sound of the breeze through the trees on a summer's day, the first bird that welcomes the morning, the cry of newborn life, water rushing over a rocky streambed, the rhythm of waves upon the shore. And, we are reminded by the psalmist, creation also speaks soundlessly: we see the wonder and the glory of God when we gaze into a star-filled night, contemplate a sunrise after a storm, or observe a solar eclipse. We marvel at God's handiwork when we consider soaring mountains, ancient sequoia trees, the Grand Canyon, and the intricate detail in a tiny leaf. Often, we are moved to silence.

How can we learn moral wisdom from the voice of creation? As Christian ethicist Cynthia Moe-Lobeda reminds us concerning Genesis 1, "God declares that creation is 'good' long before human creatures appear in the story"; she recognizes that the Hebrew word *tov* translated here as "good" also contains the implications of "life-furthering."[7] We are a created *part* of the universe created by God to show forth God's glory, and we live in relationship with God and with *all* of creation. Indeed, we are called to participate in God's ongoing, life-furthering work of creation—but instead, humans have acted in ways that undo the "life-generating capacity" of the earth, as evidenced by species extinction and loss of biodiversity.[8] If we seek to faithfully participate in the rule of Christ, then we must learn to act in ways that contribute to God's creating work, rather than acting in ways that "uncreate." Listening to the voice of creation itself can help in that process. After years of caution regarding causal links, climate scientists began to offer conclusions regarding the impact of climate change on storm severity, size, and rainfall amounts in Hurricane Florence.[9] The increasing severity of such storms serves as a "warning light" challenging us to consider carefully how our actions and lifestyles are affecting creation; we might respond similarly to shifting or shrinking habitats for different plants, animals, insects, and marine creatures. All creatures have intrinsic worth because they were created by God, and we can also hear their voices: the canary

---

[6] Turvey et al., "First Human-Caused Extinction of a Cetacean Species?"

[7] Moe-Lobeda, *Resisting Structural Evil*, 54-55, 123.

[8] Moe-Lobeda, *Resisting Structural Evil*, 56. Another example of this "uncreating" is the "terminator seed" developed by Monsanto, which makes it impossible for farmers to save seeds from year to year, requiring instead that they purchase new seed each year (ibid., 79 n. 24). The natural cycle of life, death, and new life from the seed is abnormally truncated through this technology.

[9] Parker, "Hurricane Florence's Rains May Be 50% Worse Due to Climate Change."

that sings so beautifully in the wild once served as a sentinel species warning coal miners of dangerous levels of carbon monoxide.[10] While there are ethical issues in intentionally *using* other living creatures as sentinel species to ensure human safety, attending to their voices in nature is a responsible part of our relationship with creation. Learning to interpret these voices well requires that each of us develop a more intimate relationship with the place we inhabit—the kind of relationship that has long been a part of traditional cultures. When we know the normal rhythms, sounds, and movements of our place, we will be more attuned to changes and their significance. We will also be better equipped to appreciate the beautiful songs of creation that encourage us to join in their hymns of praise to the Creator of all.

2. Christian Responses to the Ecological Crisis

Attending to the voice of creation is essential, but it is not sufficient in developing a faithful Christian response to the ecological crisis. Christian ecotheologians and ethicists provide another source of light that will help us to walk more faithfully with, and within, creation. Although Christian reflection on our place within and interactions with creation began long before the beginning of the environmental movement in the West[11] (generally dated to the publication of Rachel Carson's *Silent Spring* in 1962), Christian scholars have been considering our relationship to the rest of creation more intentionally and specifically in the last thirty years. Their approaches are diverse, but the vast majority of these scholars contend that humanity's negative impact on our planet calls Christians to a practical, theologically-informed response, beginning with the recognition: "We do not know our place." This recognition entails acknowledging that (1) we do not recognize our place *within* (not above) creation; (2) we do not understand the role that God has given us in using our own moral capacity to live in ways that help creation to flourish; (3) we lack humility; and (4) we are not well acquainted with the particular places in which we live.

2.1 Our Place within Creation. Evangelical theology's focus on "accepting Jesus as personal Lord and Savior" distracts us from recognizing that our God is not merely the God of humans, but the Lord of all creation. It therefore runs the risk of leading us to believe that human history is the only significant thing and that the physical world is merely a canvas upon which what really matters—the drama of human life and our redemption—is painted.[12] When this is coupled with a view of

---

[10] This practice has been discontinued, and canaries replaced with detection equipment. See Eschner, "The Story of the Real Canary in the Coal Mine."

[11] For examples of earlier Baptist and Mennonite sources, see Shenton, "Baptist Agrarians"; idem, "They Were Right."

[12] Wirzba, *The Paradise of God*, 27.

salvation primarily as a future event in which those who are "saved" will live in some far-off heaven after their earthly bodies die, we are easily deceived into treating God's good creation as "resources" for our own human endeavors—because humans are all that really matters.[13] First, we need a thicker understanding of creation theology—one treating creation as more than a story of origins and recognizing that humans have a unique place within (not above) creation.[14]

Norman Wirzba asserts that "we understand creation in a proper manner when we see God's creative work as *continuous* and *responsive*....God wants to be involved in the life of creation...[and creation] has not yet achieved its complete perfection."[15] A rich theology of creation is informed by texts throughout Scripture: Genesis 1 and 2, to be sure, but also Job, Psalms, the Gospels, Ephesians, and Revelation. *Job's* recognition that creation is God-centered, rather than human-centered, teaches *us* to shift from an anthropocentric to a theocentric view of creation.[16] God is concerned for all of God's creatures, and God delights in all of creation—even the parts that we cannot understand or do not value highly, like stinkbugs or centipedes. God knows us intimately—but also knows the sparrow, feeds the ravens, and dresses the lilies in royal splendor (Luke 12). On the seventh day, the Lord rested, delighting in the creation—and in the practice of the Sabbath, we are invited "to enter into the happiness, delight, and stillness of God."[17]

Humans are not at the center of creation, but neither are we above it. Some interpretations of the dominion mandate (Gen. 1:28) have placed humanity, as "rulers," *over* creation—not recognizing that we are a *part* of creation. Recognizing our "rootedness within God's ecological order"[18] is an essential part of understanding our place. From within creation, we exercise our God-given role, to which we turn next.

2.2 Our God-Given Role in Creation. Wirzba sees the Genesis 2 account as definitive for understanding our unique role in creation. This account shows our dependence upon the soil: the man, the trees, and all the animals are made "from the dust of the ground" or "out of the ground" (Gen. 2:7, 9, 19), and the produce of the ground provides sustenance for humans. Not only is "our fate...tied to the fate of the soil," but our unique human role is "to till [the garden] and keep it" (Gen. 2:15); this "keeping" involves the concept of service, in the sense of "the necessary and ennobling work that promotes growth and health," and for humans, it is "a

---

[13] Wirzba, *The Paradise of God*, 20.

[14] Providing this re-examination of the theology of creation is at the heart of Wirzba's project in *The Paradise of God*.

[15] Wirzba, *The Paradise of God*, 16, 17 (emphasis added).

[16] Wirzba, *The Paradise of God*, 45-47.

[17] Wirzba, *The Paradise of God*, 36.

[18] Mustol, *Dusty Earthlings*, 206.

participation in and a continuation of God's own life-giving creativity."[19] Thus, we fulfill the vocation given to us by God at creation by caring for the earth in a way leading to creaturely flourishing. This secures our own future—since we are entirely dependent upon this planet for our own sustenance and well-being—but we do not focus on our own needs and desires. This vocation is uniquely fitted to humans, who have the ability to observe, plan, analyze, collaborate, and use our intelligence and moral capacity to determine what will best serve the creation we are charged with keeping. Our work, Wirzba notes, "leads directly to the formation of moral and religious virtues that are proper for human development"—primarily (but not limited to) humility and gratitude.[20]

2.3 Humility. Development of humility is essential. Enamored of our own creativity, problem-solving ability, inventiveness, and technological prowess, we are building our own twenty-first-century tower of Babel. While our ancestors realized a bountiful harvest required careful attention to the soil's health, we have used technology to ensure high "productivity" without regard for the natural limitations of the land or the health of the soil. Irrigation makes the desert into a garden. Technologically-created problems (such as the development of "superweeds" by repeated use of certain pesticides) can be solved by new technology. We need to develop humility: we live in God's garden (not one of our own making), and ultimately, rain and snow, seedtime and harvest—all of these are in God's hands.

Humility teaches us to be mindful of our place as creatures within the created order. We have been given an important and unique task within creation, but the world belongs to God. As any gardener knows, gardening develops humility: even if we do everything properly, a late-spring freeze or a heavy rainfall can destroy the crop. We learn to be thankful for sunny days and gentle rains, and we recognize that our work is bigger than us: we cannot control it.

We need humility lest we "get too big for our britches," thinking that we are in control. "Since the beginning of the modern era," John Mustol writes, "we have been more or less committed to a command-and-control approach, seeking to overpower feedbacks and control natural processes....This...has given us the illusion that we are exempt from ecological feedbacks."[21] We are not exempt; we (in the global north) have used technology to insulate ourselves from these ecological feedbacks. For example, although topsoil erosion was recognized as a problem of national importance in the US prior to World War II, and soil conservation prac-

---

[19] Wirzba, *The Paradise of God*, 31.

[20] Wirzba, *The Paradise of God*, 31. Mustol (*Dusty Earthlings*, 206) notes that other virtues required for Christian ecological practice include "self-control, kenosis, and justice,...wisdom, prudence, sufficiency, frugality, [and] love."

[21] Mustol, *Dusty Earthlings*, 161-62.

tices were employed as a response during the war, in the long term, we have compensated for declining soil fertility through the use of synthetic fertilizers. This "solution" has led to other problems (e.g., nitrogen run-off affecting rivers and bays), but most importantly, it uses our God-given abilities to *overcome* natural systems and processes, rather than using those abilities in humility to *promote the flourishing of* creation.

2.4 Our Particular Places. As noted above, we have viewed creation as a "resource"—something to be used to benefit humanity. We extract its benefits rather than attending to its welfare. We may recognize that the earth is our home, and that we need to take care of it—but "caring for the planet" is such a huge, abstract task. To make progress, each of us must come to know and love the particular place that we inhabit. Mennonite S. Roy Kaufman reminds us that if each of us cares for our place, then together, we care for the whole of creation—we make decisions differently in our communities when we know those whom our choices affect, and we recognize that our actions (even though we cannot see it) impact other communities.[22] We can only come to love our place when we know our place, and this requires a commitment to our local communities and the ecosystems of which they are a part unfamiliar to our mobile mindsets. Being rooted in the earth, after all, requires being rooted in a particular place, with particular people and particular plants, animals, insects, waterways, and soil. Appropriately knowing our place does not set one place above another—my place is not any better than yours just because it is *mine*—but it makes manageable the work that God has entrusted to us.

Ecotheologians provide light that enables us to see creation much more clearly. They help us understand our place within creation, given a unique and significant responsibility—not as the masters of creation, but attending to the particular places we inhabit and seeking their flourishing. They situate ecological concerns within the context of loving neighbors near and far, illuminating the close relationship between our economic actions and their ecological impacts.[23] They address the intersection of Christian ethics and global climate change and propose faithful Christian responses to our planet's decreasing biodiversity.[24] Faithfully following Jesus requires considering all of creation—and human structures, systems, and actions that impact creation—theologically.

---

[22] Kaufman, *Healing God's Earth*, 115-16.

[23] Moe-Lobeda, *Resisting Structural Evil: Love as Ecological-Economic Vocation*.

[24] Northcott, *A Moral Climate*; O'Brien, *An Ethics of Biodiversity*.

3. Light from the Sciences and the Environmental Movement

As Christians, Scripture and theology shape our interactions with creation. However, although we might not share convictions or even strategies with other groups, they provide light for us to engage more faithfully in our vocation of helping creation flourish. Scientists aid us in gaining deeper understanding of the systems of which we are a part and our impacts on them. The environmental movement raises our awareness of possible implications of our daily actions and political decisions, such as proposed changes to legislation and regulation. Social science fills in gaps concerning the human impact of environmental choices. These sources help us see the possibilities for changing our practices; they help us translate our theology into action.

3.1 Light from Science. Science's bright light can illuminate the extent of our ecological problems and in some cases, point in the direction of actions that will reduce our negative impact on creation and lead to greater flourishing. Discernment is required in obtaining accurate and well-researched information, as rumor and misinformation abound. The Intergovernmental Panel on Climate Change (IPCC), including representatives from 195 member countries, regularly produces extensive peer-reviewed reports on global climate change, drawing upon the work of thousands of scientists worldwide. The Fifth Assessment Report was published in 2014, and it includes data to support the conclusions that "human influence on the climate system is clear, and recent anthropogenic [human-caused] emissions of greenhouse gases are the highest in history. Recent climate changes have had widespread impacts on human and natural systems" and "warming of the climate system is unequivocal."[25] IPCC reports are especially helpful not only because they are scientifically researched and extensively reviewed, but also because input is sought throughout the process from both developed and developing countries, ensuring that all voices have an opportunity to be heard. More accessible to the layperson, NASA's Global Climate Change website[26] provides educational materials (including graphics, photos, interactives, and videos) for children and adults about topics related to climate change and its impacts, including global temperature trends, rising sea levels, ocean acidification, melting sea ice and glaciers, and atmospheric changes.

Science not only helps us see negative consequences of our changing climate and other environmental/ecological issues, such as reduced biodiversity and the

---

[25] IPCC Core Writing Team, R. K. Pachauri, and L. A. Meyer, eds., "Climate Change 2014."

[26] Earth Science Communications Team of the NASA Jet Propulsion Laboratory, Global Climate Change: Vital Signs of the Planet, online https://climate.nasa.gov.

effects of air and water pollution. It also teaches how we can help creation flourish. Environmental science and ecology textbooks can provide light to help us see the planet and its creatures more clearly and respond in more life-giving ways; numerous peer-reviewed journal articles can inform those who have a scientific background. We would benefit from engaging scientists and science teachers who are members of our congregations or communities in our discussions regarding ecological matters. Without a scientific understanding of what is happening in our world, we are unable to respond appropriately; we may be deceived by craftily-written propaganda, leading to well-intentioned action that harms creation rather than helping it.

3.2 Light from the Environmental Movement. The environmental movement itself also provides light: the Sierra Club, Greenpeace, the Audubon Society, and The Nature Conservancy work in advocacy and education. Some organizations, such as iLoveMountains.org, which aims to "end mountaintop removal coal mining,"[27] have a very specific focus; this is helpful when we consider problems and challenges affecting our particular place. Although some might act before scientists find consensus on a particular issue, these organizations play a vital role in raising our awareness of possible implications of our way of life, for good or ill. Their work helps to sharpen our vision, so that we can imagine different ways of being in the world and of acting.

3.3 Light from the Social Sciences. In his 2015 papal encyclical on the environment, Pope Francis draws on the social sciences to stress the importance of attending to the needs of the poor in responding to the ecological crisis.[28] Specialists within the social sciences help us see the impacts of our lifestyles and legislation on other *human* members of creation—particularly people of color, the poor, and the marginalized. Environmental sociologist Robert Bullard has been called the "father of environmental justice"; his work as an activist-scholar over the last forty years has addressed systemic injustice in locations selected for industrial facilities and garbage dumps, racial disparities and unequal treatment following natural disasters such as Hurricane Katrina, and sustainable planning.[29] Environmental justice issues are not limited to the United States—often, poorer communities worldwide are located in areas more susceptible to flooding, and some island communities are already making plans for relocation or adaptation as sea levels rise, as is noted by

---

[27] ILoveMountains.org, "End Mountaintop Removal Coal Mining." According to their website, mountaintop removal coal mining is used throughout Central Appalachia, including West Virginia, Virginia, and Kentucky.

[28] Francis, *Laudato Si'* (On Care for Our Common Home), e.g., § 30.

[29] Bullard, "Biography—Dr. Robert Bullard," Dr. Robert Bullard: Father of Environmental Justice, online http://drrobertbullard.com/biography.

anthropologist David Lipset.[30] Social scientists focus on human communities, but their work also includes the health of ecosystems; for example, some address issues related to sustainable agriculture, land use and its environmental impact, and how power imbalances affect agricultural decision-making. While the "environmental movement" has largely focused its attention on uncultivated spaces—and agricultural ethics has been a separate field of study—a rich understanding of our God-given vocation in caring for creation includes not only sparrows and ravens, but also corn and cows. How we farm—and the policies that guide our agricultural practices—are a vital part of tending to the flourishing of God's good earth and the people and other creatures who live upon it. The work of rural sociologists, food studies scholars, rural geographers, and other social scientists and practitioners helps us see connections between people, power, places, and nonhuman creation.

Scientists, environmental activities, and social science help us engage our responsibility to God's creation more intentionally. They illuminate challenges facing the inhabitants of particular places and those facing the entire planet. They call attention to injustices that inequitably affect people marginalized by skin color, national origin, geographic location, or socio-economic status. These sources of light are essential if we are going to aid the flourishing of creation in ways that transcend good intentions.

4. The Voices of the Marginalized

Moe-Lobeda, Bullard, and Pope Francis remind us that we have neglected one set of voices for too long: while we might ask how our actions might affect various marginalized groups, we often fail to listen to *their* voices. We must listen to the long-ignored voices of women, who—especially through their traditional responsibilities of providing food and water for their families—are particularly sensitive to impacts of mining, climate change, and development.[31] A word of caution is in order: we must engage with the persons and communities—the *subalterns* themselves—and not merely treat them as objects or data. More than that, as George Zachariah reminds us, we must learn to live in responsible solidarity with our subaltern kin as they resist the status quo and the totalizing gaze that denies the existence of alternatives to globalization.[32] My treatment here is too brief and insufficient to the importance of this endeavor; hopefully, it will open our ears and eyes to those whose lived experiences often remain hidden from our sight.

---

[30] Lipset, "The New State of Nature."

[31] See, for example, Meyer, "Environmental Activism in the Philippines."

[32] Zachariah, *Alternatives Unincorporated: Earth Ethics from the Grassroots* (London: Equinox, 2011), 131-33.

5. Congregational Action and Transformation

Virtue ethicists and neuroscientists alike remind us that what we *do* has a powerful effect on who we *become*: our practices form us, both spiritually and physiologically. Thus, if we want to join in the Spirit's work of redeeming creation—rather than contributing to its groaning—we need to act in ways consistent with redemption. Actions like turning off unnecessary lights, using reusable shopping bags, conserving water, and recycling are necessary in this formation process. These actions are not, in themselves, sufficient for "changing the world," so we must understand their function. True, the impact of many people engaging in such actions can be significant on a practical level. But from a formation perspective, these teach us to pay attention to how we relate to all of creation. We listen to creation's voice—crying, groaning, singing, and resting.

> This is my Father's world.
> On the day of its wondrous birth
> The stars of light in phalanx bright
> Sang out in heavenly mirth.
>
> This is my Father's world.
> E'en yet to my listening ears
> All nature sings, and around me rings
> The music of the spheres.
>
> This is my Father's world.
> I rest me in the thought
> Of rocks and trees, of skies and seas,
> His hand the wonders wrought.
>
> This is my Father's world.
> The birds that their carols raise,
> The morning light, the lily white,
> Declare their Maker's praise.
>
> This is my Father's world.
> He shines in all that's fair.
> In the rustling grass I hear Him pass,
> He speaks to me everywhere.[33]

---

[33] These stanzas from a poem by Maltbie Davenport Babcock adapted as the familiar hymn "This Is My Father's World" (the complete poem has 16 stanzas) express well this listening to the

We prayerfully consider our role in contributing to the flourishing of that creation by knowing our place and working for its flourishing, paying particular attention to those in our communities whose voices might usually go unheard. In so doing, we engage with scientists, social scientists, and environmental activists, learning what is at stake and what actions will have the greatest positive change. In that process, we become different. We unite in solidarity with the marginalized. And as New Testament scholar N. T. Wright reminds us, these actions participate in God's redemption of creation, and "in the Lord [our] labor is not in vain" (1 Cor. 15:58). "We are called," Wright writes, "to bring forth real and effective signs of God's renewed creation even in the midst of the present age."[34] What we do *now* matters in God's economy (and ecology), even though we cannot see the big picture and we recognize that creation's redemption is ultimately God's work. God pronounced creation *good*. We have marred it through our actions, but we have been given the opportunity to participate in its redemption, thus developing virtues that lead to the flourishing of creation, including ourselves.

6. For Further Reading

Francis. *Laudato Si'* (On Care for Our Common Home). May 24, 2015. Online http://w2.vatican.va/content/francesco/en/encyclicals/documents/papa-francesco_20150524_enciclica-laudato-si.html.

Moe-Lobeda, Cynthia. *Resisting Structural Evil: Love as Ecological-Economic Vocation*. Minneapolis, MN: Fortress, 2013.

Mustol, John. *Dusty Earthlings: Living as Eco-Physical Beings in God's Eco-Physical World*. Eugene, OR: Cascade Books, 2012.

Northcott, Michael S. *A Moral Climate: The Ethics of Global Warming*. Maryknoll, NY: Orbis Books, 2009.

O'Brien, Kevin J. *An Ethics of Biodiversity: Christianity, Ecology, and the Variety of Life*. Washington, DC: Georgetown University Press, 2010.

Wirzba, Norman. *Food and Faith: A Theology of Eating*. 2nd Edition. New York: Cambridge University Press, 2019.

_____. *The Paradise of God: Renewing Religion in an Ecological Age*. New York: Oxford University Press, 2007.

---

voice of creation (*Thoughts for Every-Day Living from the Spoken and Written Words of Maltbie Davenport Babcock*, 180).

[34] Wright, *Surprised by Scripture*, 106.

Part II

LIGHT FROM OUR LIFE-IN-COMMUNITY

15

Light from Ancient Confessions of Faith

Curtis W. Freeman

The Baptist World Alliance held its first Congress in 1905 at Exeter Hall in London. When BWA president Alexander Maclaren addressed the opening session, he suggested that the Congress should begin their assembly with an "audible and unanimous acknowledgment of [the] Faith" that made clear where they stood "in the continuity of the historic Church." He then invited his fellow participants to rise to their feet and confess the Apostles' Creed, "not as a piece of coercion or discipline, but as a simple acknowledgment of where we stand and what we believe." The whole gathering instantly rose and repeated the creed.[1] When the BWA held the centenary meeting of the Congress on July 27, 2005, the opening assembly also repeated the creed together.[2] These two important acts bear repetition by Baptists from the congregational to the global level, because they recognize the recitation of the ancient ecumenical creeds as an important resource for connecting Baptist Christians with the faith as it has been believed and confessed through the centuries, and around the world.

1. Confessional Faith

Baptists have historically been nervous about creeds because of the ways that established churches have used them as instruments of coercion. Edward Wightman (d. 1612), an early Baptist and the last heretic burned in England, defended what he believed to be the true faith against the "false doctrine" of the Nicolaitans, which he claimed was enshrined in the creeds.[3] By opposing the creeds, Wightman believed he was not simply refuting the doctrines of the Church of England, but was setting straight the Christian faith in what he contended had been a sixteen hun-

---

[1] Shakespeare, ed., *Baptist World Congress, London, July 11-19, 1905*, 19-20 and vii.

[2] Freeman, Harmon, Newman, and Thompson, "Confessing the Faith"; DeVane, "Educators Ask, BWA Agrees to Recite Apostles' Creed"; Allen, "Proposal Sparks Debate Over Baptists and Creeds."

[3] James I, "Narration of the Burning of Edward Wightman"; Burrage, *Early English Dissenters*, 1:216–20; Atherton and Como, "The Burning of Edward Wightman."

dred-year heretical declension from apostolic Christianity. With notable exceptions like Wightman, Baptists have seldom expressed disagreement with the articles of the Apostles' and Nicene Creeds, denoted here as the "ancient ecumenical creeds" because of their continuity with the apostolic tradition.[4] The Baptist aversion to creeds is principally rooted in the conviction that prioritized the experience of faith over the exactness of the statement of faith. Baptists have often resonated with the argument made by Tertullian that people "are made, not born, Christians."[5] Their insistence on a confessional faith has its roots in the Puritan tradition that held to the necessity of "the experience of grace." Experienced Christians were those who offered a personal confession of their faith.[6] Reciting a creed, no matter how well stated, is no substitute for a personal confession of faith. This experiential emphasis is simply expressed in the gospel song which exclaims, "not my brother, not my sister, but it's me, O Lord."[7] In more precise language, Baptists emphasize the *fides qua creditur* (the faith by which it is believed, i.e., personal faith or trusting obedience) more than the *fides quae creditur* (the faith which is believed, i.e., the deposit of faith or knowledge of truth revealed in Christ).[8]

Both the *fides qua* and *fides quae* are necessary, as together they maintain a tension between liberty of conscience and fidelity to the gospel. As the early twentieth-century British Baptist leader John Clifford explained, "it is not creeds as creeds" that is the issue. Rather, "it is coercion through and by creeds" that is the problem.[9] Clifford recognized the historic connection between personal and creedal faith. He noted that the apostles transmitted their pattern of the faith in three creedal statements. The first is Petrine: "You are the Messiah, the Son of the living God" (Matt 16:16). The second is Johannine, uttered from the lips of the apostle Thomas: "My Lord and my God!" (John 20:28). The third is Pauline: "Because if you confess with your lips that Jesus is Lord and believe in your heart that God raised him from the dead, you will be saved" (Rom. 10:9). In the words of these three apostolic witnesses, the experiential reality of primitive Christian faith given once and for all in Christ was, Clifford argued, "indisputably established." These three proto-creeds provide a biblical pattern for all subsequent confessions of faith

---

[4] Williams, *Retrieving the Tradition and Renewing Evangelicalism*, 71-99.

[5] Tertullian *Apology* 18 (ET, *Ante-Nicene Fathers of the Christian Church*, ed. Roberts and Donaldson, 3:32).

[6] *Westminster Confession of Faith*, art. 10; Vavasor Powell, *Spirituall Experiences, of Sundry Beleevers* (1653); Jane Turner, *Choice Experiences of the Kind Dealings of God* (1653); and Katherine Sutton, *A Christian Womans Experiences of the Glorious Working of Gods Free Grace* (1663), in Freeman, ed. *A Company of Women Preachers*, 305-68 and 587-646.

[7] "Standing in the Need of Prayer," Traditional.

[8] Rahner, ed., *Encyclopedia of Theology*, s.v. "Faith," 500.

[9] Bateman, *John Clifford*, 148.

by holding the personal and creedal together.[10] Indeed, the personal and creedal were combined in the early church. The Apostles' Creed arose as a baptismal confession that may be traced to the second-century baptismal creed of Hippolytus, and the Nicene Creed came to be almost universally used as a eucharistic confession of faith by the sixth century.[11] When framed in this way, it does not come down to a choice between personal confession and creedal recitation, but rather to seeing that personal faith coheres with the ancient ecumenical creeds when freely and faithfully offered as an act of confession, beginning with the declaration, "I believe."

2. Trinitarian Center

One of the chief reasons that Baptists should recite the ancient ecumenical creeds is that doing so keeps the focus on the Trinitarian center of historic Christian faith. The Apostles' Creed begins with the declaration, "I believe *in God*." This declaration notably does not end with a period, which might be left to drift into an abstract generic theism. Instead the creed invites an affirmation of trust in the God of Israel, who is made manifest in Jesus of Nazareth, his Abba, and their Spirit. It is in the name of this "three-personed God" that the church joins the mission of making disciples by baptizing and teaching them (Matt. 28:19). It is this name of this Triune God that the church receives benediction (2 Cor. 13:13). Indeed, every article of faith affirmed in the creed and every act of faith performed by the church is grounded in and related to this three-in-one God. Without this Trinitarian center, faith and practice become incoherent. Reciting the words of the creed enacts the most basic Christian conviction stated with simplicity and clarity by Gregory of Nazianzus, that "when I say God, I mean Father, Son, and Holy Ghost."[12] To put it plainly, confessing the ancient ecumenical creeds keeps Christians connected with the most basic and fundamental grammar of the faith of historic Christianity—the Trinity.

Baptists, whose worship tends toward extemporaneity and away from formality, may find it a bit awkward to employ a set pattern for their confession of faith. Yet the recitation of the creed provides a Trinitarian grammar for their confession to be offered freely and faithfully. The penchant for liturgical liberty can easily drift from Trinitarian faith as liberals tilt toward a unitarianism of the first person, while evangelicals lean in the direction of unitarianism of the second person, and charis-

---

[10] Clifford, "The Great Forty Years."

[11] Hippolytus of Rome 21.12-18 (ET, *The Apostolic Tradition of St. Hippolytus*, 2nd ed., ed. Dix and Chadwick, 36-37); Kelly, *Early Christian Creeds*, 3rd ed., 113-19 and 348-57.

[12] Gregory of Nazianzus *Oration* 38.7 (ET, *Nicene and Post-Nicene Fathers: Second Series*, ed. Schaff and Wace, 7:347).

matics seem prone to a unitarianism of third person.[13] Given the looseness of theological language, it might seem from the standpoint of historic Trinitarian Christianity that Baptists are simply Unitarians that simply have not yet gotten around to denying the Trinity. By freely and faithfully reciting the ancient ecumenical creeds, Baptist confess their faith in the Trinitarian language shared by Christians throughout the ages.[14]

3. Hermeneutical Guidance

The stated belief of the early Baptists was that the meaning of the Bible as the revealed word of God is sufficiently plain to be understood by each and all, affirming that "in this written Word God hath plainly revealed whatsoever he hath thought needful for us to know, beleeve and acknowledge, touching the Nature and Office of Christ, in whom all the promises are Yea and Amen to the praise of God."[15] The gospel song puts it even more simply: "Jesus loves me this I know, for the Bible tells me so."[16] W. B. Johnson, the first president of the Southern Baptist Convention, when speaking at the inaugural gathering in Augusta, Georgia declared: "We have constructed for our basis no new creed, acting in this manner upon a Baptist aversion for all creeds but the Bible."[17] He was not the first, nor was he the last, to invoke the motto "no creed but the Bible." The rhetoric of "the Bible and the Bible only," while accurately reflecting a deep conviction, nevertheless leaves Baptists open to the imposition of alternative creed-like statements that have no connection to the historic Christian faith, thus making them ill equipped to discern the deep logic of the Bible as the unfolding story of the Triune God.

The Baptist suspicion of creeds is rooted in a confidence that the Bible alone is a sufficient ground for faith and practice. Yet this assumption does not seem to understand that they have a stake the whole Christian tradition. It masks a hermeneutical naiveté that presumes readers can leapfrog from the primitive Christianity of the Bible to the contemporary situation with relative ease. It seemingly ignores the fact that the basic core of apostolic doctrine was preserved and passed on in the post-apostolic era through the patristic writings and that this apostolic tradition may be retrieved by carefully reading the early church sources. Of particular im-

---

[13] Niebuhr, "The Doctrine of the Trinity and the Unity of the Church"; Wright, *The Old Testament and Theology*, 24.

[14] Freeman, "God in Three Persons," chap. 3 in Freeman, *Contesting Catholicity*, 143-90; Yarnell, "Baptists, Classical Trinitarianism, and the Christian Tradition."

[15] *First London Confession*, art. 8, in *Baptist Confessions of Faith*, 2nd ed., ed. Lumpkin, 158.

[16] "Jesus Loves Me!" Anna Bartlett Warner.

[17] Johnson, "The Southern Baptist Convention, To the Brethren in the United States; To the Congregations Connected with the Respective Churches; and to All Candid Men."

portance is the patristic rule of faith which, although like the creed, was a more elastic summary of the basic body of apostolic doctrine. The rule functioned as a hermeneutical guide for reading Scripture, serving as more of an intrinsic précis that disclosed the central teachings of the Bible than an extrinsic standard that was arbitrarily imposed.

Baptists have often found this need for the creed difficult to incorporate. For example, when the Oxford graduate John Biddle published his heterodox *Confession of Faith* in 1648, many of his Baptist contemporaries were sympathetically inclined because of his commitment to a simple biblicism. Yet Biddle's biblicism led him to conclude that the Father is the "Most High God, Creator of Heaven and Earth" and that Jesus Christ "hath no other than a Humane Nature" and is "not the Most High God, the same with the Father, but subordinate to Him."[18] When Biddle found himself in conflict with Parliament, the Baptists circulated a petition on his behalf. Their support was not a referendum on his anti-trinitiarianism, though they shared his suspicion of the ontologically saturated language of the so-called Athanasian Creed as well as his preference to confess the faith in "words that are found in the holy Scriptures."[19] Yet this "Bible only" hermeneutic led Biddle directly to an anti-Trinitarian Socinianism. It is important to note that the historic Trinitarian and Christological doctrines, which the Baptists affirmed and Biddle denied, were not derived from Scripture alone but by reading the Scriptures through the lens of the ancient ecumenical creeds.[20] And the track record for those committed to "just reading the Bible" is not encouraging, as it has too often led down paths that depart from the apostolic tradition.[21] The free and faithful confession of the creed provides the hermeneutical guidance to learn how to read the Bible as the unfolding story of the Triune God.

4. Historical Continuity

This stance of "no creed but the Bible" has other down sides. It has been a driving force in propagating the sectarian divisions that mark modern Christianity. Each new sect claims to restore apostolic faith and practice where the others have failed, but they have succeeded only in further dividing the church. Baptists from the beginning drew on this restorationist vision. John Smyth argued in his book *The*

---

[18] Biddle, *A Confession of Faith Touching the Holy Trinity According to the Scripture*, art. 1, 3, and 4 (pp. 1, 19, 29).

[19] *The Petition of Divers Gathered Churches, and others wel affected, in and about the city of London, for declaring the ordinance of the Lords and Commons, for punishing blasphemies and heresies, null and void* (London, 1655), 4.

[20] Williams, *Retrieving the Tradition*, 95-99.

[21] Holmes, "The Dangers of Just Reading the Bible: Orthodoxy and Christology."

Character of the Beast, written in 1609, that infant baptism invalidated the churchly status of those that practiced it.[22] His followers believed that by returning to the biblically warranted practice of believer baptism as instituted by Jesus (Mark 16:16), they were restoring apostolic Christianity.[23] John Williamson Nevin pointed out that this restorationist approach too easily assumes that primitive Christianity springs directly from the Bible without historical mediation.[24] The end result is a sectarianism that lacks a sense of continuity with the historic church prior to the Reformation except in occasional flashes of light in the "dark ages." In its worst expressions there is only the New Testament and the present. Nevin worried about the power of every congregation "to originate a new Christianity for its own use, and so may well afford to let that of other ages pass for a grand apostasy."[25] Nevin's colleague Philip Schaff argued similarly that sectarianism leads to "not the single pope of the city of the seven hills, but the numberless popes...who would fain enslave Protestants once more to human authority, not as embodied in the Church indeed, but as holding in the form of mere private judgement and private will."[26]

Even William H. Whitsitt, the president of the Southern Baptist Seminary in Louisville, Kentucky, who showed that the claim tracing the Baptists in an unbroken succession back to the time of Christ lacked any historical basis, argued that Baptist ecclesiology rested on the Bible alone. [27] Though Whitsitt assured readers that his concern was "purely a question of modern historical research," his contention that the Baptist view of the church was the clear teaching of the Bible did little to convince critics.[28] The biblicism shared by Baptist restorationists and historicists alike assumed a declension narrative of the church's history that failed to resolve the lingering question of how Baptists still might legitimately claim continuity with apostolic Christianity. A more nuanced approach, as James William McClendon, Jr. proposed, is the recognition that "the present church, like the New Testament community of disciples, is often errant or fallen, often restored."[29] Such an outlook leaves room for continuity despite the recognition of discontinuity. When Maclaren led the BWA in confessing the Apostles' Creed, he suggested that it would manifest their continuity with the historic church. Following this example,

---

[22] Smyth, *The Character of the Beast*, in *Works of John Smyth*, ed. Whitley, 2:565.
[23] Helwys, *Short Declaration of the Mystery of Iniquity*, ed. Groves, 132.
[24] Nevin, "The Theology of the New Liturgy."
[25] Nevin, "The Sect System," in *Catholic and Reformed*, 146.
[26] Schaff, *Principle of Protestantism*, 121.
[27] Carroll, *The Trail of Blood Following Christians Down through the Centuries*. Carroll drew from earlier sources, including Jones, *The History of the Christian Church*, and Orchard, *A Concise History of the Baptists*.
[28] Whitsitt, *A Question in Baptist History*, 5.
[29] McClendon, *Systematic Theology*, vol. 1, *Ethics*, rev. ed., 31.

the voluntary confession of the ancient ecumenical creeds by Baptists steps away from the autistic sectarianism of biblicist restorationism and voices the conviction that their gathered communities stand in continuity with apostolic Christianity and thus are visible manifestations of the church catholic. Such an approach is both quantitatively catholic, because it participates with the *consensus fidelium* in mystical and historical continuity with the faith of the apostolic church, and qualitatively catholic in that it joins voices with the apostolic witness to the Bible as the unfolding story of the Triune God.[30]

5. Ecumenical Unity

The same biblicism that has driven the sectarian impulse in Baptist life which severs the historical continuity with apostolic Christianity also fosters a fragmentation of Christian unity. To put it differently, the commitment to a "no creed but the Bible" approach has consequences, not only for the diachronic catholicity of the church (continuity through time), but also for the church's synchronic catholicity (connection throughout the world). It should not be surprising, then, that when the inaugural assembly of the World Council of Churches met in 1948, just eight Baptists unions joined as founding members and that in 2006 the membership roster of the WCC included only twenty-five Baptist unions.[31] In the United States, American Baptists have been full participants in national and global ecumenical organizations, whereas Southern Baptists have not.[32] Baptist church historian William Estep explained that the Southern Baptist resistance to ecumenism was due to a concern that visible unity would result in compromise on the non-negotiable convictions of believer baptism and congregational ecclesiology as well

---

[30] The distinction between "quantitative" and "qualitative" catholicity is helpfully made by Congar, *Chrétiens désunis*, 115-17; ET, *Divided Christendom*, 93-94.

[31] Harmon, "The Baptist Tradition and Ecumenism"; Payne, "Baptists and the Ecumenical Movement," chap. in Payne, *Free Churchmen, Unrepentant and Repentant*.

[32] Hill and Torbet, *Baptists North and South*, 27-34. In 1914 the SBC voted to decline an invitation to participate in the Federal Council of Churches (later renamed the National Council of Churches). In their report to the Convention, the study committee affirmed a Bible-only position on ecumenism, stating that "*the only genuine basis of true Christian unity is a unity on the teachings of the Bible as commonly accepted and commonly understood*" (*Annual of the Southern Baptist Convention* [1914], 73-78). The American Baptist Churches USA has participated in the NCC since its founding as the Northern Baptist Convention in 1908 and has been a member of the WCC since its formation in 1948; it created an Office of Ecumenical Relations in 1966 to maintain ecumenical dialogue. See Barr, *Oneness in Christ*, and McBeth, *The Baptist Heritage*, 600-02.

as disregard for the Baptist aversion to creeds.[33] At the Baptist World Alliance Congress in 1947, Henry Cook, British pastor and chair of the BWA Committee on Evangelism, made a fervent appeal for Baptists to participate in the WCC. His plea was met with fierce resistance by Southern Baptists, including former convention president M. E. Dodd.[34] The strong opposition to ecumenical relations by Southern Baptists led Australian Baptist theologian Edward Roberts-Thomson to conclude that "the Baptist world, ecumenically, can be divided into two groups: those who are of the Southern Baptist point of view, or are closely influenced by it, and those who are not."[35]

This tension moved James Wm. McClendon, Jr. in 1968 to wonder aloud: "What is a Baptist ecumenism?" He suggested that there can never be real unity where there is "rivalry, enmity, distrust, hatred between Christians." Ecumenism is based on love for one another in spite of differences that seeks to live into a vision of identity in Christ.[36] Ecumenical work, McClendon observed, is simply another way of describing the attempt to discover in one another what is authentically Christian because it includes within its scope "those apostolic qualities that make Christianity Christ-like."[37] Such a vision of Christian unity can be traced to the earliest Baptists, in John Smyth's *Confession of Faith*, which breathed an ecumenical

---

[33] Estep, *Baptists and Christian Unity*, 168–88. More recently Albert Mohler has reiterated similar concerns as a reason for why the SBC does not participate in ecumenical organizations, stating that "the Convention has avoided entanglements that would compromise doctrine, restrict the freedom and independence of the Convention, or violate basic issues of Baptist conviction." Mohler concluded, "Southern Baptists stand unalterably opposed to any ecumenical or interchurch union not based upon common convictions and practices drawn from the teachings of the Bible. That is, Southern Baptists will not negotiate a union that would violate our understandings of regenerate church membership, local church autonomy, free church polity, the ordinances, etc." (Mohler, "The Southern Baptist Convention and the Issue of Interdenominational Relationships").

[34] Patterson and Pierrard, "Recovery from the War and the Advance to Maturity," 108. In 1948 the Baptist Union of Great Britain approved a statement on the church, which declared: "Although Baptists have for so long held a position separate from that of other communions, they have always claimed to be part of the one holy catholic Church of our Lord Jesus Christ. They believe in the catholic Church as the holy society of believers in our Lord Jesus Christ, which He founded, of which He is the only Head, and in which He dwells by His Spirit, so that though manifested in many communions, organized in various modes, and scattered throughout the world, it is yet one in Him" (Baptist Union of Great Britain and Ireland, "The Baptist Doctrine of the Church," § 2 [March 1948], in *Baptist Union Documents 1948-1977*, ed. Hayden, 5-6).

[35] Roberts-Thomson, *With Hands Outstretched*, 94.

[36] McClendon, "What is a Southern Baptist Ecumenism?" (*Collected Works of James Wm. McClendon, Jr.*, 1:237-43).

[37] McClendon, *Systematic Theology*, vol. 3, *Witness*, 336.

spirit into the Baptist vision by declaring that "all penitent and faithfull Christians are brethren in the communion of the outward church, wheresoever they live, by what name soever they are knowen, [be they Roman Catholics, Lutherans, Zwinglians, Calvinists, Brownists, Anabaptists, or other pious Christians], which in truth and zeale, follow repentance and faith." He continued, "we salute them all with a holie kisse, being hartilie grieved that wee which follow after one faith, and one spirit, one lord, and one God, one bodie, and one baptisme, should be rent into so many sects, and schismes: and that only for matters of lesse moment."[38] May Baptists, as McClendon urged, "congregation by congregation, local church by local church, Christian group by Christian group, seek to embody the completeness that is found in Christ Jesus and in his true saints ancient and modern," because when they embody that catholicity which is authentically Christian, they "shall of necessity come closer to one another."[39] Let all Baptists, then, manifest that catholicity by freely confessing their faith in the words of the ancient and ecumenical creeds of the church: We believe in God the Father Almighty...and in Jesus Christ the Son...and in the Holy Spirit...Amen.

6. For Further Reading

Barth, Karl. *Credo*. Translated by J. Strathearn McNab. New York: Scribner's, 1962.

Freeman, Curtis W. *Contesting Catholicity: Theology for Other Baptists*. Waco, TX: Baylor University Press, 2014 [chapters 3-4, 93-190].

Jenson, Robert W. *Canon and Creed*. Louisville: Westminster John Knox, 2010.

Kelly, J. N. D. *Early Christian Creeds*, 3rd ed. New York: Longman, 1972.

Myers, Ben. *The Apostles' Creed: A Guide to the Ancient Catechism*. Bellingham, WA: Lexham Press, 2018.

Pelikan, Jaroslav. *Credo: Historical and Theological Guide to Creeds and Confessions of Faith in the Christian Tradition*. New Haven: Yale University Press, 2003.

---

[38] Smyth, *A Confession of Faith*, § 69, in *Works of John Smyth*, ed. Whitley, 2:745. The bracketed reference to "Roman Catholics, Lutherans, Zwinglians, Calvinists, Brownists, Anabaptists, or other pious Christians," is included in the version of Smyth's *Confession* LXXI that appears as an appendix in Evans, *Early English Baptists*, 1:267.

[39] McClendon, *Systematic Theology*, vol. 3, *Witness*, 336.

16

Light from Pre-Reformation
Women's Theological Contributions

Kate Hanch

In an era before the printing press, from Christ's resurrection to the Protestant Reformation, men's voices prevailed in theological literature and formulations. The "Great Tradition," at least as it has been presented in some theological works, has often meant a *ressourcement* of male theologians only. Limited opportunities, combined with patriarchal norms of the era, meant that women's voices were often supplanted, silenced, or forgotten. In our contemporary moment, this continues to be the case. Nonetheless, women contributed to theological discourse, whether it was through influencing male relatives (Monica's prayers for and catechesis of her son Augustine and Macrina's mentoring of her brothers Gregory of Nyssa and Basil of Caesarea); music and plays (such as Hildegard von Bingen's *Symphonia* and *Ordo Virtutum*); dictated spiritual autobiographies (as with Margery Kempe's *Life*); and letters written to clergy and laity (Catherine of Siena).

Of the era, Rosemary Radford Ruether remarks: "Although women could not be priests, they could be prophets."[1] They were prohibited from presiding over the sacraments and becoming clergy, but could theologize in other capacities, including their writings. As prophets (often not recognized by the church), women both spoke with authority and directed people toward the Divine. Many women throughout church history, from the early church martyr Perpetua to the nineteenth century African American preacher Jarena Lee, adopted prophetic discourse to validate their voices. They alluded to biblical texts in their imagery, cadence, or diction. In doing so, they placed themselves on a plane close to that of biblical authors. They believed their words and visions, like the Hebrew prophets, were ordained by God for the good of their communities. The English late medieval mystic Julian of Norwich (1342-1416) exemplifies this and serves as a case study for this chapter. Julian's "bodying" of John's Gospel, particularly in her use of "oneing," offers Baptists novel ways of theologizing and interpreting Scripture that con-

---

[1] Ruether, *Women and Redemption*, 81.

sider context, the fecundity of the Scriptures, and the multilayered, multidimensional character of God.[2]

1. Contextual Notes

Knowing the context is important when reading *any* theologian. For pre-Reformation women especially, realizing that direct interpretation of Scripture was often forbidden gives us permission to look for allusions to Scripture without direct references. Julian utilizes themes from the farewell discourse in John to depict God's one-ing of humanity to God's self, which is a soteriological motif.[3] To use "one" as a verb and not a number was not unique to Julian—other medieval English mystics utilized this term.[4] However, more than other theologians of her time, Julian utilizes the term to describe how the Triune God saves humanity. The word "atonement" contains the idea of being oned with God—at-one-ment.[5] Specifically, Julian employs themes of friendship, indwelling, and a love that sustains this indwelling. These themes overlap one another, indicating a perichoretic trend inherent in John and sustained by Julian. This one-ing has a social dimension, as persons are not only oned with God, but each other. In her play with this Johannine theme of oneing, Julian reveals how doctrinal loci always already interconnect with one another.

Julian's emphasis of humanity's oneing to God comes as good news to her contemporary listeners. She records her revelations while the Black Death still lingered in Norwich's memory. This plague killed anywhere from thirty to sixty percent of Europe's population, last striking Norwich when Julian was young. A shortage of labor from the plague prompted peasant unrest, and a peasant uprising occurred and was viciously crushed by the bishop in Norwich during Julian's adulthood. Corrupt friars preyed upon the misery of the people, and the Lollard controversy, along with the multiple popes aligned with different political factions,

---

[2] I use the term "body" as a verb instead of "embody" because "embody" implies we can theologize without a body.

[3] Much of this work comes from a paper I presented titled "Oneing as *Theōsis*: Julian of Norwich's Use of the Johannine Farewell Discourse" at a meeting of the Society of Biblical Literature in Boston, Massachusetts in November 2017 in a section on "Recovering Female Interpreters of the Bible." For an examination of how Julian may have utilized the Johannine epistles, see Stovell, "Oned and Grounded in Love: Julian of Norwich and the Johannine God of Love." Modern translations of the Middle English will use the word "knit," "unite," or "join" instead of "one."

[4] The anonymous author of *The Cloud of the Unknowing*, a contemporary of Julian, uses "oned" to describe how God unites with humanity, but does not develop the concept.

[5] While the term "atonement" itself arises in the sixteenth century, it comes from the medieval verb "one." See Stevenson, ed., *Oxford Dictionary of English*, 3rd ed., s.v. "Atonement."

jeopardized the stability of the established church.[6] In addition, England was engaged in the 100 Years' War with France, and extra taxes from the war and the plague burdened the most vulnerable populations.[7] Julian, in the large town of Norwich, with her anchorite attached to the church of St. Julian's, would be familiar with the heartaches of her day. From her window, she would encounter people coming to Mass, and during the week they would come to her for spiritual wisdom.

It is in this context that Julian develops the idea of God as one-ing humanity to God's self. Suffering an illness that almost killed her at age 30 in 1373, Julian experienced a series of visions depicting Christ's Passion. She records them in what is called the Short Text (ST). Thirty years later, she rewrites and expands them to share additional insights and a deepened theological understanding, known as the Long Text (LT).[8] Scholars debate the extent of Julian's familiarity with Scripture: it was through access either to the Vulgate (written or in the context of the mass) or perhaps to the vernacular English, as the Wycliffe Bible had been translated during Julian's lifetime. The Wycliffe translations from Latin into English would have been considered heretical, and Julian would certainly have looked upon them with suspicion, if she had encountered them at all. However, there was a possibility that Julian may have encountered English translations of scriptural snippets.[9] Julian likely did not have access to a written Latin text, but perhaps knew Latin to a degree through spiritual advisors and the mass. Brant Pelphrey describes the commonality of medieval mystics alluding to or paraphrasing scripture, while not mentioning the source or context, such as Walter Hilton or Richard Rolle. However, he remarks that these medieval writers usually identify the source "at least once," something absent in much of Julian's writing.[10] Julian may have learned Scripture through other mystical or devotional literature, such as the *Ancrene Wisse*, the guidebook for anchoresses. This text contained multiple Scripture passages; both in Latin and English.[11] Even if Julian did not have access to a written biblical text, she received ideas and scriptural themes in varied ways.

The way Julian interprets Scripture is through employing the ideas or mimicking the style or syntax rather than a direct paraphrase. For instance, Julian refer-

---

[6] The Lollards were a group of lay preachers considered heretical by the official church of their day. Julian's anchorite was near the place were Lollards were persecuted and executed. See Jantzen, *Julian of Norwich*, 11.

[7] Goldberg, *Medieval England*, 65.

[8] All my quotations are from the Long Text.

[9] Deanesly, *The Lollard Bible*, cited in Pelphrey, *Love Was His Meaning*, 343.

[10] Pelphrey, *Love Was His Meaning*, 343.

[11] Sutherland, "Julian of Norwich," in *Handbook of Women Biblical Interpreters*, ed. Taylor and Choi, 300; cf. Pelphrey, *Love was His Meaning*, 346.

ences humanity being created out of the "slime of the earth,"[12] alluding to the Genesis creation account.[13] Julian's parable of the lord and the servant, where she articulates her notion of sin, is in the style of parables found in the synoptic Gospels and may allude to either the suffering servant of Isaiah 53 or to the vision of Joshua appearing before the Lord in Zechariah 3.[14] With the term "one-ing," Julian, in bodying the cadence and structure of John, demonstrates the fullness of ways in which God saves humanity. By closely reading John's farewell discourse alongside Julian, we glean from Julian how to live out Scripture's call, be faithful to our own community, and construct theology in creative and life-affirming ways.

2. Friendship in Oneing

John 15:12-16 depicts Jesus as offering a new way for the disciples to relate with him: instead of a subordinate status (servant or slave), Jesus now refers to them as friends. This is the first time he calls to the disciples as friends—only in John 11:11 does he give Lazarus this distinction. In John 15, the friendship is marked by mutual abiding, the disciples' following the ways of Jesus, and Jesus' giving of his life for the disciples. Gerard Sloyan remarks that Jesus initiates and maintains this new mutual relationship. Jesus becomes the "lover and the friend" who models the truest form of *agape* love.[15] He initiates the friendship, while the disciples are to respond and imitate. Julian picks up on John's notion of friendship in oneing, particularly in describing how humanity is to follow Jesus' ways. For Julian, we are to hold to the guidance of Jesus, who is our "blessed friend."[16] Our friend Jesus loves us when we worship him and when we sin and wants us to cling to him regardless. Julian's pastoral motives come to play here—she claims that the enemy (Satan) will tempt us with false fear and anxiety because we are unworthy to contemplate our friend Jesus. In an era in which the plague was blamed on God's wrath over humanity's sin, this fear was keenly felt. However, the friendship between Christ and humanity, Julian suggests, prevails over evil and death, for nothing can separate God from the Christian. Julian declares "power of our enemy is shut in the hand of our friend, and therefore a soul which knows this to be certain will fear nothing but him whom she loves."[17] This fear is what Julian calls a "reverent fear" that en-

---

[12] Julian of Norwich, *Showings*, trans. Colledge and Walsh, 14.53 (p. 284).

[13] See Pelphrey, *Love Was His Meaning*, 330-49 for more on how Julian views Scripture.

[14] Julian of Norwich, *Showings* (LT), 14.51 (p. 278). James Walsh refers to the suffering servant in *The Revelations of Divine Love of Julian of Norwich*, 31-32. Pelphrey refers to Zechariah 3 in *Love Was His Meaning*, xi.

[15] Sloyan, *John*, 189.

[16] Watson and Jenkins, eds., *The Writings of Julian of Norwich*, 363.

[17] Julian of Norwich, *Showings* (LT), 15.65 (p. 309).

courages Christians to flee evil and "fall into our Lord's breast."[18] For Julian, Christ as friend means both compassion and embrace. Like John, Julian's friendship suggests a mutuality beyond a disciple-master relationship—she refers to "our courteous Lord" as "familiar," or intimate. The familiar Christ leads us "into the fullness of joy."[19] Julian borrows the friendship motif from John, and then expands it to apply to her community. The sharing of the friendship focuses pastorally on how God saves humanity, focusing less on humanity's anxiety over sin and more on the Triune God's desire for union with humanity. The onus in salvation is on God; humanity is lured by God's friendship.

3. Mutual Indwelling Characterizing Oneing

For John, as well as Julian, oneing depicted through friendship includes mutual indwelling. The Gospel author depicts two kinds of mutual indwelling in John 14-15: of Father and Son, and of Son and the disciples. The third is a one-way dwelling, that of the Advocate or the Spirit within the disciples as sent by the Father through the Son. Regarding the Father-Son indwelling, Jesus tells his disciples that because they have seen Jesus, they have also seen the Father, because Jesus states, "I am in the Father and the Father is in me" (John 14:11). Jesus then urges the disciples to "abide in me as I abide in you." The abiding begins within the Father and Son dyad, and then Jesus in turn opens to the concept of mutual indwelling between him and the disciples. He sends the Advocate who indwells the disciples as signal of the presence of Jesus and his Father.

Julian applies the mutual indwelling found in John with a Trinitarian framework. She declares that we are "enclosed in the Father, and we are enclosed in the Son, and we are enclosed in the Holy Ghost. And the Father is enclosed in us, the Son is enclosed in us, and the Holy Ghost is enclosed in us."[20] While the Trinity is a post-biblical theological development, the Gospel does lend itself to this interpretation, though indirectly. If the Father and the Son mutually abide in one another, and the Son and the disciples mutually indwell each other, and the Son sends the Spirit of the Father to indwell the disciples, then the indwelling occurs not just within the pairs mentioned in the discourse, but implicitly among the Trinitarian persons and the believers. While the indwelling may be mutual, for John, as well for Julian, the divine still takes precedence and initiative. The metaphor of the vine and branches demonstrates Jesus as creating and sustaining the mutual indwelling. Jesus as the vine and the disciples as the branches characterizes the friendship as

---

[18] Julian of Norwich, *Showings* (LT), 16.74 (p. 357).

[19] Julian of Norwich, *Showings* (LT), 16.77 (p. 331).

[20] Julian of Norwich, *Showings* (LT), 14.54 (p. 297).

begun by the divine. If the disciples do not abide in Jesus, they can "do nothing" (John 15:5). Not abiding in Jesus leads to the disciples becoming withered and fallen away to destruction (John 15:6).

Likewise, though the abiding of the Trinity and Christians is mutual for Julian, God initiates and preserves this relationship. Julian claims that the soul is "so deeply grounded in God, so endlessly treasured" that we do not know it unless we know God. In a way, the soul does not exist unless it is grounded in God. Julian describes the soul as "naturally rooted in God in endless love."[21] The words "grounded" and "rooted" bear conceptual similarity with John's vine and branches—the branches do not exist or have purpose without the vine; likewise, the soul is nothing if it is not rooted within God. This mutual Trinitarian indwelling and rootedness connects also to 1 John 3:23-25, where the disciples are charged to love one another, and in doing so, they, through the Spirit, will abide in Christ.[22] This echoes the sending of the Advocate in John's Gospel, who points the disciples to the Father (14:16-17, 26; 15:26; 16:13-14). For Julian, taking cues from the Johannine Gospel, it is in this mutual enclosure that Christians are oned to the Triune God. Baptist theologian Paul Fiddes, reflecting upon Julian, argues that this indwelling should be understood actively, as humans participate in the movements of God. Dwelling, he suggests, like the word "one," should be considered a verb rather than a noun.[23] This ensures the participatory function of both the indwelling and the oneing—while God may initiate the movement, God lures and welcomes humanity to respond in joy. The indwelling serves as another angle in describing how God ones with humanity—a oneing that locates humanity *in* God's very heart. To borrow a metaphor from Julian's first revelation, we can imagine ourselves as a hazelnut, held in the palm of God's hand, knowing that God creates us, loves us, and sustains us. Not only do we body the Word, but the Word bodies us. Because we are located within God, for Julian, echoing the Apostle Paul, nothing can separate us from the love of God.

4. Love in Oneing

Both the Gospel writer and Julian see love as the motivation for God's oneing with humanity. This love is not only a human-divine love, but a love that overflows for what Julian calls "fellow creatures." In John, Jesus places the initiative of love with the divine, declaring "As the Father has loved me, so I have loved you, abide in my love" (John 15:9). Then, he declares his love for his disciples, urging them to fol-

---

[21] Julian of Norwich, *Showings* (LT), 14.56 (p. 289); Watson and Jenkins, eds., *The Writings of Julian of Norwich*, 301.

[22] Stovell, "Oned and Grounded in Love," 12.

[23] Fiddes, "Covenant and Participation," 126.

low such love: "love one another as I have loved you." (15:12). How are the disciples to love Jesus, and one another? By laying down their lives (15:14), and keeping Jesus' commands (14:21-24, 15:10, 12). Love and care marks Jesus' farewell discourse, even when not specifically mentioned. For instance, he describes himself in parental terms, declaring to his disciples "I will not leave you orphaned, I am coming to you" in relation to his upcoming death and resurrection (John 14:19). He continues this affectionate stance with his urging "do not let your hearts be troubled" (John 14:27). Not only does the gospel author mention love specifically, but Jesus' tone in the farewell discourse connotes love and care for the disciples.

Julian, like John, sees love as God's reason for oneing both in divine-human love, and human relations with one another. In fact, she identifies love as the motivation for Christ's suffering and passion: "love was his meaning. Who reveals it to you? Love. What did he reveal to you? Love. Why does he reveal it to you? For love....I was taught that love is our Lord's meaning."[24] The Trinity's motivation in oneing with humanity is love, and the Trinity is revealed as love to humanity.

Julian also uses parental imagery in her description of God, claiming "God almighty is our loving Father, and God all wisdom is our loving Mother, with the love and the goodness of the Holy Spirit."[25] The commonality among the Trinitarian persons is love. It is a love that both affirms and destabilizes kinship metaphors, as the various persons of the Trinity are described as lovers, brothers, parents, and friends. In whatever way humanity conceives of love, Julian has thought of it and sees its origins within the divine. God's love is cataphatic (what we can know about God)—as God is described in multiple relational metaphors. Yet, God's love is apophatic (the mystery of the divine)—the multiplicity of such metaphors assures her audience there is always something more to discover.

The love in which God ones us to God's self spills over to the love we have for our neighbor.[26] Julian claims that humanity's goodness and love toward neighbor reflects Christ's indwelling of humanity: "every natural compassion which one has for one's fellow Christians in love is Christ in us."[27] Further, she asserts: the "love of God creates in us such a unity that when it is truly seen, no [person] can separate [themselves] from another [person]."[28] An individual's well-being is bound up with the community's well-being. Love for God overflows for love for neighbor.

---

[24] Julian of Norwich, *Showings* (LT), 16.86 (p. 342).
[25] Julian of Norwich, *Showings* (LT), 14.58 (p. 293).
[26] Pelphrey, *Love Was His Meaning*, 192.
[27] Julian of Norwich, *Showings* (LT), 13.28 (p. 237).
[28] Julian of Norwich, *Showings* (LT), 15.65 (p. 309).

For Julian, a Christian's oneing with God plays out in one's care, love, and oneing with the other.[29]

5. Baptist Takeaways

To describe the nuances and contributions of pre-Reformation women would take multiple books. Julian of Norwich serves as an example, or perhaps entry point, by which we can interrogate the role pre-Reformation women play in our own theological and spiritual development. What does it mean, as I cited Ruether in the beginning, for pre-Reformation women to be prophets, and how might we emulate them today? Biblically, prophets represent an in-between space, speaking on behalf of God while attending to the needs of the community. Women as prophets faced additional marginality, as the patriarchal constructs compelled women to proclaim and theologize creatively, subversively, and gently. In Julian's case, she held some privilege, as her position as an anchoress meant she had time to pray, reflect, and counsel the outside world. Yet, as a woman, she was prohibited from interpreting Scripture and was subject to the church authorities. As Baptists, we tend to do our best theological work in these intermediary or marginalized spaces, where the absence of privilege and prestige compel us to do the same. This space, whether chosen or forced upon us, shapes our pastoral and theological practices and prompts us to attend to marginalized persons and perspectives we would otherwise overlook and ignore.

What can Baptists take away from Julian and other pre-Reformation women, and how can Julian's theology illumine Baptists' own? First, the practice of seriously engaging pre-Reformation women—not only in *lectio divina* or spiritual devotion, but as *theologians* and biblical interpreters called by God to speak a good word to their communities—helps disrupt boundaries of who is counted as a theologian and who can create theology. All along, beginning with Mary's discovery of the empty tomb in the Gospels to today, Christian women continually make invaluable contributions to theological discourse. Historical and systematic theological treatments, as well as sermons, should consider Julian alongside Anselm, or Angela of Foligno alongside Aquinas. To read women on the same playing field as the "church fathers" expands our theological imaginations and resists gradations of knowledge. Like all eras, we realize in studying women in the early and medieval church contained multiple, and sometimes conflicting, perspectives on doctrinal loci such as Christology and soteriology that complicate traditional or straightfor-

---

[29] Julian most likely picks up this theme of love for God leading to love for neighbor, either directly or indirectly, from Augustine's *De Trinitate*. Augustinian monks were close to her cell and perhaps influenced her intellectually. For more on this theme in Julian, see Hanch, "Participation in God, Oned by Love."

ward approaches. For instance, Julian of Norwich's Christology resists Gustav Aulén's neat categorization of theories of atonement[30] because she simultaneously embraces Christ as defeating sin and death (13:33), his death as having some sort of substitutionary focus (14:51), and Christ as the moral model whom we should emulate (16:83). Julian intuits that atonement theories are not necessarily theories per se—they are *metaphors* intended to point toward the overwhelming mysterious love of God that draws humanity to the divine. She struggles with, and never fully answers, questions of theodicy and why Christ suffered and died. She stands firm with what she does know—that the Triune God initiates and sustains a loving relationship with humanity.

From pre-Reformation women, including Julian, we learn that the absence of Scriptural citations does not mean these theologians are not seriously engaging the texts. Often, women body the spirit of Scripture in their prophecy, as the way they write invokes the whole canon of Scripture. For instance, Hildegard of Bingen's judgment on the church's corruption echoes the Old Testament prophets' condemning the sins of Israel. The twelfth-century Mechtild of Hackeborn relies upon the scriptures that accompany the liturgical year to describe God's desire for her. Julian reveals to us the multiple ways Scripture can be interpreted—through adopting its cadences, expanding on its ideas, and using its terms in new and creative ways. Prohibitions against women interpreting the Bible allow them to approach the text in creative and contextually appropriate ways. Julian carries the themes of John's Gospel and makes them alive for the people who come to her anchor hold window at Norwich. In a way, she retells the story that resonates with the anxieties and concerns of her community. The Word becomes bodied anew in Julian's retelling and expansion. As such, Julian may be considered a preacher, bringing the good news to her aching community.[31] Her engagement with Scripture not only establishes authority from God in a prophetic way; it is a didactic strategy following Yahweh's declaration in Deut. 6:1-8: to keep God's commands, to continually discuss with the community, to body them daily.

Underlying Julian's proclamation is love. Julian reminds us that love is and should be the motivation for all theological discourse. As Julian ponders how God saves her, she declares: "I saw no difference between God and our substance, but, as it were, all God; and still my understanding accepted that our substance is in God, that is to say God is God, and our substance is a creature in God."[32] The level of intimacy between the soul and God is characterized by friendship, mutual indwelling, and love—all themes also present in the Johannine Gospel. Becoming "oned"

---

[30] Aulén, *Christus Victor.*
[31] Cf. McCray, *The Censored Pulpit.*
[32] Julian of Norwich, *Showings* (LT), 14.54 (p. 285).

or "knitted" with God, for Julian, is how God saves humanity. Julian's "evenchristens" (what she calls her fellow Christians) experience a transformation, a new status or reality—not unlike John's declaration of the disciples as "friends." Further, for Julian, seeing salvation primarily through the lens of oneing demonstrates pastoral sensitivities to her context. In a turbulent political and ecclesial context, and in the face of overwhelming grief lingering from the Black Plague, the idea of becoming "oned" with God stood as hopeful news for the people who came to Julian's window. As Jesus uses kinship and an intimate tone in John, so Julian utilizes notions of friendship, motherhood, and fatherhood. Just as Jesus declare that he and the Father are one in John 10:30, so now Julian could apply that her soul and God were one.[33] Her notion of oneing, and rooting oneing in John's Gospel, expands soteriology beyond the Passion and Resurrection narratives. Rather, Julian, utilizing Johannine themes, anchors soteriology in the context of relationships marked by love, joy and mutuality—love *is* the Lord's meaning. This oneing has a social dimension, as Christians are oned with God, they are also oned with each other. We learn from Julian that the motivation for evangelism is not to save souls but out of the overwhelming love God has for us and the recognition that we are bound together as we dwell in God. For Julian, perhaps taking clues from John's Gospel, to become oned with God is to feel at home in God with others—what she describes as God's kindly homeliness.[34] For her, becoming oned with God is a continual process, akin to sanctification, where humanity become continually transformed into the likeness of Christ.

More so than her male contemporaries, Julian's theology gives a poetic or metaphorical rendering of doctrines in an accessible way to her community. She reminds us that theology—our God talk—should be beautiful as well as didactic, expansive as well as useful. We as the church can and should retrieve this from Julian and other pre-Reformation women in our sermon preparation, church education, and spiritual practices. In my role as a lay leader and supply preacher in Baptist churches, I incorporate the writings of pre-Reformation women in various ways. While preaching on John 17, I referenced Julian to describe the role of the Trinitarian persons in the Ascension. I brought the female medieval mystics into adult education, utilizing Hildegard of Bingen's artistic depiction of the universe as an egg to lead a discussion on how we understand the doctrine of creation. When I pray alone or in group settings, I recall the myriad of ways in which Catherine of Siena, Mechtild of Magdeburg, and Angela of Foligno describe God's surpassing

---

[33] More recently, Byers, *Ecclesiology and Theosis in the Gospel of John*, has made a connection between "The Father and I are One" in John 10:30 and applied it to *theōsis*.

[34] "Homely" is another term not retained in modern translations but that holds theological significance for Julian.

love for them. Understanding pre-Reformation women's intermediary contexts, and their prophetic roles in such contexts, can inform how we can be attuned to the Holy Spirit in ministering to and with our churches and our world today.

6. For Further Reading

Cohick, Lynn H. and Amy Brown Hughes. *Christian Women in the Patristic World: Their Influence, Authority, and Legacy in the Second Through Fifth Centuries.* Grand Rapids, Mich.: Baker Academic, 2017.

Julian of Norwich. *Showings.* Translated by Edmund Colledge and James Walsh. New York: Paulist Press, 1978.

Oden, Amy, ed. *In Her Words: Women's Writings in the History of Christian Thought.* Nashville: Abingdon Press, 1994.

Ruether, Rosemary Radford. *Women and Redemption: A Theological History.* Minneapolis, MN: Fortress Press, 1998.

Taylor, Marion Ann and Agnes Choi, eds. *Handbook of Women Biblical Interpreters: A Historical and Biographical Guide.* Grand Rapids, MI: Baker Academic, 2012.

Watson, Nicholas, and Jacqueline Jenkins, eds. *The Writings of Julian of Norwich: A Vision Showed to a Devout Woman and a Revelation of Love.* University Park, PA: Pennsylvania State University Press, 2006.

17

Light from the Confessions of the European Reformations

Rady Roldán-Figueroa

By one classic account of the Protestant Reformation, Martin Luther stood against the corruption of Rome and the moral decay of medieval Christianity. Among his reforming manifestos was the *Babylonian Captivity of the Church* of 1520. He rallied against medieval sacramental practices, which exemplified for him the church's captivity under a corrupt papacy. In using the phrase "Babylonian captivity of the church," he was drawing on the biblical narratives associated with the captivity of the people of Judah. He was also drawing on the discursive practice of the poet and seminal figure of the Italian Renaissance, Francesco Petrarca (1304–1374), who used the phrase to denounce the corruption of the Avignon papacy.[1] If we follow his representation of medieval Christianity, then we could say that up to Luther the people of God had endured three great Babylonian captivities; namely, that of the people of Judah, that of the papacy of Avignon, and lastly that of Rome under the House of Borgia.

1. Baptists and the "Fourth Babylonian Captivity"

A "Babylonian captivity" is a state of affairs in which the moral judgment and ethical commitments of the people of God are clouded, dimmed, and eclipsed as they are held captive and transfixed by overriding powers and principalities. Thus, following the logic of mythico-allegorical discursive modalities, we could say that there is a fourth Babylonian captivity hovering over conservative Baptist churches as well as American evangelicalism. There is no single way of describing this fourth captivity. However, it became profoundly evident during the 2016 electoral cycle and its aftermath as the churches failed—as they continue to fail—to bear witness to the gospel of Jesus Christ by surrendering their moral judgment to the political enticements of the brand of populist authoritarianism known as Trumpism.[2]

---

[1] Boyle, *Petrarch's Genius*, 96-97.
[2] See for example, Viefhues-Bailey, "Looking Forward to a New Heaven and a New Earth Where American Greatness Dwells."

Authoritarian creeds are ideologies based on the cult of personality that tend to exalt the all-mighty leader as cusp of all decision-making and the unquestionable source of authority. Not only are authoritarian movements against the democratic traditions of this country, but they are also inspired by idolatrous ideologies. Currently, we have seen intolerance rise to levels not seen or experienced in decades. Further, it is not only that the churches have failed to stand up with unanimous voice of denunciation. Instead, many Baptist churches, Baptist leaders and scholars, have also been compromised and complicit by lending their support and enabling the unfettered rise of such demonic powers and principalities.

Of greater concern is that Trumpism's appeal among Baptists is probably the result of the correspondence between certain Baptist "distinctives," on the one hand, and the core ideas of populist authoritarianism on the other. In fact, Baptist distinctives such as "congregational polity" and "biblical authority" are not unequivocal theological concepts. Both depend on ideas and notions that can be confused and mixed up with analogous political terms. For instance, Baptists have for long explained congregational government on the basis of a social analogy that describes it as a form of "democracy," or government by many. The 1963 *Baptist Faith and Message* describes the church as "an autonomous body, operating through democratic processes under the Lordship of Jesus Christ."[3] When the notion of a church governed by "democratic processes" is coupled with those of "priesthood of believers" and "soul freedom," the result is an inescapable symmetry with the political principles, not of libertarianism, but of populism. Interestingly, "individualism" and "libertarianism" are the two most common designations used to describe Baptist social ethics and political orientation. However, the populist proclivity of the movement is as prominent, if not even more pervasive.

One of the great challenges posed by populist movements in the twenty-first century is that they tend to be anti-democratic and anti-pluralist. As Jan-Wemer Muller has pointed out, populism is "a degraded form of democracy that promises to make good on democracy's highest ideals."[4] The egalitarianism that characterized populist movements in the nineteenth-century was inspired by the promising political potential of republicanism. In contrast, populism today is inspired by the perceived failure of republicanism and reacts with repulsion towards the ideals of liberal-democracy.

Another important aspect of Baptist belief and practice that makes the movement susceptible to the seductive influence of populism is that of theological authoritarianism. Paradoxically, conservative Baptist have displayed a perplexing fascination with the notion of authority. Indeed, it could be argued that it is this

---

[3] Southern Baptist Convention, "Baptist Faith and Message" (1963), art. 6.
[4] Muller, *What Is Populism?*, 6.

beguilement with authority that separates conservative from progressive Baptists. The Baptist Faith and Message Study Committee responsible for the drafting of the 2000 *Baptist Faith and Message* explained the changes introduced in 1963 as a response to "assaults upon the authority and truthfulness of the Bible."[5] Similar seemingly innocuous statements on "biblical authority" hide a corrosive and caustic corollary, for they communicate more than just a conviction about the Bible. Walter B. Shurden hinted at this question in his essay "The Problem of Authority in the Southern Baptist Convention."[6] He clearly identify the crux of the issue as the tension between authority and freedom. As he pointed out: "In fact, our problem as it pertains to the Bible is not the problem of authority at all, but the problem of freedom."[7] However, he did not see that a deeper and more profound source of this ill in Baptist life is the idea of authority itself and its uncritical acceptance.

In fact, statements on "biblical authority" are also statements about "authority." An important assumption at work is the notion that authority is self-evident and that its exercise is unquestionably good. Hidden and unexamined is the reality that authority is at odds with personal liberty and that authority often undermines it. Authority is after all about legitimately commanding personal obedience. In our daily life authority describes an asymmetrical relation of power predicated upon submission and conformity. Theological authoritarianism encloses everything in uneven and unequal relations of power and submission. The "problem of authority" that Shurden spoke of decades earlier really amounts to treating authority itself as the thing to be protected, safeguarded, and cherished.

Undeniably, "authority" is a notion that we find both in our lived experience as well as in New Testament teachings about the person and work of Christ. Hence, it is important to critically distinguish them. The central New Testament teaching on "authority" (Greek *exousia*) is that "all authority in heaven and on earth has been given" to Jesus Christ (Matt. 28:18). The Lord Jesus is above all mundane authority and authority cannot be usurped from the Lord. Hence, when there are those who ask, "by what authority are you doing these things, and who gave you this authority," the Lord has the freedom to respond, "neither will I tell you by what authority I do these things" (Matt. 21:23-27; Mark 11:27-33; Luke 20:1–8). The authority of the accuser of humankind, the authority that takes itself as the end of all things, has been vanquished by the "authority" of Christ (Rev. 12:10). If we have authority it is only in the name of Christ, and even then, we

---

[5] Southern Baptist Convention, "Report of the Baptist Faith and Message Study Committee to the Southern Baptist Convention."

[6] Shurden, "The Problem of Authority in the Southern Baptist Convention."

[7] Shurden, "The Problem of Authority in the Southern Baptist Convention," 225.

have it not as entitlement, but as the "servants" to whom authority is entrusted (Mark 13:34) and who remain utterly dependent on the power of the Lord.

However, authoritarianism takes authority as the end of all things; it treats authority as a sort of divine principle removed from history and inherently possessed of goodness, indeed as the highest good. A distinction here between civil and ecclesiastical authority is insufficient, as the difficulty is with the authoritarian principle itself. The authority that takes itself for a god is not from God and therefore Christians need not be subject and submissive to this authority (Rom. 13:1-2).

2. Baptists and the Confessions of the European Reformations

There are at least two ways in which confessional statements of the European Reformations can help pave a way out of this captivity. First, some of the confessional statements of this period illustrate the ways in which the new Christian communities sought to strike a balance between submission to political authority and Christian witness; that is, these confessions recognized that civil authority and Christian witness could be in tension. Second, some of the confessions of the European reformations are still very influential among American evangelicals and they have been important sources for theological authoritarianism. Sorting these confessions out and clarifying their teachings on ecclesiastical and civil authority, can help us identify the root sources of religious support for populist authoritarianism. The following is a discussion of some the most prominent confessions and catechisms of the European reformations, with exclusive attention to their ideas on the Christian understanding of authority.[8]

The usurpation of authority was an important concern of the Protestant Reformation. In fact, in his *Babylonian Captivity of the Church*, Luther spoke against Rome's illegitimate arrogation of ecclesiastical authority. He regarded the withholding of the cup during the celebration of mass as a "tyranny" of the clergy.[9] "It follows, further," he remarked, "that if the church can withhold from the laity one kind, the wine, it can also withhold from them the other, the bread. It could therefore withhold the entire Sacrament of the Altar from the laity and completely annul Christ's institution as far as they are concerned. By what authority, I ask."[10] He concluded that "neither pope nor bishop nor any other man has the right to impose a single syllable of law upon a Christian man without his consent; if he does, it is done in the spirit of tyranny."[11]

---

[8] For an overview see Maag, "Catechisms and Confessions of Faith," 209.

[9] Luther, "Babylonian Captivity of the Church," in *Selected Writings of Martin Luther*, ed. Tappert, 1:379.

[10] Luther, "Babylonian Captivity," in *Selected Writings of Martin Luther*, ed. Tappert, 374.

[11] Luther, "Babylonian Captivity," in *Selected Writings of Martin Luther*, ed. Tappert, 422.

However, evangelical reformers did not only have to define their theology in relation to the Catholic Church. They also had to articulate their positions in relation to radical reform movements. Chief among the latter were the Anabaptists, whose radical antiauthoritarianism posed a challenge to Catholics, Lutherans, and Reformed alike. Such questioning and rejection of ecclesiastic and civil authority was summarized in the *Schleitheim Articles* of the Swiss Anabaptists, drafted in 1527.[12] The Swiss Anabaptist posited a radical separation between those living in Christian perfection and those who didn't. While the former were governed by the "ban"—or ecclesiastical discipline as instituted in Christian perfection, the latter were to be subject to the "sword," or secular authority. God instituted the "sword" for those living outside Christian perfection and magistrates legitimately exercised this power to discipline and punish. Consequently, those living in perfection could not wield the sword in self-defense, or sit as judges, nor take positions of authority as part of the magistracy.[13] The Swiss Anabaptists held a radical view of Christ's authority among those living in Christian perfection and their beliefs earned them the despise of religious groups still holding to the idea of state churches.

During the European reformations, confessions served as norms governing the public ministry of the churches, including their teaching and preaching. Confessions were in this regard instrumental in defining the place of the new communities within territorial states. The *Augsburg Confession* (or the *Augustana*), for example, was drafted as a public statement summarizing the doctrines of Protestant preachers and theologians in Germany. Philip Melanchthon (1497–1560) oversaw the writing of the *Augustana*, which was presented in 1530 before Charles V (1500–1558) at the Diet of Augsburg. The question of authority was of paramount importance in the document. Protestants wanted to leave no doubt about their submission to the emperor's authority. Hence, they addressed the document to Charles V and sought to define their position within the Holy Roman Empire of the German Nation. In the preface, the declaration was described as "a confession of our preachers and of ourselves, the doctrine of which, derived from the Holy Scripture and pure Word of God, they have to this time set forth in our lands, dukedoms, domains, and cities, and have taught in the churches."[14] Protestants hoped to find a peaceful resolution to their doctrinal differences with Rome and, in the event this could not be accomplished in the context of the diet, then they hoped the emperor would endeavor to have the pope summon a general council of the church. In any case, they recognized and affirmed the emperor's authority to which they submitted in obedience.

---

[12] Sattler, "Schleitheim Articles," in *Radical Reformation*, ed. Baylor, 172-80.

[13] Sattler, "Schleitheim Articles," in *Radical Reformation*, ed. Baylor, 176-78.

[14] "Augsburg Confession," in *Creeds of Christendom*, ed. Schaff and Schaff, 3:4.

However, the *Augustana* also set forth the limits of imperial authority. In Article 16, it addressed all things related to the political life of Christians. In contrast to Anabaptists, whom they explicitly denounced, Lutherans asserted that Christians could hold civil office—including the administration of justice be soldiers, and own property. They did not "disallow order and government."[15] To the contrary, the *Augustana* affirmed that Lutherans had a duty to contribute to its preservation and maintenance. The ordinances of government were to be regarded as God's own (*"ordinationes Dei"*). Consequently, all ordinances should be observed with charity.[16]

And yet, the magistracy could only expect this obedience in matters that did not contradict the gospel. Undoubtedly the *Augustana* clearly stated that Christians by necessity "must obey their magistrates and their laws." Nevertheless, citing Acts 5:29 ("But Peter and the apostles answered, 'We must obey God rather than any human authority'") it demarcated the limits of the magistracy's authority as well as the obedience that it could command. Lutherans asserted that the magistracy contravenes its authority in every and all instances in which it demands the obedience that is owed to God. In this way, the *Augustana* acknowledged that the magistracy is always confronted by the potential to overstep its authority and attempt to take the place of God, thus turning demonic. Lutherans confessed that when the magistracy goes beyond its authority then it is no longer a legitimate order instituted by God. Furthermore, they also confessed that at that point the Christian "must obey God rather than any human authority."

The *French Confession*, also known as the *Gallican Confession*, was first drafted for the National Synod of Paris in 1559.[17] It was later revised and adopted in the National Synod of 1571. While it was formerly attributed to John Calvin, in reality the final form was based in two previous versions, one of them coming from Geneva.[18] The Reformed churches of France were at the time experiencing persecution under King Henry II (r. 1547–1559) and his second son, Charles IX (r. 1560–1574). Shortly after its adoption as the symbol of the French Reformed churches, Charles IX ordered the carnage of Protestants that is remembered as the Massacre of St. Bartholomew's Day (August 23–24, 1572). Thus, the *Gallican Confession* sought to observe a delicate balance between proclaiming loyalty to the crown and asserting the faith. As in the case of the *Augustana*, this balance was accomplished in part by denouncing and rejecting the views of Anabaptists and other radical

---

[15] "Augsburg Confession," in *Creeds of Christendom*, ed. Schaff and Schaff, 3:17.

[16] "Augsburg Confession," in *Creeds of Christendom*, ed. Schaff and Schaff, 3:17.

[17] "Confessio Fidei Gallicana," in *Creeds of Christendom*, ed. Schaff and Schaff, 3:56-382; "Gallican Confession," in *Encyclopedia of Protestantism*, ed. Hillerbrand, 2:514.

[18] Maag, "Catechisms and Confessions," 214.

antiauthoritarian groups. The closing section of the Gallican Confession, Article 40, declared: "Therefore we detest all those who would like to reject authority, to establish community and confusion of property, and overthrow the order of justice."[19] French Protestants avowed to obey the law, pay taxes and "bear the yoke of subjection with a good and free will," even if the rulers were "unbelievers." However, they boldly confessed that they would do so "provided that the sovereign empire of God remains intact."[20] The criterion for submission to ecclesiastical authority was summarized in Article 33, and it probably reflects their criterion of submission to civil authority as well. While they rejected all "human inventions," they resigned themselves to accept those things that were conducive to "concord and holds all in obedience, from the greatest to the least."[21] Hence, even under the great pressure of persecution, the French Reformed churches were courageous enough to set limits to ecclesiastical and political authority.

The *Belgic Confession* and the *Heidelberg Catechism* were more precise in their articulation of a Reformed understanding of civil authority and personal obedience. Like the *Gallican Confession*, these confessions were informed by the theology of John Calvin (1509–1569), Theodore Beza (1519–1605), and other leading figures of the Reformed churches. Unlike the *Gallican Confession*, the other two gained notoriety as symbols of international Calvinism and are among the most influential confessions in American evangelicalism. They sought to align Calvinist predestinarianism with the territorial claims of emerging modern nation-states in order to create state churches with the ability to impose religious conformity. In this regard, these confessions mirrored a larger European context shaped by the Peace of Augsburg (1555) and the growing acceptance of the principle of *cuius regio, eius religio* ("he who governs the territory decides its religion"). Crucial for this endeavor was the doctrine of total depravity that was concomitant with Reformed anthropological pessimism. Ironically, these Reformed confessions failed to anticipate how depravity itself would lead to the corruption of those placed in roles of authority as well as of their offices. Instead, they expressed an unqualified faith in the goodness of authority and political structures, which they treated as instituted orders of God's governance. If there was a problem with Catholic tyranny, it had little to do with the structures regulating daily life (as of yet there were no serious challenges to monarchical forms of government) and everything to do with Catholicism.

---

[19] "Confessio Fidei Gallicana," in *Creeds of Christendom*, ed. Schaff and Schaff, 3:382.

[20] "Confessio Fidei Gallicana," in *Creeds of Christendom*, ed. Schaff and Schaff, 3:382.

[21] "Confessio Fidei Gallicana," in *Creeds of Christendom*, ed. Schaff and Schaff, 3:378.

Guy de Bres (1522–1567) was the author of the *Belgic Confession*, which he drafted around 1559.[22] At the time the Low Countries were ruled by the Spanish Habsburgs and the statement was the first Protestant confession in the realm. As in France, Protestants faced severe opposition and unyielding repression under King Philip II (r. 1556–98), who was a devout Catholic. Consequently, the *Belgic Confession* summarized the beliefs of a religious minority. In some parts the *Belgic Confession* treaded very closely to the *Gallican Confession*, which was clearly used as a model. However, the view of civil authority proposed in the *Belgic Confession* was much more elaborate and revealed a more sophisticated perspective, even if significantly contributing to the long-term development of Protestant theological authoritarianism. In fact, Carel F. C. Coetzee described Article 36 of the *Belgic Confession* as setting forth a clearly theocratic model of church-state relations—a model that Coetzee himself advanced for the South African context.[23] Moreover, in his literature review on the subject, Pieter Coertzen situated Article 36 between the Constantinian and theocratic models of society and noted how both models assume an established state church.[24]

Indeed, the doctrine of total depravity is the cornerstone of the theocratic model set forth in Article 36. "We believe," reads the opening line of the article, "that our gracious God, because of the depravity of mankind, has appointed kings, princes, and magistrates, willing that the world should be governed by certain laws and policies." Moreover, the end of all government is, according to this Reformed perspective, "that the dissoluteness of men might be restrained." Quoting 1 Pet. 2:14 ("as sent by him to punish those who do wrong and to praise those who do right"), article 36 explains how God has invested the magistracy with the sword for this purpose. However, the role of the state is not only to restrain debauchery. Instead, the state is also entrusted with the mission of protecting the sacred ministry. As part of that task, the state may "remove and prevent all idolatry and false worship." In this regard, the state is also charged with the destruction of the "kingdom of antichrist" and the promotion of Christ's kingdom. The article ascertains that obedience is due to the state in everything, but it clarifies that obedience must be observed in all demands that "are not repugnant to the Word of God." The closing lines rehearse the condemnation of Anabaptists and "all those who reject the higher powers and magistrates."[25]

---

[22] "Confessio Belgica," in *Creeds of Christendom*, ed. Schaff and Schaff, 3:83-436; Raymond A. Mentzer, "Belgic Confession of 1561," in *Encyclopedia of Protestantism*, ed. Hillerbrand, 1:48–49.

[23] Coetzee, "Godsdiensvryheid in die lig van Artikel 36, NGB."

[24] Coertzen, "Relationship Between Church and State in a Democracy with Guaranteed Freedom of Religion."

[25] "Confessio Belgica," in *Creeds of Christendom*, ed. Schaff and Schaff, 3:432-33.

As in the case of the *Belgic Confession*, the teachings of the *Heidelberg Catechism* on obedience were consistent with Reformed anthropological pessimism and were undermining of personal liberty. Written in 1562 by Zacharias Ursinus (1534–83) and, probably, Caspar Olevian (1536–1587), the *Catechism* was presented to Elector Frederick III and it became the confessional standard of the state church. Ursinus addressed the subject of obedience to authorities in the section of the *Catechism* dedicated to the Ten Commandments, specifically in the exchange generated around the fifth commandment: "Honor your father and your mother, as the Lord your God commanded you" (Deut. 5:16).

The Reformed view on obedience is summarized as a response to the question, "What is God's will for you in the fifth commandment?"[26] The response presages the kind of theological argumentation that informs today's theological authoritarianism and buttresses sympathies for political populist authoritarianism. First, it collapses all intervening institutions found in civil society that mediate between the human person and the state, including families, under a single generic form and category, namely "those in authority over me." Thus, the duty of the Christian is to "honor, love, and be loyal to my father and mother and all those in authority over me." While the *Catechism* underscores the obedience that is owed to all "those in authority," it does not even contemplate the limits of authority, nor even the possibility that authority might behold itself idolatrously. The emphasis is on the obedience and submission of the human person, with no regards for conscience or personal liberty. Perhaps, it couldn't be otherwise in a document predicated upon the idea of the absolute bondage of the human will on account of sin. Yet, it must be remembered that the *Belgic Confession* had greater political realism and, thus, the historical contexts in which these documents were written is to be credited for the different ways in which the idea of obedience was construed. Nevertheless, the *Catechism* failed to recognize the corrupting influence of power and how those with authority over others could abuse and exploit those under them; for there are no qualifications nor restrictions placed on authority. Furthermore, authority is taken as inherently good. "That I submit," the *Catechism* continues, "myself with proper obedience to all their good teaching and discipline." Here is found one of the hallmarks of authoritarianism; authority is taken as intrinsically good, its utterances as good principles, and the correction it administers as always sound, fair, and just. The best that the Christian can do against the abuse of power is to be "patient": "that I be patient with their failings." Those "in authority over

---

[26] I am following the translation approved by the 2011 Synod of the Christian Reformed Church: *Heidelberg Catechism*, online https://www.crcna.org/welcome/beliefs/confessions/ heidelberg-catechism; "Heidelberg Catechism," in *Creeds of Christendom*, ed. Schaff and Schaff, 3:345.

me" may fail, but their shortcomings are nothing more than flows and deficiencies. The possibility that authority may be corrupted, perverted, debauched, and even go wayward is not even envisaged. The basis for this absent mindedness about the malleable and supple character of authority is faulty biblical reasoning: "for through them God chooses to rule us." [27] God may have chosen to rule humanity through them, but God never intended for them to become like God, nor to take God's place.

The *Westminster Confession* was of greater consequence for Baptists. Drafted by the divines gathered at the Westminster Assembly, it was completed by December 1646 and sanctioned by Parliament in 1648. Together with the *Directory of Public Worship* (1645), the *Westminster Larger Catechism* and the *Westminster Shorter Catechism*, the *Westminster Confession* provided the blueprint for the reformation of the Church of England under the "Long Parliament" (1640–60). The theology of the *Westminster Confession* was in line with continental Reformed orthodoxy. However, it had a marked Erastian (from Thomas Erastus, 1524–83) influence resulting in the greater ascendancy it gave to the civil authority over the church.[28]

The *Westminster Confession* exceeded the *Belgic Confession* in its comprehensive treatment—quite extensive for a confessional statement—of civil authority.[29] Moreover, as in the *Belgic Confession*, it posited that civil authority had a positive responsibility to govern in matters of religion. In chapter 20, the *Westminster Confession* described civil and ecclesiastical authority as "powers" ordained by God and concluded that "they who, upon pretense of Christian liberty, shall oppose any lawful power, or the lawful exercise of it, whether it be civil or ecclesiastical, resist the ordinance of God." Furthermore, it confined Christian liberty to a sort of spiritual realm, defining it solely as the "freedom from the guilt of sin, and condemning wrath of God." Any possible contradictions between Christian liberty and "the powers which God has ordained" were preemptively disallowed as both were declared to have been intended by God not to destroy but to uphold each other.[30]

The divines and laypersons gathered at Westminster were gravely concerned with the preservation of "the external peace and order which Christ has established in the Church." Consequently, they exalted the power of the civil magistrate to defend both civil and ecclesiastical order. In chapter 23, the *Westminster Confession* declared that God has ordained the civil magistrate to be "under [God], over the

---

[27] "Heidelberg Catechism," in *Creeds of Christendom*, ed. Schaff and Schaff, 3:345.

[28] Morrill, "The Puritan Revolution."

[29] "Westminster Confession of Faith," in *Creeds of Christendom*, ed. Schaff and Schaff, 3:600-73.

[30] "Westminster Confession of Faith," in *Creeds of Christendom*, ed. Schaff and Schaff, 3:643-45.

people, for [God's] own glory, and the public good." Drawing on Rom. 13:1–4, it asserted that God "armed" the civil magistrate with the power of the sword. The ultimate purpose of this power and authority was to promote the observance of piety, the practice of justice and the prevalence of peace. In order to accomplish this, the civil magistrate could lawfully wage war "upon just and necessary occasion." The civil magistrate could not as such preach or administer the sacraments, nor implement ecclesiastical discipline. However, the Westminster Assembly declared that the civil magistrate could take all necessary actions to ensure that these activities be carried out correctly, according to good doctrine, and for the health of the realm. The authority of the civil magistrate to extirpate heresy and even enforce religious conformity, according to the *Westminster Confession*, was ordained by God and, therefore, it was the duty of all Christians to simply obey.[31]

Interestingly, the Westminster Assembly made explicit its faith and trust in the inherent goodness of authority and the political structures that it assumed to be of divine origin and inspiration. Obedience to the civil magistrate was unconditional, with no indication that disobedience could ever be considered a legitimate option. Moreover, the Assembly did not regard obedience as a contingent matter dependent upon the religion of the civil magistrate. To the contrary, it asserted that "infidelity, or difference in religion, does not make void the magistrates' just and legal authority."[32] In fact, of the Reformed confessions only the *Scottish Confession* (1560) spoke of "repressing tyranny" as a duty.[33]

Lastly, it is necessary to keep in mind that seventeenth century Baptists were terribly worried about the usurpation of Christ's authority. Thomas Helwys (c. 1570–1616) challenged the Reformed understanding of civil authority as a divinely instituted order that is beyond questioning. Instead, he asserted the preeminence of conscience. As he wrote: "It is spiritual obedience that the Lord requires, and the king's sword cannot smite the spirits of men."[34] He acknowledged the authority of the king, but not in matters of conscience. He regarded as a "great cruel tyranny" for the king to "force men's consciences in their religion to God." [35]

---

[31] "Westminster Confession of Faith," in *Creeds of Christendom*, ed. Schaff and Schaff, 3:652–55.

[32] "Westminster Confession of Faith," in *Creeds of Christendom*, ed. Schaff and Schaff, 3:652–55.

[33] "Confession Fidei Scoticana," in *Creeds of Christendom*, ed. Schaff and Schaff, 3:437–79, 454 (art. 14).

[34] Helwys, "Short Declaration of the Mystery of Iniquity," in *Life and Writings of Thomas Helwys*, ed. Early, 193.

[35] Helwys, "Short Declaration of the Mystery of Iniquity," in *Life and Writings of Thomas Helwys*, ed. Early, 193.

Hanserd Knollys also voiced this apprehension in his writings. In his *A Moderate Response* (1645) he characterized the Diotrephes mentioned in 3 John 9-10 as one who committed an "evil" deed by "usurping authority over the church and those brethren whom he cast out of the church." Furthermore, this usurper of authority would "lord it over the church, and have the pre-eminence above his brethren, whether fellow elders or fellow saints."[36] In *Mystical Babylon Availed* (1679), he blamed the papacy for wrongfully assuming authority. He poured typical Protestant anti-popery vitriol in this track, which he wrote when rumors of the Popish Plot where still dominating popular imagination throughout England. He argued that the papacy was not a "lawful power ordained of God." While the papacy had power, it did not have authority because it did not have "God's approbation" to function as an order of magistracy. The papacy effectively "usurped" the power of the "Roman kingdom."[37]

Yet, early English Baptists also had to negotiate authority in their daily lives. They were not radical antiauthoritarians, but understood that authority, especially stately authority, was to be limited. Hence, in their *Public Dispute* (1645), Benjamin Coxe, Hanserd Knollys, and William Kiffin confessed their submission to civil authority. They avowed to be "ready to obey our civil magistrates, as to profess our subjection to his authority in all lawful commands." They offered to publicly display their "willing and loyal subjection to the magistrate's civil authority," but only within the limits of the magistrate's "lawful power." [38] A similar perspective on the authority of, and the obedience owed to, civil authority was summarized in "A Brief Confession or Declaration of Faith" of 1660. In fact, the General Baptists followed the pattern of other Protestant communities of setting forth their core beliefs in summary statements. They, however, departed from the norm of assuming the inherent goodness of authority and structures of government. In this regard, they made clear their "whole, and holy intent and purpose, that (through the help of grace)" they would "not yield, nor [...] in the least actually obey" any impositions in matters of religion that did violence to their conscience. Citing Acts 5:29, they confessed that it was better to obey God rather than humans.[39] In this way, they placed crucial limits on civil authority and the kind and degree of obedience that it can require.

---

[36] Knollys, "A Moderate Response," in *Collected Works of Hanserd Knollys*, ed. Pitts and Roldán-Figueroa, 54.

[37] Knollys, "Mystical Babylon Availed," in *Collected Works of Hanserd Knollys*, ed. Pitts and Roldán-Figueroa, 134.

[38] Coxe, Knollys, and Kiffin, "A Public Dispute," in *Collected Works of Hanserd Knollys*, , ed. Pitts and Roldán-Figueroa, 79.

[39] "A Brief Confession or Declaration of Faith," in *Baptist Life and Thought*, rev. ed., ed. Brackney, 72.

3. Confessing the Faith Against Populist Authoritarianism

Early English Baptists had the ability to distinguish the rightful exercise of authority from the unjust arrogation of power. They developed a critical understanding of authority because this was their first order of the day. Baptists today must rediscover the ability to confess the faith against populist authoritarianism and any form of idolatry that seeks to usurp the authority of Christ. The ability to confess is a practical ability and thus it can be cultivated by all congregations. Concrete steps include reflection about roles and figures of authority in worship and communal life. The most transformative questions in this regard always start with "why." Why do we talk about the authority of the Bible? Why does the pastor have authority in the church? Why do people tend to recognize the authority of male and heterosexual leaders? Why do people tend to disregard the authority of women and queer leaders? Why do persons with disabilities seldom occupy positions of authority? Why are children always subject to authority and expected not to question authority? In fact, the best practice to confess the faith against populist authoritarianism is to question and interrogate authority. There is no better place to learn to do this than in the Christian church.

4. For Further Reading

Bell, Marty. "James Robinson Graves and the Rhetoric of Demagogy: Primitivism and Democracy in Old Landmarkism." Ph.D. diss., Vanderbilt University, 1990.

Gunnoe, Charles D., Karin Maag, Paul W. Fields, and Lyle D. Bierma. *An Introduction to the Heidelberg Catechism: Sources, History and Theology*. Grand Rapids, MI: Baker Academic, 2005.

Diefendorf, Barbara B. *Beneath the Cross: Catholics and Hughuenots in Sixteenth-Century Paris*. Oxford: Oxford University Press, 1991.

Gootjes, Nicolaas Hendrik. *The Belgic Confession: Its History and Sources*. Grand Rapids, MI: Baker Academic, 2007.

Schroeder, Edward H. *Gift and Promise: The Augsburg Confession and the Heart of Christian Theology*. Minneapolis: Fortress Press, 2016.

Weaver, C. Douglas. *In Search of the New Testament Church: The Baptist Story*. Macon, GA: Mercer University Press, 2008.

Wills, Gregory A. *Democratic Religion: Freedom, Authority, and Church Discipline in the Baptist South, 1785-1900*. Oxford: Oxford University Press, 2003.

18

Light from Baptist Confessions of Faith

Stephen R. Holmes

Baptist Christianity begins in confession. This is true historically in multiple ways. The little fellowship of John Smyth and Thomas Helwys, in exile in Amsterdam, produced no less than four significant confessions between 1609 and 1611 in their efforts to understand who they had become by submitting to (re)baptism at Smyth's hand. The first three of these[1] were negotiations with the Waterlander Mennonites which grew out of Smyth's concern that his se-baptism had been inappropriate and was invalid, and that he should instead have sought baptism from the Mennonites. The last, Helwys's 1611 *Declaration of Faith*, is an attempt to distinguish the (tiny) church remaining from the Mennonites and is generally considered the first Baptist confession.[2] Its twenty-seven articles are rich in Scripture and offer a condensed account of the chief heads of theology (Trinity, creation, Christology, redemption, etc.) and an extended ecclesiology. It is clear that the it is intended to distinguish the English Church from the Mennonites: anabaptist posi-

---

[1] The text of John Smyth's "Short Confession of Faith in XX Articles" can be found in Burrage, *Early English Dissenters in the Light of Recent Research*, 2:182-84, and Lumpkin, ed., *Baptist Confessions of Faith*, 2nd ed.,100-01. (Page references to the Lumpkin edition of *Baptist Confessions of Faith* throughout this chapter are to the second edition; an updated revised expansion of the second edition edited by Bill J. Leonard, which has a different pagination for the corresponding confessions, is listed in the "For Further Reading" bibliography at the end of this chapter. The revised second edition includes a substantial revision of the Southern Baptist Convention's *Baptist Faith and Message* adopted in 2000 as well as additional recent statements and confessions from various unions and institutions in the global Baptist community.) Helwys's party sought to prevent Smyth and others joining the Mennonites, and drew up their own confession, titled "Synopsis fides, verae Christianae Ecclesiae Anglican, Amsterdamiae." This may be found in Burrage, *Early English Dissenters in the Light of Recent Research*, 2:182-84. Smyth and others agreed to sign the 1610 *Short Confession*, which is largely an English translation of a 1580 Mennonite confession (with, however, some important omissions) which Smyth and others agreed to sign; see Burrage, *Early English Dissenters in the Light of Recent Research*, 2:187-200 for the original text and Lumpkin, ed., *Baptist Confessions of Faith*, 102-13, for a version rendered into modern English (curiously claiming to be translated from a Dutch original).

[2] Lumpkin, ed., *Baptist Confessions of Faith*, 116-23.

tions on the magistracy (art. 24) and taking oaths (art. 25) are rejected explicitly (and Menno's idiosyncratic Christology is quietly but explicitly repudiated as well in art. 8³). The ecclesiology is common enough to the English Separatist tradition—the account of baptism excepted, of course—but as such is already recognizably Baptist in all points. The local congregation is fully church in its own right and has power and responsibility to elect its own officers, both elders and deacons (interestingly, the confession specifies that both men and women can be deacons); excommunication is the only mode of church discipline. In a nice polemical swipe, the long article asserting (against the Mennonites) that the magistracy is ordained by God, an appropriate Christian vocation, and properly bears the power of the sword, is mostly a quotation from an earlier publication of Smyth. The publication of this confession, demonstrating that Helwys's congregation stands in a different tradition to the Mennonites, might be regarded as the decisive moment in the beginnings of the Baptist movement. Might such decisive moments in which Baptists have offered this sort of confession of their faith shed light on the efforts of Baptist churches to practice theology today? This chapter seeks to answer that question by (1) tracing the history of Baptist confessions of faith and their varied purposes, forms, and reception; (2) suggesting principles that might guide our listening to the varied voices of these confessions; and (3) gesturing toward what we might actually do with the light—and limitations—of the products of these confessional practices of theology by previous Baptist communities.

1. The History and Variety of Baptist Confessions

Of course, Helwys's 1611 *Declaration of Faith* is far from the last confession written by Baptists in the seventeenth century. Another again demonstrates that, in a different historical sense this time, Baptist Christianity begins in confession. Just as Helwys's church was negotiating its particular position in dialogue with Robinson's church, Johnson's "Ancient Church," and the Waterlanders, so in London in the 1640s a number of proto-Baptist congregations that had mostly split off from the Jacob-Lathrop-Jessey church were beginning to coalesce into a self-consciously single movement. The 1644 *London Confession*,[4] affirmed together by seven congregations (which we would now term Particular Baptists, but they owned themselves

---

³ Menno—and so, presumably, the Amsterdam Waterlanders, although I know of no explicit evidence for this—held to a "heavenly flesh" Christology, according to which the human nature that was assumed into union with the divine Logos was created *ex nihilo* by God. Helwys writes that Jesus is "the Sonne of Marie the Virgine, made of hir substance, Gal. 4.4." (Lumpkin, ed., *Baptist Confessions of Faith*, 119). This ("made of hir substance") is a direct denial of Menno's doctrine of *ex nihilo* creation of the human nature.

⁴ Lumpkin, ed., *Baptist Confessions of Faith*, 153-71.

then simply to be "Churches of Christ in London"[5]), stands as a decisive marker of this growing sense of self-identity.[6] Shared confession made them a distinctive group ("denomination" may not be too strong), with doctrinal agreement and boundary, where before they had merely been similar streams of something larger and more amorphous. Confessing together made them distinctively Baptist.

A consideration of some other seventeenth-century English confessions demonstrates the variety of uses of symbolic documents for Baptists. The 1660 *Standard Confession* of the General Baptists[7] is less theologically adroit than the 1644 Particular Baptist document; it also comes from a group that was already self-consciously formed into a national organization. The first General Assembly of General Baptists[8] had been held in 1654, and meetings were held annually from then on. 1660 saw the unhappy collision of two crises, however: externally the political turmoil that culminated in the Restoration led to a rekindling of rumors about Baptists being dangerous revolutionaries; internally a debate about Christology was threatening the unity of the movement.[9] The *Standard Confession* was therefore an attempt to protect internal unity and external reputation (it ends, remarkably, with an emphatic insistence that rumors that Baptists have "gotten knives, hooked knives, & the like, & great store of Arms besides"[10] are false).

The 1677 *Second London Confession* (often known as the 1689 Confession in the USA because it was re-affirmed by a Particular Baptist national assembly that met soon after Toleration was extended) is another interesting document. It is an edited version of the famous 1646 Presbyterian *Westminster Confession*, which was also the basis of the Congregationalist 1658 "Savoy Declaration." When published in 1677, the Confession was explicitly stated to be written "making use of the very same words with them both, in these articles (which are very many) wherein our faith and doctrine is the same with theirs…to manifest our consent with both in all

---

[5] From the preface: Lumpkin, ed., *Baptist Confessions of Faith*, 156.

[6] On this see Birch, *To Follow the Lambe Wheresoever He Goeth*.

[7] Lumpkin, ed., *Baptist Confessions of Faith*, 224-35. I have written on the various editions of the "Standard Confession," and their textual variants, in Holmes, "Note Concerning the Text, Editions, and Authorship of the 1660 Standard Confession of the General Baptists."

[8] The term might be anachronistic, but it is not significantly so. The first reference to "General Baptist" as a title that I can find is in 1661: Adis, *A Fannaticks Addresse Humbly Presented*, 12, where he describes his co-religionists as "General Baptists."

[9] I have argued that the *Standard Confession* was written in part to respond to the first stirring of arguments about Caffyn's Christology in Holmes, "Note Concerning the Text, Editions, and Authorship of the 1660 Standard Confession of the General Baptists," 6-7.

[10] Emphasis original.

the fundamental articles of the Christian Religion...."[11] The Confession, that is, in time of persecution, was a deliberate attempt at pan-protestant ecumenism, written to demonstrate and emphasize just how much was shared by the three Calvinistic Dissenting denominations.[12] A group of General Baptists were inspired by this example to write their own "pan-protestant" confession, the *Orthodox Creed* of 1678. Its full title demonstrates the ambition: "An Orthodox Creed, or A Protestant Confession of Faith, Being an Essay to Unite and Confirm all True Protestants in the Fundamental Articles of the Christian Religion Against the Errors and Heresies of Rome." It is clear that the *Orthodox Creed* was at the same time an attempt to repudiate Matthew Caffyn's heterodox Christology, and so it had an eye on internal differentiation at the same time as proclaiming broad external unity. Its reception amongst the General Baptists was not generally positive (Thomas Grantham re-published the 1660 *Standard Confession* with addenda in opposition to the *Orthodox Creed*, for example), and there is no evidence of which I am aware for any recognition beyond the denomination.

In the seventeenth century, then, English Baptists used confessional documents to:

1. Distinguish themselves from other church traditions;

2. Find shared identity between like-minded congregations;

3. Address external slanders;

4. Patch up internal divisions;

5. Demonstrate their similarity to other church traditions; and

6. Demand conformity to one side of internal divisions.[13]

This is a very varied list and contains two pairs of uses that appear to be in fairly direct opposition (which is of course not a problem; the same literary form can be used for different, even opposing, purposes). It is also a list that would be expanded in some surprising ways if we moved beyond seventeenth-century England—some Scandinavian Baptists produced confessional material because they were required

---

[11] Anonymous, *A Confession of Faith put forth by the Elders and Brethren of Many Congregations...*(1677) from the prefatory letter "To the Judicious and Impartial Reader," which is unpaginated, but I count the location as p. iv.

[12] "...hereby declaring before God, Angels, & Men, our hearty agreement with them, in that wholesome Protestant Doctrine..." (*Confession of Faith put forth by the Elders and Brethren of Many Congregations*," p. v).

[13] McBeth, *The Baptist Heritage*, 66-67 claims that early Baptists never used confessions in a prescriptive sense; the evidence does not support this, however.

to by the governing authorities, for instance.[14] However, it might give us pause when we seek to make an appeal, as I have been invited to do by the set theme of this chapter, to "Baptist confessional resources" as a whole: we will need to find some unifying feature amidst the diversity to make the appeal credible.

The variation in purpose of Baptist confessional material also leads to a variation in form. Even amongst the seventeenth-century English confessions so far mentioned, some can be fitted on two pages, others run to dozens; some focus on controversial material, others are irenic attempts to locate Baptists within a broader tradition. This variation only grows wider as we extend beyond England and beyond the seventeenth century. My own denomination, the Baptist Union of Scotland, unites around a *Declaration of Principle* dating from 1908, that contains three clauses totaling 127 words;[15] the largest Baptist denomination in the world, the Southern Baptist Convention, updated its confessional document, the *Baptist Faith and Message*, in 2000, to a version that runs to over 5,000 words, and comes complete with almost half as much text again in a commentary on the final article on the family.[16]

Regarding variety, we must note finally the variety of reception. Some documents are controversial even within the community that produced them; others are generally welcomed. Some are adopted as models by other Baptist organizations.[17] Some function as important identity markers, repeatedly reflected on and appealed to; others are largely ignored.[18]

If a document is received neither widely nor generally, we must query its status as a relevant confessional text. The 1678 *Orthodox Creed* is perhaps a good example here: although well-known to historians now, and whatever judgement is made of its quality as a piece of theological writing, it was controversial on publication (as noted above) and was never received as a confessional document by any denominational body. It is therefore perhaps better read as a private theological treatise (akin, perhaps, to Thomas Monck's *Cure;*[19]). Some sense that a confession-

---

[14] Johnson, *A Global Introduction to Baptist Churches*, 390.

[15] Baptist Union of Scotland, "Declaration of Principle."

[16] Southern Baptist Convention, "Baptist Faith and Message (2000)."

[17] The 1963 "Baptist Faith and Message" was for a time received as a confessional document by the European Baptist Federation, and by Baptist denominations in Spain, Portugal, and Greece, for example. See Parker, *Baptists in Europe*, 243.

[18] It is striking, for example, that in scholarly discussions of Baptist identity in various parts of the world, there is often little or no mention of any confessional material, suggesting that those documents that do exist are not "live" in any sense. See for example the various papers in Randall, Pilli, and Cross, eds., *Baptist Identities*, or the various discussions of "evolving traditioning sources" around the Baptist world in Johnson, *Global Introduction to Baptist Churches*.

[19] Monck, *A Cure for the Cankering Errors of the New Eutychians*; Monck was involved in the writing of the *Orthodox Creed*.

al text has been received by a Baptist church or organization seems necessary before we consider it to be adequately confessional.

2. Listening to the Witness of the Confessions: Principles

This variety of form, content, and reception of the confessional documents creates a problem for us: how do we appeal to such a varied collection of documents in a responsible way? There is, however, a prior question: should we so appeal? On what argument might we claim that we Baptists should pay attention to our earlier denominational confessional documents?

We might assert that there is something pristine or basic, about our foundational confessional documents. Such an assertion must be based on a suggestion that there is something pure or decisive about the origins of the Baptist movement, and so that foundational documents carry weight that nothing later can achieve, but this argument does not work in any formulation I can construct. There is a proper conservatism in Baptist and Christian traditions, a constant looking back to the apostles, and certainly this impulse to do church as church was done in the New Testament times is central to Baptist beginnings, and to virtually every Baptist renewal movement since.[20] That said, Thomas Helwys or John Spilsbury or Sabine Staresmore were not apostles, and a Baptist commitment to living as the apostles lived will not highlight the first half of the seventeenth century as particularly decisive. We seek to live as Thomas and John and Mary Magdalene did, not as Helwys and Spilsbury and Staresmore did, and we expect to revise our accounts of how best to live up to that ideal over time. The testimony of the seventeenth-century founders was, to quote Smyth's sometime co-pastor John Robinson, that "the Lord hath more truth yet to break forth out of His Holy Word."[21]

This leads to a second suggestion: perhaps, because of this continual gift of new insight given by God, we should prioritize our most recent confessional documents. Baptists are pilgrim people, constantly journeying forward into new truth and light; our refusal to settle on a foundational historical confession (as, say, our Presbyterian sisters and brothers have done) is evidence of this. We frame and re-frame as more light and more truth come, sometimes writing new confessions, sometimes editing old ones. To take only one example, the *Baptist Faith and Message* was first written in 1925 and was a revision of the 1833 *New Hampshire Con-*

---

[20] Underwood, *Primitivism, Radicalism, and the Lamb's War*, draws out an interesting distinction in this connection: he suggests that early Quakers believed that, in the Spirit, they could enter the "Great Time" and share experience with the apostles, whereas early Baptists admitted historical distance from the apostles, but tried to live as the apostles had lived.

[21] Robinson's words (perhaps apocryphal) are recounted in Winslow, *Hypocrisie Unmasked*; see George, *John Robinson and the English Separatist Tradition*, vii.

fession of Faith; it was revised in 1963, amended in 1998, and again revised completely in 2000; it is a living document, responsible to the changing convictions of the Southern Baptist Convention. Is it the case that, because God is leading us on, the 2000 edition is necessarily better than the one written in 1925?

If we believed that every changed Baptist conviction was simply a reflection of new truth found in Scripture, we would be right to prioritize our newest documents, as containing our purest perception of divine truth; few of us would be completely confident about this, however. Sometimes our changed sense of what is right has been a capitulation to the spirit of the age, not a faithful following of the prompting of God's Spirit. We also have to acknowledge that there have been moments in our history when competing confessional documents have been proposed, solidifying honestly differing beliefs about the truths that God is making known amongst us.[22] Giving priority to the newest document is not an acceptable Baptist practice any more than giving priority to the oldest is. New documents can be controversial and rapidly forgotten; even if initially successful, they might eventually be judged to be inadequate.

If neither our most ancient nor our most recent attempts at confession are to be privileged, is there any reason to privilege any attempt at confession? There may be documents to which a given Baptist writer or fellowship is required to give attention to by virtue of their ecclesial context. As an elder of St. Andrews Baptist Church, I have indicated my consent to our fellowship's *Basis of Faith*, and it would be wrong of me to teach in opposition to that confession without first remitting my office. Similarly, as an accredited minister of the Baptist Union of Scotland, I am committed in some sense to respect the *Declaration of Principle* of that Union. Again, my local fellowship is clearly responsible to its own *Basis of Faith*, and it is also responsible to the foundational document of the Union of which it is a part. Such commitments are to be taken significantly, of course, but beyond such particular local contexts, is there any reason for me (or my church fellowship) to give more attention to specifically confessional documents than to other documents of Baptist history?

Let me specify the question to demonstrate its force. I closed the last section with passing reference to Monck's *Cure*, which may be the most theologically-accomplished treatment of the doctrine of God by a seventeenth-century General Baptist and shows a remarkable grasp of classical Trinitarianism (particularly given Monck's lack of formal education). There is no question in my mind that it is a much more serious theological document than the 1660 *Standard Confession*. Its length helps, of course, as does the fact that it is the work of a single writer, and so

---

[22] Grantham's republication and expansion of the 1660 *Standard Confession* in response to the writing of the *Orthodox Creed* is an obvious example, already referenced in this chapter.

not a text that is forced to codify compromise (which every confessional text does to some extent, and which the *Standard Confession* was written in part at least to do), but more than that it just displays a sure grasp of classical Christian doctrine which is absent from the *Confession*. Why, then, should we pay more attention to the *Confession* than to the *Cure*?

Were we not Baptists, that question would be relatively easy to answer. We would have some account of how God guides the church through synods and councils, and so we would privilege the *Confession* as having been agreed (and repeatedly re-affirmed) by responsible synods. I do not regard that as a strong argument for Baptists, however.[23] Instead, we might argue that, whatever our private views on the quality of the two documents, the reception history of the Confession gives it a privileged status. I have argued before that the broad reception of a confessional text gives it a de facto authority within the receiving community:[24] consider this argument as applied to the *Standard Confession*. Written in 1660, it was re-affirmed in 1663, returned to by Grantham in 1678 as a place to stand in opposing the *Orthodox Creed*, and then re-published in the 1690s as a definition of the limits of acceptable orthodoxy in the debates over Caffyn's doctrine of God. It crossed the Atlantic and was sporadically appealed to by American Free Will Baptists until the writing of the 1812 *Former Articles* (which themselves owed something to the *Standard Confession*). That is to say, it is a document that successive generations of General/Free Will Baptists recognized themselves in for a century and a half, in a series of very different contexts: in England, under the Commonwealth, after the Restoration, during the persecution of the Clarendon Code, and under toleration; in America, either side of the War of Independence, at least.

This broad historical and cultural reception, I propose, should lead us to regard the document as peculiarly worthy of our attention. Whatever our private judgements as to its worth, a remarkably wide variety of Baptists found it adequate as a description of who they were, and so we must regard it as a particularly successful piece of Baptist self-description, which is therefore worthy of the sustained attention of anyone who is concerned with the question of what it is to be Baptist. I might launch an argument that Monck's *Cure* (or Grantham's *Christianismus Primitivus*, or whatever) should be regarded as a powerful account of what it is to be a General/Arminian Baptist, but the *Standard Confession* has that status already by virtue of its reception history.

If we move beyond this particular example, we might note that, of the seventeenth-century English texts mentioned above, several vanished into obscurity,

---

[23] Even if national conventions are regarded as having ecclesial status, it is weak. See Jones, *The European Baptist Federation*, 27-31.

[24] Holmes, *Listening to the Past*, 153-64.

known only to historians, if to them. The four confessions produced by Smyth and Helwys around 1610 and the *Orthodox Creed* fall into this category. Others had an afterlife, sometimes lengthy, becoming touchstone documents which were returned to again and again by Baptist communities over decades and even centuries because they were found to express powerfully something of what it meant to be Baptist. The two *London Confessions* and the *Standard Confession* fall into this category. If Baptists in widely varying historical, cultural, and geographical contexts have often found in these particular texts an authentic and useful expression of what it is to be Baptist, then that is already an argument—not decisive, but significant—that the text expresses something powerful about Baptist identity, and so should be taken seriously.

On this basis we might identify a handful of texts as being key markers of Baptist identity because of their reception over the years: the two seventeenth-century *London Confessions*; the 1660 *Standard Confession*; and the 1833 *New Hampshire Confession* would be in the first rank here in the English-speaking world. Other confessional documents have not been as widely received, and so may be held to be less significant.

This argument privileges texts of a certain age, of course, but only in terms of recognition or proof. There is nothing in this argument to deny that a more modern text may be a better expression of Baptist identity than any of the above-named confessions; but its worth cannot yet be said to be proved with the same level of certainty. (That said, the breadth of cultural and geographical reception is also a part of the argument above: suppose a document were produced tomorrow which was quickly adopted as a new doctrinal standard by the Southern Baptist Convention, the National Baptist Convention, the Baptist Union of Great Britain, the Baptist World Alliance, and Anglophone Baptist groups across Africa, Asia, and Australasia; my argument would recognize it as having very significant authority, even though it was very young.)

All this suggests a series of principles as to how we might make and judge appeals to our varied confessional inheritance:

> a. The relative importance of any given confessional document may be determined by its breadth of reception, and we should give more significance to more important documents.

> b. We should give more significance to positions advanced in a number of documents, particularly if they come from diverse contexts (where "diverse" might mean: historically separated; geographically widespread; crossing major cultural barriers; or similar).

> c. Any position of even moderate significance on these criteria must be acd. cepted as a possible "Baptist" position.

d. On this basis, there will be many topics on which Baptists have disagreed and do disagree, and no side in those disputes may claim that their opponents are less than authentically Baptist.

e. Nonetheless, there are topics on which there is a remarkable unanimity in the confessional material, and this unanimity must be heard with profound seriousness given the general diversity on display.

f. We should, finally, give attention to any sustained witness to seriously counter-cultural positions advanced in confessional documents, because the points where we have felt the need to visibly reject our home culture carry particular weight.

It will be noted that these principles, particularly b, but also f, allow not just for the witness of what I termed the "first rank" documents above, but also less influential documents, particularly if an impressive number of them speak with the same voice, or if a noticeable minority assert the same counter-cultural position. If Baptists across the world and down through history have affirmed substantially the same point in a series of different confessions, that point carries great weight according to my argument, even if each individual confession which affirms it is relatively minor. The burden of proof here is low.

This line of reflection also leads us to ways of recognizing regional or historical differences in Baptist identity. I once argued that British Baptist confessional material has been persistently unusual—from sixteenth-century Separatist precursors through to the confessional documents of today—in locating its Scripture-principle under its Christology (rather than in prolegomena, or under pneumatology);[25] if this is right, then it allows us to assert something about specifically British Baptist identity which sets it in some distinction to broader streams of Baptist life. Similarly, we might be able to argue that there is something specific about nineteenth-century Baptist identity, or about General/Arminian Baptist identity, on the basis of shared doctrines in significant confessional material that are not found more widely.

3. The Witness of our Confessions

At this point it would be natural to turn to an extended synoptic comparison of a wide variety of confessional documents, together with an analysis of their historical, geographical, and cultural significance, in order to investigate what is on this evidence core to Baptist identity, and where allowable diversity lies. Such a project must wait for another day. On the one hand, it is far too ambitious in scope to

---

[25] Holmes, "Baptists and the Bible."

essay in a brief chapter such as this; on the other, the prior work of collecting, and narrating the reception of, the documents remains to be done, at least beyond the narrow confines of the U.K. and North America.[26] (In noting the cultural limitations of the confessional material that has been received and celebrated in our denomination, we must also note that it displays all the standard biases of European/Western history: it was written, utterly disproportionately, by straight, white, able-bodied men.)

That said, what can we do with the material we have? There are assertions that we may make as at least true of the transatlantic Anglophone movement, with their broader applicability undecided pending better investigation of broader streams of Baptist confessional material. We would find many doctrines simply affirmed by this: some sort of doctrine of the Trinity, a confession of the incarnation, a commitment to the authority of Scripture, an account of the necessity of the new birth for salvation, baptism as a mark of salvation, church membership as the proper place for Christian discipleship and sanctification; the incompetence of civil rulers to demand particular practices of belief and worship, and so some account of freedom of conscience—all this would be very broadly confessed, and so properly regarded as essential to being Baptist.

Again, there are other issues on which we find genuine diversity in our confessional material, with enough weight on either side to force us to say that, at least historically, both positions have been authentically Baptist. It is clear that the Calvinist-Arminian debate fits here, but other, perhaps more surprising issues, do so also. Consider the controverted question of where Baptists stand in relation to other Protestants: do we identify as a strand of a broader Reformed movement, or as something much more separate and distinctive? Our confessional heritage would suggest that both are authentically Baptist positions. We cannot deny the importance of the 1677/1689 *Second London Confession*, which (as noted above) is an intentional attempt to locate Baptists in a pan-Protestant alliance; equally, we have to acknowledge that, as such, it is unusual amongst our confessions, and that (again, to use the example already narrated), the General Baptist preference for the *Standard Confession* over the *Orthodox Creed* is a powerful and sustained witness in the other direction.[27]

---

[26] Parker, *Baptists in Europe*, offers a very helpful collection of (English translations of) Baptist confessional material from across Europe, but no data on which to evaluate the reception of the various documents, which I have argued is crucial.

[27] The 1610 *Short Confession*, being adapted from an earlier Mennonite text, is the only confession (known to the author) that would suggest an attempt to locate Baptists as part of a broader Anabaptist tradition; given its context (opposed by Helwys and his congregation) and lack of later reception, it is hard to use it for an argument that this is also a position attested to confessionally.

Finally, there are what we might term "significant idiosyncrasies"—positions, or constructions, that are by no means universal in our Baptist confessional heritage, but that are sufficiently visible that we have to accept them as authentically Baptist, and that are unquestionably eccentric when compared to the wider doctrinal tradition. The attempt, visible in the 1644/1646 *London Confession* and other less well-known documents, to construct the whole economy of salvation under the threefold office of Christ (as prophet, priest, and king) would be an example: it is borrowed from Separatist writings, but it stands in confessional terms as a uniquely Baptist attempt to organize doctrine. The 1677/1689 *Second London Confession* follows a different pattern, learned *from* its Presbyterian precursor, and so we cannot pretend that the distinctive pattern of 1644/1646 is the only Baptist way, but it stands as a pregnant suggestion of a different and authentically Baptist way of thinking about the economy of salvation. On the criteria developed in this chapter, it cannot command our assent, but it can require us to consider its claims. To be forced to consider a different approach is often a gift indeed.

4. For Further Reading

Freeman, Curtis W., ed. *Perspectives in Religious Studies* 29, no. 4 (Winter 2002) [Thematic issue on Baptist confessions of faith with articles by Freeman, Philip E. Thompson, Steven R. Harmon, Barry Harvey, Mikael N. Broadway, J. Deotis Roberts, E. Frank Tupper, and William L. Hendricks].

Lumpkin, William L., ed. *Baptist Confessions of Faith*. Rev. ed. Valley Forge, PA: Judson Press, 1969.

_____, ed. *Baptist Confessions of Faith*. 2nd rev. ed. Revised by Bill J. Leonard. Valley Forge, PA: Judson Press, 2011.

Parker, G. Keith. *Baptists in Europe: History and Confessions of Faith*. Nashville: Broadman Press, 1982.

19

Light from Catholic Magisterial Sources

Coleman Fannin

This chapter proposes that Baptist congregations should study the documents and other statements issued by the Catholic magisterium, the teaching authority of the Catholic Church, in order to address the perennial challenge posed by the subjectivity of the theological and ethical judgments of individuals, a challenge intensified by consumerism and the decline of Baptist associations and conventions. It further encourages Baptist congregations to study the deliberative processes employed by the Catholic magisterium in order to renew their own practice of thinking and teaching with the church beyond their own tradition.

1. Preliminary Considerations

Before making these arguments, three things are worth noting. First, although the resources of the Catholic Church merit special consideration because they represent a singularly historical and global communion, those of other communions and organizations such as the World Council of Churches may be beneficial as well. Second, the analysis of Catholic statements in this chapter should be seen as complementary to the analyses of creeds, confessions, and catechisms, including those of the Baptist tradition, in other chapters. Third, of all the resources or "sources of light" recommended in this book, those of the Catholic magisterium would undoubtedly be some of the most difficult for Baptists to consider, given their history of anti-Catholicism—not to mention their "tradition of rejecting tradition."[1] To be sure, many Baptists no longer denounce the Catholic Church or evangelize Catholics, but anti-Catholic attitudes linger even among Baptists who regard Catholics as fellow Christians and themselves as "ecumenical." These attitudes stem from significant theological differences, but they are also inseparable from the ways in which Baptists have both shaped and been shaped by American democracy.

After nearly two centuries of advocating for religious freedom, Baptists helped achieve it in the United States and therefore strongly identified with the new na-

---

[1] Thompson, "Re-Envisioning Baptist Identity," 302.

tion. Moreover, they were well suited to take advantage of the conditions that accompanied disestablishment and democracy, including revivalism. By the early twentieth century, they had become the largest Protestant denomination in an overwhelmingly Protestant America and were sending more and more missionaries abroad, and their own apparent success and their country's growing influence in world affairs had convinced them that Baptist theology and American democracy were in harmony and indeed would spread around the globe together.[2] Because it remained hierarchical and opposed to religious freedom (in the American sense), the Catholic Church served as a perfect foil for Baptists. Polemics between Protestants and Catholics were nothing new, of course, but the fact that the burgeoning Catholic population was largely composed of immigrants who set about building separate schools gave rise to anti-Catholic sentiment that was nativist as well as theological. Not until the election of John F. Kennedy, the nation's first Catholic president, did Baptists stop questioning the political loyalty of Catholics, who by that time were moving up the economic ladder and venturing out of their institutional subculture. Then, in the mid 1960s, the Second Vatican Council (Vatican II), an assembly of Catholic bishops, promulgated a series of documents, notably *Dignitatis Humanae* (the Declaration on Religious Freedom) and *Unitatis Redintegratio* (the Decree on Ecumenism), that addressed major concerns of Protestants and stimulated dialogue, formal and informal, with Protestants, including Baptists.[3] Such dialogue is partly responsible for the improved relations and greater familiarity that inform this chapter.

Nevertheless, in addition to lingering anti-Catholicism, two factors would complicate the study of Catholic magisterial resources by Baptist congregations. One is a simplistic or "lowest common denominator" approach to Christian unity that minimizes the importance of doctrines, sacraments, and other theological matters. This approach can have several motivations, including an admirable desire for cooperation, but it can lead to blaming Catholicism for perpetuating division (e.g., by not allowing Protestants to receive the Eucharist) or to treating the Catholic tradition as a mere repository of useful concepts and practices. The other factor is political and cultural polarization, which can lead to abstracting Catholic resources from their contexts and selecting only those aspects that accord with a certain ideology. Conflicts in Baptist life have fueled such polarization, not least by producing versions of Baptist identity defined by biblical inerrancy or individual and congregational freedom, each of which can lead to perceiving the Catholic Church, particularly its magisterium, as the antithesis of Baptist theology. Baptists who are

---

[2] See Canipe, *A Baptist Democracy.*
[3] See Freeman, "Baptists and Catholics Together?"

open to receiving light from the Catholic tradition must be willing to question this perception.

2. The Nature and Function of the Catholic Magisterium

With these factors in mind, it is appropriate to examine the nature and function of the Catholic magisterium from the perspective of Catholic theology. The magisterium—a Latin term meaning "the office of master," a title given to medieval scholars—is the Catholic Church in its role as the authoritative teacher of divine revelation. It designates both the function of teaching and those who exercise this function, namely, the bishops, the successors of the apostles, in communion with the pope, the successor of Peter and the bishop of Rome. One key to understanding this role is the centrality of the Incarnation in Catholic theology. According to Robert Barron, a bishop and theologian, "*the* great principle of Catholicism is the Incarnation, the enfleshment of God," meaning that "*the Word of God*—the mind by which the whole universe came to be—did not remain sequestered in heaven but rather entered into this ordinary world of bodies, this grubby arena of history, this compromised and tear-stained human condition of ours."[4] Protestant and Orthodox Christians likewise affirm the doctrine of the Incarnation, but they do not share what Barron regards as essential to the "Catholic mind," namely, "a keen sense of the prolongation of the Incarnation throughout space and time, an extension that is made possible through the mystery of the church."[5] To the Catholic mind, revelation primarily concerns not private insight or illumination, although these do occur, but the action and communication of God in history, which are recorded in Scripture but continue in and through the church.

Another key to understanding the role of the magisterium is the communal character of Catholicism. Theology begins with revelation, which requires faith, but it uses reason to interpret revelation, and Catholic theology treats both faith and reason as communal. Theologians Frederick Bauerschmidt and James Buckley explain that "Catholic theology, while being deeply personal, is not reducible to the faith of individual Catholics. Engaging in Catholic theology involves not simply thinking for myself, it also involves thinking with others....Our theological language belongs to the Catholic tradition before it belongs to any individual, and individuals come to own that language to the degree that they become part of the community that bears that tradition."[6] The role of the magisterium, then, is to guard and teach the faith of this community, which is extended through time. The

---

[4] Barron, *Catholicism*, 1.
[5] Barron, *Catholicism*, 3.
[6] Bauerschmidt and Buckley, *Catholic Theology*, 5.

idea of this role is implied by Scripture, particularly Matthew 28, where Jesus shares his authority with the apostles in order for them to share the gospel with the world by teaching, baptizing, and giving commands. According to the late cardinal Avery Dulles, the Great Commission shows that "the Apostles and their successors have the power to teach all nations the way of Christ, to sanctify the faithful through sacraments and other forms of worship, and to exercise pastoral government over the community of Christian believers."[7] This power corresponds to the threefold office of Christ—prophet, priest, and king—with the magisterium corresponding to the prophetic office. The rationale behind the magisterium is that the church received the revelation of Christ as a body and therefore has a responsibility to transmit it as well as to defend and explain it, and it needs persons who are competent to perform these tasks. "Anyone who wants to ascertain the word of God must obtain it directly or indirectly from the persons to whom it was entrusted," Dulles argues. "Jesus selected and trained the Twelve for this function. The Bible itself is the work of qualified witnesses who wrote with a special divine assistance known as inspiration."[8] To the Catholic mind, God has given believers the freedom to have faith, but faith involves not belief in something found through unaided reason or experience but acceptance of something received from the "qualified witnesses" of Scripture and tradition.

2.1 Scripture, Tradition, and Magisterium. From the perspective of Catholic theology, the revelation of Christ has been transmitted from the apostles through two fundamental forms, Scripture and tradition, which together comprise a single "deposit of faith." As Bauerschmidt and Buckley remark, "In a sense Scripture *is* tradition inasmuch as it grows out of the handing-on (in Greek, *paradosis*; in Latin, *traditio*) of the story of Israel, Jesus, and the Church from one generation to the next."[9] The leaders of the early church first accepted the sacred books of Israel, then received certain texts from the apostolic period as canonical and authoritative, texts written after the message of revelation had been handed on orally for some time. Scripture is both a product of tradition, in the sense of the process of "handing-on," and the center of tradition, in the sense of the content that is handed on. The process involves preaching, worship, and the institutions of the church, and the content includes creeds and liturgies as well as Scripture. Scripture does not change, but tradition does, making the Catholic tradition a living tradition, both literally and figuratively. According to Bauerschmidt and Buckley, "'Tradition' is simply another way of speaking of the communal life of Christians, of the fact that we do not think or pray or teach or serve or work for peace and justice as isolated

---

[7] Dulles, *Magisterium*, 1.
[8] Dulles, *Magisterium*, 4.
[9] Bauerschmidt and Buckley, *Catholic Theology*, 19.

individuals, but as members of a community who are constantly in conversation with each other. What 'tradition' adds to 'community' is the recognition that this conversation is not simply taking place with the living, but also with all those who have come before us and now live with Christ."[10]

The Catholic Church describes its living tradition in terms of "development of doctrine," a concept that originated with nineteenth-century theologian John Henry Newman. Although the deposit of faith is complete, it develops over time, meaning that, as stated in *Dei Verbum*, Vatican II's Dogmatic Constitution on Divine Revelation, "there is a growth in the understanding of the realities and the words which have been handed down."[11] Given that theological language cannot simply mean whatever an individual chooses it to mean, the development of tradition must be normed by Scripture and guided by the church, specifically the bishops, themselves guided by the Holy Spirit. As summarized in *Dei Verbum*, "the task of authentically interpreting the word of God, whether written or handed on, has been entrusted exclusively to the living teaching office of the Church, whose authority is exercised in the name of Jesus Christ." Importantly, the text adds that the magisterium "is not superior to the word of God, but is its servant" and "teaches only what has been handed on to it."[12] After the apostolic period, theologians such as Irenaeus of Lyons perceived the need for a continuing authority to preserve the apostolic message and explicated the biblical idea of apostolic succession, attempting to maintain a universal consensus of doctrine while allowing for growth in the understanding of doctrine. This view of authority was assumed by the time of the ecumenical councils, but it was not a subject of systematic reflection until the eleventh century. Conflict between the papacy and secular rulers, then between Catholics and Protestants, heavily influenced that reflection until the First Vatican Council (1869-70), which defined the nature and function of the teaching office, using the term "magisterium" to designate members of the hierarchy with the authority to teach publicly.

2.2 "Ordinary" and "Extraordinary" Magisterium. The magisterium is not in fact an office or department in the Roman Curia, the administrative body of the Vatican, but the "college" (from the Latin *collegium*, meaning "partnership") of Catholic bishops throughout the world, currently over 5,000 in number. The unity of the bishops has two sources, the visible source of the pope and the invisible source of the Spirit, and their office has two tasks, set out by the First Vatican Council: to "religiously guard and faithfully expound the revelation or deposit of

---

[10] Bauerschmidt and Buckley, *Catholic Theology*, 21.
[11] Vatican Council II, *Dei Verbum*, § 5.
[12] Vatican Council II, *Dei Verbum*, § 10. ·

faith transmitted by the apostles."[13] The first task, known as the "ordinary magisterium," is concerned with pastoral matters such as liturgy and catechesis. It is sometimes exercised by the bishops, sometimes by the pope, when they teach doctrines that are central to the Catholic faith through homilies and documents such as pastoral letters and encyclicals. They do not do so in isolation; Bauerschmidt and Buckley assert that "in this task, not only priests, but also in a certain sense all baptized Catholics, are co-workers with the bishops when they fulfill their duties as parents, catechists, or public witnesses to their faith."[14] The second task, known as the "extraordinary magisterium," is specifically concerned with interpretation and, when necessary, definition. It is also exercised by both the bishops and the pope, the former when, typically as a council, the bishops "solemnly" define a matter of faith and morals (i.e., a doctrine), the latter when, in consultation with the bishops, the pope defines a doctrine to be held by the church. Handing on the deposit of faith requires interpreting it in new and changing circumstances; occasionally there is a conflict between possible interpretations, and the task of the magisterium is to determine which interpretation is suitable. This task is also constructive, however; Dulles notes that "in condemning misinterpretations of the faith, the Magisterium inevitably gives a more precise interpretation to what has been handed down in the doctrinal tradition, and thus 'develops' the doctrine."[15] Here, too, lay Catholics have a role, known as "the sense of the faithful," which involves being consulted by the magisterium and, once a doctrine is proclaimed, being obliged to accept it, while acknowledging that not every doctrine has equal weight. The sense of the faithful is not the same as public opinion; rather, it is developed by growing in holiness and in understanding of the teaching of the church, even as the magisterium seeks to clarify that teaching.

Although the extraordinary magisterium may be more well known, owing to the often-misunderstood dogma of papal infallibility, the ordinary magisterium is responsible for the resources that would be beneficial to Baptists. These resources are the products of a participatory approach to theology; bishops are required to earn a licentiate (a postgraduate degree) in theology or a related discipline, but their teaching role is pastoral, not academic, and they customarily consult theologians and other scholars, including those serving on commissions convened by the Roman Curia and episcopal conferences such as the United States Conference of Catholic Bishops (USCCB). Consultation extends to the conciliar level; at the invitation of voting bishops, almost 500 *periti* ("experts") attended the sessions of Vati-

---

[13] Vatican Council I, *Pastor Aeternus*, § 4.5, in *Decrees of the Ecumenical Councils*, ed. Tanner, vol. 2, *Trent to Vatican II*, 816.

[14] Bauerschmidt and Buckley, *Catholic Theology*, 24.

[15] Dulles, *Magisterium*, 62-63.

can II, where they participated in the difficult and sometimes contentious process of preparing the conciliar documents. Moreover, these resources typically incorporate knowledge and insight from earlier theologians and magisterial teaching as well as Scripture, meaning that participation is not limited to the present. In other words, to study them is to study more than what a particular pope or group of bishops in a particular place happens to think at a particular time. The voice of the magisterium is to some extent the voice of the Catholic Church as a historical and global communion.

3. Help for Baptists from Catholic Magisterial Sources

The accessibility of magisterial resources partly depends on the intended audience. *Forming Consciences for Faithful Citizenship*, issued by the USCCB prior to each of the last three presidential election cycles, is directed to all Catholics, clergy and laity (along with "all people of good will") "to help form their consciences; to teach those entrusted to their care; to contribute to civil and respectful public dialogue; and to shape political choices in the coming election in light of Catholic teaching."[16] The *Catechism of the Catholic Church*, promulgated in 1992, is intended as a source for developing shorter summaries of doctrine to be used in preparing people for confirmation or reception into the Catholic Church, but it can still be read profitably by non-Catholics. Other magisterial resources, such as the documents of Vatican II and encyclicals issued by popes since the late nineteenth century, are more theologically sophisticated. However, their ideas have considerable practical application, a point illustrated by the development of what has come to be known as "Catholic social teaching."

3.1 Catholic Social Teaching. Catholic social teaching is generally considered to have begun with the encyclical *Rerum Novarum*, issued by Pope Leo XIII in 1891. At the time, Europe was dealing with the effects of capitalism and the conflict brought on by the responses of socialism and communism. Large-scale industrialization and consequent urbanization had contributed to widespread poverty and social dislocation, resulting in a labor class who were largely uneducated and increasingly dissatisfied with the harsh conditions in which they lived and worked, to the point that a number of European nations were on the verge of revolution. After briefly describing the situation, Leo asserts that a solution must be found for the "misery and wretchedness" of the majority of the working class, especially after the abolishment of the guilds that had protected them:

---

[16] United States Conference of Catholic Bishops, *Forming Consciences for Faithful Citizenship*, 6.

Hence, by degrees it has come to pass that working men have been surrendered, isolated and helpless, to the hardheartedness of employers and the greed of unchecked competition. The mischief has been increased by rapacious usury, which, although more than once condemned by the Church, is nevertheless, under a different guise, but with like injustice, still practiced by covetous and grasping men. To this must be added that the hiring of labor and the conduct of trade are concentrated in the hands of comparatively few; so that a small number of very rich men have been able to lay upon the teeming masses of the laboring poor a yoke little better than that of slavery itself.[17]

Leo's criticism was directed at capitalists who, even if they did care about the plight of workers, refused to see it as related to systemic problems. At the same time, it was also directed at socialists who saw this plight as *entirely* related to such problems, which could be solved only by eliminating private property in favor of state control. The pope contends that "their contentions are so clearly powerless to end the controversy that were they carried into effect the working man himself would be among the first to suffer. They are, moreover, emphatically unjust, for they would rob the lawful possessor, distort the functions of the State, and create utter confusion in the community."[18] Against both of these theories, socialism and laissez-faire capitalism, Leo utilizes Scripture and tradition, including figures such as Tertullian and Thomas Aquinas, to outline the proper relationship between capital and labor. Private property is a fundamental principle of natural law and is affirmed by liberalism, not socialism. However, a truly liberal economy is concerned with more than profit:

Let the working man and the employer make free agreements, and in particular let them agree freely as to the wages; nevertheless, there underlies a dictate of natural justice more imperious and ancient than any bargain between man and man, namely, that wages ought not to be insufficient to support a frugal and well-behaved wage-earner. If through necessity or fear of a worse evil the workman accept harder conditions because an employer or contractor will afford him no better, he is made the victim of force and injustice.[19]

Among other things, Leo encourages the formation of "workingmen's unions" and insists that employers and workers alike have both rights and duties, such as the right to a fair wage and the duty to refrain from violence. The church and the state

---

[17] Leo XIII, *Rerum Novarum*, § 3.
[18] Leo XIII, *Rerum Novarum*, § 4.
[19] Leo XIII, *Rerum Novarum*, § 45.

likewise have duties; the former to teach principles that promote class harmony, the latter to protect rights that promote justice.

Although this analysis remains relevant, the crucial point is that *Rerum Novarum* marks the first stage in the Catholic Church establishing its independence from particular social orders, not only to critique them but also to reestablish its own foundation on Scripture and tradition in a way that enables Catholics to engage the modern world critically and constructively. Subsequent encyclicals follow a pattern of analyzing a pressing social problem and outlining a distinctively Christian response that builds on previous documents. In *Quadragesimo Anno* (1931), Pope Pius XI acknowledges that Leo's teaching has been regarded as suspect, even by many Catholics, because it "boldly attacked and overturned the idols of Liberalism, ignored long-standing prejudices, and was in advance of its time beyond all expectation," to the point that it was regarded as "a kind of imaginary ideal of perfection more desirable then attainable."[20] Yet Pius is more radical than Leo in calling for changes in economic systems, and he makes a point of distinguishing between communism and a moderate socialism that "inclines toward and in a certain measure approaches the truths which Christian tradition has always held sacred."[21] For the pope, the pillars of private property, economic cooperation, and community are essential for maintaining peace, but the resulting bonds are fully realized only in the body of Christ:

> For justice alone can, if faithfully observed, remove the causes of social conflict but can never bring about union of minds and hearts. Indeed all the institutions for the establishment of peace and the promotion of mutual help among men, however perfect these may seem, have the principal foundation of their stability in the mutual bond of minds and hearts whereby the members are united with one another. If this bond is lacking, the best of regulations come to naught, as we have learned by too frequent experience. And so, then only will true cooperation be possible for a single common good when the constituent parts of society deeply feel themselves members of one great family and children of the same Heavenly Father; nay, that they are one body in Christ, "but severally members one of another" [Rom 12:5], so that "if one member suffers anything, all the members suffer with it" [1 Cor 12:26].[22]

Recent encyclicals also follow this pattern, with different emphases depending on their respective contexts. For example, Pope John Paul II promulgated *Centesimus Annus* (1991) in the wake of the fall of communism (and to commemorate

---

[20] Pius XI, *Quadragesimo Anno*, § 14.

[21] Pius XI, *Quadragesimo Anno*, § 113.

[22] Pius XI, *Quadragesimo Anno*, § 137.

Rerum Novarum), leading him to focus on the positive aspects of free markets, whereas Pope Benedict XVI promulgated *Caritas in Veritate* (2009) in the wake of the global financial crisis, leading him to be more critical of such markets, despite citing *Centesimus Annus* more than 20 times. As evidenced by Pius' comment about *Rerum Novarum*, reception of encyclicals has always been somewhat mixed. Some Catholics have disagreed with them, others have been inspired by them, and most have never read them. As Catholic theologian Kenneth Himes says, however, "the importance of the material cannot be measured by the size of the readership. Its influence comes from how the texts have been 'translated' into sermons, lectures, public programs, social movements, acts of charity, just deeds, and peacemaking."[23] Given the complexity of the political and economic spheres and the diversity of a worldwide church, Catholic social teaching has been remarkably consistent in presenting a vision of human life as an integrated whole with a supernatural purpose, as opposed to ideologies that isolate or subordinate certain aspects of human life. That is, it does not make a sharp distinction between the social and the personal or spiritual. For example, although its primary theme is evangelization, Pope Francis' apostolic exhortation *Evangelii Gaudium* addresses a range of topics, including the reform of the church, the preparation of homilies, the inclusion of the poor in society, the dignity of unborn children, and the imitation of the Virgin Mary. As Francis says, this can seem quite strange:

> Despite the tide of secularism which has swept our societies, in many countries—even those where Christians are a minority—the Catholic Church is considered a credible institution by public opinion, and trusted for her solidarity and concern for those in greatest need. Again and again, the Church has acted as a mediator in finding solutions to problems affecting peace, social harmony, the land, the defense of life, human and civil rights, and so forth….Yet, we find it difficult to make people see that when we raise other questions less palatable to public opinion, we are doing so out of fidelity to precisely the same convictions about human dignity and the common good.[24]

3.2 Thinking and Teaching Ecclesially. The unity of the social and the personal is just one of many things that Baptists might glean from Catholic magisterial resources. They might also learn a great deal from the deliberative processes that have produced those resources about how to think and teach with the church. For all their blind spots, Baptists once understood that individuals do not simply acquire the Christian faith through the Bible and personal experience but must be formed

---

[23] Himes, "Introduction," in *Modern Catholic Social Teaching*, ed. Himes, 3.
[24] Francis, *Evangelii Gaudium*, § 65.

in that faith by congregations, who receive it from "all those who have come before us and now live with Christ," and they also understood that congregations must be bound together by confessions and covenants to accomplish such formation. Otherwise, their emphasis on freedom can undermine both commitment to a congregation and discernment in relation to the culture. At the same time, a magisterial role is not foreign to Baptists. As Steven Harmon states, "the very concept of a definable Baptist identity and the possibility that it could be betrayed point in the direction of an unacknowledged Baptist magisterium."[25] Moreover, acknowledging that "Baptist churches, like all Christian communities, discover that as they make disciples they must teach something," Harmon describes the practice of theology by Baptist churches as an exercise of what he terms "Free Church magisterium":

> Though this is a clumsy English coinage, one might call this the "magisterium-hood of all believers"—which seems to be the implication of reading the gospels as manuals of discipleship, which therefore means that all who become disciples of Christ are commissioned by him in Matthew 28:18ff to participate in the church's teaching office. But just as in the Catholic configuration of magisterium the bishops do not exercise magisterium only in association with the bishop of Rome and the other bishops, but also with the faithful who participate in various ways in the nonhierarchical dimension of the magisterium, so in the Free Church practice of teaching authority, it is not the local congregation alone that authorizes its teaching, nor is the membership of the congregation undifferentiated in its participation in this practice. In the best expressions of Baptist ecclesiology, the independence of local congregations is not absolute. Local Baptist congregations are interdependent in their relations with one another, in local associations but also in various national and international associations of Baptists.[26]

Recognizing that the question is not whether to have a teaching authority but what kind of teaching authority to have, especially in the midst of competing cultural authorities, is a crucial step in receiving light from the Catholic tradition and indeed from the church as a whole. The burden of reception or "translation" falls primarily on ministers and the professors who train them, a burden that is only increasing in a post-Christian society. "The Church must always be on guard against being taken in by the spirit of the age," Dulles notes. "One of the great values of the hierarchical magisterium is that it gives the Church a body of teachers who are deeply immersed in Holy Scripture and Tradition, who are trained in ways of prayer and worship and qualified by the grace of sacramental ordination to speak in the name of Christ the Lord. The indispensable task of the Magisterium is to

---

[25] Harmon, *Baptist Identity and the Ecumenical Future*, 167-68.
[26] Harmon, *Baptist Identity and the Ecumenical Future*, 169, 177.

bear witness to the truth 'in season and out of season' (2 Tim. 4:2)."[27] Although the Free Church magisterium certainly differs from the Catholic magisterium, its teachers should have similar training and a similar commitment to bringing congregational life under the rule of Christ by carefully weighing ideas and interpretations from various sources, including those recommended in this chapter and throughout this book. All these ideas and interpretations deserve to be considered, but not all will be compatible with each other or with Scripture and tradition, and the task of the Baptist magisterium is to make this determination, lest powerful social forces shape their faith and practice by different means. If this task is performed well, with intellectual humility and generosity, Baptists may receive light that will enable them to be the church in this age.

4. For Further Reading

Catholic Church. *Catechism of the Catholic Church*. 2nd ed. Washington, DC: United States Conference of Catholic Bishops, 2000.

Dulles, Avery. *Magisterium: Teacher and Guardian of the Faith*. Naples, FL: Sapientia Press, 2007.

Flannery, Austin, ed. *Vatican Council II: The Basic Sixteen Documents*. Collegeville, MN: Liturgical Press, 2014.

Gaillardetz, Richard R. *By What Authority? Foundations for Understanding Authority in the Church*. Rev. ed. Collegeville, MN: Liturgical Press Academic, 2018.

O'Brien, David J. and Thomas A. Shannon, eds. *Catholic Social Thought: Encyclicals and Documents from Pope Leo XIII to Pope Francis*. 3rd ed. Maryknoll, NY: Orbis Books, 2016.

---

[27] Dulles, *Magisterium*, 107.

20

Light for Navigating Moral Disagreement

Myles Werntz

This chapter explores the question of how churches may navigate ongoing moral disagreement. Among Baptists, there has been no shortage of moral divisions which have not only separated Baptist denominations but split particular churches as well.[1] The presence of conventions and associations has helped to facilitate divergent theological opinions among churches, but the more difficult question is how to approach moral ambiguity in a local Baptist congregation. Exploring moral difference must entail more than simply passing over moral divisions as "optional"; it must work through the difficult moral divisions which, if left unattended, become the seeds for ecclesial division.[2]

The reasons that Baptists think primarily about morals as individuals and not communally has any number of sources. We could locate the problem in the way that "conscience" is articulated in Baptist life as fundamentally a safeguard for the individual over against the tyranny of other opinions.[3] We could name the problem as one of misunderstanding Baptist origins, forgetting that Baptist origins are more communal than individualist.[4] But fundamental to any genealogy of Baptist moral thought is the question of how the individual came to have priority over the life of the community. This all simply leads, however, to a new tyranny: that of the individual, unable to hear the wisdom, pain, or concerns of others unless it directly

---

[1] Moral issues which have divided Baptists include (but are not limited to) slavery, war, race, and sexuality. See Kidd and Hankins, *Baptists in America* for an overview of the denominational histories of some of these issues.

[2] Consider, for example, how privatized decisions about sex and food are connected to schisms in the Corinthian church (1 Cor. 5 and 10). 1 Corinthians echoes what we find to be true throughout the Scriptures: acts of volition which we tend to see as "individual" choices always have communal effects.

[3] Leonard, *Baptists in America*, 82: "In other words, God alone is judge of conscience, and thus all human beings are responsible to God alone for the religious and spiritual choices they make. As the Baptists who wrote the *Propositions and Conclusions* (1612) saw it, a personal experience of grace brought religious knowledge that transcended all 'outward' resources."

[4] See Freeman, *Contesting Catholicity*, 225-72.

concerns me. This tyranny of the individual is contradictory to the gospel, for the concerns and suffering of one part of the body intimately affects all of the body: "If one member suffers, all suffer together with it; if one member is honored, all rejoice together with it" (1 Cor. 12:26). That we are unable to hear the concerns and suffering of others to affect us speaks to the ways in which we have deformed the life of faith to be a purely individualist venture.

To help reframe how churches can better hear ethical voices, I will provide a framework which re-narrates three hallmarks of Baptist life around the question of moral deliberation: (1) conversion, (2) contemplation and prayer, and (3) corporate life.[5] In doing so, it is my hope that we will see that what Baptist churches already do includes a way forward for churches which are struggling with moral disagreement. What I will propose here is more than simply "deliberation," for that leaves us with the idea that what we do when engaging moral questions is only engaging in practical reason on the basis of certain scriptural texts. In Baptist churches, the question of moral division is intimately (and rightly) related to theological division and the practice of discipleship, and so accounting for moral division and hearing other voices is not as simple as resolving a practical difference of opinion.[6]

In taking this approach, I am not suggesting that Christians ignore wisdom from sources outside Scripture, as Christian moral wisdom is not generated purely by internal resources, but rather by subjecting all things to the Lordship of Christ. There is no prize for ignoring the questions generated by society, but likewise, there is no prize in simply adopting wholesale the frameworks and assumptions by which society generates moral questions. Christians, as Augustine reminds us, are constantly in the business of reframing, working with, and renewing the "Egyptian gold," melting down the pagan idols into goods worthy for the temple of God.[7] It is by pointing to these three aspects of Baptist congregational practice that I hope to provide a framework for forging provisional answers in ways which will open our ears to voices we might have otherwise missed.

---

[5] I am borrowing this three-fold typology from Furr and Freeman, eds., *Ties That Bind*, 3.

[6] In the modern period, the division of theology from ethics stems back to the assumption that our questions about God's being are fundamentally separate from questions about human action, that there is no relation between humans and the divine. The splitting off of "speculative" from "practical" questions has many roots, but is typically traced back to the German Enlightenment, and summed up in Immanuel Kant's *Religion within the Boundaries of Mere Reason*.

[7] Augustine, *On Christian Doctrine*, 2.40 (ET, *Teaching Christianity (De Doctrina Christiana) I/II*, 2nd rev. ed., trans. Hill, ed. Rotelle, 159-60).

1. The Moral Agent:
Conversion and the Baptist Congregation

Foundational to the Christian life is the assumption that those who are in Christ are participants in the new creation that Christ has brought (2 Cor. 5:17). In this, Baptists hold that salvation is in many respects an unnatural event by which our allegiances to the world are ruptured and remade around Christ. Acknowledging this means that, for Christians, negotiating the moral life is not something which can be done on the basis of native intuitions, and that the moral life is not something which simply builds on the basis of cultural assumptions. By contrast, conversion assumes that our moral lives must be remade by looking to Christ through the Scriptures first.

This has any number of implications for moral disagreements. As we come to Christ, we are all shaped by our culture and families of origin, and this is not a thing to be forsaken; at no point does Paul ask that Gentiles or Jews cease being Gentiles or Jews in order to be Christian, calling them instead to be of one mind in and through their differences (Phil. 2:2). From the early days of the English Separatists, personal conversion accompanied by believer's baptism has always been the precursor to the moral life, for only as we have our lives remade by God in Christ can we hope to have anything to offer to the world. For Baptists, it is not solely by knowledge of the Scriptures that we are able to bear witness well, but by our continually converted and transformed lives.

By beginning our ethics with this emphasis on conversion, we will hopefully find that many of the terms of our moral debates are unconsciously framed by modes of thought which have been shielded from the light of the Scriptures.[8] For example, by entering the world of Scripture, we see that "conscience" is God's gift to both affirm and convict our actions, and not just an inner light which provides justification for something which we have decided to do already. Or we might learn that "priesthood of the believers" is not meant as an absolute right to be used over against others but a designation of service. Conversion as the first movement of a Baptist ethic means acknowledging that a witness in the world is something which proceed apart from critical engagement with Christ and the Scriptures.

This conversion is both personal and corporate, meaning that our conformity to Christ occurs both in the intimate contours of a person's social location, and in their connections to other members of the body of Christ. Negatively, these could

---

[8] I do not mean to revert here to a naïve form of biblicism, but to suggest that, in any moral engagement, even our most worthy extrabiblical assumptions should be brought into explicit conversation with the Scriptures, if only to be honest about our sources and influences.

be pit against one another as opposing forces; constructively, however, conversion to Christ means that all parts of Christ's body are being conformed together into the one body of Christ. As such, being conformed to the likeness of Christ will entail both unity and difference; as a father of two, my discipleship will entail different considerations, productive possibilities and limitations than would be incumbent for a person without children. And yet, my conversion to Christ is not complete if I divorce myself from the rest of Christ's body (Eph. 4:1-6).

Conversion, then, is not a singular event, but an ongoing process in which our lives and witness are not only deepened within the contours of our own lives; conversion is a process by which our lives are knit together with the lives of other saints. The incorporation of other voices of moral witness into this process proceeds fundamentally from this assumption—that the Spirit is operative in the witness of others—but it would be naïve to assume that this is sufficient for a community to listen to these voices. To be sure, certain voices alien to the Baptist tradition have resonance within a congregation's popular imagination, such as the Lutheran Dietrich Bonhoeffer or the Reformed John Calvin, as their influence has been pervasive on both theological and moral levels for multiple generations.[9] But even with someone as well-appreciated as Bonhoeffer, certain Lutheran assumptions about the nature of communion, ecclesiology, or the process of salvation will pose roadblocks for Baptists.

The stories of how these voices with such alien assumptions to Baptist congregations became incorporated into Baptist imagination is beyond this chapter, but rests broadly upon two assets of these figures: the fruits of their ministries, and their engagements with Scripture. Given that theological and moral arguments for Baptists stem from the wellspring of Scripture, the Scriptural reasoning engaged in by both thinkers provided inroads to Baptist congregations which prioritize fidelity to the Scriptures over (and over against for the most part) fidelity to the broader theological tradition: Consider, for example, the innumerable commentaries upon Scripture by Calvin, or the ways in which Bonhoeffer's moral example provides a touchstone for Christians far beyond Lutheran circles. [10] In other words, Baptists have always found wisdom beyond their own explicit confessional voices, and recognized those voices on the basis of the common love of Christ and the Scriptures present within those witnesses.

---

[9] Figures such as Bonhoeffer have such a polyphonic corpus that their work has been claimed by multiple theological frameworks; see Haynes, *The Bonhoeffer Phenomenon*. Likewise, a figure like Calvin, who makes various ecclesiological and soteriological moves which run counter to dominant Baptist practice, has maintained wide (albeit controversial) appropriation among Baptists; see Wagoner and Clendenen, *Calvinism*.

[10] For why this should not be an either/or argument for Baptists, see Harmon, *Towards Baptist Catholicity*.

Calvin and Luther provide easy examples of those outside the Baptist world, but what about those voices whose work digs deeper into the foundations of Baptist practice? There are many examples of those whose work and witness has interrogated our moral assumptions, but let me point to Martin Luther King, Jr., a figure whom Baptists would presently count as a saint, but in his time was counted otherwise. In his "Letter from a Birmingham Jail," King chastises two kinds of Christians; the first—segregationist Christians—he knows will not listen, but the second kind—the moderate white Christians—King chastises for not being open to examining their own unconscious racism.

King writes, "I had hoped that the white moderate would understand that law and order exist for the purpose of establishing justice and that when they fail in this purpose they become the dangerously structured dams that block the flow of social progress...we who engage in nonviolent direct action are not the creators of tension. *We merely bring it out in the open*, where it can be seen and dealt with."[11] In appealing to the white moderates as a fellow Christian, King introduces hidden foundations central to their moral disagreement which the white Christians could not hear. But as a fellow member of the body of Christ, King's words could not be so easily dismissed, arguing as he did from Scripture and the theological tradition.

So, given divergent claims concerning the moral life, how do we move forward, particularly when our divergences are rooted in Scripture? In Romans 12:1-2, we find one of the key exhortations ("to be transformed by the renewing of your minds") bookended by communal context on both ends. In v. 1, Paul exhorts the plural "you" of the congregation "to present [their] bodies as a living sacrifice," as their act of "spiritual worship," depicting the work of conversion as both one which is undergone by a community of persons in the context of that community's worship. The transformation of the mind—the experience of conformity of the individual's moral and intellectual faculties to Christ—is likewise ordered toward a common discernment of "what is the will of God." Then in v. 3 Paul cautions in this process "everyone among you not to think of yourself more highly than you ought to think, but to think with sober judgment, each according to the measure of faith that God has assigned."

The link here between the process of conversion and the inclusion of those voices in the process of conversion which we would rather not hear is clear, then; the renewal of the mind occurs in a way which is both deflationary and comparative. As we are converted to Christ, in a communal context, our understanding of the will of God involves both a proper assessment of where we rightly stand, a process which cannot occur apart from hearing and seeing those who are joined to us

---

[11] King, Jr., "Letter from Birmingham Jail," in *The Radical King*, ed. West, 135, emphasis mine.

in that process. Paul here does envision unanimity of judgment but what is indispensable for Paul is that conversion *requires* the acknowledgment of others who are themselves members of the same body of faith which I belong to, and that—if there is only one body of Christ—breaking faith over moral disagreement is not an option for Christians.

2. The Moral Action: Prayer and Listening

As we consider then *how* to incorporate other voices of moral witness—both dead and living—into our moral deliberations, conversion also provides the proper frame. Conversion is a theme assumed by the New Testament, but lightly touched on; put differently, conversion occurs, but the dynamics of its occurrence do not receive any great analytic treatment.[12] It is here that we turn beyond the claims of others, to the process in which we listen: the contemplative.

As Gary Furr and Curtis Freeman point out, a second major mark for Baptists is our cultivating of our relationship to God in prayer, meditation, and acts of devotion.[13] One of the best examples of this is the work of John Bunyan, who in his journals and *The Pilgrim's Progress* exhibits an openness in prayer to God.[14] This contemplation is not for the sake of ecstatic experiences, but that in being laid open before God in prayer and contemplation, we might be made into the people God has called us to be. Whether spoken of in terms of revivalism, prayer meetings, Sunday School or spiritual direction, Baptists have always held that prayer and spiritual belonging constitutes an indispensable aspect of the Christian life.

The major objection here is quite plainly that prayer and moral argument of different species: that appeals to prayer are simply dodging the process of rational deliberation. But as we saw with Romans 12:1-3, Christians do not approach deliberation as a purely rational exercise, but within the context of prayer and worship. If, as Paul exhorts the Romans, our moral conversion occurs alongside others, the "transformation of the mind" is not a kind of self-construction or "self-disciplining" (a notion of prayer bordering on the Pelagian), but a being-led by God.[15]

---

[12] As described by Gallagher, "Conversion and Community in Late Antiquity," earlier twentieth-century accounts of conversion were misinformed by William James' account of individual religious psychology, neglecting the communal and institutional aspects of religious conversion.

[13] Furr and Freeman, eds., *Ties That Bind*, 3.

[14] Bunyan, *Grace Abounding to the Chief of Sinners*; idem, *The Pilgrim's Progress*.

[15] It is exceedingly common to think of both moral formation and prayers as what Michel Foucault, and many modern theologians after him, have called "techniques of the self": that in prayer, we discipline the self and engage in the *askesis* of prayer; see Foucault, *Technologies of the*

Prayer, as Sarah Coakley has argued, has the effect of allowing us to release hardened notions of the self, such that we may—as Paul exhorts in Romans—receive from God that which is good and true.[16] It strikes us as strange to think of moral argument as having a strong "contemplative" dimension, but, if ethics is ultimately a life of discipleship before God, then prayer is, among other things, that indispensable act which prevents our moral judgments from being presumptuous. Our prayer aligns our actions with God in Christ, inflecting the pursuit of God with the virtues of faith, hope, love, and Lord willing, justice, temperance, prudence, and fortitude.

The contemplative context, Coakley argues, allows us to release our notions of ourselves to God, that we might receive from God that which is true and good, or as Paul puts it, "the will of God" that is "perfect" (Rom. 12:2). Most often, in Baptist circles, the Spirit is associated with individual piety or with action within society,[17] but contemplative prayer is significant here in three ways. First, in the context of moral argument works to help us to release ourselves to God, that we might receive from God the gift of ourselves (freer from anxiety and guilt) as well as the gift that is other people, receiving their presence not as a threat to moral witness but as part of what must be considered in our moral witness. Secondly, prayer, in joining us together in God, Coakley suggests, reveals an equality of persons before God which, in turn, subverts our unconscious ways of subjugating some voices to other voices; in prayer, we realized that God is *our* Father, the one to whom we all pray and to whom we are all equally joined.[18] Prayer in the Scriptures—whether in the Psalms, Gospels, or the epistles—is envisioned as a communal act, performed by believers together both in times of agreement and disagreement.

Finally, prayer opens up our moral deliberations to the dimensions of our arguments which are not explicitly "rational." Traditionally, emphasizing aspects of moral argumentation such as emotions, empathy, compassion, and in this case, contemplation, have been dismissed as "sub-rational." But this is to ignore both the model of Scripture and recent developments in moral psychology. If we allow that,

---

Self. For two modern appropriation of this approach, see Jordan, *Convulsing Bodies*, and Schuld, *Foucault and Augustine.*

[16] Coakley, *Powers and Submissions*, 3-39, and *God, Sexuality, and the Self*, 100-90. In both places, Coakley argues for prayer as a release of the self toward God which undoes our hardened presuppositions about the self and surrenders them to God.

[17] Consider, for example, Walter Rauschenbusch's conviction that the Spirit of God was breaking forth in the conversion of society's structures, or in Martin Luther King Jr.'s belief that the moral arc of the universe bent toward justice.

[18] Coakley, "Living into the Mystery of the Holy Trinity." I have criticized Coakley as needing to be more explicit about the ecclesiology in her work on this point in Werntz, "The Body and the Body of the Church."

with Paul, the renovation of the human is not simply something which restores the mind, but all aspects of our person, then our engagements with God and one another cannot neglect these integral aspects of human personhood. To attempt to make moral arguments *apart from* more "experiential" aspects is not only to engage sub-humanly in our arguments, but to forget that reason itself is interlaced with experience and affection.[19] In the humility of prayer, we find ourselves able to receive witness that consists in reasons which we ourselves have not reasoned.

3. The Moral Context: The Church Deliberating

Third and finally, Furr and Freeman point to the corporate dimension of Baptist life, observing that part of what distinctively marks the Baptist tradition is its congregational, localist structure.[20] From our earliest days, Baptists have emphasized the ways in which confessing the faith is best done in the company of believers, and that to be of Christ was to be of the community of the baptized. The significance for a Baptist ethic is that, both as Baptists and as Christians, we are not condemned to draw only upon our individual resources to live faithful lives, but that we live, worship, and deliberate about our moral lives as a worshiping community.

As we have seen in the previous two marks, the context of a worshiping community draws together diverse persons, even in demographically homogenous situations. As Kathryn Tanner has pointed out, simply having the same practice in place does not mean that all persons in a place perform it the same way; the same object, practice, or idea is handled differently by persons within the same community.[21] Because I grew up with the parents I did and have the history that I do, I hear phrases such as "Jesus is Lord" differently than someone else, and build out my life of discipleship in a different way. But through the practices which we intrinsically *share*—for example, preaching, baptism, communion, missions, and Christian education—these different understandings come out and must be negotiated: such is the work of being church together. As we encounter the Scriptures together and seek to bear witness together to the same Lord, this will inevitably involve negotiation of differences.[22]

---

[19] The work of Martha Nussbaum has been essential in retrieving the role of love and the affections in the moral life; see in particular her *Love's Knowledge* and *Upheavals of Thought*. These insights are reminiscent of the patristic insight that our knowledge of God is interlaced with our love of God, such that we can only truly know our object (God) as our reason is joined to our affections; see Williams, *The Wound of Knowledge*.

[20] Furr and Freeman, eds., *Ties That Bind*, 3.

[21] Tanner, *Theories of Culture*, 104-10.

[22] Yeager and Herman, "The Virtue of 'Selling Out'," have made a compelling argument for why moral negotiation is not intrinsically a bad thing, but a moral behavior to be performed.

The local, gathered nature of church, then, allows us—necessitates, even—hearing of different voices than our own, voices who will be different for reason more complicated than that they are not myself. This commitment to the local church complicates another aspect of Baptist ecclesiology, in that it very possible to simply ignore anything from beyond our local church, even if spoken by fellow Baptists. A commitment to local church autonomy makes Baptists eminently flexible, able to respond to local issues without waiting on cumbersome structures, this also means that Baptists have always been and will likely offer no single answer on any number of moral questions, as they have no other body to answer to other than their own local body.[23] The autonomy of local congregations presents itself as a problem in arguably no greater way than in times of moral division. Other Christian traditions—Protestant, Catholic, and Orthodox—have long traditions of moral pronouncements; because there is an assumed denominational unity among congregations, there can be some common and indispensable framework within which to argue about the moral life.

But we should not despair! Autonomy of the local congregation may very well lead to ethical fragmentation and may mean that denominational or associational statements on moral questions lack binding force in ways present in other traditions—but let me propose a different way to view this. One approach is certainly to call for local congregations to view the pronouncements of Baptist denominational bodies as binding, and in this way, create a common framework for Baptists to work within. Another way, however, is to retain these pronouncements as outside voice of conscience to local congregations in this way, calling far-off Baptist congregations to hear voices that may not be immediately obvious to them. As we saw earlier, voices external to the congregation can be included in the moral discussions of a congregation, provided they are recognized as the wisdom of fellow Christians. Such recognition does not require a local congregation to cede its autonomy, but simply to open its ears to the voices of other faithful Christians.

This emphasis on the local congregation has, I think, actually produced great possibility for Baptists to hear these voices. Because of the great Baptist missional emphasis, theological and cultural plurality is simply what Baptists have *always* had, as local congregations take root in different contexts. From Howard Thurman to Charles Spurgeon to Billy Graham to Roger Williams, Baptists have a diverse heritage and a witness that is not always singular, but contextual to its time and place. Because of our global heritage, Baptists have the blessing and curse of having various genealogies which can genuinely be called Baptist, many of which have

---

[23] This is not to discount pronouncements made by associational or denominational bodies, but ecclesiologically, Baptists hold to an autonomy of the local church which renders these statements as non-binding.

been only been selectively read. We are in the early stages, I think, of recovering global voices of Baptists in India (which currently has the largest population of Baptists outside the United States), in Lebanon, and in the Philippines. In other words, this final aspect of a Baptist ethic—congregationalism—has produced a diversity of responses which provide Baptists with a rich diversity of resources from which to draw and learn. If we can learn to hear these voices, and to pray in ways which recognize the equality of these voices, as I have suggested, the locality of these voices does not become an obstacle to overcome, but a gift to receive. For it is *because* of their locality, their freedom to be who they are in context, that these plural voices are able to grow strong, not in spite of their locality. What is needed is not an overarching structure to channel them, but the discipline of prayer and deliberation to be able to receive them as part of the same body of Christ.

4. Conclusion

Emphasizing these three strands together—the conversionist, the contemplative, and the corporate—does two things. First, it paints a picture of moral deliberation which supersedes rational deliberation alone. Because God forms us as moral beings not only with respect to our reason but with respect to our bodies, experiences, emotions, and relationships, it is essential that we draw all of these resources to bear on the question of moral deliberation. Secondly, it grounds the process of moral deliberation in the practices of the Christian life which are both familiar to us and essential to our growth as Christians. Placing moral deliberation as a second-order practice to the Christian life runs the risk of making it optional; seeing it as intrinsic to the things which we *already do* as Christians, however, makes such processes less alien. When drawn together, these three strands of the Christian life open space for those voices which are alien to us. In being more fully converted to Christ, we are able to see others as likewise on the journey toward God; in prayer, we are freed from the idolatries which plague our journeys to God; in journeying together toward Christ, we see others (both in our own congregations and from beyond) as fellow sojourners, and not strangers to be feared.

In this chapter, I have said absolutely nothing of specifics about what kinds of policies or procedures Baptists ethics should promote, for three reasons. First, Baptist ethics begins at home, by which I mean the life of the congregation. And so, it is important, before we engage the many opportunities for discipleship in the world, we do a little bit of necessary throat-clearing about where we begin, and the ways in which we are able to listen to plural voices of moral witness within the church. The second reason follows from the first: as a Baptist, I do not want to shortcut the place of the congregations in ethical formation. Those of you who are pastors and ministers will be among your congregation's first ethics teachers. It falls to those who are not simply among the ordained, but who are among laypersons in places of teaching, instruction, mentoring, or missions to guide the congregation well, modeling the proper openness of Christ, teaching our congregations to negotiate our moral questions well together.

5. For Further Reading

Carson, Merrie Schoenman. "Stewardship, Discernment, and Congregational Decision Making." *The Covenant Quarterly* 71 (2013): 73-95.

Cleveland, Christena. *Disunity in Christ: Uncovering the Hidden Forces that Keep Us Apart.* Downers Grove, IL: IVP Academic, 2013.

Dougherty, Rose Mary. *Discernment: A Path to Spiritual Awakening.* New York: Paulist Press, 2009.

Furr, Gary A. and Curtis W. Freeman, eds. *Ties That Bind: Life Together in the Baptist Vision.* Macon, GA: Smyth & Helwys, 1994.

Keiser, Joshua A. *Becoming Simple and Wise: Moral Discernment in Dietrich Bonhoeffer's Vision of Christian Ethics.* Eugene, OR: Pickwick Publications, 2015.

Moses, Sarah M. "The Ethics of 'Recognition': Rowan Williams' Approach to Moral Discernment in the Christian Community." *Journal of the Society of Christian Ethics* 35 (2015): 147-65.

Tyra, Gary. *Pursuing Moral Faithfulness: Ethics and Christian Discipleship.* Downers Grove, IL: IVP Academic, 2015.

21

Light from Saintly Sources

Derek C. Hatch

To invoke the saints in a Baptist context might be a perilous deed. For their part, Baptists have said very little about saints and have tended to avoid serious discussion of the subject altogether. For instance, few congregations have the word "saint" in their title, a practice that is common among Catholic and some Protestant traditions.[1] There is no calendar of saint observances, and no persons are officially remembered as "saints." Moreover, it is not merely the absence of certain "saintly" emphases that marks Baptist faith and practice. Indeed, many Baptists are even suspicious of those who have embraced a robust economy of sanctity (especially Catholics). The invocation of saints in prayers prompts worries about replacing Jesus as the object of our prayers. At the very least, Baptists grow concerned that the saints might function as a necessary stepping stone for the religious life. Further, devotional practices related to particular saints are occasionally cited as a sign of something patently unscriptural and unchristian.

Of course, as Baptists do acknowledge, the word "saint" does appear in the New Testament, primarily as a substantive version of the adjective *hagios* ("holy"). The term is almost always found in the plural within the New Testament, and it is quite prominent in the Pauline literature (though there are thirteen occurrences in the Apocalypse). Baptist confessions of faith, such as the London Confession of 1644 and the Second London Confession of 1689, also utilize the term. W. T. Conner sums up a representative Baptist view when he writes that "saints" is used in the New Testament in a sense that indicates people (i.e., all Christians) set apart for God.[2] He views this notion of sanctity as part and parcel of the sanctification undergone by all believers who are linked to Christ, resulting in "a righteous life [that] grows out of the indwelling Spirit."[3] Boldly Conner declares, "We have no

---

[1] There are several notable exceptions, including St. John's Baptist Church in Charlotte, North Carolina. It should be noted that using "saint" to name a congregation seems far more likely to occur in an African-American Baptist church.

[2] Conner, *What Is a Saint?*, 9-10.

[3] Conner, *What Is a Saint?*, 11-12.

ground in either Scripture or reason for maintaining that we have any living connection with those who have gone on before."[4]

In what follows, I will tease out what it might mean for Baptists to embrace the saints as a source of theological light. To do so, I will engage with the reflections of our Catholic brothers and sisters concerning the role of the saints in the Christian life and what the Second Vatican Council calls the universal call to holiness. Only when this wider picture is in view can we truly take up the question of this chapter. Therefore, after situating our conversation within that context, I will discuss several avenues by which saints' significance might be celebrated within Baptist life and thought. It is hoped that this chapter will contribute to our greater participation in the church catholic on pilgrimage with and toward the Triune God.

1. Saints and the Universal Call to Holiness

While Baptists have tended to underemphasize saints, preferring to use the term only in the strictest New Testament sense of "fellow believers," Catholics have maintained a prominent place for saints.[5] Certainly, specific saints do play a role in the Catholic notion of holiness (e.g., through specific modes of patronage), but that is not the end of the story. Saints are part of what might be called an economy of sanctity that extends to all of the faithful without limit.[6] In short, the faithful are called upon, as those who follow Jesus, to embrace a path of sanctity. This path is described in the Second Vatican Council's Dogmatic Constitution on the Church (*Lumen Gentium*) as the universal call to holiness in the church. The Council states that "all in the Church, whether they belong to the hierarchy or are cared for by it, are called to holiness."[7] Drawing on the Apostle Paul's admonition to the Thessalonians that holiness makes up the fabric of all our lives, the text reiterates, "all Christians in any state or walk of life are called to the fullness of Christian life and

---

[4] Conner, *What Is a Saint?*, 17. Later he acknowledges that, if all Christians are saints, then the departed may still hold that status: "They belonged to God while living; surely they still belong to him" (27).

[5] I have argued elsewhere that the theological concept by which a majority of this underemphasis is derived—the priesthood of all believers—does not in fact rule out a robust notion of saints, even as a set-apart class of people within the ecclesia. See Hatch, "The Universal Call to Holiness and the Priesthood of All Believers."

[6] See Matt. 5:48 ("Be perfect, therefore, as your heavenly Father is perfect."). Gregory of Nyssa stated, "Christian perfection has but one limit, that of having none" (*Life of Moses*, quoted in the *Catechism of the Catholic Church* § 2028 (p. 490).

[7] Vatican II, *Dogmatic Constitution on the Church (Lumen Gentium)*, § 39, in *Vatican Council II*, rev. ed., ed. Flannery, 396.

to the perfection of love."[8] The focus of such a vocation is Christ himself, the one who called us to be perfect and the one who modeled this holiness in his earthly sojourn, primarily in the two greatest commandments. Concerning his disciples, *Lumen Gentium* says, "The followers of Christ, called by God not by virtue of their works but by his design and grace, and justified in the Lord Jesus, have been made sons of God in the baptism of faith and partakers of the divine nature, and so are truly sanctified."[9] Thus, like Christ himself, all of the faithful will be "marked by love both of God and of [their] neighbor."[10] With Christ as the exemplar, then, the goal of the discipleship imaged by the saints becomes Christologically shaped.

Thus, in the Catholic view, there is no doubt that this call is universal, but the ways that it can be manifested and developed are multiple. In other words, as the Council states, "The forms and tasks of life are many but holiness is one—that sanctity which is cultivated by all who act under God's Spirit and, obeying the Father's voice and adoring God the Father in spirit and in truth, follow Christ."[11] This sanctity is broader than simply a handful of people. Instead, all the faithful (in all stations of life) are part of the same journey and headed in the same direction, even in the midst of great diversity. Aiming to illustrate the breadth of this chorus, *Lumen Gentium* discusses the manner in which several classes of people share in this call, including bishops, priests, ministers of lesser rank, married couples and parents, widows and single people, humanitarians and activists, and all people, especially those "weighed down by poverty, infirmity, sickness and other hardships."[12] What we see here, then, is not a superhuman sense of sanctity. Rather, the council, by appealing to people of all stations of life, offers through Christ's example what it calls "a more human manner of life" to the world.[13]

More recently, popes have highlighted the centrality of the universal call to holiness. In January 2001, John Paul II offered *Novo Millennio Ineunte*, an apostolic letter on the occasion of the new millennium. In it, he aimed to outline the church's priorities going forward. Not surprisingly, he focused primarily on holi-

---

[8] Vatican II, *Dogmatic Constitution on the Church (Lumen Gentium)*, § 40, in *Vatican Council II*, rev. ed., ed. Flannery, 397.

[9] Vatican II, *Dogmatic Constitution on the Church (Lumen Gentium)*, § 40, in *Vatican Council II*, rev. ed., ed. Flannery, 397.

[10] Vatican II, *Dogmatic Constitution on the Church (Lumen Gentium)*, § 42, in *Vatican Council II*, rev. ed., ed. Flannery, 400.

[11] Vatican II, *Dogmatic Constitution on the Church (Lumen Gentium)*, § 41, in *Vatican Council II*, rev. ed., ed. Flannery, 398.

[12] Vatican II, *Dogmatic Constitution on the Church (Lumen Gentium)*, § 41, in *Vatican Council II*, rev. ed., ed. Flannery, 400.

[13] Vatican II, *Dogmatic Constitution on the Church (Lumen Gentium)*, § 40, in *Vatican Council II*, rev. ed., ed. Flannery, 397.

ness, which he described as "a message that convinces without the need for words" and as "the living reflection of the face of Christ."[14] Continuing, he stated, "Holiness, whether ascribed to Popes well-known to history or to humble lay and religious figures, from one continent to another of the globe, has emerged more clearly as the dimension which expresses best the mystery of the Church."[15] Recalling *Lumen Gentium*, he noted that the council document rediscovered this mystery when it recognized the church as a people gathered together in the unity of the Father, the Son, and the Holy Spirit.[16] This holiness, though, is more than a state; it is a task as well, one that deserves the utmost attention and effort: "all pastoral initiatives must be set in relation to holiness."[17] Further, John Paul II connected baptism to holiness: "To ask catechumens: 'Do you wish to receive Baptism?' means at the same time to ask them, 'Do you wish to become holy?'"[18] He reiterated the council's point that holiness is not a condition reserved for a few special persons. Instead, John Paul II declared, "The time has come to re-propose wholeheartedly to everyone this *high standard of ordinary Christian living*."[19] To do so requires "training in holiness," which includes the art of prayer, Eucharistic practice, penitential contrition, and listening to and proclaiming the word of God.[20]

In a November 2014 general audience in St. Peter's Square, Pope Francis also invoked the theme of holiness as discussed in *Lumen Gentium*. Grounded in baptism, "all Christians…share in the same vocation," one that he described as a "universal vocation to being saints."[21] Like John Paul II and the Second Vatican Council, Francis refuted the notion that sainthood is something obtained through determined effort. Instead, sanctity is always received as a gift, "granted to us by the Lord Jesus."[22] It involves "rediscover[ing] oneself in communion with God, in the fullness of his life and of his love."[23] Consequently, sanctity is not the "preroga-

---

[14] John Paul II, *Novo Millennio Ineunte*, § 7.

[15] John Paul II, *Novo Millennio Ineunte*, § 7.

[16] John Paul II, *Novo Millennio Ineunte*, § 30. Cf. Vatican II, *Dogmatic Constitution on the Church (Lumen Gentium)*, § 4, in *Vatican Council II*, rev. ed., ed. Flannery, 351-52.

[17] John Paul II, *Novo Millennio Ineunte*, § 30.

[18] John Paul II, *Novo Millennio Ineunte*, § 31.

[19] John Paul II, *Novo Millennio Ineunte*, § 31; emphasis added.

[20] John Paul II, *Novo Millennio Ineunte*, §§ 32-41.

[21] Francis, General Audience (November 19, 2014). In Graham Greene's novel *The Power and the Glory*, the wayward whiskey priest is caught up in a story of persecution. His journey through this period, which includes performance of his clerical sacramental duties and ultimately the sacrifice of martyrdom, results in a changed outlook and a conclusion similar to what was spoken by Francis: "He knew now that at the end there was only one thing that counted—to be a saint" (Greene, *The Power and the Glory*, 210).

[22] Francis, General Audience (November 19, 2014), § 1.

[23] Francis, General Audience (November 19, 2014), § 1.

tive of the few."[24] Francis gave more texture to this claim by walking through various states of life (consecrated, married, unmarried, parent or grandparent, catechist, educator, volunteer).[25] In short, he declared, "[E]very state of life leads to holiness, always! In your home, on the street, at work, at church, in that moment and in your state of life, the path to sainthood has been opened."[26] To pursue that path, Francis suggests that progress might be found in small acts consisting of patience, prayer, generosity, and hospitality.[27]

Throughout all these reflections, it is clear that in the Catholic view holiness or sainthood is the path of the entire church. As *Lumen Gentium* states, "In the Church not everyone marches along the same path, yet all are called to sanctity."[28] This general call to sanctity, however, does not exclude a place for specified saints. After all, the fullness of this universal vocation received by the whole church is manifested in the life and witness of these particular persons, as *Lumen Gentium* makes clear: "[T]he authentic cult of the saints consists not so much in the multiplying of external acts, but rather in the greater intensity of our love, whereby, for our own greater good and that of the whole Church, we seek from the saints 'example in their way of life, fellowship in their communion, and aid by their intercession.'"[29] Baptist theologians Paul Fiddes, Brian Haymes, and Richard Kidd make a similar observation: "[I]n some lives there appears to be a particular disclosure that calls for attention."[30] To be sure, this disclosure—a certain intensity of the love of God and love of neighbor—is not based on the merits or abilities of the individuals, but on the grace of the Holy One within them. We recognize such grace perhaps due to special circumstances that make it visible in a peculiar manner, not only captivating our gaze, but beckoning us to imitation. Highlighting the role of ecclesial judgment and recognition, they state, "the church corporately has *found* them to be a focal point for reflecting on the generosity of God in human

---

[24] Francis, General Audience (November 19, 2014), § 1.

[25] Francis, General Audience (November 19, 2014), § 2. Francis even imagines a potential dialogue objecting to this claim: "'But, father, I work in a factory; I work as an accountant, only with numbers; you can't be a saint there....' Yes, yes you can! There, where you work, you can become a saint" (ibid.).

[26] Francis, General Audience (November 19, 2014), § 2.

[27] Francis, General Audience (November 19, 2014), § 3.

[28] Vatican II, *Dogmatic Constitution on the Church (Lumen Gentium)*, § 32, in *Vatican Council II*, rev. ed. Flannery, 389.

[29] Vatican II, *Dogmatic Constitution on the Church (Lumen Gentium)*, § 51, in *Vatican Council II*, rev. ed. Flannery, 412. Elsewhere, *Lumen Gentium* links the holiness of the faithful with the saints by stating, "[T]he holiness of the People of God will grow in fruitful abundance, as is clearly shown in the history of the Church through the lives of so many saints" (ibid., § 40, pp. 397-98).

[30] Fiddes, Haymes, and Kidd, *Baptists and the Communion of Saints*, 23.

life."[31] Therefore, it is not impossible to see potential points of intersection, as well as places where Baptists might learn from their Catholic counterparts as they strive to better account for the sanctity of the holy faithful within and without their tradition.

2. Can Baptists Welcome the Saints?

In a blog post on the occasion of All Saints Day in 2013, Baptist World Alliance General Secretary Neville Callam wrote:

> Shouldn't Baptist churches retrieve the practice of venerating the saints, that is, engaging in corporate worship acts designed not to worship the saints, but to remember, honor, learn from, and celebrate saints from our Baptist family and from other Christian communions? Until we regularly include commemoration of the saints in our worship celebrations, we will continue to neglect the opportunity to give proper value to those from our past who have borne courageous witness to faithful discipleship.[32]

James McClendon echoes this question, emphasizing the role of the Holy Spirit within the saints' ecclesial presence: "[I]f we remember, and relive, and so tell the stories that great Christians are discovered among us again in our own day, then the saints are alive *and the Spirit once again informs the people of God*."[33] But what does this look like? How might Baptists begin to consider the role of saints not only in ecclesial activity writ large, but in liturgical acts more specifically?

One way to celebrate the saints is to create the occasion for honoring their lives. British Baptist pastor Andy Goodliff presents a case for the development of a Baptist sanctoral, a calendared cycle commemorating the stories of particular witnesses to the Christian faith.[34] As Goodliff states, such a device would help Baptists in "remembering with thankfulness and learning with openness from the lives of those that have gone before and now number among the saints of God."[35] Once assembled, this calendar would provide organization and rhythm to the life of Baptist churches. That is, as observing the seasons of the Christian year places Baptist congregations on shared liturgical ground with other Christians, a common cycle

---

[31] Fiddes, Haymes, and Kidd, *Baptists and the Communion of Saints*, 95; emphasis added.

[32] Callam, "General Secretary's Blog" (October 31, 2013), quoted in Harmon, "Baptists and the Veneration of the Saints."

[33] McClendon, "Do We Need Saints Today?", 2:294; emphasis added.

[34] Goodliff, "Towards a Baptist Sanctoral?" In this article, Goodliff does great work in summarizing other Baptist theologians' work (e.g., that of McClendon, Harmon, Stephen Holmes, and John Colwell, among others) that points toward greater need for a Baptist embrace of the saints both theologically and liturgically.

[35] Goodliff, "Towards a Baptist Sanctoral?," 28.

of saintly persons would certainly deepen these ties further. Moreover, by scattering these exemplary lives throughout the year, rather than concentrating them at liturgical zeniths, the invitation to follow their Christ-like lead is ongoing and not haphazard or uneven.[36]

Even with the construction of a calendar, the question of celebration is not fully answered. Taking seriously the ancient church axiom, *lex orandi, lex credendi* ("the rule of praying is the rule of believing"), we might look for paths of remembrance that are woven into the prayer and worship of the body of Christ. After all, a great deal of Baptist theologizing, for instance, occurs in the singing and worship of the congregation. Moreover, in prayers of thanksgiving or prayers of remembrance, particular theological convictions come to the fore. Indeed, our understanding of such convictions may be transformed by being woven into the story of a specific life. The first suggestion for pursuing such a goal is to simply name saints in worship. This can be accomplished in several ways, including a simple identification of a particular saintly occasion (e.g., "Today is the Feast of Saint...."), marking the occasion of All Saints Day,[37] and the use of the many extant prayers we have received from the saints of old.[38] It should be noted, though, that the use of visual images (even icons) could be adopted as well and as something akin to parish festivals in memory of a particular saint.[39]

Steven Harmon has suggested that more might be done with the saints if churches provided liturgical space for a brief vignette marking the faithful life of a saint. Additionally, he writes, "When the life of the model Christian being commemorated on a given Sunday serves to illustrate the living of the stories told in the lectionary texts for the day, the lives of the saints would serve as ideal sermon illustrations—lived biblical stories rather than anecdotes that parallel sermonic ideas."[40]

---

[36] Cf. *Catechism of the Catholic Church*, § 2030: "It is in the Church, in communion with all the baptized, that the Christian fulfills his vocation....From the Church he learns the *example of holiness* and...discovers it in the spiritual tradition and long history of the saints who have gone before him and whom the liturgy celebrates in the rhythms of the sanctoral cycle."

[37] When visiting a Baptist church in Austin, Texas, on All Saints Day, I observed a shared remembrance of the faithful Christians who had died during the past year. After the pastor named well-known persons, he invited the congregation to participate by adding more names to the list prior to offering a pastoral prayer.

[38] Fiddes, Haymes, and Kidd, *Baptists and the Communion of Saints*, 164-65.

[39] The Evangelical Baptist Church of the Republic of Georgia has begun using icons in worship (Fiddes, Haymes, and Kidd, *Baptists and the Communion of Saints*, 166-67).

[40] Harmon, *Towards Baptist Catholicity*, 170. Occasionally, one can find similar depictions of saints from the Scriptures and the tradition in stained glass, usually as exemplifications of one of the virtues. For example, in Baylor University's Robbins Chapel, each of the intellectual, moral, and theological virtues is named and associated with a biblical hero of the faith as well as an

In this way, these lives speak to us and continue to shape the contours of Christian existence, much like G. K. Chesterton spoke of tradition as the "democracy of the dead." Along these lines he elaborated, "Tradition means giving a vote to the most obscure of classes, our ancestors….Tradition refuses to submit to the small and arrogant oligarchy of those who merely happen to be walking about."[41] Harmon's suggestion brings our ancestors into the conversation concerning how to faithfully bear witness to the truth of the gospel.

Each of these actions shines a spotlight on the faithful life lived and potentially offers inspiration and imagination for believers in the contemporary context. This is certainly admirable, but more might be considered. In other words, agreeing on the importance of celebrating the lives of faithful Christians who have gone before us is good, yet not too difficult. After all, Baptists have never shied away from some such remembrances. From universities to annual offerings to general conversation, Baptists have highlighted the exemplars of their regions and particular denominations. For instance, Southern Baptists remember Lottie Moon every December and Annie Armstrong every Easter. Baptists from Texas recall the importance of Mary Hill Davis, and George W. Truett's name marks several Baptist structures and institutions, as does John Leland's and William Carey's in other locales. Moreover, collections of stories, such as *Foxe's Book of Martyrs* or the Anabaptist *Martyrs Mirror*, elevate specific lives as particularly exemplary for Christian living in sometimes harsh climates. Such remembrances are notable for their role in the collective memory of a regional Baptist body. Yet, rarely are invocations of these figures intended as more than an *illustration* of holiness.

How can saints serve as more than an object lesson? For instance, might the saintly figures remembered also be viewed as sharing in the mystical body of Christ even after death (as is indicated by a full notion of the communion of saints)? We might recall that early Christian martyrs (the first people recognized as saints) were commemorated on the date of their death, though it was called their "birthday," highlighting their full embrace of new life. In short, they were alive in God and remained active in the life of the church. Fiddes, Haymes, and Kidd echo this conclusion, discussing these faithful ones in the context of memory. Indeed, understanding the "memory of God" as a useful metaphor for conceptualizing the abiding relationship between the creator and the creature, they see the memory of God as binding all the saints together as all are alive in Christ.[42] Thus, even beyond

---

exemplar from the rest of Christian history (e.g., Solomon and Boethius for wisdom; Hannah and Dorothy Day for hope).

[41] Chesterton, *Orthodoxy*, 48.

[42] Fiddes, Haymes, and Kidd, *Baptists and the Communion of Saints*, 69-70; "To be remembered by God would be nothing less than being alive in God" (ibid., 90).

death, these beloved disciples continually serve the church and are signs of Jesus' life and work. Because of this, Fiddes, Haymes, and Kidd note, "To remember them and others is to be inspired by the Spirit."[43] Moreover, the authors welcome the intercession of these who live in God, these whose prayers (like all prayers), "ride upon the praying of Christ into the most holy place."[44] To be certain, they avoid any sense that Mary and the saints are a necessary conduit for our prayers, but they do affirm that we offer our prayers with Mary and the saints such that our prayers are never alone.[45]

The idea that these saints may be active within the life of God beyond the grave opens up new horizons for Baptists and their nascent reflections on sanctity. Even though Baptists might dispute aspects of a Catholic view of sanctity that may ascribe merit to saints that they retain after death, we might recall McClendon's work, which points to the mediatory character of these lives. They are not mere ornamentation or illustration of the Christian life; rather, they carry that life to us. That is, these saints mediate God's presence to the people of God but also to the temporal plane in what Dom Gregory Dix has described as the sanctification of time.[46] Insofar as this is the case, it seems that these lives make possible saintly intercession in a manner similar to intercessory petitions offered by the living. While they are distinct from Christ and his role, these saints are Christ to us. As such, we might welcome their ongoing prayers, and we might with McClendon recognize the place of honoring (i.e., venerating) these people.[47]

3. Receiving Light from the Saints

The development of a Baptist sanctoral offers a great deal of promise for receiving the saints, and many lives have been (informally) proposed as candidates for such a calendar, such as Martin Luther King, Jr., Muriel Lester, Fannie Lou Hamer, Thomas Helwys, and John Bunyan, among others. McClendon urges additional reflection on who we might celebrate, noting that such questions are not insular or self-serving: "To ask about the lives we will celebrate is to ask what is the character of life worth celebrating—in the end it is to ask about the character of the Christ."[48] To be sure, such remembrance requires truthfully telling the stories of the saints, including their blemishes, because "to tell the whole truth about our

---

[43] Fiddes, Haymes, and Kidd, *Baptists and the Communion of Saints*, 24.
[44] Fiddes, Haymes, and Kidd, *Baptists and the Communion of Saints*, 75.
[45] Fiddes, Haymes, and Kidd, *Baptists and the Communion of Saints*, 92-93.
[46] See Dix, *The Shape of the Liturgy*, 303-96.
[47] McClendon, Jr., *Biography as Theology*, 180.
[48] McClendon, *Biography as Theology*, 180.

saints is in the end to unite them with ourselves...."[49] Goodliff mentions the need to expand the list of candidates beyond the bounds of the UK and North America to include lesser-known persons as well as women.[50] This begs a further question: does a Baptist sanctoral consist of a cycle wholly populated by Baptists or does it include the lives of certain Baptists along with all other lived witnesses to the gospel of Jesus Christ? In other words, if we fill the calendar entirely with Baptist folk, how will this sanctoral accomplish the aims described by Harmon as "both distinctively Baptist and broadly ecumenical"?[51]

A calendar wholly made up of Baptists could potentially increase the ties between Baptist churches, but it might simply recreate Baptist struggles regarding unity with the broader Christian family. McClendon understood this as well. The core of his theology—the baptist vision—has always been broader than the churches that call themselves Baptist. For instance, in *Ethics* (the first volume of his systematic theology), Jonathan and Sarah Edwards, Dietrich Bonhoeffer, and Dorothy Day stand as exemplars.[52] Interestingly, our fellow Christians in some other traditions have included several Baptists within their annual cycles.[53] Several pathways forward seem worth consideration. First, we might work to embrace earlier Christians who embodied faithfulness before the Reformation, such as Athanasius, Augustine, Perpetua and Felicity, Macrina, and Polycarp. Such recognition ties Baptists simultaneously to the early church as well as to contemporary Christians who share in remembering their lives and their participation in the whole body of Christ. Further, we might look for moments where Baptists can and should affirm the sanctity of those in other traditions (i.e., after the Reformation), such as Thérèse of Lisieux, Archbishop Oscar Romero, Bonhoeffer, André Trocmé, and Mother Teresa.[54] Occasionally, our commemoration of their lives could contribute to our greater unity not only with Christians of one neighboring tradition but also with all Christians across the world.[55] A Baptist sanctoral, then, must not be solely

---

[49] McClendon, *Biography as Theology*, 178-79.

[50] Goodliff, "Towards a Baptist Sanctoral?," 28.

[51] Harmon, *Towards Baptist Catholicity*, 170.

[52] McClendon, *Systematic Theology*, vol. 1, *Ethics*, rev. ed.

[53] Several Anglican communions honor John Bunyan. In the Episcopal Church in the United States, Walter Rauschenbusch has a feast day (July 2), as do Roger Williams (February 5), Martin Luther King, Jr. (April 4), William Carey (October 19), Adoniram Judson (April 12), and Lottie Moon (December 22). The Evangelical Lutheran Church in America honors King on January 15.

[54] Fiddes, Haymes and Kidd, *Baptists and the Communion of Saints*, 114-25, hold up Thérèse as a witness to the significance of specific saints.

[55] Consider, for instance, the potential impact of remembering the twenty-six Catholic Martyrs of Nagasaki (February 6 in the General Roman Calendar) or Charles Lwanga and his companions (June 3 in the General Roman Calendar).

Baptist. Instead, it must include non-Baptist voices and draw into it a wider chorus of Baptists who echo and extend that which we have inherited from the whole tradition. In McClendon's terms, it must reflect the character of the mystical body of Christ.[56]

Moreover, even on a logistical level, it is easy to discern that the number of people who might be suggested as saints vastly outnumbers the potential occasions for remembrance. For other traditions, part of the resolution of this issue has involved engagement of a wider notion of ecclesial authority. That is, the Catholic canonization process does limit the number of people who are officially recognized as saints. However, it is notable that Catholics and Anglicans do allow for some distinction between those whose lives are of significance for the entire church and those for whom that particular intensity of sanctity touches only a specific locality or region (thereby limiting the scope of their celebration). This distinction may prove helpful in sorting through even the Baptist candidates for recognition. Theologically speaking, it also does important work for how space and time are consecrated. Dix points out that the development of a more robust cult of saints in the fourth century brought local martyrs to the fore as witness to the Lordship of Christ. The result was that "their cultus enabled the church to set forth Jesus as the Lord not only of universal history but of homely local history as well...."[57] In short, in these local and regional saints, the Word became flesh in their midst.

The Latin root for cult (*cultus*) has a sense of "to care for"; thus, "agriculture" involves care for what is grown in the ground. In this manner, the "cult of the saints," a phrase that has terrified many Baptists for centuries, might simply point to the ways in which the living church cares for those who have gone before us. Such work certainly involves remembering their stories, but that may not be sufficient. Much like recent sacramental discussions about recovering a deeper sense of our Eucharistic remembrance, the memory of the saints must involve participation. We must actively share with all of this holy communion. Thus, the vast array of

---

[56] Additional questions remain, though they must be tabled until later discussion. For instance, a wider embrace of the church's annual cycle of sanctity leads to reservations about Marian feast days. While perhaps Baptists will have to struggle through the feasts of the Assumption (August 15), Immaculate Conception (December 8), or those dedicated to Marian apparitions, such as Our Lady of Guadalupe (December 12) and Our Lady of Lourdes (February 11), what about the feast of the Annunciation (March 25), which finds its basis wholly in scripture and is appropriately oriented toward Jesus, whose birth will be celebrated exactly nine months later? Or the Solemnity of Mary, the Mother of God (January 1 for Western Christians; December 26 in the East)? It seems that at least these occasions should be considered as candidates for celebration, in part in order to receive the gift of Mary from our fellow Christian pilgrims, but also to augment Baptist understanding of the mother of God.

[57] Dix, *Shape of the Liturgy*, 333.

saints across the centuries "serve[s] as models for new styles of being Christian, opening paths which many others will follow."[58] Additionally, we must look for more subtle saints in the post-Enlightenment era, whether they be found in homes, offices, and factories as well as monasteries and churches. Altogether, such saints help people of each generation "take up the way of practical holiness in daily life."[59] When the church celebrates the saints, it cares for—it cultivates—the ties within the *ecclesia* and the church's witness to the world. Finally, to receive the saints should deepen our worship and further direct our lives toward Christ, the one whom all the saints imitate (cf. 1 Cor. 11:1).

4. For Further Reading

Ellsberg, Robert. *All Saints: Daily Reflections on Saints, Prophets, and Witnesses for Our Time.* New York: Crossroad, 1997.

Fiddes, Paul, Brian Haymes, and Richard Kidd. *Baptists and the Communion of Saints: A Theology of Covenanted Disciples.* Waco, TX: Baylor University Press, 2014.

McCarthy, David Matzko. *Sharing God's Company: A Theology of the Communion of the Saints.* Grand Rapids, MI: William B. Eerdmans, 2012.

McClendon, James Wm., Jr. *Biography as Theology: How Life Stories Can Remake Today's Theology.* 1974. Reprint, Eugene, OR: Wipf and Stock, 2002.

McClendon, James Wm., Jr. "Do We Need Saints Today? (1986)." In *The Collected Works of James Wm. McClendon, Jr.: Volume Two,* edited by Ryan Andrew Newson and Andrew C. Wright, 285-94. Waco, TX: Baylor University Press, 2014.

Rothaus Moser, Matthew A. *Love Itself is Understanding: Hans Urs von Balthasar's Theology of the Saints.* Minneapolis: Fortress Press, 2016.

---

[58] Dix, *Shape of the Liturgy,* 156-57.
[59] Dix, *Shape of the Liturgy,* 57.

22

Light from Traditional Liturgical Sources

Philip E. Thompson

While I believe Baptists should receive light from the reform of worship known as the Liturgical Movement, how this should look is not a simple matter. My goal is not to persuade Baptists to adopt a particular "worship style," to embrace "high church" worship, nor to become more "refined" by borrowing from the liturgies of other churches, as though the prayers of earlier times and other cultures are more "meaningful." If that were what I hoped to accomplish, this chapter would have an air of superficiality about it of which I want no part. My hope, rather, is briefly to gesture toward something I envision being enacted in a range of styles from shaped note hymnody to the masterworks of classical repertoire, from gospel to jazz to rock, with prayers spanning extemporized offerings to texts of other centuries and places and churches. To be clear, it is a call for reform within that embodiment of the Christian faith called "Baptist," particularly in North America. More, however, is at stake than the quality of prose we employ in our worship.

1. Worship as Theology

Worship and liturgy are not like the other sources of light to which we might attend. Indeed, to call them "sources" is to regard them wrongly. As Aidan Kavanagh observed, worship is "not one theological source among others."[1] Worship is not a datum of theology. It *is* theology.[2] In saying this, I do not mean this topic above all the others treated in this volume is alone "really" important. Still, there is a qualitative difference. Many of the other conversations reflected and envisioned in this collection may be characterized as "secondary theology," reflection on the faith, illuminated by light from various sources, imparted through dialogue, yielding enriched understanding and practices. Kavanagh noted that this is what we most often mean when we speak of theology.[3] What emerges in worship, however, he

---

[1] Kavanagh, *On Liturgical Theology*, 7.
[2] Kavanagh, *On Liturgical Theology*, 75-76.
[3] Kavanagh, *On Liturgical Theology*, 74-75.

said, "is *theologia* itself," primary theology.[4] In worship, our understanding of God, ourselves, and the world is given shape. "The human activity of listening for and addressing God shows something of what may be said and known about God."[5] Our prayers and worship establish our belief (*lex orandi est lex credendi*, as the medieval maxim is often summarized).

It is important that we worship well. Worship is the site of confrontation with the disorder of the world, a disorder often described as liturgical and religious.[6] Dietrich Bonhoeffer noted that, fallen from God, human life has lost its sense of "the real," God revealed in Jesus Christ.[7] This loss is manifested and perpetuated in ways properly called "liturgical." James K. A. Smith has persuasively set forth an interpretation of human being as "*homo liturgicus*," engaged in the aiming of our love toward visions of the good. Simply to be human is to do this, to enact what Smith calls "rituals of ultimate concern," or "liturgies."[8] Apart from God in Christ, ultimate concern is directed toward lesser goods, other gods. Among these Smith includes cultural liturgies of consumerism and nationalism.[9] He is not alone. Stanley Hauerwas cites Peter Leithart's claim that the state has been resacralized in modernity.[10] Scott Waalkes has described the commercial parody of the liturgical calendar in the United States.[11] That misplaced ultimacy has uncritically been allowed to coopt the formation of churches, particularly those identified as Evangelical, is

---

[4] Kavanagh, *On Liturgical Theology*, 75.

[5] Saliers, *Worship as Theology*, 69. Kavanagh, *On Liturgical Theology*, 88-89, noted that western Christians talk a great deal about secondary theology, but about the primary form hardly at all. This is not to imply that worship is not talked about at great length. Sadly, it is often about the more superficial aspects of it that are most ardently discussed. Kavanagh contended, 173-74, that this is the result of "the secularization process in the West—a process which Hanna (*sic*) Arendt thinks…threw people not into the world but back upon themselves. This in turn has given rise to a defensive privatism which emphasizes the sovereignty of the individual…." Baptists could be so characterized, I believe.

[6] Kavanagh, *On Liturgical Theology*, 39.

[7] Bonhoeffer, *Ethics*, 66–100. Bonhoeffer did not draw firm connections to worship, but that is not to say such should not be drawn. Hauerwas and Wells, *The Blackwell Companion to Christian Ethics*, 2nd ed., is an ambitious exploration of Christian ethics from the perspective of the liturgy.

[8] Smith, *Desiring the* Kingdom, 39-88. Gouldbourne, "Liturgical Identity Carriers for Ecclesial Transformation," 379-91, explores this dynamic helpfully from a Baptist context, citing several other thinkers who reflect on this topic.

[9] Smith, *Desiring the Kingdom*, 93-112.

[10] Hauerwas, "The End of Sacrifice," 431. See too Cavanaugh, *The Myth of Religious Violence*, and idem, *Migrations of the Holy*.

[11] Waalkes, *The Fulness of Time in a Flat World*, 149-50.

one of the concerns at the heart of the present volume.[12] A coopted church becomes unable truly to preach the gospel. "What good is a church," asks Byron Anderson, "that can neither critique nor console the world?"[13]

Baptists have tended to think in the other direction, from belief to worship. "As men believe," noted Franklin Segler in a widely-used textbook, "so they worship. The doctrines we hold determine the nature of our worship."[14] This reflects an obscuring of worship's formative power in much Baptist writing in North America. Yet this is not a stark either/or. The relation of primary and secondary theology is indeed a complex dynamic. They are, as Anderson has pointed out, "mutually causative."[15] A study of nineteenth century Baptists in both England and the United States shows that the practice and understanding of worship underwent changes because of developments in Baptist theology.[16] We cannot think, therefore, that making wholesale changes in worship will cure all our theological and ethical ills apart from hard work on the level of secondary theology as well. We should address both.

Worship embodies the gospel.[17] Faithfully enacted, it becomes what Johann Baptist Metz has called the "dangerous memory" of the suffering and passion of Christ in the world.[18] Right worship should constitute the church as a sign of the Kingdom of God.[19] Nearly sixty years ago, J. V. L. Casserley observed:

> We know very little about the Kingdom of God, for the eye has not seen and the ear has not heard it…yet of this we may be sure, the Kingdom of God will be much more like the liturgy, which indeed anticipates and participates in the Kingdom, than like anything else we know on earth.[20]

---

[12] Churches that identify as more "mainline" or "progressive" are liable to their own forms of this coopting. See Mikael Broadway et al., "Re-Envisioning Baptist Identity," 303-10.

[13] Anderson, *Worship and Christian Identity*, 39.

[14] Segler, *Christian Worship*, 57.

[15] Anderson, *Worship and Christian Identity*, 29.

[16] Thompson, "Re-Envisioning Baptist Identity"; Ellis, *Gathering*.

[17] Williams, "Structure and Form in Church Worship," 293.

[18] Richter, "Liturgical Reform as the Means for Church Renewal," 119. Metz does not explore the liturgical aspects of his potent idea, leaving that task for others. A sterling example of this is Morrill, *Anamnesis as Dangerous Memory*.

[19] Kavanagh, *On Liturgical Theology*, 3-4 et passim. In keeping with his definition of worship as primary theology, Kavanagh insisted that "orthodoxy" means primarily "right worship," and only derivatively "doctrinal accuracy." This implies, however, that there are boundaries within which worship must remain to be "right."

[20] Casserley, "The Significance of the Liturgical Movement," 216.

Kavanagh put it well in his inimitably terse prose. A community that practices right worship, he asserted, should understand itself to be "the world rendered normal" because it has been restored to communion with God.[21]

2. The Liturgical Movement and Baptists

The Liturgical Movement has sought to renew the church in accordance with precisely this vision. It is, however, often misconstrued as being about the recovery of ancient liturgical texts. Admittedly, there is some truth to this. The liturgical movement arose in the nineteenth century in the wake of early biblical text criticism, with the aim of reconstructing the most accurate version of the text possible.[22] Until around the Second World War, it was primarily a phenomenon within Roman Catholicism, with parallels within Anglican and Reformed churches such as the Oxford Movement in England and the Mercersburg theology in the United States.

Yet, from the mid-twentieth century on, a confluence of the Liturgical Movement and the Ecumenical Movement had the twin effects of sharing the riches of the liturgy among more Protestant bodies and shifting Catholic focus more fully to reform of the various rites of Christian worship, often responding to concerns raised by the reformers of the sixteenth century.[23] The liturgical reform of the Second Vatican Council, and parallel renewal within several Protestant bodies, are often seen as the flowering of the Liturgical Movement's achievements and as a work of the Holy Spirit.[24] Casserley summarized matters beautifully:

> At first sight the liturgical movement appears to be animated by a primarily historical, indeed almost archaeological temper of mind....[A]n effort to recover something of the riches and values of the worship of the early church....[B]ut it would be a great mistake to suppose that the liturgical movement is simply concerned with the rites and ceremonies of the worshiping church. On the contrary in its most important aspects it is primarily a movement for the reformation of the whole life of the Church, it is at once a movement, a biblical revival, and a prophetic outburst.[25]

---

[21] Kavanagh, *On Liturgical Theology*, 159.

[22] Franklin, "Nineteenth Century Liturgical Movement"; Richter, "Liturgical Reform as the Means for Church Renewal," 128.

[23] Tillard, "Liturgical Reform and Christian Unity," 227, 236.

[24] Casserley, "Significance of the Liturgical Movement," 211; Wainwright, "Word and Table," 332.

[25] Casserley, "Significance of the Liturgical Movement," 211.

Prophetic outbursts cannot leave the self-understanding of the people of God unaffected. Liturgy and ecclesiology are inseparable, contends Klemens Richter. Therefore, there is an unbreakable connection between liturgical reform and church reform.[26] Quoting Reiner Kaczynski, "an *ecclesia semper reformanda* requires a *liturgia semper reformanda*," Richter concludes that liturgical reform cannot be separated from a more far reaching reform of the church.[27] Otherwise "it will ultimately remain only a cosmetic treatment of the Church's image."[28]

This raises pointed questions for Baptists. What I have sketched here does not "fit" with the way Baptists in North America have understood worship for many decades now. Baptists in North America have remained almost entirely aloof from the Liturgical Movement, hardly availing themselves of this source's light, received by Episcopal, Reformed, Methodist, and Lutheran communions.[29] Worse, worship has not received the thoughtful consideration it deserves.[30] What James Carter noted about Southern Baptists describes Baptists in North America generally. "*That* (their) worship has always been important. *How* they worship has not been that important."[31] This is not a trivial matter. If what I have described about the formative power of worship and the risk of worship being coopted is correct, should we not ask how susceptible to malformation our worship may have left us? While Baptists are not the only ones who could be so described, Baptists have been described as "churches in cultural captivity."[32] I believe that the reform of our worship should be one of the ways in which we go about confronting our various captivities.[33]

---

[26] Richter, "Liturgical Reform as the Means for Church Renewal," 121.

[27] Richter, "Liturgical Reform as the Means for Church Renewal," 127.

[28] Richter, "Liturgical Reform as the Means for Church Renewal," 141.

[29] Some Baptist scholars and churches, it should be noted, have sought to draw from the insights that have come from the Liturgical Movement. See, for example, many of the recommendations given by Harmon, "Praying and Believing" reflect themes of the liturgical movement, as do several of the essays in Kennedy and Hatch, eds., *Gathering Together*. Jeff Brumley reports on a Baptist church which employs the liturgical book of another communion which has been significantly influenced by the liturgical movement: Brumley, "Virginia Church May Look Anglican, but It's Fully Baptist."

[30] Carter, "What Is the Southern Baptist Heritage of Worship?" 38; Hinson, "Theology and Experience of Worship,"423; Segler, *Christian Worship*; McNutt, *Worship in the Churches*; Dana and Sipes, *A Manual of Ecclesiology*, 2nd rev. ed.; Dobbins, *The Church at Worship*; Pearce, *Come, Let Us Worship*.

[31] Carter, "What Is the Southern Baptist Heritage of Worship?" 38. Emphasis in the original.

[32] Eighmy and Hill, *Churches in Cultural Captivity*.

[33] While reform of worship would not be the sole key to such reform among Baptists, neither is it mere wishful thinking to suppose that reform of worship could play a role. Saliers, *Worship Come to Its Senses*; Anderson, *Worship and Christian Identity*; and Westerfield Tucker,

To be sure, there has been among Baptists for some time a fairly widespread sense that worship needs to be given more careful attention. In England, H. V. Larcombe declared to the London Baptist Association in 1950, "If Baptist Advance is to be anywhere real and abiding, it must most of all, and first of all, speak to us in relation to our practice and theory of worship."[34] Writing in 1962, Gaines Dobbins expressed concern about what he perceived to be lacking in Baptist worship.[35] About the same time, Paul Rowntree Clifford, an English Baptist teaching in Canada, observed an uneasy disquiet about the prevailing forms of worship in Baptist churches.[36] Nearer our own time, we might add to Carter's voice those of Raymond Bailey and Daniel Day observing not only the lack of reflection devoted to worship by Baptists in North America, but deleterious changes in worship in the absence of this reflection.[37]

Concerning what was required, Neville Clark cautioned against seeking change merely in the demeanor of worshipers. "To call for more reverence and solemnity, as if that will answer the need (for renewal of Baptist worship), is to misconceive the problem and underestimate its radical nature."[38] Nearly a quarter century later, Michael Walker showed similar urgency. "Not for the first time in the history of the church, liturgy is the focal point of deeper theological issues...."[39]

What produced the condition that creates in some a profound dissatisfaction? Wayne Dalton rightly noted in 1969, "The problem of worship in Baptist churches has had a peculiar history."[40] In North America, it stems in very large part from the widely acknowledged legacy of frontier revivalism in the eighteenth, and especially nineteenth, centuries.[41] This has, in some instances bequeathed, and in others joined with, a number of problematic characteristics of Baptists since that time. Prominent among them we would note individualism, in particular what has been

---

"North American Methodism's Engagement with Liturgical Renewal"; all relate aspects of reform that took place in Methodist congregations through change in worship.

[34] Clark, *Call to Worship*, 7.

[35] Dobbins, *The Church at Worship*, 2–7.

[36] Clifford, "Baptist Forms of Worship," 221.

[37] Bailey, "The Changing Face of Baptist Worship," 47–48; Day, "A Word about...Worship," 161-62.

[38] Clark, *Call to Worship*, 9–10. See too Winward, *The Reformation of Our Worship*, 6.

[39] Walker, "Baptist Worship in the Twentieth Century," 30; Casserley, "Significance of the Liturgical Movement," 212.

[40] Dalton, "Worship and Baptist Ecclesiology," 7.

[41] See for just two examples Walker, "Baptist Worship in the Twentieth Century," 21-22; and Nettleton, "Baptist Worship in Ecumenical Perspective," 72-76. It exceeds the scope of this essay to attend to this aspect of British Baptist history. There were similar developments, though with significant differences and brought about by other cultural dynamics.

called "expressive individualism."[42] Worship, even corporate worship, is seen primarily as an individual endeavor consisting of the expression of one's devotion to God.[43] Joining this I would add the paired characteristics of an overweening emphasis on personal, spiritual experience and the loss of a sense of the spiritual importance of material creation.[44]

Together, these have created what I call an "aesthetic calculus" in worship. What is most important is what appeals to worshipers as enabling "meaningful experiences" of God. In this light, the words "liturgy" and "liturgical" have come predominantly for Baptists to designate a style of worship marked by formality of ministerial attire (i.e. robes and stoles) and speech (prepared texts), even musical instrumentation, all of which is for the creation of experience.[45] Wayne Ward thus suggested that the reason some Baptists leave for churches where the Eucharist is more central is the aesthetically pleasing and spiritually moving "Anglican or Roman Catholic worship experience."[46] However accurate this description may be, it is lamentable. If Baptists leave Baptist churches, better reasons than taste should be determinative. Or perhaps genuinely theological reasons for departure cannot be perceived. Glenn Hinson rightly observes, "The gap between (Baptists) and liturgical churches is so great that we fail to comprehend the meaning of the word liturgical."[47] Failing this comprehension, Kavanagh's observation seems apt, if caustic, "Something seems to have been enthusiastically trivialized."[48]

One often senses a different quality of reflection on worship in writings from English Baptists, one not fettered by the individualist-expressivist assumptions so

---

[42] Bellah, *Habits of the Heart*, 32–35 and passim.

[43] Stanfield, *The Christian Worshiping*, 1-7; Dana and Sipes, *A Manual of Ecclesiology*, 201, 279; Pearce, *Come, Let Us Worship*, 11-29, 66-67; Clifford, "Baptist Forms of Worship," 228; Dalton, "Worship and Baptist Ecclesiology," 8; Hustad, "Baptist Worship Forms," 35; Ellis, "Gathering Struggles," 13-15. He calls for a more "impressive" understanding of prayer and worship as well.

[44] See for examples of either critique of these tendencies, or manifestations of them, Thompson, "Re-Envisioning Baptist Identity"; Harmon, "Trinitarian *Koinōnia* and Ecclesial *Oikoumenē*," 7; Stamps and Emerson, "Liturgy for Low-Church Baptists," 84-85; Ellis, *Gathering*, 65–66; McNutt, *Worship*, 7, 30-31; Hinson, "Theology and Experience of Worship," 422; Hustad, "Baptist Worship Forms," 35; Day, "A Word about...Worship," 162; Segler and Bradley, *Christian Worship*, 47.

[45] Bailey, "The Changing Face of Baptist Worship," 53, asserts that liturgical services may feature flute, oboe and harp. See also Basden, *The Worship Maze*, 41–54. Casserley, "Significance of the Liturgical Movement," 211, indicates that this identification with style is not limited to Baptists.

[46] Ward, "The Worship of the Church," 69.

[47] Hinson, "Theology and Experience of Worship," 423.

[48] Kavanagh, *On Liturgical Theology*, 47.

widely present in North America. Through more consistent involvement in the Ecumenical Movement than most Baptists in North America, some English Baptists came earlier and more enthusiastically to the insights of the Liturgical Movement.[49] Anthony Cross and Christopher Ellis note that Baptists have been key figures in the work of the Joint Liturgical Group, which has played an important role within British church life more broadly than simply the Baptists.[50] This work has yielded a number of Baptist worship books and/or hymnals over the last fifty years.[51] These books have provided texts for prayers, but with the insistence that liturgical reform is not about the use of particular texts, but a certain pattern of worship, what scholars of liturgy call the *ordo*.[52] "The essential mark of liturgy," noted Clark, "is not that it enshrine fixed and unvariable forms of words in an endlessly repetitive cycle, but that it possess a theologically grounded structure and pattern...."[53] This is especially true for Baptists, whose emphasis has been on the freedom of the Holy Spirit rather than the use of set forms of prayers and other liturgical formulae.[54]

3. Light for Reforming Baptist Worship

Baptist worship cannot be made more faithful simply by using prayers from other traditions, incorporating them into "traditional style" worship for the sake of making worship more "meaningful." To do this alone is simply to capitulate to the aesthetic calculus. Besides, what is often thought to be "traditional" Baptist worship, sometimes panned as a "hymn sandwich," developed in the nineteenth century.[55] Nothing more compelling than force of habit makes this ordering of worship in any way normative. To change would not mean the abandonment of Baptist

---

[49] Walker, "Baptist Worship in the Twentieth Century," 23; Baptist Union of Great Britain, *Patterns and Prayers for Christian Worship*, 3.

[50] Cross, *Baptism and the Baptists*, 439; Ellis, *Gathering*, 34.

[51] Three significant titles are: Payne and Winward, eds., *Orders and Prayers for Church Worship*; Baptist Union of Great Britain, *Patterns and Prayers for Christian Worship*; idem, *Gathering for Worship*.

[52] Payne and Winward, *Orders and Prayers*, xiii-xvi; Baptist Union of Great Britain, *Patterns and Prayers for Christian Worship*, v, 1-8; and Baptist Union of Great Britain, *Gathering for Worship*, xiii-xv.

[53] Clark, *Call to Worship*, 10. Numerous examples of the dialogical pattern of worship may be found in Hickman, Saliers, Stookey, and White, eds., *The New Handbook of the Christian Year*; Presbyterian Church (USA), *Book of Common Worship*; and Episcopal Church (USA), *The 1979 Book of Common Prayer*.

[54] See Payne and Winward, *Orders and Prayers*, xiii-xiv; Baptist Union of Great Britain, *Patterns and Prayers for Christian Worship*, v; and idem, *Gathering for Worship*, xiv.

[55] Ellis, *Gathering*, 56-57; Ellis, "Gathering Struggles," 11-12.

heritage.[56] Indeed, I do not believe there is a good reason to make the Baptist worship of any period normative. We should ask whether there is in our own tradition that which will enable faithful formation through the patterns of the liturgy, perhaps offering witness to others in the process. I argue that the worship shaped by the commonly held Baptist "secondary theology" is incapable of bearing the weight of the best of our heritage. We might ask if we could approach the reform of Baptist worship by adopting the pattern of worship commended by the Liturgical Movement, (which can be done using any "style" of music) together with recovering historic Baptist insights so that the formation that takes place would be thoroughly Baptist.[57]

Far more can be, and needs to be, said. I must let the barest gestures suffice with the assurance that the central insight of the Liturgical Movement, the aim of worship according to its pattern, is not alien to historical Baptist understandings. Casserley encapsulated this insight:

> (The liturgy forms) a community which binds itself to conform to the will and grace of God revealed in Jesus Christ, that will and grace of God which makes each one of us free with a kind of creaturely participation in the freedom of God which is in fact the only true freedom there is. In the liturgical community we conform to this will of God and to nothing else beside it[58]

He might have been describing the self-understanding Baptists embodied in their worship historically.

Through much of their history, Baptists understood themselves to be set apart in the world, called to be conformed to Christ through following in the path of Jesus. This took place for them, not solely but significantly, by the power of the Holy Spirit through the ministry of Word and sacrament. Theirs was an embodied and practiced theology and spirituality of discipleship. In following, they would know the Triune God who was present in Christ. Above all this was apparent in their gatherings to practice baptism and the Lord's Supper. We see it in the hymns and chants with which they accompanied these rites.[59] Thus, noted A. J. Gordon, "The church is formed from within. Christ present by the Holy Ghost...organizing (persons) into himself as the living center. The Head and the body are therefore one, and predestined to the same history of humiliation and glory."[60]

---

[56] See Clifford, "Baptist Forms of Worship," 222.

[57] Hicks, *The Worship Pastor*, 156-72.

[58] Casserley, "Significance of the Liturgical Movement," 217.

[59] Several Baptist hymnals in the nineteenth century included selections for congregational chanting, consisting of Psalms, the great Canticles of the Church, and various baptismal and spiritual chants.

[60] Gordon, *The Ministry of the Spirit*, 53.

Baptism serves as a pertinent test case for how Baptists might receive light from the Liturgical Movement. "A major impulse at work in the liturgical movement," notes Joseph Mangina, "was to restore to baptism something of the dramatic, boundary-crossing character that marked Christian initiation."[61] While present in a number of texts from earlier Baptist history, we see this in striking fashion in two eighteenth century sources. In a baptismal prayer we find the following:

> Behold the suppliant of pardon, sanctification, and salvation on coming to that which encourages his expectation of the necessary blessings! Accept his person....Henceforth, be thou his, and he thine; for it is his will to put on Christ by baptism; to become a christian openly; to take thy yoke and burden on his shoulder; and to learn obedience of the meek and lowly Jesus! Let his life be alike figure to his baptism....[62]

The baptismal prayer implored, "Lamb of God, which taketh away the sins of the world meet thy disciples! We know that thou art present every where (*sic*), but ah! let it not be here as at the first on the banks of the Jordan when thou didst stand among the croud (*sic*), and they knew it not! O let us find the messiah here!"[63] Every baptismal "here" was the place where disciples met their Lord.

And in a baptismal chant adapted from a hymn by the English Baptist, Samuel Stennett:

> On Jordan's stormy banks I stand,
> And cast a wishful eye
> To Canaan's fair and happy land,
> Where my possessions lie.
>
> Oh, the transporting, rapturous scene,
> That rises to my sight;
> Sweet fields arrayed in living green,
> And rivers of delight.[64]

The boundary envisioned is nothing less than eschatological. "[W]hat could be more essential to baptism," asks Mangina, "than the public display of Satan's kingdom overthrown?"[65]

---

[61] Mangina, "Baptism at the Turn of the Ages," 388.

[62] Edwards, *The Customs of Primitive Churches*, 82.

[63] Edwards, *The Customs of Primitive Churches*, 81.

[64] "Selections for Chanting," in American Baptist Publication Society, *The Baptist Hymn Book*, sec. 25.

[65] Mangina, "Baptism at the Turn of the Ages," 389.

This is the direction, I believe, for the reform of Baptist worship. The insights of the Liturgical Movement paired with a Baptist *ressourcement* suggest that Baptist worship has the capacity to form persons not as those who seek to experience God in a meaningful way, but who "learn obedience of the meek and lowly Jesus" daily.

Toward this end, Baptists could integrate into their worship the formative practices of the catechumenate more fully than many other churches that have reformed their initiatory rites. To do so will, however, require serious reflection on the history and theology both of Baptists and the wider church. The catechumenate "restores the essential place of faith at the heart of baptism."[66] Listening to their ancestors from before the age of revivalism, Baptists again may see conversion to faith more as a process of formation than as a decision in response to a crisis of soul.

This would in turn require re-conceptualizing baptism as something other than the symbolization of an individual's faith or conversion experience. Both to assist this process of re-conceptualization and as an element of a re-conceptualized baptism, Baptist worship services might regularly incorporate prayers for those preparing for baptism. More difficult for many congregations, Communion might be restricted to those who are baptized. It would, however, provide occasion for teaching about baptism and Christian life. It would also enable baptism and First Communion to be observed as a unified rite, as was the case in the early church.

Kavanagh said that God is not present to the church by faith, but in reality. It is the church that is present to God by faith. The beams of light from the Liturgical Movement and the Baptist past offer the hope that Baptists can be more faithfully present to God.

4. For Further Reading

Ellis, Christopher J. *Gathering: A Theology and Spirituality of Worship*. London: SCM Press, 2004.

Ellis, Christopher J. and Myra Blyth, eds. *Gathering for Worship: Patterns and Prayers for the Community of Disciples*. Norwich, UK: Canterbury Press, 2005.

Hickman, Hoyt L. *The New Handbook of the Christian Year: Based on the Revised Common Lectionary*. Nashville: Abingdon Press, 1992.

Hicks, Zac. *The Worship Pastor: A Call to Ministry for Worship Leaders and Teams*. Grand Rapids, MI: Zondervan, 2016.

Kavanagh, Aidan. *On Liturgical Theology*. Collegeville, MN: The Liturgical Press, 1992.

---

[66] Tillard, "Liturgical Reform and Christian Unity," 239.

Kennedy, Rodney Wallace and Derek Hatch, eds. *Gathering Together: Baptists at Work in Worship*. Eugene, OR: Pickwick Publications, 2013.

23

Light from Contemporary Liturgical Sources

Jennifer W. Davidson

A young, white woman wearing a tan trench coat, Chuck Taylor sneakers, and carrying a sonic screwdriver wanders into the quiet room off the main concourse of the convention center. She is dressed up as the tenth doctor from the long-running BBC science fiction program Doctor Who. The space in this room is markedly different from anywhere else in the convention, and she is grateful for it. A few other people are in the room; several of them are clergy from different faith traditions including a Wiccan, a priest of Dionysus, and two Baptists. One of them greets her and smiles warmly. She smiles back, but she chooses to settle down by the finger labyrinth. She's not here for more interaction—there has been plenty of that right outside the room at the vast Sci-Fi convention. She is here for the silence, for a chance to reflect, to re-center and re-energize before engaging the conference again. The room is sponsored by the Oasis Project, and she is grateful for it.[1]

A gathering of about thirty people organized by members of Second Acts[2] have assembled near the entry to the Alameda County Superior Court in Oakland, California. It is Good Friday in April 2017. A significant number of them are clearly clergy members, identified by the stoles they are wearing, or by their clergy collars. They begin speaking one-by-one, calling out confessions of complicity with social systems of oppression and racism. They dip their hands in buckets filled with red liquid, made to look like blood. People of different races, ethnicities, gender identities, faith traditions, and ages immerse their hands in the bucket and pull them out again, dripping red. They confess their sins as they place their bloody handprints on the courthouse wall. Several stand to the side holding a large banner between them. On it, printed in large block letters, are the words "Stop the Crucifixion of Black Lives." Passers-by stop and watch, astounded to see clergy engaged

---

[1] See The Oasis Project, *The Oasis Project: Creating Safer Spaces and Providing Interfaith Spiritual Care for Conventions,* online https://oasis4conventions.wordpress.com/about/ (downloaded December 6, 2017).

[2] For more information about Second Acts and to view photos and videos of previous actions, see their Facebook page: online https://www.facebook.com/SecondActs/ (downloaded December 6, 2017).

in these actions. Others keep moving, eyes averted. Police gather along the edges, keeping an eye on everyone, waiting to see if arrests will be necessary.

An urban church has its doors open on a Saturday afternoon, and live music pours out toward the street as people walk by on their way to the farmers market. A few people filter in the doors. The sanctuary is darkened, but candles are lit around the room. There are about a dozen people throughout the space. Some are lying down in pews listening to the music, others are distributed around different inter-active worship stations. Some are sitting at a table coloring. Others are writing in journals. A small group in the corner are being led through yoga poses. Someone walks a labyrinth. This interfaith worship is called PAUSE,[3] and it is offered four afternoons a year at Lakeshore Avenue Baptist Church in Oakland, California. For some, it is the only time they feel connected to worship or church. It is the only chance they have to catch their breath. They need this wide-open space to feel the freedom to listen to and respond to God's invitation. Others, longtime church-goers, go to PAUSE even though the worship stations baffle them. They sense something inside themselves that is drawn to this contemplative experience. They want to support the efforts of the young adults who craft these services in an effort to provide connection to the divine without the messiness of religion.

These are glimpses into the worship lives of three very different emerging li-turgical communities rooted in free-church, Baptist communities.[4] In this chapter I will explore the ways these communities engage in experimental worship practices, paying particular attention to how they each interpret their practices from theolog-ical perspectives informed by Baptist sensibilities. I will highlight the contribution that consideration of these forms of worship might make to Baptist liturgical the-ology and liturgical practice in local churches.

1. A Word about Method

Before exploring these specific communities, it is essential to say something about the peculiar work of doing Baptist liturgical theology. Rooted in the conviction that Baptist theology is collegial, provisional, and contextual,[5] I contend that Bap-

---

[3] For more about PAUSE, see Tanner, "In Formation."

[4] While Second Acts is not a Baptist community, one of its founding members was raised in a Southern Baptist congregation and explicitly names the Baptist tradition as informing the backbone of her work with Second Acts.

[5] I owe much in this section to an essay written by British Baptist theologian Brian Haymes, "Theology and Baptist Identity," in Fiddes, Haymes, Kidd, and Quicke, *Doing Theolo-gy in a Baptist Way*, 1-5. Haymes suggests that "Baptist distinctives...imply a way of doing theol-ogy" which he expresses in terms of four interrelated affirmations namely, that a Baptist ap-proach to theology is continuously renewed and remade; collegial in formation and practice;

tist liturgical theology must therefore be multi-vocal, dialogical, and local.[6] In the following section I will briefly explore each of these aspects before turning to the experimental liturgical communities that will form the heart of this chapter.

Baptist liturgical theology is multi-vocal. When studying contemporary worship practices, it seeks to incorporate others' perspectives intentionally through the use of ethnographic methods including interviews of participants. Baptist liturgical theology preserves multiple, even contradictory viewpoints when doing so most accurately represents the diversity present within Baptist worship life. Baptist liturgical theology also intentionally engages ecumenical liturgical scholarship as equal conversation partners, understanding not only that every tradition has its own gifts, but that free-church worship also has beautiful gifts to contribute to the conversation.[7] Rather than emphasizing a reforming agenda when investigating Baptist liturgical practices, the Baptist liturgical theologian aims first and foremost to understand the theological meaning-making enterprise as it emerges from those practices.

Baptist liturgical theology is dialogical. More conversational than commanding in tone, it invites communal reflection and self-reflection as an integral part of the theological process. It seeks to ask what wisdom already exists within the community and is open to amendment based upon that wisdom. Baptist liturgical theology offers its contribution humbly, always understanding that every theology carefully crafted by one Baptist community can be understood quite differently and even be contradicted by another Baptist community. It speaks from practices and perspectives rooted in local congregations, and it offers the insights gathered there as authentic witness to the actions of the Holy Spirit in particular communities that may well have bearing on other communities. With this in mind, Baptist li-

---

informed through biblical narrative and lived experience; and provisional or tentative, and thereby marked by plurality and multivocality. I am also strongly influenced by Broadway, Freeman, Harvey, McClendon, Newman, and Thompson, "Re-Envisioning Baptist Identity," and the ensuing dialogue in the pages of that journal. As has been mentioned in the introduction to this book, the "Baptists Manifesto," as this statement has come to be known, itself also serves as a catalyst for this present volume of essays.

[6] For a more thorough explanation of my methodology for Baptist liturgical theology see Davidson, *River of Life, Feast of Grace.*

[7] Ellis, *Gathering*, 256, warns that there is an almost dire need for affirmative liturgical theologies to be written from Free Church perspectives in order to better foster a healthy dialogue between "liturgically formal traditions" and free-church traditions. "Such dialogue would enrich ecumenical understanding of Christian worship because it would begin to release the stuttering Free Church voice, which has either been silent, or else has not been heard by those whose liturgical voices have for so long been so eloquent. It is in exploring the riches of *each* tradition that we gain a larger vision of the worship of *all* God's people. This exciting and nourishing adventure is only just beginning" (ibid.).

turgical theologians might offer their insights in full voice, with conviction, while not claiming ultimate authority for other contexts.[8]

Baptist liturgical theology is local. Our ecclesiology deeply informs our theological method. If the local church is the Body of Christ, then we must pay attention to how the Body of Christ is manifest in location. Central to a Baptist way of doing theology are the stories communities tell about themselves in relation to the biblical witness, shared experiences, and local traditions. James Wm. McClendon, Jr. writes, "Story will transform story."[9] In telling our stories about worship (a communal event that centers itself in the stories of Scripture), we articulate a liturgical theology that is uniquely Baptist. Approached in this way, as Christopher Ellis points out, "theological reflection will be based on the actuality of that worship rather than on principles developed away from it and then applied to it."[10]

In this chapter I amplify the voices and perspectives of the three experimental communities identified earlier. Through interviews conducted with the individuals who are the leaders of these communities, I have sought to uncover their theological commitments, rootedness in Baptist convictions, and the gifts that their forms of worship might offer to the renewal of Baptist liturgical life. The liturgical practices of the Oasis Project, Second Acts, and PAUSE cultivate communities that seek to be a presence to the marginalized, offer practice in discernment, and reveal the radical nature of the gospel for the world today.

2. Presence to the Marginalized

"We have a tendency to want to listen to the people who use the same words that we do, who use the same code, right?" Paul Schneider remarks as he talks about some of the reasons he started the Oasis Project. "But what I've found over and over again is that the people who have different codes are the ones who can really open my eyes, really make me hear something new, or look at something in a way that I've never looked at it before." Schneider founded the Oasis Project to provide

---

[8] Baptists are equally circumspect of any theology that makes monolithic or ultimate claims by others upon them. Because theology is constantly being worked out in every gathered assembly by every generation in unending contexts and circumstances, Baptists are "properly wary of those who wish to squeeze us into their own mould." See Haymes, "Theology and Baptist Identity," 5.

[9] McClendon explains that in the baptist vision the big "S," which is the Story of Scripture, is used to interpret the community's own story (small "s") that it tells about its convictions of faith. In this sense, the biblical Story becomes our story. Embedded within this approach is a critical function that is essential to the theological task. "For theology is also the mirror that confronts today's church if here it recognizes itself not as it *is* but as *it must be* to be faithful to Jesus Christ" (emphasis added). See McClendon, *Systematic Theology*, vol. 1, *Ethics*, 1st ed., 31-35.

[10] Ellis, *Gathering*, 35.

safer space and interfaith spiritual care for sci-fi and fantasy conventions. "People who are serious about their science fiction and fantasy are often a lot more spiritual than people give them credit for," he told me. But as one who was already attending and volunteering at conventions, Schneider knew a different story.

> Science fiction and fantasy have become such a pop-culture thing that people tend to think of it as very shallow. But it's really not. It's really very deep, very complex, very layered. A lot of people whom I think of as being at the core these conventions, even the ones who would say they are not particularly religious, all of them acknowledge a need for some sort of spiritual health in their lives.

Schneider created the Oasis Project while a student in seminary. "I saw that conventions sometimes brought out moments of spiritual crisis in certain people...I conceived of the Oasis Project not only as a way to create the safer recharge space I desired, but also a way to allow there to be a clear place one could come for spiritual and emotional support during a convention."[11] Schneider knew that an explicitly religious presence at conventions would have to be offered gently and unobtrusively. "A lot of the people at these conventions have been for one reason or another rejected and hurt by the church. If I can in some small way help mitigate that, help overcome that, help them maybe be less hurt by the church, then I see that as my responsibility as part of the church." Through his work with the Oasis Project, Schneider remarks:

> I've had some truly amazing conversations with different writers, regular convention goers, even vendors—people who are at the convention selling things—talking with me about their own spiritual journeys and their own struggles with the divine. These are things that would have never come up if I weren't standing there wearing a cross in that sort of clergy role. But because I've taken on that role, they are willing to talk with me.

"Church can have such a negative stigma to it," says Allison J. Tanner, minister of Christian formation at Lakeshore Avenue Baptist Church. "If people don't have a positive experience with the traditional rituals of church, then that negative stigma unfortunately prevents people from encountering God." The young adults who designed PAUSE wanted to create a spiritually rich and welcoming space for their non-churched friends. "Many of our young people feel like the church service on a Sunday morning isn't really where they would invite their friends to come. They wouldn't get a lot of meaning out of it." Tanner is clear, "It's not that people aren't encountering God apart from the church, but it is rarely named and recog-

---

[11] Schneider, "The Oasis Project Origin."

nized outside of institutions. We are trying to provide a way to experience the divine that is not institutionalized, especially for the non-churched and the nonreligious."

Taking out her notes from a recent meeting in which the young adults behind PAUSE met to review the goals of their experimental liturgical community, Tanner reported to me, "They said very specifically, 'We want to provide a religion-free church experience, a sanctuary from church.'" Tanner sits quietly for a moment as she continues to collect her thoughts:

> I recognize as a pastor that there is a deep connection between religious institutions and the divine. And in trying to break down some of those walls, messing with what we do as a religious institution is really important. People are longing to encounter God as a separation from the busyness of life. And church isn't answering that need in many ways.

On the other hand, Tanner observes, "the voice of God is very present in the world as people are doing yoga, listening to music, and pausing to really think and reflect. I want to elevate the spiritual exercises that help people find God in their lives. I want to tap into what's happening outside the church, and bring that into the church."

Cherri Murphy, core member of Second Acts, a community that engages in nonviolent liturgical direct action, says that people who become involved in their actions soon find that it "requires every particular aspect of a person, every identity they are linked to. This is different than the church. The church says generally that all are welcome, but mostly that is not true." As a same-gender-loving woman, Murphy is painfully aware of the ways people are excluded from churches for intentional and unintentional reasons. In order to be fully involved in a congregation's life, some people must "check parts of their identities at the door. But in movement work we say, yeah, all are really welcome. There is something about this work that allows people to come in and bring all of themselves, and feel like they can contribute all that they are, no matter what they're wearing, what their past is."

Second Act's openness to centering the marginalized in their liturgical actions makes their events accessible and appealing to millennials, those with disabilities, non-faith-related community organizers, gender nonconforming individuals, and others who have been hurt by traditional church life. "We are coming to this liturgy where we are not concerned about who we are and whether we will be included in this worship. And that's what it's really about!"

The organizers of all three of these communities are deeply aware of the ways institutionalized churches have done harm in the past or have become obstacles for people who desire an encounter with God. Through their experimental liturgical offerings, they seek to provide a safe and healing space for the marginalized to experience a sense of healing and sacred presence.

3. Practice in Discernment

Even as PAUSE seeks to provide a sanctuary from church, the organizers are well aware that the PAUSE experience is itself offered in the sanctuary of a church building. Tanner sees this as a generative opportunity not only for non-churched people to experience a more accessible worship experience, but also for life-long church members to discover for themselves a new way of being in worship together. It's the "lifers" who Tanner finds are often most uncomfortable. They want to know, "What am I supposed to do here?" She says, "That's why we give them many different things to choose from. But a lot of people just choose to do nothing, because they say afterward, 'I can't remember the last time I did nothing for two hours.' And that experience itself was just so profound for them. That's really a goal and focus of PAUSE."

The organizers of PAUSE offer a simple program that lists about a dozen different ways that participants can engage the service. "The program lists who the musician is, says you can sit and do nothing, or invites you to engage in the labyrinth, the meditative movement, the coloring, or journaling. It articulates some of the reasoning behind each action so that when people say, 'So why would I color?' the program helps provide a spiritual framework for the event."

"It's funny," Tanner remarks, "because I get in trouble with some of the older folks at church who recognize the irony that I'm trying to make Sunday morning worship more engaging, interactive, and upbeat. And yet the young adults are asking for this escape from the busyness of the world to have the intentional stillness of PAUSE. But I see both of these as very real needs, and not as contradictory ones."

Tanner observes that Sunday morning worship often requires people to conform to the expectations embedded in each moment of worship. But PAUSE "removes some of those expectations. It's much more of a free-for-all, and intentionally so! It's a collection of individual experiences, but we are all in there together. We are all having a sacred experience, but in very individualized ways." In a real sense, for Tanner, this model captures something about the Baptist principle of soul freedom.

> There are multiple opportunities, but you find your own way. There isn't one right way of engaging in worship at PAUSE. It's okay if you want to listen to music, or just do nothing. You can do what your spirit leads you to do. And people aren't used to that. Church folks really struggle with it. They want to be told what they are supposed to do. It's as if they don't know how to allow themselves to do whatever they want, or to just listen to a voice inside them that says, 'Hm, let me try this for a while.' You know?

PAUSE helps church folks to kind of let go of 'what is this *supposed* to be?' and embrace 'what might my soul want to do right now?'"

The opportunity to practice discernment in the midst of experimental liturgies fulfills what Tanner sees as a great need particularly of lifelong Baptists. She believes the discomfort some participants feel is revealing of a lack of experience with active discernment. "The soul can't be leading and guiding," she says, "if we feel like we always have to be in control." PAUSE offers participants an opening to the Spirit's leading in the midst of worship in a way that a programmed service with its usual orderly flow may not. Tanner admits:

I long personally for these spiritual places where I can really hear my own voice within me. How we find ourselves amidst culture allows us to act, but also *not* to act. In fact, in many ways, we use the noisiness of culture to prevent ourselves from doing what we really want to do. So to undo that and escape from it, we need the space to separate, to slow down, and hear our own voices. We need the space to allow our souls to speak to us, and give us the power and agency to speak through culture, rather than allowing culture to control what we say and how we say it.

4. Revealing the Radical Nature of the Gospel

"The goal is not to recruit people at our public liturgical actions," Murphy laughs, "or even to bring them to the altar where we get a membership. The goal is to change a consciousness about the way people are living. That doesn't necessarily require someone to join a church in response." Murphy describes the role of non-violent liturgical direct action as "public liturgies that disrupt the narratives of our own oppressions that we have been complicit with. They disrupt the sense of hyper-individualism prevalent in North American culture. And they provide an opportunity for freedom—a way to envision and participate in the beloved community that we talk about and sing about."

The public liturgical actions planned by the Second Acts community members emerge from a sense of urgency.

The bell is tolling in this country. But many of us are still not worshiping in a way that frees us. Worship for Second Acts is about disrupting the sleep of our complicity. So when we meet to plan our liturgical actions, we are thinking about our goal of disruption that will get people to think outside their own boxes. Our intention behind our Good Friday service on the courthouse steps last April was to bring folks to an awareness of police brutality and state-sanctioned killings of people of color. People are still being crucified today, and our worship needs to wake people up to that fact.

Murphy knows that clergy can gain greater visibility and have greater access to power brokers. But this is a privilege that is not always leveraged in the pursuit of justice.

Clergy were largely missing-in-action in the fight for Black liberation up until about two years ago. I think the movement continued without us, and faith-based institutions stopped doing the work that love obligates us to do. But we are back on the force. We have reincorporated ourselves back into public witnessing in ways that are grounded in faith. So when you see a bunch of clergy on courthouse steps, putting their hands in blood, and putting their bloody hands on the walls, and then pouring those buckets of blood down the courthouse steps while talking about racism? That gets people's attention. And I think that's what it's about. If it stops people for a moment, you know, whether or not they sing a song with us, or even if they look away, or they look strangely at us—those actions they witness are disrupting their consciousness for a moment in a way that will continue to be unveiled.

While growing up in Virginia, Murphy witnessed the power of the gospel to transform lives and awaken liberation by attending Wednesday night testimony services in her black, Southern Baptist church. "From my perspective as a descendent of slaves in the freedom fight for black lives, I learned that at one point we had to claim freedom. In the South, Black Southern Baptists took a unique and very risky lead in claiming that freedom before they experienced it. I grew up in a former plantation state going to a Baptist church with people who testified in worship to the faithful resilience of obtaining freedom."

Murphy learned from "watching women, *particularly women*, testifying to their resiliency. They were testifying to what was happening in their lives in that moment. But at the end they always testified that it was going to change." The testimony of "faithful resiliency" and the "commitment to change" is what "put the cement in my back," says Murphy. And it shapes the public liturgies she plans today. "That was what anointed me: this commitment not to the way things look at any given moment, but to the belief that our circumstances will change. So whenever something happens here locally or nationally, my mind goes back to those testimony services. I remember my ancestors, and their making it. And I know that in my moment, I shall make it, too." Empowered by the witness and memory of her ancestors, Murphy knows the power that imagination, honed in light of the resurrection, can have to transform people's vision of what is possible. Along with the other members of Second Acts, Murphy engages in nonviolent direct liturgical action to testify to the radical vision of the gospel for the world today.

Schneider's creation of the Oasis Project stemmed from the radical vision he perceived in Jesus' command to his disciples to go "to the lost sheep of the House of Israel" (Matthew 10:5). "When Jesus sends the disciples out in Matthew, he doesn't send them to foreigners or to Romans. He sends them to talk to their own people. I was already a part of these sci-fi and fantasy communities. So I was able to see a need, and I sensed there could be something I could do to fill that need." But to meet the need of such diverse convention participants with deep authenticity, Schneider knew that the Oasis Project should not be a Christian space only but had to be interfaith. "That the interfaith commitment has always been a core component of the Oasis Project strikes me as uniquely Baptist," Schneider remarks. "We are talking about freedom of religion here. I recognized that not everyone was going to walk into that room with the same religious convictions that I have. I wanted to actively build a team that came from multiple faith traditions, and not just say on paper, 'All faiths are welcome in this room.' That to me feels like it is very in line with the best of the Baptist tradition." Like the liturgical actions designed by the Second Acts community, Schneider's Oasis Project is not about recruiting new church members; rather, he offers a space of radical hospitality to which people are invited to come and rest a while, to find peace, to feel connected, to be heard, or simply to be seen.

5. Sources of Light

Throughout this chapter we have heard the voices of those who engage in experimental liturgical practices in response to a sense of the Spirit's leading in the lives of their communities. Their voices have served as sources of light for us, illuminating their own journeys while also shedding light for us to reflect upon our own journeys. We find in these three communities the powerful desire to provide liturgical experiences with and for those who have been marginalized, alienated, or hurt by more traditional expressions of church. How might congregations with more "traditional" worship practices look to these emerging communities as sources of light to illuminate new, previously unseen possibilities for their own liturgical life? I will identify three invitations below, grounded in the work and witness of the communities explored in this chapter.

First, traditional worshiping congregations are invited to look for the ways in which they might better identify and facilitate practices of discernment in the midst of worship. Discernment may already be present, but not necessarily identified as such. Congregations that practice the rite of Altar Prayer or Joys and Concerns are already inviting worship participants to discern how the Holy Spirit may be leading them to stand and request prayer for themselves or others. Other moments may also be incorporated: a Lenten service might provide two simple worshiping stations that participants could be invited to engage. Perhaps one could be a station with a bowl of water for affirming one's baptism. Another could be a station with slips of paper to write out prayers for the world. Asking congregants to notice which station they feel led to engage will give them an opportunity to listen for what God is doing within their own spirits. Naming this as a practice of discernment rooted in soul freedom may allow more traditional congregations to embrace this new experiment.

Second, traditional worshiping congregations are invited to seek out opportunities for interfaith worship. Rooted deeply in the Baptist commitment to freedom of religion, congregations can engage interfaith space in a radically welcoming manner. Further, with increasing numbers of people identifying as "nones" (those who consider themselves spiritual, but do not affiliate with a particular religious tradition)[12], congregations can seek out alternative expressions of spirituality that are likely happening within their own context. Churches might use science fiction books for book groups, or Sci-Fi films as the basis of a discussion forum to explore theological and spiritual themes found in the genre. Churches might consider commissioning a few likeminded congregation members to attend a Sci-Fi/Fantasy Convention to experience the spiritual themes there. They would be sent not with the intention of converting others, but with an openness to perceiving new ways the Spirit is moving in people's lives today.

Finally, traditional worshiping congregations are invited to interrogate whether their current worship practices sufficiently awaken participants to the radical demands of the gospel, to their complicity with systems of oppression, and to the resurrection imagination that testifies to the possibility for change. A worship committee might be tasked with reading through bulletins, hymns, any printed prayers, and scripture passages used over the previous year to analyze how well the congregation is doing at keeping in mind systemic sin in balance with individual constructions of sinfulness. Congregations might look for certain patterns in its prayer life: who is most often made the object of prayer and what is neglected. For example, does the church pray for an end of poverty, but never for the dismantling of white supremacy?[13] Does the congregation name the suffering in present day headlines while failing to celebrate the places of resurrection happening through literacy programs, cease-fire initiatives, community organizing, and other grassroots movements ignored by the 24-hour news cycle? Interrogating worship in this manner can uncover implicit bias and illuminate the potential for deeper resurrection practices.

None of the experimental liturgical practices in this chapter is offered as a replacement of Sunday morning worship. They do, however, speak to us afresh of

---

[12] See Drescher, *Choosing Our Religion*.

[13] To learn how to uncover bias within congregational prayers, churches might study the chapter "Liturgy: Church Worship and White Superiority," in West, *Disruptive Christian Ethics*, 112-40.

the sometimes unexpected and surprising ways the Spirit continues to move among Baptists today. By responding to the invitations extended here, congregations might discover life-giving ways to participate in the Spirit's movement.

6. For Further Reading

Drescher, Elizabeth. *Choosing Our Religion: The Spiritual Lives of America's Nones*. New York: Oxford University Press, 2016.

Francis, Leah Gunning. *Ferguson and Faith: Sparking Leadership and Awakening Community*. St Louis, MO: Chalice Press, 2015.

Lightsey, Pamela R. *Our Lives Matter: A Womanist Queer Theology*. Eugene, OR: Pickwick Publications, 2015.

White, Vera and Charles Wiley. *New Worshiping Communities: A Theological Exploration*. Louisville, KY: Westminster John Knox Press, 2018.

Mathews, Michael-Ray, Marie Clare P. Onwubuariri, and Cody J. Sanders. *Trouble the Water: A Christian Resource for the Work of Racial Justice*. Macon, GA: Nurturing Faith, 2017.

24

Light from/for Ecumenical Convergence

Steven R. Harmon

The opening chapter of this book expressed the goal of the practice of theology by local Baptist churches partly in terms of language drawn from one of the most significant recent voices of ecumenical convergence—*The Church: Towards a Common Vision*, a document issued to the churches by the World Council of Churches in 2013 that will be introduced more fully later in this chapter:

> The Church, as the body of Christ, acts by the power of the Holy Spirit to continue his life-giving mission in prophetic and compassionate ministry and so participates in God's work of healing a broken world. Communion, whose source is the very life of the Holy Trinity, is both the gift by which the Church lives and, at the same time, the gift that God calls the Church to offer to a wounded and divided humanity in hope of reconciliation and healing.[1]

The capacity of the local church for participating in the Triune God's communion-creating work in the world is diminished by the degree to which ecclesial division marks its life locally and in relation to the whole church. Jesus' prayer in John 17:20-21 suggests that the rule of Christ among his followers is partial so long as their life together is not a participation in and embodiment of the communion that characterizes the life of the Triune God, with consequences for the world's reception of the church's proclamation of the Good News. This chapter points Baptist ministers to the resources that will help them bring these voices of ecumenical convergence—voices not of "soloist" ecumenical theologians but of "choruses" of joint commissions to ecclesial ecumenical dialogues—to bear on the congregation's participation in the quest for more visible Christian unity and suggests ways in which they might be employed in the life of the congregation.[2]

---

[1] World Council of Churches, *The Church: Towards a Common Vision* § 1 (p. 5).

[2] Cf. Pelikan, *The Vindication of Tradition*, 17: "the history of tradition requires that we listen to the choruses and not only to the soloists—nor only to the virtuosi among the soloists."

1. Formation for the Practice of Christian Unity

Ecumenical engagement is therefore along with evangelism one of the first-order practices of the church whose members have been paradoxically baptized both into the one body of Christ and into its numerous divisions. For this reason, there is now a wide-ranging ecumenical consensus regarding the importance of ecumenical formation in educational preparation for ministry, even if not always reflected in the curricula of Baptist institutions of theological education.[3]

Baptist ecclesiology renders ecumenical formation important not only for Baptist ministers but also for the members of the congregations they serve. Among the responsibilities of bishops in traditions with episcopal ecclesial polity has been safeguarding the unity of the church. In most configurations of Baptist congregational ecclesiology, the New Testament designations "pastor" and "bishop" are regarded as synonymous (with Acts 20:28 and 1 Pet. 5:2 frequently cited for support). The pastor/bishop then has the function not only of shepherding the flock but also of overseeing it. But the task of oversight is not only that of the pastor: she shares with the whole congregation the responsibility of mutual "watch-care"— supporting one another as fellow travelers on the way of Jesus Christ.[4] Therefore for Baptists it is both local church pastors and local church members who bear primary responsibility for the episcopal task of safeguarding the unity of the church, and it is both pastors and church members who must be formed for this task.

---

[3] The *Directory for the Application of Principles and Norms of Ecumenism* issued by the Catholic Church's Pontifical Council for Promoting Christian Unity in 1993 recommended that all Catholic seminarians be required to complete a course in ecumenism (Pontifical Council for Promoting Christian Unity, *Directory for the Application of Principles and Norms of Ecumenism*). The World Council of Churches Programme on Ecumenical Theological Education working document "Magna Charta on Ecumenical Formation in Theological Education in the 21st Century" (2008) insists that leadership in ecumenical engagement is an essential ministry skill and that formation for such leadership is integral to the theological curriculum (Werner, "Magna Charta on Ecumenical Formation in Theological Education in the 21st Century"). A few years ago I taught a required Master of Divinity core curriculum course in Ecumenical Theology for a seminary affiliated with the Evangelical Lutheran Church in America, a denomination which both mandates that ecumenism receive attention in the preparation of its clergy and employs a full-time chief ecumenical officer to foster ecumenical engagement in the life of this communion with ecclesial origins at the initial fault line of the sixteenth-century fragmentation of the church in the West.

[4] Cf. McClendon, *Systematic Theology*, vol. 1, *Ethics*, rev. ed., 49-53.

2. Key Documents for Ecumenical Formation

When the modern missions movement of the nineteenth century gave birth to the modern ecumenical movement early in the twentieth century, some of its pioneers recognized that visible unity in mission would not be possible apart from addressing divisive issues of doctrine and church order. Charles Brent, an Episcopal bishop and missionary to the Philippines who was one of the speakers at the Edinburgh World Missionary Conference in 1910, proposed soon thereafter the creation of an international commission on faith and order.[5] In 1927 this took shape as the World Conference on Faith and Order in Lausanne, Switzerland, at which all major Christian communions, with the exception of the Catholic Church but including the Orthodox churches, were represented. When the World Council of Churches (WCC) was formed in 1948, this annual conference became the Commission on Faith and Order of the WCC, which is the principal forum for international multilateral ecumenical dialogue (conversations between representatives of multiple—i.e., three or more—Christian world communions) and is responsible for all but one of the multilateral texts treated in this chapter. Subsequently, the Second Vatican Council (1962-65) committed the Catholic Church to full participation in the modern ecumenical movement that originated beyond its communion. This development initiated and inspired the bilateral dialogues that burgeoned over the next five decades. The Catholic Church began dialogues with other communions, which then encouraged these non-Catholic communions to enter into dialogue with one another. The Baptist World Alliance (BWA) has participated in such bilateral dialogues (conversations between representatives of two Christian communions), both with the Catholic Church and with other Christian world communions, and the reports from these conversations are likewise introduced in this chapter.

2.1. Multilateral Ecumenical Convergences

Eight Baptist unions were founding members of the World Council of Churches in 1948, and today twenty-seven Baptist unions are WCC members.[6] Representatives of these Baptist national-level trans-local associations, as well as representatives of the Baptist World Alliance, have served on the WCC Commission on Faith and Order working groups responsible for drafting the convergence texts and study documents mentioned here. Baptist theological voices have made

---

[5] Zabriskie, *Bishop Brent, Crusader for Christian Unity.*

[6] Payne, "Baptists and the Ecumenical Movement," 263; World Council of Churches, "Church Families: Baptist Churches."

themselves heard throughout the process of the development, publication, and reception of these documents, as members of the WCC Commission on Faith and Order and as members of the global Baptist community from which input was solicited. When ministers and members of Baptist congregations listen to these multilateral "choruses" of ecumenical convergence, they are hearing the work of Baptist composers and choristers collaborating with their counterparts from other churches, in addition to hearing the voices those other churches contribute to the chorus.

2.1.1. Baptism, Eucharist and Ministry (1982). One of the two major success stories of the modern ecumenical movement proposed to the divided churches possible convergences on the primary ecclesiological differences between them. In 1982 the WCC Commission on Faith and Order issued a "convergence" statement on *Baptism, Eucharist and Ministry (BEM)*.[7] *BEM* was the fruit of fifty years of multilateral work on Faith and Order, and it received input from representatives of multiple Protestant denominations, including the Free Church or Believer's Church traditions, along with the Eastern Orthodox churches and the Catholic Church. Its most significant achievement was in its section on baptism. On the one hand, partly because of the constructive contributions of consultations with representatives of the Free Church/Believer's Church traditions, *BEM* definitively articulated what is now the current ecumenical consensus that "baptism upon personal profession of faith is the most clearly attested pattern in the New Testament documents" and that believer's baptism by immersion is the normative biblical practice from which the later practice of infant baptism derives its significance.[8] On the other hand, *BEM* commended two legitimate patterns for uniting baptism, personal faith, and Christian formation in the churches' work of making disciples in a way that has encouraged much progress toward mutual baptismal recognition, between churches that baptize only those who have embraced the faith of their own volition and churches that also baptize infants whom the church nurtures in faith. *BEM* likewise treated the Eucharist and the ministry of the church in ways that invited mutual recognition of the essential features of Eucharistic practice and the exercise of ministry in one another's churches in the midst of our significant remaining differences regarding the Eucharist and ministry, though the convergences proposed regarding these latter two aspects of ecclesiology have not been as influential in their reception as the section on baptism.[9] *BEM*'s recognition of the histori-

---

[7] World Council of Churches, *Baptism, Eucharist and Ministry.*

[8] Vischer, "The Convergence Texts on Baptism, Eucharist and Ministry," 442-43; World Council of Churches, *Louisville Consultation on Baptism.*

[9] The World Council of Churches has published six volumes of official ecclesial responses to *BEM* (Thurian, ed., *Churches Respond to Baptism, Eucharist and Ministry*, 6 vols.).

cal and theological priority of believer's baptism is an ecumenical gift contributed by the Free Church tradition.[10] Many Baptist congregations are seeking to make the unity of the church more visible by revisiting the relation of their policies on church membership to the baptismal practices of other traditions from which candidates for membership may come. *BEM* can offer these Baptist churches that are practicing theology in taking up this conversation the gift of a theological rationale for recognizing the infant baptisms of candidates for church membership that have been joined with post-baptismal catechesis and personal faith, without abandoning their own commitment to the disciple-making practice of believer's baptism.

2.1.2. One Baptism: Towards Mutual Recognition (2011).[11] Building on the achievements of *BEM* regarding baptism and taking into account the responses of the churches to the convergences it proposed, in 2011 the WCC Commission on Faith and Order issued *One Baptism: Towards Mutual Recognition* as a "study text."[12] Rooted in a rich engagement of Scripture and a thick account of the diversity of baptismal practices and theologies in the Christian tradition, *One Baptism* helpfully shifted the emphasis of ecumenical discussions of baptism from chronological orderings of faith, baptism, and formation in faith to a focus on the whole journey of Christian initiation in the company of the church, an improvement on *BEM* in identifying ways for both believer-baptizing and infant-baptizing churches to discern in one another's baptismal practices common journeys of Christian experience.

On the question of rebaptism, "One Baptism" calls churches that require those previously baptized as infants to be rebaptized as a condition of membership and churches that require the same of those previously baptized as believing adults but in a church of differing faith and order to reflect on the implications of those requirements. The document fails, however, to address a variation of the latter scenario with which many Baptist congregations must deal: members of Baptist churches who were baptized as believers, but at rather young ages, who later in life question whether they really understood the commitment they were making and now wish to be baptized following their more mature embrace of faith. Baptists may nonetheless find help in "One Baptism" for addressing such cases pastorally, for both the steps toward faith taken by young children who are then baptized and

---

[10] According to Methodist ecumenical theologian Geoffrey Wainwright (one of the architects of *BEM*), in particular Morris West, a Baptist Union of Great Britain member of the WCC Commission on Faith and Order during the years of work on *BEM*, was influential in seeing that Baptist/Free Church voices were heard in regard to the "Baptism" section of *BEM* and incorporated into its convergence (Wainwright, e-mail message to Steven R. Harmon, January 12, 2012).

[11] Material in this section has been adapted from Harmon, "One Baptism," 9-10.

[12] World Council of Churches, *One Baptism*.

the mature faith of adults can be related to the baptism near the beginning of their journeys, which need not be repeated.

Careful study of "One Baptism," along with *BEM*, will help everyone involved in the aforementioned deliberations about the relation of church membership to baptism to think through the implications of their decisions about this matter for their stances on the legitimacy of non-Baptist churches and their members' faith. Whether all Baptists find agreement with it or not, the study of "One Baptism" by Baptist ministers, laypersons, and whole congregations will yield a greatly enriched Baptist theology of baptism and potentially a more powerful baptismal practice.

2.1.3. The Church: Towards a Common Vision (2013). Two years after the publication of *One Baptism*, the WCC Commission on Faith and Order issued *The Church: Towards a Common Vision* (*TCTCV*), which joined *BEM* as one of only two documents to be designated as a "convergence text" among the approximately 300 documents produced by the WCC Faith and Order Commission across its history.[13] The 186 responses to *BEM* from member communions of the WCC had surfaced some ecclesiological themes that needed further study: (1) the role the church plays in God's salvific goals; (2) the implications for ecclesiology of the concept of Trinitarian *koinonia*; (3) the manner in which the church is created by the word of God; (4) the nature of the church as a sacrament by which the world comes to experience God's love; (5) the church's identity as a pilgrim community; and (6) the church as prophetic sign and servant of the coming reign of God.

A new project to address these broader issues of ecclesial vision evolved in several stages, beginning with a draft text titled *The Nature and Purpose of the Church: A Stage on the Way to a Common Statement*.[14] As with *BEM*, again the churches offered responses to this draft document that were taken into account in the next phase of the Commission's work. At the 2006 WCC Assembly in Porto Alegre, Brazil, the Commission presented a new draft, *The Nature and Mission of the Church*, again subtitled *A Stage on the Way to a Common Statement*, and again the Commission submitted the text to the churches for response. Further input came from the Plenary Commission on Faith and Order meeting in Crete in October 2009, in which I participated as the representative of the Baptist World Alliance on the Commission. Several addresses on the program offered global perspectives on the ecclesial vision of *The Nature and Mission of the Church*. One by Syrian Orthodox Metropolitan Geevarghese Mar Coorilos of India critiqued the way the draft text on *The Nature and Mission of the Church* treated biblical images of the church in purely doctrinal terms without sufficient attention to their sociological dimen-

---

[13] World Council of Churches, *The Church*.

[14] World Council of Churches, *The Nature and Purpose of the Church*.

sions and implications for the liberation of the dispossessed and the disempowered, which Metropolitan Coorilos called "the actual church amongst communities of people in their struggle for the fullness of life." He said:

> In India, for the ["untouchable" members of the Dalit caste] who form the majority of the Indian church, the body of Christ is a Dalit body, a 'broken body' (the word Dalit literally means "broken" and "torn asunder"). Jesus Christ became a Dalit because he was torn-asunder and mutilated on the cross. The Church as "body of Christ," in the Indian context, therefore, has profound theological and sociological implications for a Dalit ecclesiology....[*The Nature and Mission of the Church*], however, fails to strike chords and resonate with such contextual theological challenges...In other words, the text fails to encounter the real *ecclesia* among communities of people in pain and suffering.[15]

In addition to feedback offered in such addresses, in smaller working groups, and in general discussions, we recommended that those responsible for drafting "shorten the text and...make it more contextual, more reflective of the lives of the churches throughout the world, and more accessible to a wider readership."[16] The drafting committee took this feedback into account along with a 2011 inter-Orthodox consultation on the text and the churches' earlier responses to *The Nature and Mission of the Church*. It underwent three more drafts that made improvements in light of continued feedback, and in September 2012 the WCC Central Committee officially received the new convergence statement, now titled *The Church: Towards a Common Vision*. It was published in 2013, presented at the 10th Assembly of the World Council of Churches in Busan, South Korea that October, and commended to the churches for study and response.

In its final form, *TCTCV* represents an advance beyond *BEM* in three primary ways. First, it reengages the roots of the modern ecumenical movement in the modern missions movement by framing the quest for Christian unity as a participation in God's mission in the world. Second, it roots the unity of the church in the unity of the Triune God. especially in terms of the biblical concept of *koinonia*, which the subsequent Christian theological tradition has developed both as Trinitarian concept and as an ecclesiological concept, and it is influenced in particular by recent constructive retrievals of these developments.[17] Third, it offers a more robustly eschatological development of the church's ecumenical imperative, which *TCTCV* sees as inseparable from the mission of the Triune God, who is the source of ecclesial unity. The three strands come together in the selection from the open-

---

[15] Coorilos, "The Nature and Mission of the Church," 188-92.

[16] World Council of Churches, *The Church*, 45.

[17] E.g., Fuchs, *Koinonia and the Quest for an Ecumenical Ecclesiology*.

ing paragraph of the text's first section quoted in the opening paragraph of the present chapter. *TCTCV* portrays the church as "an eschatological reality, already anticipating the kingdom, but not yet its full realization." Therefore, it is also "a pilgrim community" on a "journey towards the full realization of God's gift of communion."[18] Listening to—and responding to—the ecumenical convergence on the mission of the church voiced by *TCTCV* can help Baptist communities make further progress in this journey together with other churches for the sake of "a wounded and divided humanity in hope of reconciliation and healing" (§ 1).

    2.1.4. Joint Declaration on the Doctrine of Justification (1999). One significant voice of ecumenical convergence began as a Catholic-Lutheran bilateral convergence but became multilateral with other Christian world communions joining the chorus: the *Joint Declaration on the Doctrine of Justification* (*JDDJ*) issued by the Catholic Church and the Lutheran World Federation (LWF) on October 31—Reformation Day—in 1999.[19] Regarded by some as the second major success story of the modern ecumenical movement and its Faith and Order stream in particular (with *BEM* as the first), the *JDDJ* is the outcome of the bilateral dialogue initiated by the Catholic Church immediately following the Second Vatican Council with the LWF. The first two phases of the dialogue (1967-72 and 1973-84) paved the way for concentrated work in Phase III (1986-93) on the theological issue at the root of the sixteenth-century divisions between Catholics and Lutherans—the doctrine of justification—detailed in the report *Church and Justification* (1993). Much of the heavy lifting in terms of shared biblical, historical, and theological work on justification had been done by the joint commission to the American national dialogue between representatives of the United States Conference of Catholic Bishops and American Lutherans that began meeting in 1965 and in 1983 produced the report *Justification by Faith.*[20]

    Following the lead of the U.S. Lutheran-Catholic dialogue, the *JDDJ* articulated what has been termed a "differentiated consensus" on justification. The two communions arrived at a fundamental consensus on justification as God's gracious initiative that both declares humanity to be righteous and is at work to make humanity in character and conduct. This consensus is "differentiated" in terms of remaining differences regarding the ecclesiological and sacramental outworkings of justification, but the remaining differences are regarded as matters that do not imperil the fundamental consensus and are not church-dividing, though they warrant ongoing dialogue. Thus, the great achievement of the international Lutheran-

---

[18] World Council of Churches, *The Church*, §§ 33, 35, 37 (pp. 21-22).

[19] Lutheran World Federation and Catholic Church, *Joint Declaration on the Doctrine of Justification.*

[20] United States Lutheran-Roman Catholic Dialogue, *Justification by Faith.*

Catholic dialogue was an authoritative agreement almost 500 years after their initial division that while there remain important church-dividing disagreements between the two communions, the central doctrine at stake in the debates of the sixteenth century is no longer considered to be among them.

What began as the most significant outcome of all the international bilateral dialogues of the past half-century has become a five-party multilateral convergence. In 2006 the World Methodist Council (WMC) officially joined the *JDDJ*, followed by the World Communion of Reformed Churches (WCRC) in 2017, and on October 31, 2017, the Anglican Communion also became official signatories to the *JDDJ* in a service in Westminster Abbey with representatives of the Catholic Church, the LWF, the WMC, and the WCRC participating. While the BWA is not yet among the world communion signatories of the *JDDJ*, a paper presented by a Baptist delegate to exploratory "pre-conversation" consultations prior to Phase II of the Baptist-Catholic international bilateral dialogue concluded that there are no theological barriers to the BWA joining the *JDDJ*,[21] and there have been informal communications among the members of the BWA Commission on Baptist Doctrine and Christian Unity about such a possibility. The Baptist-Methodist International Dialogue Joint Commission explicitly recommended that the BWA "consider responding appropriately to the *JDDJ*."[22] But whether or not the global communion of Baptists joins it, Baptists may learn from the *JDDJ* at least two things that should shape their relationships with their Catholic sisters and brothers in Christ at the grassroots. First, Baptist pastors may no longer preach and teach that the Catholic Church does not teach justification by faith, for the *JDDJ*'s "differentiated consensus" on the doctrine is officially embraced by the Catholic Church. Second, in light of the *JDDJ* Baptists should not observe Reformation Day as a triumphalistic celebration of the superiority of Protestant understandings of salvation (or of our "salvation" from supposed Catholic "false teachings" about salvation), but rather as a grateful celebration of ecumenical convergence on the

---

[21] This paper, presented during "pre-conversations" preceding Phase II of the Baptist-Catholic international bilateral (2006-2010) in Rome in December 2003, was subsequently published as a journal article: Toom, "Baptists on Justification."

[22] Baptist World Alliance and World Methodist Council, *Faith Working through Love*, section V. Recommendations: "4. We found the emerging ecumenical consensus around the Joint Declaration on the Doctrine of Justification to be very helpful in our dialogues, and noted that the World Methodist Council has formally adopted it. We recommend that the Baptist World Alliance consider responding appropriately to the JDDJ."

doctrine that divided the church in the sixteenth century as well as an occasion for lamenting our remaining divisions and praying for the unity of the church.[23]

2.2. Bilateral Ecumenical Convergences with Baptist Participation

The fruit of a half-century of the post-Vatican II international bilateral dialogues in the form of their reports and agreed statements, along with some of the key documents of multilateral ecumenical convergence such as those introduced above, is published in the *Growth in Agreement* series sponsored by the World Council of Churches in four thick volumes to date.[24] Among them are the reports from international bilateral dialogues with Baptist participation introduced briefly here.[25] Concrete suggestions for their use in congregational practices of theology are offered in section 3 of this chapter, "Formative Practices of Ecumenical Reception."

2.2.1. BWA and World Alliance of Reformed Churches (1973-1977). The first international bilateral in which representatives of the BWA engaged was with the World Alliance of Reformed Churches (now known as the World Communion of Reformed Churches). Not all Baptists are Reformed with a capital "R" (i.e., Calvinist), but since the seventeenth century significant segments of Baptist life have identified with that expression of the Reformation. Whether one claims the heritage of Particular (Calvinistic) or General (Arminian) Baptists, the report from the dialogue is an excellent entrée to stimulating theological conversation with local Presbyterians and members of other Reformed churches on matters addressed in the dialogue: the centrality of the Scriptures in both traditions, ecclesiological differences as well as convergences, and theologies and practices of baptism.[26] Such study also has the potential to help Baptist communities address the attraction of

---

[23] For helpful guidance for ecumenically attentive observances of Reformation Sunday, see Lutheran World Federation and Pontifical Council for Promoting Christian Unity, *From Conflict to Communion*.

[24] Meyer and Vischer, eds., *Growth in Agreement*; Gros, Meyer, and Rusch, eds., *Growth in Agreement II*; Gros, Best, and Fuchs, eds., *Growth in Agreement III*; Best, Fuchs, Gibaut, Gros, and Prassas, eds., *Growth in Agreement IV, Books 1 and 2*.

[25] While all of these reports from international dialogues with Baptist participation except for those from Phase II of the dialogue with the Catholic Church and the dialogue with the World Methodist Council have been published in the *Growth in Agreement* series, for the purposes of this chapter they are cited as the electronic documents in PDF that are freely available for download on the BWA web site (URLs included in the full bibliographical references at the end of the book). There have also been numerous national and regional bilateral dialogues with Baptist participation; see Neville Callam, "Baptists in Bilateral Theological Dialogue."

[26] Baptist World Alliance and World Alliance of Reformed Churches, *Report of Theological Conversations Sponsored by the World Alliance of Reformed Churches and the Baptist World Alliance, 1973-77.*

some of their members to certain expressions of Reformed theology that their Reformed dialogue partners might agree are less than salutary.

2.2.2. BWA and Catholic Church (1984-1988, 2006-2010, 2017-2021). It would be difficult to imagine a more polarized pair of ecumenical dialogue partners than Baptists and Catholics. Yet when the BWA and the Catholic Church engaged in a series of international conversations from 1984 through 1988 to see what they might be able to say together, the two communions were actually able to say a great deal about their agreement on "God's saving revelation in Jesus Christ, the necessity of personal commitment to God in Christ, the ongoing work of the Holy Spirit, and the missionary imperative that emerges from God's redemptive activity on behalf of humankind," as paragraph 2 of the report *Summons to Witness to Christ in Today's World* summarized the matters on which Baptists and Catholics were able to say something together about our common commitment to the good news of our testimony that "Jesus Christ is Lord."[27] That report also identified deep differences evident in those conversations that warranted continued exploration: theological authority and method; the shape of ecclesial *koinonia*; the relationship between faith, baptism, and Christian witness; and the place of Mary in faith and practice. When I served as a member of the Baptist delegation to a second series of conversations with the Catholic Church from 2006 through 2010, we directly addressed those ongoing differences. The nearly 100-page report *The Word of God in the Life of the Church* is not a description of our differences.[28] It is rather a statement of our surprisingly substantial consensus on the church's participation in the *koinonia* of the Triune God, the authority of Christ in Scripture and tradition, baptism and the Eucharist/Lord's Supper, Mary as a model of discipleship, and the ministry of oversight (*episkopē* and unity in the life of the church. We presented these agreements as a "differentiated consensus": paragraphs set in bold type expressed our basic consensus, followed by paragraphs set in regular type that offered commentary on the natures of that consensus and/or identified the ways in which there are remaining differences in how each communion understands and embodies what Baptists and Catholics have been able to say together. Phase III of this dialogue, for which I serve as Co-Secretary of the joint commission is currently underway (2017-2021). It returns to the challenge of Phase I to work toward "the framing of concrete ways to witness together at the present time."[29] The overarching theme of Phase III is "The Dynamic of the Gospel and the Witness of the

---

[27] Baptist World Alliance and Catholic Church, *Summons to Witness to Christ in Today's World*.

[28] Baptist World Alliance and Catholic Church, *The Word of God in the Life of the Church*.

[29] Baptist World Alliance and Catholic Church, *Summons to Witness to Christ in Today's World*, § 58.

Church." During the first four years of this series, we are addressing four aspects of this theme: "Sources of Common Witness," "Contexts of Common Witness," "Challenges of Common Witness" and "Forms of Common Witness," with year five reserved for work toward the report summarizing our findings. The report will likely be published in 2022 or 2023.

2.2.3. BWA and Lutheran World Federation (1986-1989). While Baptists represent a distinctively different stream of the Protestant tradition, its Reformation tributaries flow from the Lutheran beginnings of Protestantism. Baptists may join Lutheran neighbors in digging down to common roots by reading the report from the international dialogue between the BWA and the Lutheran World Federation.[30] In the process, they may receive some of the gifts of a tradition that, despite its beginnings in ecclesial division, has devoted much energy to the modern ecumenical movement and its proposals for convergence, including its convergences with the Catholic tradition on justification and other matters.

2.2.4. BWA and World Mennonite Conference (1989-1992). The Mennonites are Baptists' closest denominational kissing cousins. If there is a Mennonite fellowship in your area, members of your Baptist congregation can get to know them by exploring together the report from the Baptist-Mennonite international dialogue.[31] While this particular report is more a brief comparative summary of what Baptists and Mennonites have in common as well as their differences, it can be useful to Baptist congregations in learning about their relation to the larger Free Church tradition and in identifying what gifts they could receive, or re-receive, from their Anabaptist forebears and Mennonite kindred. Such gifts might include some of the Mennonite distinctives listed under "Divergences" between the two communions in the report, such as the emphasis on peace as essential to the way of Jesus Christ, the accountability of followers of Christ to one another in the community of the church, and service as a means of engaging in missions.[32]

2.2.5. BWA and Anglican Consultative Council (2000-2005). Dissent from the Church of England birthed the Baptists, but more recent dialogue between representatives of the traditions has helped them discover that they now have much more in common and many gifts to share with one another. The international Baptist-Anglican bilateral represented a novel experiment in ecumenical conversations at this level. Rather than appointing two delegations with relatively fixed membership that met annually across the span of the dialogue, this was a regionally contex-

---

[30] Baptist World Alliance and Lutheran World Federation, *Baptists and Lutherans in Conversation.*

[31] Baptist World Alliance and World Mennonite Conference, *Baptist-Mennonite Theological Conversations.*

[32] Baptist World Alliance and World Mennonite Conference, *Baptist-Mennonite Theological Conversations*, 18, 27-28, 38-39.

tualized dialogue that met in six different regions of the world in which there are opportunities for encounter between Baptists and Anglicans at the grassroots, with the majority of the membership for each regional phase of the dialogue drawn from churches in that region and a small continuation committee with three members from each communion that participated in all six rounds of the dialogue. One of the major fruits of this approach was the dialogue report's inclusion after Part One, which contained the more traditional summaries of convergences and remaining differences, of Part Two, "Stories"—a thick narration of the ways Anglicans and Baptists in different contexts have been able to envision and embody various local expressions of Christian unity in relation to one another.[33] Surely being able to tell this concretized story together is one of the most significant achievements of the dialogue, along with its proposal of a Baptist-Anglican convergence on baptism. It seeks to move beyond the impasses inevitably confronted by infant-baptizing and believer-baptizing communions when "common baptism" is the ecumenical paradigm proposed for convergence between them by proposing instead the recognition "that the 'beginning' of the Christian life—or initiation—is not so much a single event, but a process or journey which may extend over a considerable time" (§ 42). As with *One Baptism: Towards Mutual Recognition*, hearing the voices of this bilateral choral ensemble proposing a way past older conflicts about baptism can help Baptists discern how their church membership policies might contribute to a more visible unity through the recognition of the baptisms administered by churches of other communions, and not only by Anglicans and Episcopalians.

2.2.6. BWA and World Methodist Council (2014-2018). The report from the most recently completed international bilateral with Baptist participation both builds on the results of previous dialogues with other communions and offers new features in a dialogue report that can encourage the process of reception.[34] Among the ways it draws on and extends the work of other ecumenical dialogue commissions is its effort to develop more fully what both the Baptist-Anglican dialogue and Phase II of the Baptist-Catholic dialogue have proposed as the possibility of recognizing common features in comparable whole journeys of Christian beginnings, with particular reference to the journeys of Christian beginnings that are typical for Baptists and Methodists (§§ 70-80). In addition to baptism and Christian initiation, the report explores the history and heritage of both communions; ecclesiology, authority, and salvation; and the practices of worship and witness/mission. Each section of the report ends with one or more stories of Baptist-Methodist ecumenical encounter and cooperation in various contexts and the texts

---

[33] Baptist World Alliance and Anglican Consultative Council, *Conversations Around the World 2000-2005*.

[34] Baptist World Alliance and World Methodist Council, *Faith Working through Love*.

of hymns that are among the gifts offered and received by each tradition. The report concludes with eleven concrete recommendations for implementation by Baptists and Methodists and their local churches and finally a responsive prayer for Baptists and Methodists to pray together in joint worship services. Two members of the Joint Commission, a French Baptist and a German Methodist, prepared a study guide to accompany the report as a means of encouraging its reception at the grassroots—the most important level of ecumenical convergence.[35]

3. Formative Practices of Ecumenical Reception

In the Free Church tradition, local church pastors play a key role in facilitating "ecumenical reception," which is the process by which worldwide Christian communions, denominations at the national level, local churches, and individual Christians become informed about, consider, and act upon the proposals and agreements that result from bilateral and multilateral ecumenical dialogue.[36] In the final chapter of my book *Baptist Identity and the Ecumenical Future*, I suggested some ways in which pastors might do this:

> In local churches, pastors can study reports of ecumenical dialogues with Baptist participation as part of their ongoing ecumenical formation. They can share them with ministers from the churches of Baptists' dialogue partners along with fellow Baptist pastors, and perhaps form local clergy discussion groups to work through the texts together. Ministers can share these dialogue texts also with church members, who have day-to-day relationships with members of other churches in which they live out visible Christian unity—and who may already be doing so in the context of their marriages and other family relationships....[R]eports and agreed statements from ecumenical dialogues can easily serve as the basis of local church formation study groups, which ideally might also involve members of a neighboring church affiliated with a dialogue partner communion. Reception of ecumenical convergences may involve recognition that a concretely altered relationship is possible between neighboring churches. On the basis of that recognition and in light of the rich tradition of covenant-making as a Baptist ecclesial practice, it may be possible to formalize a local ecumenical covenant between neighboring churches, with members and ministers pledging to abide by it in their local relations and in the calling of future ministers, who will pledge to continue the pattern of ecumenical relationships speci-

---

[35] Duval-Poujol and Schuler, eds., *Faith Working through Love: Study Guide*.

[36] Adapted from Harmon, *Ecumenism Means You, Too*, 116 ("Appendix B: Glossary of Key Ecumenical Terms," s.v. "reception"). For a book-length treatment of ecumenical reception, see Rusch, *Ecumenical Reception*; cf. also Rusch's earlier, shorter book *Reception*.

fied by the covenant as a condition of accepting their calling to serve in these congregations.[37]

When pastors lead congregations to receive the light offered by these voices of ecumenical convergence through such practices of grassroots ecumenical engagement, they are helping them participate more fully in the Triune God's communion-creating work in the world.

4. Conclusion: Discerning Listening as Receptive Ecumenism

Ecumenical reception is one means by which churches may engage in the similarly-named but distinct practice of "receptive ecumenism." Receptive ecumenism is a more recent approach to ecumenical dialogue according to which the communions in conversation with one another seek to identify the distinctive gifts that each tradition has to offer the other and which each could receive from the other with integrity, but in which "the primary emphasis is on learning rather than teaching....each tradition takes responsibility for its own potential learning from others and is, in turn, willing to facilitate the learning of others as requested but without dictating terms and without making others' learning a precondition to attending to ones' own."[38] Ecumenical reception of the convergences reached in bilateral and multilateral dialogue is one means of identifying the gifts in other traditions that Baptists might receive with integrity into their own, but Baptists have also practiced receptive ecumenism whenever they have received into their worship, devotion, and Christian living aspects of the faith and practice of other Christian traditions. They have been doing so for a long time, as the ecumenical makeup of Baptist hymnals and the increasingly numerous Baptist churches that observe the seasons of the full Christian year illustrate.[39] Local Baptist churches may also engage in receptive ecumenism by attending to the sources of light offered by the diverse voices of the whole church in its varied historical and contemporary contexts. In that sense, the intention of this book is to encourage the receptive ecumenism by which the church can become most fully the church in which "the body is one and has many members, and all the members of the body, though many, are one body" (1 Cor. 12:12). Our concluding chapter proposes ways in which ministers might help that happen.

---

[37] Harmon, *Baptist Identity and the Ecumenical Future*, 264-66. The practice of entering into local ecumenical covenants is commended in Kinnamon, *Can a Renewal Movement Be Renewed?*, 15-16, 83-84.

[38] See Murray, ed., *Receptive Ecumenism and the Call to Catholic Learning*.

[39] See Harmon, "How Baptists Receive the Gifts of Catholics and Other Christians," 1/81-5/85; idem, *Baptist Identity and the Ecumenical Future*, 152-64.

7. For Further Reading

Gros, Jeffrey, Eamon McManus, and Ann Riggs. *Introduction to Ecumenism.* Mahwah, NJ: Paulist Press, 1998.

Harmon, Steven R. *Ecumenism Means You, Too: Ordinary Christians and the Quest for Christian Unity.* Eugene, OR: Cascade Books, 2010.

_____. *Baptist Identity and the Ecumenical Future: Story, Tradition, and the Recovery of Community.* Waco, TX: Baylor University Press, 2016.

Nelson, R. David and Charles Raith II. *Ecumenism: A Guide for the Perplexed.* New York: Bloomsbury T&T Clark, 2017.

Rusch, William G. *Ecumenical Reception: Its Challenge and Opportunity.* Grand Rapids, MI: William B. Eerdmans, 2007.

Wainwright, Geoffrey and Paul McPartlan, eds. *The Oxford Handbook of Ecumenical Studies.* Oxford: Oxford University Press, 2018- (while the print version of this Handbook is currently in development, chapters are being made available online as they are prepared for publication, including the chapter on the Baptist tradition by Steven R. Harmon).

25

Conclusion: Light from Converted Listening

Amy L. Chilton and Steven R. Harmon

The goal of this book, we wrote in the first chapter, is to encourage the formation of Baptists in the convictions and practices of Trinitarian communion that mark life under Christ's rule, that they might be equipped for engaging in cruciform acts of solidarity with and ministry to those on the margins. [1] Toward that end, we have pointed Baptist ministers and theological students, as well as their theological educators, to the sources of light found in the whole church through which Baptists congregations may receive the illumination of the Spirit necessary for this urgently needed formation.

1. Illumination for/from Seeing *and* Hearing

Open my ears, that I may hear voices of truth Thou sendest clear;
and while the wave-notes fall on my ear, everything false will disappear.
Silently now I wait for Thee, ready, my God, Thy will to see;
open my ears, illumine me, Spirit divine![2]

The Spirit has been providing this formative illumination since the church's creation at Pentecost. In the story of Pentecost recounted in Acts 2, the Spirit provides light that enables people to see things: divided tongues as of fire, visions and dreams, portents in heaven and signs on earth (vv. 3, 17, 19-20). Yet in the narrative much of this illumination is related to that which is heard rather than seen: the

---

[1] Here we echo again World Council of Churches, *The Church*, § 1 (p. 5), quoted in a note in our introductory chapter and once more here: "The Church, as the body of Christ, acts by the power of the Holy Spirit to continue his life-giving mission in prophetic and compassionate ministry and so participates in God's work of healing a broken world. Communion, whose source is the very life of the Holy Trinity, is both the gift by which the Church lives and, at the same time, the gift that God calls the Church to offer to a wounded and divided humanity in hope of reconciliation and healing."

[2] Scott, "Open My Eyes, That I May See." Scott, a Baptist hymn writer, was the first woman to publish a collection of choral anthems (idem, *The Royal Anthem Book*); a subsequent collection was titled *Truth in Song: For the Lovers of Truth Everywhere*.

sound of violent wind (v. 2), the speaking of other languages by the gathered disciples (v. 4), the hearing by the gathered crowd of multinational pilgrims from the Jewish diaspora "in the native language of each" (vv. 6, 8, 11) Peter's repeated summons to "listen" to what he has to say (vv. 14, 22), and the hearing by which the crowd heeded Peter's summons to listening (vv. 37, 41). In the first volume published in the Perspectives on Baptist Identities series in which the present book also appears, Ryan Newson notes that while James Wm. McClendon, Jr. repeatedly appeals to the Pentecost narrative in his account of a "baptist vision"[3] in which "the future and the past mystically converge on the present, such that circumstances now are seen under a different aspect," it is the auditory motif that predominates in that story:

> The metaphor of vision is important, of course, but Acts 2 explicitly focuses on the changes that occur in people's ability to hear each other when the Spirit comes. What is seen is not altered as much as their ability to hear the disciples' speech—or better, understand the conversation in each one's native tongue....[I]t is at least as illuminating to describe this "type" of Christianity in auditory terms; to speak, in other words, not just of "the baptist vision," but a "baptist" way of listening.
>
> This kind of shift bears fruit because, for Christians searching for faithful ways of inhabiting a postmodern context, *listening* is a particularly helpful posture that describes what it looks like to be open and discerning to the world....But even more, listening is a helpful metaphor because, in approaching the incredibly diverse Baptist stream, one's ears must be opened in order that "from the many voices there will emerge, not a Babel, but a symphony, a theological Pentecost."[4] Simply *hearing noises* is not listening; one must learn to hear aright, and *understand* what is heard. What McClendon's "baptist" tradition really has to offer, I posit, is a way of listening—to self, to others, and to God—that "hears a different aspect" of the story than is typically told.[5]

---

[3] In Newson's usage and elsewhere in this chapter, the lower-case "b" references to "baptists" follow the convention employed by McClendon (*Systematic Theology*, vol. 1, *Ethics*, rev ed., 19) to refer collectively to the Free Church heirs of the radical reformation that include Baptists (upper-case "B").

[4] Newson is quoting McClendon, "A baptist Millennium?" in *Collected Works of James Wm. McClendon, Jr.*, ed. Newson and Wright, 1:300.

[5] Newson, *Inhabiting the World*, 22-23. We have engaged Newson's proposals in *Inhabiting the World* more fully in Harmon, Lipsett, Norris, Chilton, and Newson, "Ryan Newson's *Inhabiting the World*," 327-54; Steve's response "'Quick to Listen, Slow to Speak'" appears on pp. 327-33, and Amy's response "Converted Listening" appears on pp. 343-48.

In this baptist way of listening rooted in the Pentecost story, the sources of light by which the Spirit illuminates the church's path to God's future for the world are voices of difference that speak and are heard inter-contextually. Voices speaking from one context are heard by hearers from other contexts, in this case participating in a shared context, and the Spirit brings about new understanding precisely through this encounter with difference.[6] We and our collaborators have written this book to encourage Baptist churches to engage in this baptist way of inter-contextual listening to voices from the whole church, throughout its history and throughout the world today, which are introduced in the preceding chapters.

We are convinced that this kind of listening is a formative ecclesial practice. The simple act of listening to voices that come from contexts other than one's own can help the church to become a more faithful community of followers of Jesus Christ, even when we do not yet know precisely how our hearing of these voices ought to shape our faith and practice. This kind of listening is a journey of transformation, often embarked upon with an insufficiently detailed map. It is not without reason that Scripture prioritizes listening in relation to doctrine (defined by McClendon as "a church teaching"[7]): "let everyone be quick to listen, slow to speak" (James 1:19). Newson's development of McClendon's "baptist vision" in terms of a "baptist way of listening" called attention to McClendon's treatment of American composer Charles Ives as one of the subjects of his book *Biography as Theology*.[8] It was theologically significant for McClendon that Ives attributed his formation as a composer to his openness in listening to a wide range of musical pieces "that he was able to draw…into a harmonious and yet creatively dissonant composition in his own work."[9] We conceive of the ecclesial practice of listening as

---

[6] Our theological account of the importance of difference and diversity to the church's practice of congregational discernment has important similarities to the proposals of "radical democracy" theorists such as Romand Coles (e.g., Coles, *Beyond Gated Politics*). Radical democracy "regards liberal democracy, to which both 'left' and 'right' on the American political spectrum belong, as being insufficiently democratic because its structures resist direct democratic participation and work against the full incorporation of diverse others into a community in which the contestation of difference is essential to the common good. Radical democracy insists that genuinely democratic communities depend on their inclusion of genuinely different voices" (Harmon, "'Quick to Listen, Slow to Speak'," 330). If these insights are applied ecclesiologically, "a stance of epistemologically humble, receptive listening to others not like us is indispensable both for the church's internal practice of discernment and for its inhabitation of the world" (ibid.). Such Baptist ecclesiological applications have been made by Newson, *Inhabiting the World*; idem, *Radical Friendship*; and Schelin, "The Contestable Church."

[7] McClendon, *Systematic Theology*, vol. 2, *Doctrine*, 24.

[8] Newson, *Inhabiting the World*, 115; McClendon, *Biography as Theology*, 114-40.

[9] Harmon, "'Quick to Listen, Slow to Speak'," 332.

playing a similar role in forming the local church community's capacity for practicing theology:

> Analogously, there is a formative power in the practice of listening to diverse voices, whether or not they seem directly applicable to a particular question addressed by the community. Hearing deeply the voices of others forms us gradually for eventually crafting theological compositions that envision living more Christianly in relation to issues seemingly unrelated to a particular voice we may hear. For the contexts from which each voice speaks—those we have heard and are hearing, and those we have yet to hear—are intersectionally connected.[10]

This simple practice of listening, however, not only needs the assistance of God's Spirit for forming hearers in the capacity to move beyond encountering difference as "hearing noises" to learning "to hear aright, and to *understand* what is heard."[11] Listening is a practice that, like all practices of the church, is susceptible to corruption. Therefore, our listening is always in need of conversion, and conversion comes in part through the re-examination occasioned by the inter-contextual hearing of voices of difference:

> If *listening* to oneself, God, and others is a goal and also a set of practices that stands in need of conversion, and if we accept that the Spirit moves as the Spirit will in the church catholic in which members are themselves simultaneously inhabiting the same church (in different local churches) and a complex myriad of worlds, then it behooves us to engage in a conversion of *our* listening so that the church might contradict a world which actively shuts its ears to *songs from different lands*....[W]hat does a rightly oriented powerful practice of listening that has been converted to the cover story of the "lamb that was slain" look like? At a basic level this rightly oriented powerful practice actively seeks out the voices that seem most cacophonous, that on first listen *ring as untrue.* This seeking is not in order to synchronize those voices to one's own, but rather because the listener must discern

---

[10] Harmon, "'Quick to Listen, Slow to Speak'," 332. Susan Shaw introduced intersectionality theory in chapter 8 of the present book (see subsection 1.3 Intersectionality and Feminist Theologies); Kimberlé Crenshaw coined the term "intersectionality" and pioneered the concept in her article "Demarginalizing the Intersection of Race and Sex." Baptist minister and theologian Martin Luther King, Jr. anticipated the emphases of intersectionality theory in his insistence that "Injustice anywhere is a threat to justice everywhere. We are caught in an inescapable network of mutuality, tied in a single garment of destiny. Whatever affects one directly, affects all indirectly" (King, "Letter from Birmingham Jail," 2.

[11] Newson, *Inhabiting the World*, 23.

whether the aspect by which she hears those voices stands in need of conversion.[12]

The Pentecost-birthed community's Spirit-enabled practice of listening underwent a gradual process of conversion through encounters with difference. The outpouring of the Spirit at the feast of Pentecost did involve important elements of inclusion: the presence of people in the gathered crowd "from every nation under heaven" (v. 25) and the transcending of divisions of gender, age, and social class in the pouring out of the Spirit "upon all flesh" (vv. 16-18). But in this episode, those included by the Spirit were Jewish. The recognition that non-Jewish citizens of "every nation under heaven" were included in God's salvation would await further conversion of the early Christian community. By Acts 10, a few years after the Pentecost experience, the encounter with Cornelius and his household had led Peter to declare "I truly understand that God shows no partiality, but in every nation anyone who fears [God] and does what is right is acceptable to [God]" (vv. 34-35) and to ask "Can anyone withhold the water for baptizing these people who have received the Holy Spirit just as we have?" (v. 47). Peter's later recounting of this experience that had helped him see that God had "made no distinction between them and us" before the apostles and elders gathered for theological deliberation in Jerusalem was decisive for the church's resolution of the question of the inclusion of the Gentiles in the community (Acts 15:6-11). These encounters with difference had likewise formed the apostle Paul, who recognized in his letter to the Galatians that baptism creates a new reality, a new community in which instead of the ways the world divides humanity and grants privilege according to perceived differences—"Jew and Greek, slave and free, male and female"—now "There is no longer Jew or Greek, there is no longer slave or free, there is no longer male and female; for all of you are one in Christ Jesus" (Gal. 3:28). That text must be read in light of both Jewish and Greco-Roman texts that prized the privilege possessed by the first group in each of the three pairs of divisions noted—ethnic, socio-economic, and gender. [13] It is not difficult to imagine its application to a contemporary community in which the light provided by the Spirit through inter-contextual encounters with difference leads the church to envision a new community created by baptism in which there is no longer white or non-white, "natural born citizen" or immigrant, straight or queer, or gender binary-conforming and -nonconforming, but all are one in Christ Jesus.

---

[12] Chilton, "Converted Listening," 346-47.

[13] See Wiley, *Paul and the Gentile Women*, 15, 17, 19, 51, 95-97, 101-02, 114, 120; 125-26, n. 8; 138-39, nn. 48-49. The specific Jewish and Greco-Roman texts in the background of Gal. 3:28 are noted, e.g., in Longenecker, *Galatians*, 157.

2. Practicing Converted Listening

What, then, do we do with all these sources of light, all these voices, in the life of the congregation? How might we attend to our listening so that is not merely a hearing of noises, and not a selective hearing distorted by our predispositions and previous influences, but a deep listening open to the understanding that the Spirit may lead us toward as we hear? We must first listen—and, to make use again of the visual metaphor, we must first look. But not all of our listening and looking will initially involve noticing the things that we may come to notice later through converted listening (and looking). We may hear all the sounds within earshot, and we may look around at everything within our field of vision, but we may not notice with discernment everything that we hear and see. For example, we recently participated in an academic conference at which we both presented papers in the same classroom. In a front corner of the classroom was a table that appeared to be a medical exam table. "Must be used for classes in some area of medicine," Steve and his male colleagues thought after seeing it. "What's a gynecological exam table doing here?" wondered Amy and another female colleague. What we noticed, or failed to notice, about the specific purpose of the table was shaped by our differing social locations, we came to realize through our dialogue about what we saw differently.

2.1. The Church as Contextualized Theologizing Community

The task of local Baptist churches becoming loci of rich theological dialogue that engages difference constructively necessarily involves active participation of the whole body. While the role of the pastor in a Baptist church is often complicated by our anti-clerical beginnings and various practices of the priesthood of all believers, the reality is that in many local congregations the pastor has the most theological training (though this is certainly not the case in all congregations!). The pastor stands (or should stand) in the role of resident theological facilitator, peculiarly equipped by means of her seminary education for guiding the practices that make up a local "theologizing community": practices of listening, Scripture reading, and preaching (amongst others).

The local church's trans-local associations, at their best, participate in Trinitarian community and connect the local church to the church catholic *and make up the church as the Triune body*. Within the church catholic (i.e., the whole church), local churches quite evidently theologize differently, thus necessitating greater attention to trans-local theology and its formative practices if local faith communities are to participate well in the Trinitarian body of Christ. If the members of the community are to be shaped adequately as inter-contextual theologians, we must begin with the reality that local reading communities read and theologize differently and that *difference* in and of itself is not heretical.

298

This raises a series of questions. What must the local church do to actualize the church catholic in the local church? How does the local church maintain integrity as a local reading community without ghettoizing itself? How can local churches hear and engage other localized voices not as an exercise in cheap diversity tourism but rather as the costly practice of becoming the church together in Trinitarian unity?[14] What must the local church *do* in order faithfully to be the church together with other local churches?

One important first step is the recognition that many Baptists in the North American context are heirs of modern conservative foundationalism and its heritage of "experience blindness," pre-conditioning them to rule out as heretical some voices from other localities whose theological conclusions may initially ring as untrue—the very voices that make experiences other than their own more visibly present so that those voices challenge the presumed normativity of their own experiences.[15] The mere presence of "experience" in theology is problematic in this sense, in addition to the presence of different experiences that have heightened relief compared to our own. If the interweaving of community-embedded experience and theological voice is a given outcome for the theologizing community, the task then is to recognize the contours of this in our own local theologies and to find ways to bridge differences in experiences and voices with other local theologies. McClendon proposes one means of navigating this by using J. L. Austin's philosophical *speech act theory* to examine theological language (i.e., how a community speaks the truths it believes about God), particularly how theological language connects to the breadth of a community's knowledge, conventions, and experiences. The things we say about God do not stand apart from lives we live in response to God and our world. Speech act theory may help with this first task of recognizing the presence of the local reading community's own experience in its own theology.[16] The exploration of theologies different than our own can then begin with questions of how faithfully that theology is a practice of a local community, rather than how closely it adheres to a supposedly experience-less "orthodoxy" that mysteriously (always) mirrors our own local community. This might mean asking of the local community, "where and how is our locality present in what we understand as orthodox theology?" and asking of other communities the same.

---

[14] Martell-Otero, "From Foreign Bodies in Teacher Space to Embodied Spirit in *Personas Educadas*, 53.

[15] Kärkkäinen, *Trinity and Revelation*, 2:72, explores evangelicalism's overemphasis on propositional theological knowledge at the expense of "liberal experientialism." For a helpful outline of the modern foundational divide between conservatives and liberals that forced this "experience-blindness," see Nancey Murphy's *Beyond Liberalism and Fundamentalism*.

[16] I (Amy) explore this use of McClendon's work in Chilton, "How Do I Speak of God from This Place?"

2.2. The Church as Bible-Reading Community

Besides critical self-reflection on a community's own locatedness, in what other practices must a reading community engage in order to participate in the whole Trinitarian body of Christ together? Certainly Baptists, a "people of the book," must engage in the powerful practice of Bible reading, but if contextuality and inter-contextuality (the local church on its own and in relationship with other local churches) are both necessary aspects of Trinitarian communion, then it naturally follows that reading the Bible together *in* one's context must also mean reading the Bible together *across* contexts. If Christ is the center of the "great story" that shapes our lesser stories, the narrative that shapes and judges all of our practices, then nowhere is an inter-contextual reading practice more promising than in the reading of the Gospels together. The recent histories of "contextual" and "liberationist" theologies, many examined in this book, have brought to light the abundance of insights present in the church catholic, particularly in its readings of Jesus of Nazareth. Practices of "reading the Bible from the margins"[17] have exposed not only the historic Western (and often male) bias in academic theology, but they have also reminded local churches that many other reading communities are shedding new light on the Jesus we follow, providing additional loci in which Scripture can "offer more of itself" when communities access the "original and profound meaning" of Scripture through a deeply local reading.[18]

What does it mean to engage in the powerful practice of Bible reading inter-contextually as a local congregation? Is reading in this way possible in a deep, meaningful, and formative manner without sacrificing one's own local reading? Here the expectation is not that other local communities will read on behalf of our own, but rather that our own local reading will be shaped and informed by the voices of the church's global symphony—*voices that through our practice of listening to them help us to read anew*. Reading the Bible inter-contextually as a local community can be accomplished in multiple ways. Certainly, Scripture reading *with* persons from contexts and experiences different than our own is imaginable and desirable, perhaps even using regional and denominational associations as ready-made diverse reading communities. A local community can also read the Bible alongside of, or in the light of, the wider witness of written theological voices, such as those introduced in this volume. Both of these are practices of "reading *with*" and may be deepened when facilitating ministers bring to their congregants the tools of listening and discernment offered by the theological research skills and critical interpretive methodologies in which their own theological education has formed them, not only calling readers to a responsible reading of texts in which

---

[17] De La Torre, *Reading the Bible from the Margins*.
[18] Sobrino, "Jesus of Galilee from the Salvadoran Context," 439.

their authors are heard on their own terms but also *giving their congregants the tools by which to do so*. The reading community would then better be able to suspend the judgment of witnesses that on first hearing "ring untrue" in order to be open to hearing the voice of the Spirit through these voices of difference.[19] Alternative voices can be engaged not in order primarily to assess their "orthodoxy" (a loaded term by any stretch of the imagination), but rather in a deeper form of listening to an invisible community that forms the hearts and minds of the visible reading community alongside the reading of Scripture. The reading community can then ask how its particular reading of Scripture is faithful to the readings of believers in other contexts, not sacrificing the task of the local reading community but rather expanding it through the discipline of being formed by the faith witness of others, of having to "tune" its own instrument in order to play the heavenly orchestral pieces together well.

For example, one reading of the Bible that stands in need of significant "tuning" is the conflictual Baptist read on women in Scripture. The reading (or misreading) that prevails in many more conservative circles (particularly the reading represented by the 2000 revision of the Southern Baptist Convention's *Baptist Faith and Message*) has significant practical consequences for the faith and practices of Baptist women (and men!). Here we may think of the erasures of Mary Magdalene and Mary the mother of Jesus: the one mis-read as a prostitute and the other as a nagging and weeping woman, and here the voices of the church catholic might reshape our perceptions not only of these women but also of women in Baptist life. Although Mary Magdalene was the first preacher of the risen Christ, she became "a powerful religious leader [who] is turned into a beautiful pliant sinner, symbol of female sexuality redeemed," and depicted in religious art as a seductress.[20] Mary the Mother of Jesus becomes just that—a mother, rather than a preacher, disciple, or bearer of the God-child (the anti-Catholicism that has marked much of the Baptist tradition has made Baptists especially averse to the latter appellation). Yet, if we hear Mary the Mother of Jesus in the voice of Musa W. Dube, biblical studies scholar at the University of Botswana, she is freed from motherhood—the "most effective tool that patriarchy uses to ensure that women remain dependent, poor and at home"—and freed to be a woman disciple.[21] Reading with the women of Africa suffering from the HIV/AIDS crisis, Dube finds in Jesus' words that which frees women by his freeing of his own mother: "*Woman*, what concern is that to

---

[19] Although not directly theological, a resource I [Amy] have found particularly helpful for both my college and seminary students in gaining skills in critical reading is Adler and Van Doren, *How to Read a Book*.

[20] Johnson, *Friends of God and Prophets*, 146.

[21] Dube, "Who Do You Say That I Am?" 358.

you and to me?" (John 2:4). My own (Amy's) initial reading of this text is more along the lines of, "How rude, son!" Yet, Dube's reading shows that by calling Mary "woman," Jesus frees her from a biologically oppressive role and "counts her as a member of the community of faith."[22] By reading this Johannine text with Dube, for example, we Baptists might better address our own post-Catholic devaluing of Mary as well as our tendency to devalue women disciples, and with Mary's name spoken in a different tone might find in her a challenge to the gendered practices of our own communities of faith.[23]

2.3. Preaching as a Practice of Theology

Conversion to hearing other voices as a symphony rather than heretical cacophony and reading the Bible in the local community with the global community (both past and present) necessitates the prophetic voice of the church and its pulpits. The minister as the facilitating theologian, bringing reading and theologizing skills to congregants, engaging the plethora of voices in Bible studies, and making diverse theological resources available to the church, also has at her disposal the great poetry of ministry: the sermon. McClendon, whose "baptist vision" was the identity of the local church as part of the first century church by means of their shared practices, argued that the sermon itself was a powerful practice, a "remembering sign" that (at its best) stands opposed to the powerful practices of the world.[24] In the preparation and the delivery of the sermon, the preacher might still think of herself as the facilitating theologian, as all worship is "interactive creaturely response to what God does and requires and promises. . . [it] is two-sided conversation, dialogue, with the God of grace."[25] More than simply *involving* the pew-sitters, preaching is also a powerful means by which the congregation at the leadership of the preacher enters into the "primary theology" of the gospel as it orders its life by the narrative therein: according to McClendon, "this theology has to speak to us in story if it is to speak as deep calleth unto deep."[26]

---

[22] Dube, "Who Do You Say That I Am?" 358.

[23] John L. Thompson's observations about reading the Bible with a Christian community that is diachronically extended apply to all the voices/sources of light explored in this book, synchronically as well as diachronically extended: "We should hope to find writers in the past who argue with us, and with all our contemporaries. We should also hope to lose some of those arguments, if we are at all teachable. Sometimes we'll dissent from our forebears...At other times, our presumptions about their presuppositions will turn on us and expose our own failings...We may return from the past unpersuaded, but we will not return unchanged" (Thompson, *Reading the Bible with the Dead*, 222-23).

[24] McClendon, *Systematic Theology*, vol. 2, *Doctrine*, 374.

[25] McClendon, *Systematic Theology*, vol. 2, *Doctrine*, 376.

[26] McClendon, *Systematic Theology*, vol. 3, *Witness*, 354.

2.4. The Theology-Facilitating Preacher as Listener

But what is this "story" in which the sermon "speaks to us," and if the sermon is speaking, are the listeners really involved—and what of the preacher herself? At the conclusion of McClendon's *Collected Works*, vol. 3, is a sermon titled "How to Preach the Gospel" that was likely delivered in 1984 for a joint chapel service at the Pacific Lutheran Theological Seminary and the Church School of Divinity. In this sermon McClendon focuses his listeners on Dietrich Bonhoeffer's homiletic instructions to his seminary students in the 1930s. McClendon declares Bonhoeffer's method "(the best answer I know) to the question of how to preach the gospel."[27] That method is what McClendon labels the "present-ation" of the gospel (hyphen added by him); that is, the gospel prioritized. What this means for the preacher, according to McClendon, is that the gospel speaks "in and through you, the preacher, and not vice versa."[28] This echoes McClendon's understanding that reading the gospel in one's community is a "powerful-practice" that holds the community accountable and contains "its own corrective";[29] it is a practice that McClendon envisions the preacher herself entering into by means of prayer and meditation as essential sermon preparation. His instruction to these students was this: preacher, preach first to thyself!

What does McClendon's advice to the preacher mean in the context of this volume, in which we are asking how the church might more faithfully be the Triune body of Christ in the local congregation in relation to the global church? One thing this could mean is that as preachers engage the gospel narrative through their study of Scripture, they purposefully utilize study resources that come from contexts outside their own. Baptist theologian Stephen R. Holmes, one of the contributors to this book, took up this sort of study as a Lenten spiritual discipline:

> My Lenten discipline this year will be fasting, as far as I can, from voices like mine (white, male, Western, straight, able-bodied, cisgendered). The idea came talking to a colleague about the problem of gender imbalance on our reading lists. She (rightly, of course) stressed intentionality, which got me thinking about process. If I am writing an entire new module, I will think intentionally about reading lists, but I've done that once in the last three years. Far more often—like, more weeks than not—I give ad hoc advice. A student or colleague asks 'what's good on X?'; I reply with stuff that's in my head. Most of the time, the authors I mention are all white, male,

---

[27] McClendon, "How to Preach the Gospel," in *Collected Works of James Wm. McClendon, Jr.*, ed. Newson and Wright, 3:260.

[28] McClendon, "How to Preach the Gospel," in *Collected Works of James Wm. McClendon, Jr.*, ed. Newson and Wright, 3:260.

[29] McClendon, *Systematic Theology*, vol. 2, *Doctrine*, 35.

Western, straight, able-bodied, cisgendered....How, I wondered, do I break this circle? The answer, obviously, is to be intentional in reading authors who are not like me, to deliberately expose myself to voices not like mine. I need to work on this for all of life, but for now, it will be my discipline this Lent.[30]

Holmes's Lenten discipline exemplifies the inter-contextual listening to the voices of the whole church that we are commending as essential to preparation for preaching as a theological practice of the church. A growing body of socially-located commentary literature supplies preachers with such resources from beyond their own context. The "For Further Reading" bibliography at the end of this chapter lists selected commentary resources that offer readings of the Bible from a wide variety of social locations.[31]

2.5. Voices of the Whole Church in the Local Church

Additionally, if the gospel is both the good news *preached* and the good news *heard*, then the hearing of the Good News is intrinsically related to its *good*ness and thus its *news* is actually made up of the voices, experiences, followings, prayers, and theologizings of the church global. Thus, to preach the Good News in the local congregation is not just to preach an unadulterated/orthodox version, for there is no such access to that devoid of the listeners themselves. In order to preach the Good News, the preacher must bring to the pulpit the voices of her own congregants, the voices of the church global (such as those heard in this volume), the stories and voices of the great cloud of witnesses through time (both dead and alive), and even the *literal* voices of the church global. The preacher thus functions as an orchestra conductor whose embodied interpretation of a musical score blends varied instrumental voices into the sound of a symphony, or as a fiber artist who delivers a weaving together of the many locations of the moving of the Spirit. This

---

[30] Holmes, "Fasting from Voices Like Mine."

[31] There is also a growing body of commentary literature that helps the preacher become aware of how texts were interpreted in pre-modern exegesis. Patristic, medieval, and Reformation-era Christianity also represents social locations that are other than the social locations of the modern (and post-modern) reading community. While historical-critical methodologies have served as sources of light through which the Spirit has illuminated the church's reading of Scripture in fresh ways, they have also sometimes seemed to suggest that the only exegesis worth knowing has been produced from the mid-nineteenth century onward. The Spirit was surely shedding light on the church's reading of the Bible in pre-modern Christianity, and these projects aimed at retrieving earlier readings of Scripture may make their own contribution to making the practice of theology truly inter-contextual. See Oden, ed., *Ancient Christian Commentary on Scripture*; Wilken, ed., *The Church's Bible*; and George, ed., *Reformation Commentary on Scripture*.

could manifest itself in a variety of practical ways, all of which involve discernment and humility on the part of the preacher herself, particularly in an age in which self-imposed division as a means of protection against the other "side" is par for the course (and is, in part, the impetus for the writing of this volume).

This could mean inviting into the pulpit preachers whose voices can expand the church's listening ear. It most certainly also involves the practices of communal discernment, converted listening, and inter-contextual Bible reading. In the best of cases, the preacher is not called to be the community's stand-alone theologian, singing an *a cappella* solo with the church doors slammed against the rising symphony of the wider body of Christ. The preacher as the facilitating theologian will help her congregation practice toward being able to discern the good news in a different tune, to hear the agony and the ecstasy of the gospel story sung in a different land, so that they will become able to discern where the light from another source has illuminated a new aspect of God's character and presence and will see further even where their own light shines into the darkness of other places.

3. "Quick to Listen, Slow to Speak": Venturing a Few Concluding Words

In this final chapter we have gestured toward what it might mean for churches, and especially the pastors who facilitate their local practices of theology, to engage in a "Baptist way of listening" to the range of voices introduced in this book and to discern in them the illumination of the Spirit. We envisioned this project for a primary readership of pastors—both theological students preparing for pastoral ministry and ministers currently serving as pastors—in the Baptist and broader free church tradition (and perhaps in other Christian traditions as well). If you are a seminarian, we hope that your theological education will already be introducing you to the voices from the whole church, historically and globally, that our contributors have surveyed. During this focused time of educational preparation for ministry, we encourage you use this book as a guidebook for the long, deep theological listening that needs to precede your theological speaking as a minister. Listen to the voices that are given expression in each chapter. Follow up on the voices that most interest you—or most challenge you—in your choices for paper topics. Ask your professors and classmates (and ministers and members of your local church community) what they think about the perspectives you encounter in this book. Supplement your required reading assignments with the resources listed in the "For Further Reading" bibliographies at the end of each chapter. Add them to your wish lists for stocking your library for post-seminary reading.

For seminary graduates already engaged in the pastoral work of facilitating congregational practices of theology, we hope that this book will serve as a starting point for continuing theological education. Even though you now must do much theological speaking in this role, it is especially vital that you continue to listen deeply theologically and that you continually seek conversion in and through your listening. If you belong to a ministerial peer learning group, propose reading and discussing this book together. Intentionally incorporate the insights you gain from listening to the theological voices encountered in these chapters into the theological framework in light of which you interpret Scripture and the life of the congregation and the church's context in preparing for the act of theology that is preaching—which is the most prominent and regular role in which you will have the opportunity to facilitate the congregation's practice of theology. As you interpret the Scriptures while preparing to preach, make use of the socially-located commentary resources listed below. All biblical interpretation is socially located, but if you turn only to the commentaries you became accustomed to consulting for your seminary exegesis papers, you will likely be hearing voices that are predominately or exclusively white, European and North American, and male in your sermon preparation—and will thus preach the text along those same lines. When uninterrogated by other voices, reliance on the most frequently consulted commentaries will reinforce the fiction of a neutral, objective theology and interpretation that is privileged over "special interest" theologies and "niche" interpretations. The pastor's study may be one of the most significant locations for making theology an intercontextual practice of the church, and these tools can help that happen.

The local church's practice of theology needs the illumination that God's Spirit offers through the whole body of Christ because this is a practice of a church on pilgrimage toward a place that we cannot yet see. While we are on this pilgrimage the Spirit does not shine a spotlight all the way to the final destination or post streetlamps all along the route, but the sources of light through which the Spirit helps us see do illuminate the path just ahead of us, for the words that mediate the Word to us provide us with "a lamp to [our] feet and a light to [our] path" (Psalm 119:105). Therefore, "let anyone who has an ear listen to what the Spirit is saying to the churches" (Rev. 2:29) through these sources of light, that we might have the resources we need to practice theology, together, where we are.

4. For Further Reading: Biblical Commentary Resources for Converted Listening

Adeyemo, Tokunboh, ed. *Africa Bible Commentary: A One-Volume Commentary.* Grand Rapids, MI: Zondervan Academic, 2010.

Antonelli, Judith S. *In the Image of God: A Feminist Commentary on the Torah.* Northvale, NJ: Jason Aronson, 1997.

Blount, Brian K., Cain Hope Felder, Clarice J. Martin, and Emerson B. Powery, eds. *True to Our Native Land: An African American New Testament Commentary.* Minneapolis: Fortress Press, 2007.

Brenner, Athalya and Carole R. Fontaine, eds. *Feminist Companion to the Bible* [series; volumes individually titled]. First Series and Second Series. Sheffield, UK: Sheffield Academic Press and London: Bloomsbury, 1993-2015.

Byron, Gay L., and Vanessa Lovelace, eds. *Womanist Interpretations of the Bible: Expanding the Discourse*. Semeia Studies, no. 85. Atlanta: SBL Press, 2016.

Cardenal, Ernesto. *The Gospel in Solentiname*. Rev. one-vol. ed. Maryknoll, NY: Orbis Books, 2010.

DeYoung, Curtiss Paul, Wilda C. Gafney, Leticia Guardiola-Sáenz, George E. Tinker, and Frank M. Yamada, eds. *The Peoples' Bible*. Minneapolis: Fortress Press, 2008.

Felder, Cain Hope. *Original African Heritage Study Bible: King James Version*. Valley Forge, PA: Judson Press, 2007.

Gafney, Wilda C. *Womanist Midrash: A Reintroduction to the Women of the Torah and the Throne*. Louisville, KY: Westminster John Knox, 2017.

Goss, Robert E., and Mona West. *Take Back the Word: A Queer Reading of the Bible*. Cleveland: The Pilgrim Press, 2000.

Guest, Deryn, Robert E. Goss, Mona West, and Thomas Bohache, eds. *The Queer Bible Commentary*. London: SCM Press, 2015.

Gutiérrez, Gustavo. *On Job: God-Talk and the Suffering of the Innocent*. Translated by Matthew O'Connell. Maryknoll, NY: Orbis Books, 1987.

Melcher, Sarah J., Mikeal C. Parsons, and Amos Yong, eds. *The Bible and Disability: A Commentary*. Waco, TX: Baylor University Press, 2017.

Newsom, Carol A., Sharon H. Ringe, and Jacqueline E. Lapsley, eds. *Women's Bible Commentary*. 3rd ed. Louisville, KY: Westminster John Knox Press, 2012.

Page, Hugh R., Jr., Randall C. Bailey, Valerie Bridgeman, Stacy Davis, Cheryl Kirk-Duggan, Madipoane Masenya, Nathaniel Samuel Murrell, and Rodney S. Sadler, Jr., eds. *The Africana Bible: Reading Israel's Scriptures from Africa and the African Diaspora*. Minneapolis: Fortress Press, 2010.

Patte, Daniel, ed. *Global Bible Commentary*. Nashville: Abingdon Press, 2006.

Reid, Barbara E., Mary Ann Beavis, Amy-Jill Levine, Linda M. Maloney, Ahida Calderón Pilarski, Sarah Tanzer, and Lauress Wilkins Lawrence, eds. *Wisdom Commentary* [series; volumes individually titled]. Collegeville, MI: Liturgical Press, 2015-.

Segovia, Fernando F. and Mary Ann Tolbert, eds. *Reading from This Place: Social Location and Biblical Interpretation in Global Perspective*. 2 vols. Minneapolis: Fortress Press, 1995 and 2000.

Segovia, Fernando F. and R. S. Sugirtharajah, eds. *A Postcolonial Commentary on the New Testament Writings*. London: T.&T. Clark, 2007.

Sugirtharajah, Rasiah S. *Voices from the Margin: Interpreting the Bible in the Third World*. 25th anniversary ed. Maryknoll, NY: Orbis Books, 2016.

Wintle, Brian, Havilah Dharamraj, Jesudason Baskar Jeyaraj, Paul Swarup, Jacob Cherian, and Finny Philip, eds. *South Asia Bible Commentary: A One-Volume Commentary on the Whole Bible.* Grand Rapids, MI: Zondervan Academic, 2015.

Bibliography

Adis, Henry. *A Fannaticks Addresse Humbly Presented...*. London: 1661.

Adler, Mortimer J. and Charles Van Doren. *How to Read a Book: The Classic Guide to Intelligent Reading*. Touchstone ed. New York: Simon & Schuster, 2014.

Adeyemo, Tokunboh, ed. *Africa Bible Commentary: A One-Volume Commentary*. Grand Rapids, MI: Zondervan Academic, 2010.

Adogame, Afeosemime. "Mapping African Christianities within Religious Maps of the Universe." *The Princeton Seminary Bulletin* 33 n.s. (2016). Online http://psb2016.ptsem.edu/mapping-african-christianities-within-religious-maps-of-the-universe/#_edn1 (downloaded January 3, 2018.)

Antonelli, Judith S. *In the Image of God: A Feminist Commentary on the Torah*. Northvale, NJ: Jason Aronson, 1997.

Aguilar, Mario I. "Public Theology from the Periphery: Victims and Theologians." *International Journal of Public Theology* 1 (2007): 321-37.

Ainsworth, Maryan W. and Keith Christiansen, eds. *From Van Eyck to Bruegel: Early Netherlandish Painting in The Metropolitan Museum of Art*. New York: The Metropolitan Museum of Art, 1998.

Aldredge-Clanton, Jann. *In Search of the Christ-Sophia: An Inclusive Christology for Liberating Christians*. 2nd ed. Fort Worth, TX: Eakin Press, 2004.

Allen, Bob. "American Baptist Leaders Recall 'Other Side' of Pearl Harbor." *Baptist News Global* (December 7, 2016). Online: https://baptistnews.com/article/american-baptist-leaders-recall-other-side-of-pearl-harbor/#.WMtnEtLyt0w (downloaded March 16, 2017).

————. "CBF Relaxes Policy on Hiring LGBTQ Staff, but Maintains Some Restrictions." *Baptist News Global* (February 9, 2018). Online https://baptistnews.com/article/cbf-relaxes-policy-hiring-lgbtq-staff-maintains-restrictions/#.WpLdRWaZO8U (downloaded February 25, 2018).

————. "Proposal Sparks Debate Over Baptists and Creeds." *EthicsDaily.com* (July 16, 2004). Online https://www.ethicsdaily.com/proposal-sparks-debate-over-baptists-and-creeds-cms-4457/ (downloaded January 13, 2019).

————. "Third Baptist/Muslim Dialogue Seeks to Build Bridges between Church and Mosque." *Baptist News Global* (April 27, 2018). Online https://baptistnews.com/article/third-baptist-muslim-dialogue-seeks-to-build-bridges-between-church-and-mosque/#.W_nImC2ZOqA (downloaded November 24, 2018).

Althaus-Reid, Marcella and Lisa Isherwood, eds. *Trans/Formations*. London: SCM Press, 2009.

American Baptist Churches USA. "ABCUSA Burma Refugee Commission and IM Delegation Visits Burma Diaspora Communities in Malaysia. *American Baptist News Service* (December 13, 2017). Online http://www.abc-usa.org/2017/12/13/abcusa-burma-refugee-commission-and-international-ministries-delegation-visit-burma-diaspora-communities-in-malaysia/ (downloaded November 20, 2018).

————. "American Baptist Policy Statement on Women and Men as Partners in Church and Society (1985)." Online http://www.abc-usa.org/wp-content/uploads/2012/06/Church-and-Society.pdf (downloaded November 8, 2017).

_____. "Mission Table 2015: Case Statement on Women in Ministry." Online http://www.abc-usa.org/seven-priorities/women-in-ministry/ (downloaded November 8, 2017).

American Baptist Publication Society. *The Baptist Hymn Book*. Philadelphia: American Baptist Publication Society, 1871.

Anderson, E. Byron. *Worship and Christian Identity: Practicing Ourselves*. Virgil Michel Series. Collegeville, MN: The Liturgical Press, 2003.

Anzaldúa, Gloria. "Chicana Artists: Exploring Nepantla, el Lugar de la Frontera." In *The Latino Studies Reader: Culture, Economy and Society*, ed. Antonia Darder and Rodolfo D. Torres, 163-69. Malden, MA: Blackwell Publishers, 1998.

Aponte, Edwin David and Miguel A. De La Torre, eds. *Handbook of Latina/o Theologies*. St. Louis, MO: Chalice Press, 2006.

Aquino, María Pilar. "The Collective 'Dis-covery' of Our Own Power." In *Hispanic/Latino Theology: Challenge and Promise*, ed. Ada María Isasi-Díaz and Fernando F. Segovia, 240-60. Minneapolis: Fortress Press, 1996.

_____. "Latina Feminist Theology: Central Features." In *A Reader in Latina Feminist Theology: Religion and Justice*, ed. María Pilar Aquino, Daisy L. Machado, and Jeanette Rodríguez, 133-60. Austin: University of Texas Press, 2002.

_____. *Our Cry from Life: Feminist Theology from Latin America*. Maryknoll, NY: Orbis Books, 1993.

Aquino, María Pilar, Daisy L. Machado, and Jeanette Rodríguez, eds. *A Reader in Latin Feminist Theology: Religion and Justice*. Austin: University of Texas Press, 2002.

Aquino, María Pilar and Maria José Rosado-Nunes, eds. *Feminist Intercultural Theology: Latina Explorations for a Just World*. Maryknoll, NY: Orbis Books, 2007.

Ariarajah, Wesley. "The Challenge of Inter-faith Relations for the Christian Conference of Asia." *The Ecumenical Review* 69, no. 4 (2017): 462-73.

Atherton, Ian and David Como. "The Burning of Edward Wightman: Puritanism, Prelacy, and the Politics of Heresy in Early Modern England." *English Historical Review* 120, no. 489 (December 2005): 1215-50.

Augustine. *Teaching Christianity (De Doctrina Christiana) I/II*. 2nd rev. ed. Translated by Edmund Hill. Edited by John E. Rotelle. The Works of Saint Augustine: A Translation for the 21st Century. Hyde Park, NY: New City Press, 1996.

Aulén, Gustav. *Christus Victor: An Historical Study of the Three Main Types of the Idea of Atonement*. Translated by A. G. Herbert. London: SPCK, 1930.

Avalos, Hector, Sarah Melchor, and Jeremy Schipper, eds. *This Abled Body: Rethinking Disabilities in Biblical Studies*. Atlanta: Society of Biblical Literature, 2007.

Babcock, Maltbie Davenport. *Thoughts for Every-Day Living from the Spoken and Written Words of Maltbie Davenport Babcock*. New York: Charles Scribner's Sons, 1901.

Bailey, Raymond. "The Changing Face of Baptist Worship." *Review & Expositor* 95, no. 1 (1998): 47-58.

Baptist Union of Great Britain. *Gathering for Worship: Patterns and Prayers for the Community of Disciples*. Edited by Christopher J. Ellis and Myra Blyth. Norwich, UK: Canterbury Press, 2005.

_____. *Patterns and Prayers for Christian Worship: A Guidebook for Worship Leaders*. Edited by Bernard Green. Oxford: Oxford University Press, 1991.

Baptist Union of Scotland. "Declaration of Principle." Online https://www.scottishbaptist.com/declaration-of-principle/ (downloaded January 17, 2018).

Baptist World Alliance and Anglican Consultative Council. *Conversations Around the World 2000-2005: The Report of the International Conversations between the Anglican Communion and the Baptist World Alliance* (2005). Online https://www.bwanet.org/images/pdf/baptist-anglican-dialogue.pdf (downloaded March 22, 2019).

Baptist World Alliance and Catholic Church. *Summons to Witness to Christ in Today's World* (1988). Online https://www.bwanet.org/images/pdf/baptist-roman-catholic-dialogue.pdf (downloaded March 22, 2019).

_____. *The Word of God in the Life of the Church: A Report of International Conversations between the Catholic Church and the Baptist World Alliance 2006-2010* (2013). Online https://www.bwanet.org/images/pdf/baptist-catholic-dialogue.pdf (downloaded March 22, 2019).

Baptist World Alliance and Lutheran World Federation. *Baptists and Lutherans in Conversation: A Message to our Churches* (1990). Online https://www.bwanet.org/images/pdf/baptist-lutheran-dialogue.pdf (downloaded March 22, 2019).

Baptist World Alliance and World Mennonite Conference. *Baptist-Mennonite Theological Conversations* (1992). Online https://www.bwanet.org/images/pdf/baptist-mennonite-dialogue.pdf (downloaded March 22, 2019).

Baptist World Alliance and World Methodist Council. *Faith Working through Love: Report of the International Dialogue between the Baptist World Alliance and the World Methodist Council* (2018). Online https://www.bwanet.org/images/MEJ/Final-Report-of-the-International-Dialogue-between-BWA-and-WMC.pdf (downloaded March 22, 2019).

Baptist World Alliance and World Alliance of Reformed Churches. *Report of Theological Conversations Sponsored by the World Alliance of Reformed Churches and the Baptist World Alliance, 1973-77*. Online https://www.bwanet.org/images/pdf/baptist-reformed-dialogue.pdf (downloaded March 17, 2019).

Barr, Martha M. *Oneness in Christ: American Baptists Are Ecumenical*. Valley Forge, PA: American Baptist Churches, 1978.

Barreto, Raimundo C., Jr. "Ecumenism in the Era of World Christianity." *Unbound: An Interactive Journal of Christian Social Science* (December 8, 2015). Online http://justiceunbound.org/carousel/ecumenism-in-the-era-of-world-christianity/ (downloaded November 24, 2018).

Barreto, Raimundo C. Jr., Ronaldo Cavalcante, and Wanderley Pereira da Rosa, eds. *World Christianity as Public Religion*. Minneapolis: Fortress Press, 2017.

Barron, Robert. *Catholicism: A Journey to the Heart of the Faith*. New York: Image, 2011.

Barth, Karl. *Church Dogmatics*. Edited and translated by Geoffrey W. Bromiley and Thomas F. Torrance. Edinburgh: T. & T. Clark, 1956-75.

_____. *Credo*. Translated by J. Strathearn McNab. New York: Scribner's, 1962.

_____. *God in Action*. Translated by E. G. Homighausen and Karl J. Ernst. Edinburgh: T. & T. Clark, 1936.

Basden, Paul. *The Worship Maze: Finding a Style to Fit Your Church*. Downers Grove, IL: InterVarsity Press, 1999.

Bateman, Charles T. *John Clifford: Free Church Leader and Preacher*. London: National Council of the Evangelical Free Churches, 1904.

Bauerschmidt, Frederick Christian and James J. Buckley. *Catholic Theology: An Introduction*. Malden, MA: Wiley Blackwell, 2017.

Bays, Daniel H. *A New History of Christianity in China*. Malden, MA: Wiley-Blackwell, 2012.

Bediako, Kwame. *Christianity in Africa: The Renewal of Non-Western Religion*. Maryknoll, NY: Orbis Books, 1995.

Behar, Ruth. *The Vulnerable Observer: Anthropology That Breaks Your Heart*. Boston: Beacon Press, 1996.

Bell, Marty. "James Robinson Graves and the Rhetoric of Demagogy: Primitivism and Democracy in Old Landmarkism." Ph.D. diss., Vanderbilt University, 1990.

Bellah, Robert N. *Habits of the Heart: Individualism and Commitment in American Life*. Updated ed. Berkeley, CA: University of California Press, 1996.

Best, Thomas F. Lorelei F. Fuchs, John Gibaut, Jeffrey Gros, and Despina Prassas, eds. *Growth in Agreement IV: International Dialogue Texts and Agreed Statements, 2004-2014, Books 1 and 2*. 2 vols. Faith and Order Paper 219. Geneva: World Council of Churches Publications, 2017.

Bevans, Stephen B. *An Introduction to Theology in Global Perspective*. Maryknoll, NY: Orbis Books, 2009.

Bhakiaraj, Paul Joshua. "Forms of Asian Indigenous Christianities." In *Oxford Handbook of Christianity in Asia*, ed. Felix Wilfred. New Delhi: Oxford University Press, 2014. Online http://www.oxfordhandbooks.com/view/10.1093/oxfordhb/9780199329069.001.0001/oxfordhb-9780199329069-e-011 (downloaded March 25, 2019).

Biddle, John. *A Confession of Faith Touching the Holy Trinity According to the Scripture*. London, 1648.

Birch, Ian. *To Follow the Lambe Whereosever He Goeth: The Ecclesial Polity of the English Calvinistic Baptists 1640-1660*. Monographs in Baptist History, no. 5. Eugene, OR: Pickwick Publications, 2017.

Bingemer, Maria Clara. *Latin American Theology: Roots and Branches*. Maryknoll, NY: Orbis Books, 2016.

Bledsoe Bailey, Judith Anne. *Strength for the Journey: Feminist Theology and Baptist Women Pastors*. Richmond, VA: Center for Baptist Heritage & Studies, 2015.

Blount, Brian K., Cain Hope Felder, Clarice J. Martin, and Emerson B. Powery, eds. *True to Our Native Land: An African American New Testament Commentary*. Minneapolis: Fortress Press, 2007.

Bonhoeffer, Dietrich. *Ethics*. Edited by Clifford J. Green et al. Dietrich Bonhoeffer Works, vol. 6. Minneapolis: Fortress Press, 2005.

Boff, Leonardo. *Cry of the Earth, Cry of the Poor*. Maryknoll, NY: Orbis Books, 1997.

Boyle, Marjorie O'Rourke. *Petrarch's Genius: Pentimento and Prophecy*. Berkeley: University of California Press, 1991.

Brackney, William H. *Baptist Life and Thought: A Source Book*. Rev. ed. Valley Forge, PA: Judson Press, 1998.

Braddock, David L. and Susan L. Parish. "An Institutional History of Disability." In *Disability at the Dawn of the 21ˢᵗ Century and the State of the States*, ed. David L. Braddock, 11-68. Washington, DC: American Association of Mental Retardation, 2002.

Brazal, Agnes M. *A Theology of Southeast Asia: Liberation Postcolonial Ethics in the Philippines*. Maryknoll, NY: Orbis Books, 2019.

Brenner, Athalya and Carole R. Fontaine, eds. *Feminist Companion to the Bible* [series; volumes individually titled]. First Series and Second Series. Sheffield, UK: Sheffield Academic Press and London: Bloomsbury, 1993-2015.

Broadway, Mikael, Curtis W. Freeman, Barry Harvey, James Wm. McClendon, Jr., Elizabeth Newman, and Phillip E. Thompson. "Re-Envisioning Baptist Identity: A Manifesto for Baptist Communities in North America." *Baptists Today* (June 1997): 8-10

_____. "Re-Envisioning Baptist Identity: A Manifesto for Baptist Communities in North America." *Perspectives in Religious Studies* 24, no. 3 (Fall 1997): 303-10.

Brock, Brian and John Swinton, eds. *Disability in the Christian Tradition: A Reader.* Grand Rapids, MI.: William B. Eerdmans, 2012.

Brooks, Jerome. "The Art of Fiction No. 139: Chinua Achebe." *The Paris Review* 133 (Winter 1994). Online https://www.theparisreview.org/interviews/1720/chinua-achebe-the-art-of-fiction-no-139-chinua-achebe (downloaded November 26, 2018).

Brumley, Jeff. "Virginia Church May Look Anglican, but It's Fully Baptist." *Baptist News Global* (March 26, 2014). Online https://baptistnews.com/article/va-church-is-anglican-leaning-but-fully-baptist/ (downloaded March 28, 2018).

Bullard, Robert D. "Biography—Dr. Robert Bullard." Dr. Robert Bullard: Father of Environmental Justice. Online http://drrobertbullard.com/biography/ (downloaded January 16, 2018).

Bunyan, John. *Grace Abounding to the Chief of Sinners.* Edited by W. R. Owens. London: Penguin, 1987.

_____. *The Pilgrim's Progress.* Edited by N. H. Keeble. New York: Oxford University Press, 1984.

Burrage, Champlin. *The Early English Dissenters in the Light of Recent Research (1550-1641).* 2 vols. Cambridge: Cambridge University Press, 1912.

Burke, Kevin F. *The Ground beneath the Cross: The Theology of Ignacio Ellacuría.* Washington, DC: Georgetown University Press, 2000.

Byers, Andrew. *Ecclesiology and Theosis in the Gospel of John.* Cambridge: Cambridge University Press, 2017.

Byron, Gay L., and Vanessa Lovelace, eds. *Womanist Interpretations of the Bible: Expanding the Discourse.* Semeia Studies, no. 85. Atlanta: SBL Press, 2016.

Cabrita, Joel, David Maxwell, and Emma Wild-Wood, eds. *Relocating World Christianity: Interdisciplinary Studies in Universal and Local Expressions of the Christian Faith.* Theology and Mission in World Christianity, vol. 7. Boston: Brill, 2017.

Callam, Neville. "Baptists in Bilateral Theological Dialogue." In *Baptist Identity into the Twenty-First Century: Essays in Honour of Ken Manley,* ed. Frank Rees, 157-68. Parkville, Victoria, Australia: Whitley College, 2016.

_____. "General Secretary's Blog" (October 31, 2013). Quoted in Steven R. Harmon, "Baptists and the Veneration of the Saints," Ecclesial Theology weblog entry, November 1, 2013. Online http://ecclesialtheology.blogspot.com/2013/11/baptists-and-veneration-of-saints.html (downloaded March 22, 2018).

Campbell-Reed, Eileen. *Anatomy of a Schism: How Clergywomen's Narratives Reinterpret the Fracturing of the Southern Baptist Convention.* Knoxville: University of Tennessee Press, 2016.

Canipe Lee. *A Baptist Democracy: Separating God from Caesar in the Land of the Free.* Macon, GA: Mercer University Press, 2011.

Cannon, Katie Geneva. *Black Womanist Ethics.* Atlanta: Scholars Press, 1988.

Cannon, Katie Geneva, Emilie M. Townes, and Angela D. Sims, eds. *Womanist Theological Ethics: A Reader.* Louisville: Westminster John Knox Press, 2011.

Cardenal, Ernesto. *The Gospel in Solentiname.* Rev. one-vol. ed. Maryknoll, NY: Orbis Books, 2010.

Carroll, J. M. *The Trail of Blood Following Christians Down through the Centuries, or The History of Baptist Churches from the Time of Christ, Their Founder, to the Present Day*. Lexington, KY: Ashland Avenue Baptist Church, 1931.

Carter, James E. "What Is the Southern Baptist Heritage of Worship?" *Baptist History and Heritage* 31, no. 3 (July 1996): 38-47.

Carvalhaes, Cláudio. "Birds, People, Then Religion—An Eco-Liberation Theological and Pedagogical Approach to Interreligious Rituals." *The Journal of Interreligious Studies* 21 (2017). Online http://irstudies.org/journal/birds-people-then-religion-an-eco-liberation-theological-and-pedagogical-approach-to-interreligious-rituals-by-claudio-carvalhaes/ (downloaded November 25, 2018).

Casal, José Luis. "The Immigrant's Creed." In *Book of Common Worship*, Presbyterian Church (USA), 613-14. Louisville, KY: Westminster John Knox, 2018. Online, Calvin Institute of Christian Worship, https://worship.calvin.edu/resources/resource-library/the-immigrants-creed/ (downloaded November 28, 2018).

Casserley, J. V. Langmead. "The Significance of the Liturgical Movement." *Religion in Life* 29, no. 2 (1960): 211-19.

Catholic Church. *Catechism of the Catholic Church*. Liguori, MO: Liguori Publications, 1994.

Cavanaugh, William T. *Migrations of the Holy: God, State, and the Political Meaning of the Church*. Grand Rapids, MI: William B. Eerdmans, 2011.

————. *The Myth of Religious Violence: Secular Ideology and the Roots of Modern Conflict*. Oxford: Oxford University Press, 2009.

Charles, Mark and Soong-Chan Rah. *Unsettling Truths: The Ongoing, Dehumanizing Legacy of the Doctrine of Discovery*. Downers Grove, IL: IVP Books, 2019.

Chauncey, George. *Why Marriage? The History Shaping Today's Debate Over Gay Equality*. New York: Basic Books, 2004.

Chaves, João B. "Disrespecting Borders for Jesus, Power, and Cash: Southern Baptist Missions, the New Immigration, and the Churches of the Brazilian Diaspora." Ph.D. diss., Baylor University, 2017.

————. *The Global Mission of the Jim Crow South*. Perspectives on Baptist Identities, vol. 4. Macon, GA: Mercer University Press, forthcoming.

Chesterton, G. K. *Orthodoxy: The Romance of Faith*. London: Collins, Fontana Books, 1908; reprint ed., New York: Doubleday, 1990.

Chilton, Amy L. "Converted Listening: Practicing Our Way to Hearing the Church's Global Symphony." *Perspectives in Religious Studies* 45, no. 3 (Fall 2018): 343-48.

————. "How Do I Speak of God from This Place? Navigating Religious Language Shifts in Baptist Contexts." *American Baptist Quarterly* 25, no. 1 (Spring 2016): 52-62.

————. "Practiced Theological Diversity: Jon Sobrino and James Wm. McClendon, Jr., on Theology as a Particular, Christological, Holistically Self-Involving Practice of the Church." Ph.D. diss., Fuller Theological Seminary, 2015.

————. "Response to Steven R. Harmon's *Baptist Identity and the Ecumenical Future: Story, Tradition, and the Recovery of Community*." *Pacific Journal of Baptist Research* 11, no. 2 (November 2016): 12-15.

————. "Transformed by the Spirit: Imagining God's Future." *American Baptist Quarterly* 31, no. 2 (Summer 2012): 252-62.

————. "Unsettling Conversations: Jon Sobrino's Christo-Praxis as a Baptist Theological Method?" *Perspectives in Religious Studies* 40, no. 3 (Fall 2013): 236-50.

Ching, Wong Wai. "Negotiating for a Postcolonial Identity of 'the Poor Women' in Asia." *Journal of Feminist Studies of Religion* 16, no. 2 (Fall 2000): 5-23.

Chung, Paul S., Veli-Matti Kärkkäinen, and Kim Kyoung-Jae, eds. *Asian Contextual Theology for the Third Millennium: Theology of Minjung in Fourth-Eye Formation.* Cambridge: James Clarke & Co., 2007.

Clark, Elizabeth A. and Herbert Richardson, eds. *Women and Religion: The Original Sourcebook of Women and Christian Thought.* Revised and updated ed. San Francisco: HarperSanFrancisco, 1997.

Clark, Neville. *Call to Worship.* Studies in Ministry and Worship. London: SCM Press, 1960.

Clarke, Sathianathan, Deenabandhu Manchala, and Philip Peacock, eds. *Dalit Theology in the Twenty-First Century: Discordant Voices, Discerning Pathways.* Oxford: Oxford University Press, 2010.

Clifford, Anne M. *Introducing Feminist Theology.* Marknoll, NY: Orbis Books, 2000.

Clifford, James. "Diasporas." *Cultural Anthropology* 9 (1994): 302-38.

Clifford, John. "The Great Forty Years." In *A Baptist Treasury*, ed. Sydnor L. Stealey, 98-113. New York: Thomas Y. Crowell, 1958.

Clifford, Paul Rowntree. "Baptist Forms of Worship." *Foundations* 3, no. 3 (July 1960): 221-233.

Coakley, Sarah. *God, Sexuality, and the Self: An Essay 'On the Trinity.'* Cambridge: Cambridge University Press, 2013.

————. "Living into the Mystery of the Holy Trinity: Trinity, Prayer and Sexuality." *Anglican Theological Review* 80 (1998): 223-31.

————. *Powers and Submissions: Spirituality, Philosophy, and Gender.* Malden, MA: Blackwell, 2002.

Coetzee, Carel Frederik Christoffel. "Godsdiensvryheid in die lig van Artikel 36, NGB." *Nederduitse Gereformeerde Teologiese Tydskrif* 47, nos. 1 and 2 (2006): 143–57.

Coertzen, Pieter. "The Relationship Between Church and State in a Democracy with Guaranteed Freedom of Religion." In *Christian in Public: Aims, Methodologies, and Issues in Public Theology*, ed. L. D. Hansen, 177–90. Stellenbosch: Sun Press, COP, 2007).

Cohick, Lynn H. and Amy Brown Hughes. *Christian Women in the Patristic World: Their Influence, Authority, and Legacy in the Second Through Fifth Centuries.* Grand Rapids, Mich.: Baker Academic, 2017.

Coleman, Monica A., ed. *Ain't I a Womanist, Too? Third-Wave Womanist Religious Thought.* Minneapolis: Fortress Press, 2013.

————. *Making a Way Out of No Way: A Womanist Theology.* Innovations: African American Religious Thought. Minneapolis: Fortress Press, 2008.

Coles, Romand. *Beyond Gated Politics: Reflections on the Possibility of Democracy.* Minneapolis: University of Minnesota Press, 2005.

Collins, Patricia Hill. "Learning from the Outsider Within." In *Beyond Methodology*, ed. Mary Margaret Fonow and Judith A. Cook, 35-59. Bloomington: Indiana University Press, 1991.

Cone, James H. *Black Theology and Black Power.* New York: Seabury Press, 1969.

————. *A Black Theology of Liberation.* 40th anniversary ed. Maryknoll, NY: Orbis Books, 2010.

————. *God of the Oppressed.* Rev. ed. Maryknoll, NY: Orbis Books, 1997.

————. *Martin & Malcolm & America: A Dream or a Nightmare.* Maryknoll, NY: Orbis Books, 1991.

Congar, Yves. *Chrétiens désunis: principes d'un "oecuménisme" catholique.* Unum Sanctam, no. 1. Paris: Éditions du Cerf, 1937.

———. *Divided Christendom: A Catholic Study of the Problem of Reunion.* Translated by M. A. Bousfield. London: Geoffrey Bles/Centenary Press, 1939.

Congregation for the Doctrine of the Faith. "Instruction on Certain Aspects of the 'Theology of Liberation'." August 6, 1984. Online http://www.vatican.va/roman_curia/congregations/cfaith/documents/rc_con_cfaith_doc_1 9840806_theology-liberation_en.html (downloaded April 3, 2019).

Conner, W. T. *What Is a Saint?* Nashville: Broadman Press, 1948.

Copeland, M. Shawn. *Enfleshing Freedom: Body, Race, and Being.* Minneapolis: Fortress Press, 2009.

Coorilos, Geevarghese. "The Nature and Mission of the Church: An Indian Perspective." In *Called to Be the One Church: Faith and Order at Crete,* ed. John Gibaut, 188-92. Faith and Order Paper no. 212. Geneva: World Council of Churches Publications, 2012.

Costa, Ruy O., ed. *One Faith, Many Cultures: Inculturation, Indigenization and Contextualization.* Maryknoll, NY: Orbis Books, 1988.

Cross, Anthony R. *Baptism and the Baptists: Theology and Practice in Twentieth-Century Britain.* Paternoster Biblical and Theological Monographs. Carlisle, UK: Paternoster, 2000.

Crawford, Sidnie White. "Esther." In *Women's Bible Commentary,* ed. Carol A. Newsom and Sharon H. Ringe, 131-44. Louisville, KY: Westminster John Knox Press, 1998.

———. "The Book of Esther: Introduction, Commentary, and Reflections." In *New Interpreter's Bible,* vol. 3, 855-941. Nashville: Abingdon Press, 1999.

Crenshaw, Kimberlé. "Demarginalizing the Intersection of Race and Sex: A Black Feminist Critique of Antidiscrimination Doctrine, Feminist Theory and Antiracist Politics." *University of Chicago Legal Forum* 1989, no. 1, article 8. Online http://chicagounbound.uchicago.edu/uclf/vol1989/iss1/8 (downloaded February 12, 2019).

Crowley, Stephen. "Full Executive Order Text: Trump's Action Limiting Refugees into the U.S." *The New York Times* (January 27, 2017). Online https://www.nytimes.com/2017/01/27/us/politics/refugee-muslim-executive-order-trump.html (downloaded November 20, 2018).

Dalton, Wayne A. "Worship and Baptist Ecclesiology." *Foundations* 12, no. 1 (January 1969): 7-18.

Dana, H. E. and L. M. Sipes. *A Manual of Ecclesiology.* 2nd rev. ed. Kansas City, KS: Central Seminary Press, 1944.

Davidson, Jennifer W. *River of Life, Feast of Grace: Baptism, Communion, and Discipleship.* Valley Forge:, PA: Judson Press, 2019.

Davidson, Steed Varnyl. "Diversity, Difference, and Access to Power in Diaspora: The Case of the Book of Esther." *Word & World* 29, no. 3 (Summer 2009): 280–87.

Davies, William David. *The Cambridge History of Judaism.* Vol. 1, *Introduction; the Persian Period.* Cambridge: Cambridge University Press, 1984.

Day, J. Daniel. "A Word about...Worship." *Review & Expositor* 106, no. 2 (2009): 161–63.

Day, Linda M. *Esther.* Abingdon Old Testament Commentaries. Nashville: Abingdon Press, 2005.

Dekar, Paul R. *For the Healing of the Nations: Baptist Peacemakers.* Macon, GA: Smyth & Helwys, 1993.

De La Torre, Miguel, ed. *Hispanic American Religious Cultures.* Denver: ABC-CLIO, 2009.

_____. *Liberation Theology for Armchair Theologians*. Louisville, KY: Westminster John Knox, 2013.

_____. *Reading the Bible from the Margins*. Maryknoll, NY: Orbis Books, 2002.

De Luna, Anita. *Faith Formation and Popular Religion: Lessons from the Tejano Experience*. Lanham, MD: Rowman & Littlefield, 2002.

Deanesly, Margaret. *The Lollard Bible*. Cambridge: Cambridge University Press, 1920.

D'Emilio, John. *The World Turned: Essays on Gay History, Politics, and Culture*. Durham, NC: Duke University Press, 2002.

DeVane, Steve. "Educators Ask, BWA Agrees to Recite Apostles' Creed." *Baptist News Global* (June 30, 2004). Online https://baptistnews.com/article/educators-ask-bwa-agrees-to-recite-apostles-creed-at-2005-congress/#.XDWIqi2ZNQI (downloaded January 13, 2019).

DeYoung, Curtiss Paul, Wilda C. Gafney, Leticia Guardiola-Sáenz, George E. Tinker, and Frank M. Yamada, eds. *The Peoples' Bible*. Minneapolis: Fortress Press, 2008.

Di Liberto, Tom. "Early Summer Heat Wave in Europe" (July 13, 2017). Online https://www.climate.gov/news-features/event-tracker/early-summer-heat-wave-europe (Downloaded January 16, 2018).

_____. "Heavy Summer Rains Flood Peru" (March 10, 2017). Online https://www.climate.gov/news-features/event-tracker/heavy-summer-rains-flood-peru (downloaded January 16, 2018).

_____. "Smog Descends on India and Pakistan in Mid-November 2017" (November 15, 2017). Online https://www.climate.gov/news-features/event-tracker/smog-descends-india-and-pakistan-mid-november-2017 (downloaded January 16, 2018). "Mount Agung Erupts in Indonesia: Is It a Climate Event?," December 7, 2017, https://www.climate.gov/news-features/event-tracker/mount-agung-erupts-indonesia-it-climate-event.

_____. "Soaking Rains and Massive Snows Pile up in California in January 2017" (January 30, 2017). Online https://www.climate.gov/news-features/event-tracker/soaking-rains-and-massive-snows-pile-california-january-2017 (downloaded January 16, 2018).

_____. "Water Rationing in South Africa's Second-Largest City after Multi-Year Drought" (November 1, 2017). Online https://www.climate.gov/news-features/event-tracker/water-rationing-south-africa%E2%80%99s-second-largest-city-after-multi-year (downloaded January 16, 2018).

Diefendorf, Barbara B. *Beneath the Cross: Catholics and Hughuenots in Sixteenth-Century Paris*. Oxford: Oxford University Press, 1991.

Dingrin, La Seng. "Is Buddhism Indispensable in the Cross-Cultural Appropriation of Christianity in Burma?" *Buddhist-Christian Studies*, 29 (2009): 3-22.

Dirks, Nicholas B. *Castes of Mind: Colonialism and the Making of Modern India*. Princeton: Princeton University Press, 2001.

Dix, Dom Gregory. *The Shape of the Liturgy*, 2nd ed. London: Dacre Press, 1945; reprint, London: Bloomsbury/T&T Clark, 2005.

Dobbins, Gaines S. *The Church at Worship*. Nashville: Broadman Press, 1962.

Douglas, Kelly Brown. *The Black Christ*. Bishop Henry McNeal Studies in North American Black Religion, vol. 9. Maryknoll, NY: Orbis Books, 1994.

_____. "Womanist Theology: What Is Its Relationship to Black Theology?" In *Black Theology: A Documentary History*, vol. 2, *1980-1992*, ed. James H. Cone and Gayraud D. Wilmore, 290-99. Maryknoll, NY: Orbis Books, 1993.

Drescher, Elizabeth. *Choosing Our Religion: The Spiritual Lives of America's Nones*. New York: Oxford University Press, 2016.

Drye, Willie. "2017 Hurricane Season Was the Most Expensive in U.S. History" (November 30, 2017). Online https://news.nationalgeographic.com/2017/11/2017-hurricane-season-most-expensive-us-history-spd/ (downloaded January 16, 2018).

Dube, Musa W. *Postcolonial Feminist Interpretation of the Bible*. Atlanta: Chalice Press, 2000.

_____. "Who Do You Say That I Am?" *Feminist Theology*, 5, no. 3 (May 2007): 346-67.

_____, ed. *Other Ways of Reading: African Women and the Bible*. Atlanta: Society of Biblical Literature, 2001.

Dulles, Avery. *Magisterium: Teacher and Guardian of the Faith*. Naples, FL: Sapientia Press, 2007.

Dussel, Enrique ."Agenda for a South-South Philosophical Dialogue." *Human Architecture* 11, no. 1 (2013): 3-18.

_____. "The Epistemological Decolonization of Theology." *Concilium: International Journal of Theology* 2013, no. 2 (2013): 21-31.

Duval-Poujol, Valerie and Ulrike Schuler, eds. *Faith Working through Love: Study Guide Accompanying the Final Report of the International Dialogue between the Baptist World Alliance and the World Methodist Council*. Baptist World Alliance and World Methodist Council, 2018. Online https://www.bwanet.org/images/MEJ/Faith-Working-Through-Love-Study-Guide.pdf (downloaded March 22, 2019).

Earth Science Communications Team of the NASA Jet Propulsion Laboratory. Global Climate Change: Vital Signs of the Planet. Online https://climate.nasa.gov/ (downloaded January 16, 2018).

Edinburgh 2010 Conference. *Edinburgh 2010 Common Call*. Online http://www.edinburgh2010.org/fileadmin/Edinburgh_2010_Common_Call_with_explanation.pdf (downloaded February 28, 2019).

Edwards, Morgan. *The Customs of Primitive Churches -or- A Set of Propositions Relative to the Name, Materials, Constitution, Power, Officers, Ordinances, Rites, Business, Worship, Discipline, Government, & c. of a Church; to Which Are Added Their Proofs from Scripture, and Historical Narratives of the Manner in Which Most of Them Have Been Reduced to Practice*. Philadelphia, 1774.

Eiesland, Nancy. *The Disabled God: Toward a Liberatory Theology of Disability*. Nashville: Abingdon, 1994.

Eighmy, John Lee and Samuel S. Hill. *Churches in Cultural Captivity: A History of the Social Attitudes of Southern Baptists*. Knoxville: University of Tennessee Press, 1987.

Ellacuría, Ignacio. "The Historicity of Christian Salvation." In *Mysterium Liberationis: Fundamental Concepts of Liberation Theology*, edited by Jon Sobrino and Ignacio Ellucaría, 251-88. Maryknoll, NY: Orbis Books, 1993.

Ellis, Christopher J. *Gathering: A Theology and Spirituality of Worship*. London: SCM Press, 2004.

_____. "Gathering Struggles: Creative Tensions in Baptist Worship." *The Baptist Quarterly* 42, no. 1 (January 2007): 4-21.

Ellsberg, Robert. *All Saints: Daily Reflections on Saints, Prophets, and Witnesses for Our Time*. New York: Crossroad, 1997.

Elizondo, Virgilio. *La Morenita: Evangelizadora de las Américas*. Liguori, MO: Liguori Publications, 1981.

Elwood, Douglas J. "Asian Christian Theology in the Making: An Introduction." In *Asian Christian Theology: Emerging Themes*, rev. ed., ed. Douglas J. Elwood, 23-39. Philadelphia: Westminster Press, 1980.

_____, ed. *Asian Christian Theology: Emerging Themes*. Philadelphia: Westminster Press, 1980.

England, John C. *Asian Christian Theologies: A Research Guide to Authors, Movements, Sources*. 3 vols. Maryknoll, NY: Orbis Books, 2002-04.

Episcopal Church (USA). *The 1979 Book of Common Prayer*. New York: Oxford University Press, 2005.

Eschner, Kat. "The Story of the Real Canary in the Coal Mine." *Smithsonian* (December 30, 2016). Online https://www.smithsonianmag.com/smart-news/story-real-canary-coal-mine-180961570/ (downloaded January 16, 2018).

Estep, William R. *Baptists and Christian Unity*. Nashville: Broadman Press, 1966.

Etherington, Norman. *Mission and Empire*. Oxford: Oxford University Press, 2008.

Evans, Benjamin. *The Early English Baptists*. London: J. Heaton & Son, 1862.

Evers, Georg. "Asian Theology." In *Encyclopedia of Christianity Online*. Online http://ezproxy.ptsem.edu:2142/10.1163/2211-2685_eco_A636 (downloaded January 25, 2019).

_____. *The Churches in Asia*. Delhi: Indian Society for Promoting Christian Knowledge, 2005.

Fabella, Virginia and Sun Ai Lee Park, eds. *We Dare to Dream: Doing Theology as Asian Women*. Maryknoll, NY: Orbis Books, 1989.

Federation of Asian Bishops Conferences. *The Spirit at Work in Asia Today*. FABC Papers, no. 81. Hong Kong: Federation of Asian Bishops Conferences, 1998.

Felder, Cain Hope. *Original African Heritage Study Bible: King James Version*. Valley Forge, PA: Judson Press, 2007.

Fey, Harold C., ed. *A History of the Ecumenical Movement, Volume 2 (1948-1968)*. Geneva: WCC Publications, 2004.

Fiddes, Paul S. "Covenant and Participation: A Personal Review of the Essays." *Perspectives in Religious Studies* 44, no. 1 (Spring 2017): 119-37.

_____. *Tracks and Traces: Baptist Identity in Church and Theology*. Studies in Baptist History and Thought, vol. 13. Milton Keynes, UK: Paternoster, 2003.

_____, ed. *Under the Rule of Christ: Dimensions of Baptist Spirituality*. Regent's Study Guides, no. 14; Macon, GA: Smyth & Helwys, 2008.

Fiddes, Paul S., Brian Haymes, and Richard Kidd. *Baptists and the Communion of Saints: A Theology of Covenanted Disciples*. Waco, TX: Baylor University Press, 2014.

Fiddes, Paul S., Brian Haymes, Richard Kidd, and Michael J. Quicke. *Doing Theology in a Baptist Way*. Oxford: Whitley Publications, 2000.

Flannery, Austin, ed. *Vatican Council II: The Conciliar and Post Conciliar Documents*. Rev. ed. Vatican Collection, vol. 1. Northport, NY: Costello Publishing Co., 1992.

Florence, Anna Carter. "The Woman Who Just Said NO." *Journal for Preachers* (Advent 1998): 37–40.

Flowers, Elizabeth H. *Into the Pulpit: Southern Baptist Women and Power since World War II*. Chapel Hill: University of North Carolina Press, 2012.

Floyd-Thomas, Stacey M. *Deeper Shades of Purple: Womanism in Religion and Society*. Religion, Race, and Ethnicity. New York: New York University Press, 2006.

Foucault, Michel. *Technologies of the Self: A Seminar with Michel Foucault*. Edited by Luther H. Martin, Huck Gutman, and Patrick H. Hutton. Boston: University of Massachusetts Press, 1988.

Fox, Michael V. *Character and Ideology in the Book of Esther*. Columbia: University of South Carolina Press, 1991.

Francis. "Apostolic Exhortation on the Proclamation of the Gospel in Today's World (*Evangelii Gaudium*). November 24, 2013. Online https://w2.vatican.va/content/francesco/en/apost_exhortations/documents/papa-francesco_esortazione-ap_20131124_evangelii-gaudium.html (downloaded April 18, 2018).

_____. General Audience (November 19, 2014). Online https://w2.vatican.va/content/francesco/en/audiences/2014/documents/papa-francesco_20141119_udienza-generale.html (downloaded March 21, 2018).

_____. *Laudato Si'* (On Care for Our Common Home). May 24, 2015. Online http://w2.vatican.va/content/francesco/en/encyclicals/documents/papa-francesco_20150524_enciclica-laudato-si.html (downloaded January 16, 2018).

Francis, Leah Gunning. *Ferguson and Faith: Sparking Leadership and Awakening Community*. St Louis, MO: Chalice Press, 2015.

Franklin, R. W. "Nineteenth Century Liturgical Movement." *Worship* 53, no. 1 (January 1979): 12–39.

Freeman, Curtis W. "Baptists and Catholics Together? Making Up Is Hard to Do." *Commonweal* (January 16, 2009): 18-21.

_____. *Contesting Catholicity: Theology for Other Baptists*. Waco, TX: Baylor University Press, 2014.

_____, ed. *A Company of Women Preachers: Baptist Prophetesses in Seventeenth-Century England*. Waco, TX: Baylor University Press, 2011.

_____, ed. *Perspectives in Religious Studies* 29, no. 4 (Winter 2002) [Thematic issue on Baptist confessions of faith].

Freeman, Curtis W., Steven R. Harmon, Elizabeth Newman, and Philip E. Thompson. "Confessing the Faith." Appendix 2 in Steven R. Harmon, *Towards Baptist Catholicity: Essays on Tradition and the Baptist Vision*, 225-29. Studies in Baptist History and Thought, vol. 27. Milton Keynes, UK: Paternoster, 2006.

Fuchs, Lorelei. *Koinonia and the Quest for an Ecumenical Ecclesiology: From Foundations through Dialogue to Symbolic Competence for Communionality*. Grand Rapids, MI: William B. Eerdmans, 2008.

Fung, Jojo M. "Emerging Perspectives and Identity Negotiations of the Indigenous Christians." In *World Christianity: Perspectives and Insights*, ed. Jonathan Y. Tan and Anh Q. Tran, 287-99. Maryknoll, NY: Orbis Books, 2016.

_____. "Postcolonial Encounters with Indigenous Religions for Peace and Ecological Harmony." In *Asian Christianities*, ed. Daniel Franklin Pilario, Felix Wilfred, and Huang Po Ho, 123-34. Concilium, no. 1. London: SCM Press, 2018.

Furr, Gary A. and Curtis W. Freeman, eds. *Ties That Bind: Life Together in the Baptist Vision*. Macon, GA: Smyth & Helwys, 1994.

Gafney, Wilda C. *Womanist Midrash: A Reintroduction to the Women of the Torah and the Throne*. Louisville, KY: Westminster John Knox, 2017.

Gallagher, Eugene. "Conversion and Community in Late Antiquity." *Journal of Religion* 73 (1993): 1-15

Gaventa, William C. *Disability and Spirituality: Recovering Wholeness*. Waco, TX: Baylor University Press, 2018.

_____. "Preaching Disability: The Whole of Christ's Body in Word and Practice." *Review and Expositor* 113, no. 2 (2016): 225-42.

George, Timothy. *John Robinson and the English Separatist Tradition*. NABPR Dissertation Series, no. 1. Macon, GA: Mercer University Press, 1982.

George, Timothy, ed. *Reformation Commentary on Scripture*. Downers Grove, IL: InterVarsity Press, 2011-.

Gidla, Sujatha. *Ants among Elephants: An Untouchable Family and the Making of Modern India*. New York: Farrar, Straus and Giroux, 2017.

Goldberg, P. J. P. *Medieval England: A Social History 1250-1550*. London: Bloomsbury, 2004.

Goodliff, Andy. "Towards a Baptist Sanctoral?" *Journal of European Baptist Studies* 13, no. 3 (May 2013): 24-30.

González, Justo L. *Mañana: Christian Theology from a Hispanic Perspective*. Nashville: Abingdon Press, 1990.

_____. *Santa Biblica: The Bible through Hispanic Eyes*. Nashville: Abingdon Press, 1996.

_____, ed. *The Westminster Dictionary of Theologians*. Louisville: Westminster John Knox Press, 2006.

Gonzalez, Michelle A. *Sor Juana: Beauty and Justice in the Americas*. Maryknoll, NY: Orbis Books, 2003.

Goodman, Daniel E. "Strangers, Neighbors, and Strangers Again: The History of Southern Baptist Approaches to Jews and Judaism." *Review & Expositor* 103, no. 1 (2006): 63–89.

Gootjes, Nicolaas Hendrik. *The Belgic Confession: Its History and Sources*. Grand Rapids, MI: Baker Academic, 2007.

Gordon, Adoniram Judson. *The Ministry of the Spirit*. Philadelphia: American Baptist Publication Society, 1894.

Goss, Robert E., and Mona West. *Take Back the Word: A Queer Reading of the Bible*. Cleveland: The Pilgrim Press, 2000.

Gouldbourne, Ruth. "Liturgical Identity Carriers for Ecclesial Transformation." *American Baptist Quarterly* 31, no. 4 (Winter 2012): 379–91.

Granberg-Michaelson, Wesley. *From Times Square to Timbuktu: The Post-Christian West Meets the Non-Western Church*. Grand Rapids, MI: Wm. B. Eerdmans, 2013.

Grant, Jacquelyn. "Black Theology and the Black Woman." In *Black Theology: A Documentary History*, vol. 1, *1966-1979*, ed. James H. Cone and Gayraud S. Wilmore, 418-33. Maryknoll, NY: Orbis Books, 1979.

_____. *White Women's Christ and Black Women's Jesus: Feminist Christology and Womanist Response*. AAR Academy Series, vol. 64. Atlanta: Scholars Press, 1989.

Greene, Graham. *The Power and the Glory*. Mattituck, NY: Amereon House, 1940; reprint ed., New York: Penguin, 2003.

Greenspoon, Leonard. "The Taming of the Two: Queen Esther and Queen Vashti." In *Midrash, Women, Gender and Religion: Journal of Religion and Society*, Supplement Series 5 (2009): 155-69.

Gregory of Nazianzus. "Orations." In *Nicene and Post-Nicene Fathers: Second Series*, ed. Philip Schaff and Henry Wace, 7: 203-34. A Select Library of the Christian Church. New York: Christian Literature Publishing Co., 1887-94; reprint, Peabody, MA: Hendrickson, 1994.

Greig, Jason Reimer. *Reconsidering Intellectual Disability: L'Arche, Medical Ethics, and Christian Friendship*. Washington, DC: Georgetown University Press, 2015.

Gros, Jeffrey, Eamon McManus, and Ann Riggs. *Introduction to Ecumenism*. Mahwah, NJ: Paulist Press, 1998.

321

Gros, Jeffrey, Thomas F. Best, and Lorelei F. Fuchs, eds. *Growth in Agreement III: International Dialogue Texts and Agreed Statements, 1998-2005.* Faith and Order Paper no. 204. Geneva: WCC Publications and Grand Rapids, MI: William B. Eerdmans, 2007.

Gros, Jeffrey, Harding Meyer, and William G. Rusch, eds. *Growth in Agreement II: Reports and Agreed Statements of Ecumenical Conversations on a World Level, 1982-1998.* Faith and Order Paper no. 187. Geneva: WCC Publications and Grand Rapids, MI: William B. Eerdmans, 2000.

Grudem, Wayne. *Countering the Claims of Evangelical Feminism: Biblical Responses to the Key Questions.* Portland, OR: Multnomah, 2006.

Guest, Deryn, Robert E. Goss, Mona West, and Thomas Bohache, eds. *The Queer Bible Commentary.* London: SCM Press, 2015.

Gunnoe, Charles D., Karin Maag, Paul W. Fields, and Lyle D. Bierma. *An Introduction to the Heidelberg Catechism: Sources, History and Theology.* Grand Rapids, MI: Baker Academic, 2005.

Gutiérrez, Gustavo. *On Job: God-Talk and the Suffering of the Innocent.* Translated by Matthew O'Connell. Maryknoll, NY: Orbis Books, 1987.

Hacham, Noah. "3 Maccabees and Esther: Parallels, Intertextuality, and Diaspora Identity." *Journal of Biblical Literature* 126, no. 4 (2007): 765–85.

Hanch, Kate. "Participation in God, Oned by Love: Paul Fiddes in Dialogue with Julian of Norwich." *Perspectives in Religious Studies* 44, no. 1 (Spring 2017): 69-82.

Harmon, Steven R. *Baptist Identity and the Ecumenical Future: Story, Tradition, and the Recovery of Community.* Waco, TX: Baylor University Press, 2016.

————. "The Baptist Tradition and Ecumenism." Chap. in *The Oxford Handbook of Ecumenical Studies,* ed. Geoffrey Wainwright and Paul McPartlan. New York: Oxford University Press, 2017. Online http://www.oxfordhandbooks.com/view/10.1093/oxfordhb/9780199600847.001.0001/oxfordhb-9780199600847-e-12 (downloaded January 10, 2019).

————. *Ecumenism Means You, Too: Ordinary Christians and the Quest for Christian Unity.* Eugene, OR: Cascade Books, 2010.

————. "How Baptists Receive the Gifts of Catholics and Other Christians." *Ecumenical Trends* 39, no. 6 (June 2010): 1/81-5/85.

————. "Locating the Unity of Christ's Rule: A Response to Respondents to *Baptist Identity and the Ecumenical Future.*" *Pacific Journal of Baptist Research* 11, no. 2 (November 2016): 24-31.

————. "'One Baptism': A Study Text for Baptists." *Baptist World: A Magazine of the Baptist World Alliance* 58, no. 1 (January/March 2011): 9-10.

————. "Praying and Believing: Retrieving the Patristic Interdependence of Worship and Theology." *Review & Expositor* 101, no. 4 (September 2004): 667–95.

————. "'Quick to Listen, Slow to Speak': The Promise of a Radical Baptist Way of Hearing" *Perspectives in Religious Studies* 45, no. 3 (Fall 2018): 327-33.

————. *Towards Baptist Catholicity: Essays on Tradition and the Baptist Vision.* Studies in Baptist History and Thought, vol. 27. Milton Keynes, UK: Paternoster, 2006.

————. "Trinitarian *Koinōnia* and Ecclesial *Oikoumenē*: Paul Fiddes as Ecumenical Theologian." *Perspectives in Religious Studies* 44, no. 1 (Spring 2017): 19-37.

Harmon, Steven R., B. Diane Lipsett, Kristopher Norris, Amy L. Chilton, and Ryan Andrew Newson. "Ryan Newson's *Inhabiting the World*: A Review Symposium." *Perspectives in Religious Studies* 45, no. 3 (Fall 2018): 327-54.

Harvey, Barry. *Taking Hold of the Real: Dietrich Bonhoeffer and the Profound Worldliness of Christianity*. Eugene, OR: Cascade Books, 2015.

Haslam, Molly. *A Constructive Theology of Intellectual Disability: Human Being as Mutuality and Response*. New York, NY: Fordham University Press, 2012.

Hatch, Derek C. "The Universal Call to Holiness and the Priesthood of All Believers, Or Why the Saints Matter for Baptist Theology"" *Pacific Journal of Baptist Research* 13, no. 1 (May 2018): 2-14; online http://www.baptistresearch.org.nz/uploads/6/2/0/4/6204774/pjbr_may_2018__final_.pdf (downloaded January 13, 2020).

Hauerwas, Stanley. "The Church and Mentally Handicapped Persons: A Continuing Challenge to the Imagination." In *Religion and Disability: Essays in Scripture, Theology and Ethics*, ed. Marilyn E. Bishop, 46-64. Kansas City, MO: Sheed and Ward, 1995.

_____. "The End of Sacrifice: An Apocalyptic Politics." In *Apocalyptic and the Future of Theology: With and Beyond J. Louis Martyn*, ed. Joshua B. Davis and Douglas Harink, 422-37. Eugene, OR: Cascade Books, 2012.

_____. "Interview with Kristopher Norris." Durham, North Carolina, February 25, 2015. Cited in Kristopher Norris, "Witnessing Whiteness in the Ethics of Hauerwas," *Journal of Religious Ethics* 47, no. 1 (March 2019): 95-124; online https://doi.org/10.1111/jore.12251 (downloaded February 25, 2019).

Hauerwas, Stanley and Samuel Wells, eds. *The Blackwell Companion to Christian Ethics*. 2nd ed. Blackwell Companions to Religion. Chichester, UK: Wiley-Blackwell, 2011.

Hawley, John Stratton. *Three Bhakti Voices: Mirabai, Surdas, and Kabir in Their Times and Ours*. Oxford: Oxford University Press, 2012.

Hayami, Yoko. *Between Hills and Plains: Power and Practice in Socio-Religious Dynamics Among Karen*. Kyoto: Kyoto University Press and Melbourne: Trans-Pacific Press, 2004.

Hayden, Roger. *Baptist Union Documents 1948-1977*. London: Baptist Historical Society, 1980.

Haymes, Brian. "Theology and Baptist Identity." In Paul S. Fiddes, Brian Haymes, Richard Kidd, and Michael J. Quicke, *Doing Theology in a Baptist Way*, 1-5. Oxford: Whitley Publications, 2000.

Haynes, Stephen. *The Bonhoeffer Phenomenon: Portraits of a Protestant Saint*. Minneapolis: Fortress Press, 2004.

Helwys, Thomas. *The Life and Writings of Thomas Helwys*. Edited by Joseph E. Early. Macon, GA: Mercer University Press, 2009.

_____. *A Short Declaration of the Mistery of Iniquity*. London: 1612.

_____. *A Short Declaration of the Mystery of Iniquity* (1611/1612). Edited by Richard Groves. Macon, GA: Mercer University Press, 1998.

Hickman, Hoyt L., Don E. Saliers, Laurence Hull Stookey, and James F. White, eds. *The New Handbook of the Christian Year: Based on the Revised Common Lectionary*. Nashville: Abingdon Press, 1992.

Hicks, Zac. *The Worship Pastor: A Call to Ministry for Worship Leaders and Teams*. Grand Rapids, MI: Zondervan, 2016.

Hill, Samuel S. Jr. and Robert G. Torbet. *Baptists North and South: What Keeps Baptists Apart?* Valley Forge, PA: Judson Press, 1964.

Himes, Kenneth R., ed. *Modern Catholic Social Teaching: Commentaries and Interpretations*. Washington, DC: Georgetown University Press, 2005.

Hinson, E. Glenn. "Theology and Experience of Worship: A Baptist View." *Greek Orthodox Theological Review* 22, no. 4 (1977): 417-27.

Hippolytus of Rome. *The Apostolic Tradition of St. Hippolytus.* 2nd ed. Edited by Gregory Dix and Henry Chadwick. London: Alban, 1992.

Holmes, Stephen R. "Baptists and the Bible." *Baptist Quarterly* 43, no. 7 (2014): 410-27.

————. "The Dangers of Just Reading the Bible: Orthodoxy and Christology." In *Exploring Baptist Origins*, ed. Anthony R. Cross and Nicholas J. Wood, 122-37. Centre for Baptist History and Heritage, no. 1. Oxford: Regent's Park College, 2010.

————. "Fasting from Voices Like Mine," *Shored Fragments* [blog]. February 28, 2017). Online http://steverholmes.org.uk/blog/?p=7660 (downloaded January 8, 2019).

————. *Listening to the Past: The Place of Tradition in Theology.* Carlisle, UK: Paternoster, 2002 and Grand Rapids, MI: Baker Academic, 2002.

————. "Note Concerning the Text, Editions, and Authorship of the 1660 Standard Confession of the General Baptists." *Baptist Quarterly* 47 (2016): 2-7.

Hoover, Theressa. "Black Women and the Churches: Triple Jeopardy." In *Black Theology: A Documentary History, 1966-1979*, ed. James H. Cone and Gayraud Wilmore, 227-88. Maryknoll, NY: Orbis Books, 1979.

Hopkins, Dwight N. and Edward P. Antonio, eds. *The Cambridge Companion to Black Theology.* Cambridge Companions to Religion. Cambridge: Cambridge University Press, 2012.

Humphreys, W. Lee. "A Life-Style for Diaspora: A Study of the Tales of Esther and Daniel." *Journal of Biblical Literature* 92 (1973): 211–23.

Hustad, Donald P. "Baptist Worship Forms: Uniting the Charleston and Sandy Creek Traditions." *Review & Expositor* 85, no. 1 (1988): 31-42.

ILoveMountains.org. "End Mountaintop Removal Coal Mining." Online http://ilovemountains.org/(downloaded January 16, 2018).

International Religious Freedom Roundtable. "Purpose and Overview Statement." Online https://www.irfroundtable.org/blank-page (downloaded November 24, 2018).

International Work Group for Indigenous Affairs. Online www.iwgia.org/regions/asia (downloaded February 27, 2019).

IPCC Core Writing Team, R. K. Pachauri, and L. A. Meyer, eds. "Climate Change 2014: Synthesis Report. Contribution of Working Groups I, II and III to the Fifth Assessment Report of the Intergovernmental Panel on Climate Change." Geneva, Switzerland: IPCC, 2014. Online http://www.ipcc.ch/report/ar5/syr/ (downloaded March 6, 2018).

Irvin, Dale. *Hearing Many Voices: Dialogue and Diversity in the Ecumenical Movement.* Lanham, MA: University Press of America, 1994.

Isasi-Díaz, Ada Maria. *En la Lucha: Elaborating a Mujerista Theology.* Minneapolis: Fortress Press, 1993.

————. *Mujerista Theology.* Maryknoll, NY: Orbis Books, 1996.

————. "Mujerista Theology's Method: A Liberative Praxis, a Way of Life." In *Mestizo Christianity: Theology from the Latino Perspective*, ed. Arturo Bañuelas, 175-90. Maryknoll, NY: Orbis Books, 1995.

Isasi-Díaz, Ada Maria and Yolanda Tarango. *Hispanic Women: Prophetic Voice in the Church.* Scranton, PA: University of Scranton Press, 2006.

Jacober, Amy E. *Redefining Perfect: The Interplay Between Theology and Disability.* Eugene, OR: Cascade Books, 2017.

James I. "A Narration of the Burning of Edward Wightman." In *A True Relation of the Commissions and Warrants for the Condemnation and Burning of Bartholomew Legatt and Thomas Withman* [sic], 7-13. London: Michael Spark, 1651.

Jantzen, Grace. *Julian of Norwich: Mystic and Theologian.* New York: Paulist Press, 2000.

Jenson, Robert W. *Canon and Creed*. Louisville: Westminster John Knox, 2010.

Jimmerson, Ellin Sterne, ed. *Rainbow in the Word: LGBTQ Christians' Biblical Memoirs*. Eugene, OR: Wipf and Stock, 2017.

John Paul II. *Novo Millennio Ineunte*. January 6, 2001. Online https://w2.vatican.va/content/john-paul-ii/en/apost_letters/2001/documents/hf_jp-ii_apl_20010106_novo-millennio-ineunte.html (downloaded March 20, 2018).

Johnson, Elizabeth A. *Friends of God and Prophets: A Feminist Theological Reading of the Communion of the Saints*. New York: Continuum, 2005.

Johnson, Robert E. *A Global Introduction to Baptist Churches*. Cambridge: Cambridge University Press, 2010.

Johnson, Todd M. and Kenneth R. Ross, eds. *Atlas of Global Christianity, 1910-2010*. Edinburgh: Edinburgh University Press, 2009.

Johnson, W. B. "The Southern Baptist Convention, To the Brethren in the United States; To the Congregations Connected with the Respective Churches; and to All Candid Men." In *Proceedings of the Southern Baptist Convention in Augusta, Georgia, 8-12 May 1845*, 17-20. Richmond: H. K. Ellyson, 1845.

Jones, Keith G. *The European Baptist Federation: A Case Study in European Baptist Interdependency, 1950-2006*. Studies in Baptist History and Thought, vol. 43. Milton Keynes, UK: Paternoster, 2009.

Jones, William. *The History of the Christian Church, from the Birth of Christ to the XVIII Century: Including the Very Interesting Account of the Waldenses and Albigensis*. 4th ed. Wetumpka, AL: Charles Yancey, 1845.

Jordan, Mark D. *Convulsing Bodies: Religion and Resistance in Foucault*. Stanford: Stanford University Press, 2014.

————. *Recruiting Young Love: How Christians Talk About Homosexuality*. Chicago: University of Chicago Press, 2011.

Julian of Norwich, *Showings*, trans. Edmund Colledge and James Walsh. New York: Paulist Press, 1978.

Kachin Women's Association Thailand. "Update on the Human Rights Situation in Burma (January—June 2018)." September 10, 2018. Online https://kachinwomen.com/update-on-the-human-rights-situation-in-burma-january-june-2018/ (downloaded November 22, 2018).

Kang, Namsoon. "Re-constructing Asian Feminist Theology: Toward a Glocal Feminist Theology in an Era of Neo-Empire(s)." In *Christian Theology in Asia*, ed. Sebastian C. H. Kim, 205-26. Cambridge: Cambridge University Press, 2008.

Kant, Immanuel. *Religion within the Boundaries of Mere Reason*. Edited by Allen Wood and George di Giovanni, with introduction by Robert Merrihew Adams. Cambridge: Cambridge University Press, 1999.

Kärkkäinen, Veli-Matti. *Trinity and Revelation: A Constructive Christian Theology for the Pluralistic World*. Grand Rapids, MI: Eerdmans, 2014.

Kaufman, S. Roy. *Healing God's Earth: Rural Community in the Context of Urban Civilization*. Eugene, OR: Wipf and Stock, 2013.

Kavanagh, Aidan. *On Liturgical Theology*. Collegeville, MN: The Liturgical Press, 1992.

Kelly, J. N. D. *Early Christian Creeds*. 3rd ed. New York: Longman, 1972.

Kennedy, Rodney Wallace and Derek Hatch, eds. *Gathering Together: Baptists at Work in Worship*. Eugene, OR: Pickwick Publications, 2013.

Kidd, Thomas S. and Barry Hankins. *Baptists in America: A History.* Oxford: Oxford University Press, 2015.

Kilner, John F. *Dignity and Destiny: Humanity in the Image of God.* Grand Rapids, MI.: William B. Eerdmans, 2015.

Kim, Grace Ji-Sun and Susan M. Shaw. *Intersectional Theology: An Introductory Guide.* Minneapolis: Fortress Press, 2018.

Kim, Nami. "Cutting Edges: 'My/Our' Comfort Not at the Expense of Somebody Else: Toward a Critical Global Feminist Theology." *Journal of Feminist Studies in Religion* 21, no. 2 (Fall 2000): 75-94.

_____. "The 'Indigestible' Asian: The Unifying Term 'Asian' in Theological Discourse." In *Off the Menu: Asian and Asian North American Women's Religions and Theology,* ed. Rita Nakashima Brock, Jung Ha Kim, Pui-Lan Kwok, and Seung Ai Yang, 23-43. Louisville: Westminster John Knox Press, 2007.

_____. "Which Postcolonialism? The Relevance of Resistance Postcolonialism to Postcolonial Asia." *Asian Christian Review* 6, no. 1 (2012): 23-35.

Kim, Sebastian C. H., ed. *Christian Theology in Asia.* Cambridge: Cambridge University Press, 2008.

Kim, Sebastian C. H. and Kirsteen Kim, eds. *Christianity as a World Religion.* London: Continuum Books, 2008.

King, Martin Luther, Jr. "A Comparison of the Conceptions of God in the Thinking of Paul Tillich and Henry Nelson Wieman." Ph.D. diss., Boston University, 1955.

_____. "The Ethical Demands for Integration." In *A Testament of Hope: The Essential Writings of Martin Luther King, Jr.* ed. James M. Washington, 117-25. San Francisco: Harper & Row, 1986.

_____. "Letter from Birmingham Jail." In *The Radical King,* ed. Cornel West, 127-46. Boston: Beacon Press, 2015.

_____. "Letter from Birmingham Jail" (April 16, 1963). Online http://okra.stanford.edu/transcription/document_images/undecided/630416-019.pdf (downloaded January 2, 2019).

_____. Nobel Lecture "The Quest for Peace and Justice," December 11, 1964. Online https://www.nobelprize.org/prizes/peace/1964/king/lecture/ (downloaded January 3, 2018).

_____. *Where Do We Go From Here? Chaos or Community.* New York: Harper & Row, 1967.

King, Richard. *Orientalism and Religion: Postcolonial Theory, India and the Mystic East.* London: Routledge, 1999.

Kinnamon, Michael. *Can a Renewal Movement Be Renewed? Questions for the Future of Ecumenism.* Grand Rapids, MI: William B. Eerdmans, 2014.

Knitter, Paul. *One Earth, Many Religions: Multifaith Dialogue and Global Responsibility.* Maryknoll, NY: Orbis Books, 1995.

Kollman, Paul. "Understanding the World-Christian Turn in the History of Christianity and Theology." *Theology Today* 71, no. 2 (July 2014): 164-77.

Knollys, Hanserd. *The Collected Works of Hanserd Knollys.* Edited by William L. Pitts and Rady Roldán-Figueroa. Macon, GA: Mercer University Press, 2017.

Korschorke, Klaus. "New Maps of the History of World Christianity: Current Challenges and Future Perspectives." *Theology Today* 7, no. 2 (2014): 178-91.

Kuster, Volker. *A Protestant Theology of Passion: Korean Minjung Theology Revisited.* Leiden: Brill, 2010.

Kwok, Pui-lan. *Chinese Women and Christianity 1860-1927*. Oxford: Oxford University Press, 1992.

————. *Introducing Asian Feminist Theology*. Introductions in Feminist Theology, vol. 4. Cleveland, OH: Pilgrim Press, 2000.

————. *Postcolonial Imagination and Feminist Theology*. Louisville: Westminster John Knox, 2005.

Kyung, Chung Hyun. *Struggling to be the Sun Again: Introducing Asian Women's Theology*. Maryknoll, NY: Orbis Books, 1990.

Leach, Mark. "Down Syndrome Diagnosis at the Adoration of the Christ Child." Down Syndrome Prenatal Testing: A Resource for Information Seekers. Online http://www.downsyndromeprenataltesting.com/down-syndrome-diagnosis-at-the-adoration-of-the-christ-child/ (downloaded March 5, 2018).

————. "A Portrayal of Heaven on Earth: The Adoration of the Christ Child." Down Syndrome Prenatal Testing: A Resource for Information Seekers. Online http://www.downsyndromeprenataltesting.com/a-portrayal-of-heaven-on-earth-the-adoration-of-the-christ-child/ (downloaded March 5, 2018).

Lee, Hak Joon. *The Great World House: Martin Luther King, Jr., and Global Ethics*. Cleveland, OH: Pilgrim Press, 2011.

Leo XIII. "Encyclical on Capital and Labor" (*Rerum Novarum*). May 15, 1891. Online http://w2.vatican.va/content/leo-xiii/en/encyclicals/documents/hf_l-xiii_enc_15051891_rerum-novarum.html (downloaded April 14, 2018).

Leonard, Bill J. *Baptists in America*. New York: Columbia University Press, 2005.

Lerner, Gerda. *Women and History*. 2 vols. Oxford: Oxford University Press, 1986-1994.

Lessalle-Klein, Robert. *Blood and Ink: Ignacio Ellacuría, Jon Sobrino, and the Jesuit Martyrs of the University of Central America*. Maryknoll, NY: Orbis Books, 2014.

Levitas, Andrew S. and Cheryl S. Reid. "An Angel with Down Syndrome in a Sixteenth Century Flemish Nativity Painting." *American Journal of Medical Genetics* 116A (2003): 399-405.

Lightsey, Pamela R. *Our Lives Matter: A Womanist Queer Theology*. Eugene, OR: Pickwick Publications, 2015.

Lipset, David. "The New State of Nature: Rising Sea-Levels, Climate Justice, and Community-Based Adaptation in Papua New Guinea (2003-2011)." *Conservation & Society* 11, no. 2 (2013): 144–58. Online http://www.conservationandsociety.org/text.asp?2013/11/2/144/115726 (downloaded January 16, 2018).

Longchar, Wati. *Tribal Theology: An Emerging Asian Theology. Issue, Method, and Perspective*. Tribal Study Series, no. 8. Jorhat, India: ETC Publications, 2000.

Longenecker, Richard N. *Galatians*. Word Biblical Commentary, vol. 41. Dallas: Word Books, 1990.

Lopez, Donald S., Jr., ed. *Religions of Tibet in Practice*. Princeton: Princeton University Press, 1997.

López, Gustavo, Kristen Bialik, and Jynnah Radford. "Key Findings About U.S. Immigrants: More Than Half of U.S. Refugees in 2017 were from D.R. Congo, Iraq, Syria and Somalia." Pew Research Center (September 19, 2018). Online http://www.pewresearch.org/fact-tank/2018/09/14/key-findings-about-u-s-immigrants/ft_18-09-12_immigrantskeyfindings_more-than-half-refugees/ (downloaded November 20, 2018).

Lozano-Díaz, Nora O. "Ignored Virgin or Unaware Women: A Mexican-American Protestant Reflection on the Virgin of Guadalupe." In *A Reader in Latin Feminist Theology: Religion and Justice,* ed. María Pilar Aquino, Daisy L. Machado, and Jeanette Rodríguez, 204-16. Austin: University of Texas Press, 2002.

Lumpkin, William L., ed. *Baptist Confessions of Faith.* Rev. ed. Valley Forge, PA: Judson Press, 1969.

_____, ed. *Baptist Confessions of Faith.* 2nd rev. ed. Revised by Bill J. Leonard. Valley Forge, PA: Judson Press, 2011.

Luther, Martin. *Selected Writings of Martin Luther.* Edited by Theodore G. Tappert, trans. A. T. W. Steinhaeuser. Minneapolis: Fortress Press, 2007.

Lutheran World Federation and Catholic Church. *Joint Declaration on the Doctrine of Justification.* Grand Rapids, MI: William B. Eerdmans, 2000. Online https://www.lutheranworld.org/jddj (downloaded April 6, 2019).

Lutheran World Federation and Pontifical Council for Promoting Christian Unity. *From Conflict to Communion: Lutheran-Catholic Common Commemoration of the Reformation in 2017. Report of the Lutheran-Roman Catholic Commission on Unity.* Leipzig: Evangelische Verlangsanstalt, 2013. Online https://www.lutheranworld.org/content/resource-conflict-communion-basis-lutheran-catholic-commemoration-reformation-2017 (downloaded April 6, 2019).

Maag, Karin. "Catechisms and Confessions of Faith." In *T&T Clark Companion to Reformation Theology,* ed. David M. Whitford, 197-212. London: T&T Clark, 2014.

Mackay, John. *Ecumenics: The Science of the Church Universal.* Englewood Cliffs, NJ: Prentice-Hall, 1964.

MacKenzie, Vashti M. *Not Without a Struggle: Leadership Development for African American Women in Ministry.* Revised and updated ed. Cleveland, OH: Pilgrim Press, 2011.

Malone, Mary T. *Women & Christianity.* 3 vols. Maryknoll, NY: Orbis Books, 2000-2003.

Mangina, Joseph. "Baptism at the Turn of the Ages." In *Apocalyptic and the Future of Theology: With and Beyond J. Louis Martyn,* ed. Joshua B. Davis and Douglas Harink, 376-98. Eugene, OR: Cascade Books, 2012).

Marshall, Molly T. "Is Feminist a Baptist Word?" *Baptist News Global* (May 28, 2014). Online https://baptistnews.com/article/is-feminist-a-baptist-word/#.WgOTtWdvnXM (downloaded November 8, 2017).

_____. *Joining the Dance: A Theology of the Spirit.* Valley Forge, PA: Judson Press, 2003.

_____. *What It Means to Be Human: Made in the Image of God.* Macon, GA: Smyth & Helwys, 1995.

Martell-Otero, Loida. "From Foreign Bodies in Teacher Space to Embodied Spirit in *Personas Educadas*: Or, How to Prevent 'Tourists of Diversity' in Education." In *Teaching for a Culturally Diverse and Racially Just World,* ed. Eleazar S. Fernandez, 52-68. Eugene, OR: Cascade Books, 2014.

_____. "Women Doing Theology: Una Perspectiva Evangélica," *Apuntes* 14, no. 3 (Fall 1994): 67-85.

Martell-Otero, Loida, Zaida Maldonado Pérez, and Elizabeth Conde-Frazier, eds. *Latina Evangélicas: A Theological Survey from the Margins.* Eugene, OR: Cascade Books, 2013.

Martey, Emmanuel. *African Theology: Inculturation and Liberation.* Eugene, OR: Wipf & Stock, 2009.

Mason, Steve. "Jews, Judaeans, Judaizing, Judaism: Problems of Categorization in Ancient History." *Journal for the Study of Judaism* 38 (2007): 457–512.

Mathews, Michael-Ray, Marie Clare P. Onwubuariri, and Cody J. Sanders. *Trouble the Water: A Christian Resource for the Work of Racial Justice*. Macon, GA: Nurturing Faith, Inc., 2017.

May, Vivian. *Pursuing Intersectionality, Unsettling Dominant Imaginaries*. New York: Routledge, 2015.

McBeth, H. Leon. *The Baptist Heritage: Four Centuries of Baptist Witness*. Nashville: Broadman Press, 1987.

McCarthy, David Matzko. *Sharing God's Company: A Theology of the Communion of the Saints*. Grand Rapids, MI: William B. Eerdmans, 2012.

McClendon, James Wm., Jr. *Biography as Theology: How Life Stories Can Remake Today's Theology*. Nashville: Abingdon Press, 1974; reprint, Eugene, OR: Wipf and Stock, 2002.

————. *The Collected Works of James Wm. McClendon, Jr.* 3 vols. Edited by Ryan Andrew Newson and Andrew C. Wright. Waco, TX: Baylor University Press, 2014-16.

————. *Systematic Theology*. 3 vols. Nashville: Abingdon Press, 1986-2000. Reprint ed., Waco, TX: Baylor University Press, 2012.

————. "What Is a Southern Baptist Ecumenism?" *Southwestern Journal of Theology* 10, no. 2 (1968): 73-78.

McCray, Donyelle. *The Censored Pulpit: Julian of Norwich as Preacher*. Th.D. diss., Duke Divinity School, 2014.

McDannell, Colleen. *The Spirit of Vatican II: A History of Catholic Reform in America*. New York: Basic Books, 2011.

McFague, Sallie. *Models of God*. Minneapolis: Fortress Press, 1987.

McNutt, William Roy. *Worship in the Churches*. Philadelphia: Judson Press, 1941.

Melcher, Sarah, Mikeal Parsons, and Amos Yong, eds. *The Bible and Disability: A Commentary*. Waco, TX: Baylor University Press, 2017.

Mellon, Brad F. "John Kilner's Understanding of the *Imago Dei* and The Ethical Treatment of Persons with Disabilities." *Christian Bioethics* 23, no. 3 (2017): 283-98.

Mentzer, Raymond A. "Belgic Confession of 1561." In *Encyclopedia of Protestantism*, ed. Hans J. Hillerbrand, 1:48–49. New York: Routledge, 2004.

————. "Gallican Confession." In *Encyclopedia of Protestantism*, ed. Hans J. Hillerbrand, 2:514. New York: Routledge, 2004.

Meyer, Harding and Lukas Vischer, eds. *Growth in Agreement: Reports and Agreed Statements of Ecumenical Conversations on a World Level*. Faith and Order Paper no. 108. New York: Paulist Press and Geneva: World Council of Churches, 1984.

Meyer, Joyce Ann. "Environmental Activism in the Philippines: A Practical Theological Perspective." In *Planetary Solidarity: Global Women's Voices on Christian Doctrine and Climate Justice*, ed. Grace Ji-Sun Kim and Hilda P. Koster, 287-307. Minneapolis: Fortress Press, 2017.

Miller, Dee. *Enlarging Boston's SPOTLIGHT: A Call for Courage, Integrity, and Institutional Transformation*. North Charleston, SC: CreateSpace, 2017.

Minnesota Governor's Council on Developmental Disabilities. "Parallels in Time: A History of Developmental Disabilities." Online http://mn.gov/mnddc/parallels/(dowloaded December 12, 2017).

Minz, Nirmal. "Religion, Culture, and Education in the Context of Tribal Aspirations in India." *Journal of Dharma* 24, no. 4 (1999): 402-16.

Mitchem, Stephanie Y. *Introducing Womanist Theology*. Maryknoll, NY: Orbis Books, 2002.

Moe-Lobeda, Cynthia. *Resisting Structural Evil: Love as Ecological-Economic Vocation*. Minneapolis: Fortress Press, 2013.

Moffett, Samuel Hugh. *A History of Christianity in Asia*. 2 vols. Maryknoll, NY: Orbis Books, 1998.

Mohler, Albert. "The Southern Baptist Convention and the Issue of Interdenominational Relationships." July 16, 2009. Online https://albertmohler.com/2009/07/16/the-southern-baptist-convention-and-the-issue-of-interdenominational-relationships/ (downloaded January 7, 2019).

Monck, Thomas. *A Cure for the Cankering Errors of the New Eutychians*. London: 1673.

Moore, Rebecca. *Women in Christian Traditions*. New York: NYU Press, 2015.

Morimoto, Anri. "Asian Theology in the Ablative Case." *Studies in World Christianity* 17, no. 3 (2011): 201-15.

Morrill, Bruce T. *Anamnesis as Dangerous Memory: Political and Liturgical Theology in Dialogue*. Collegeville, MN: The Liturgical Press, 2000.

Morrill, John. "The Puritan Revolution." In *The Cambridge Companion to Puritanism*, ed. John Coffey and Paul C. H. Lim, 67–88. Cambridge: Cambridge University Press, 2008.

Moss, Candida and Jeremy Schipper, eds. *Disability Studies and Biblical Literature*. New York: Palgrave MacMillan, 2011.

Muller, Jan-Wemer. *What Is Populism?* Philadelphia: University of Pennsylvania Press, 2016.

Muñoz, José Esteban. *Cruising Utopia: The Then and There of Queer Futurity*. New York: New York University Press, 2009.

Murphy, Nancey. *Beyond Liberalism and Fundamentalism: How Modern and Postmodern Philosophy Set the Theological Agenda*. Harrisburg, PA: Trinity Press International, 2007.

Murray, Paul D., ed. *Receptive Ecumenism and the Call to Catholic Learning: Exploring a Way for Contemporary Ecumenism*. Oxford: Oxford University Press, 2008.

Mustol, John. *Dusty Earthlings: Living as Eco-Physical Beings in God's Eco-Physical World*. Eugene, OR: Cascade Books, 2012.

Myers, Ben. *The Apostles' Creed: A Guide to the Ancient Catechism*. Bellingham, WA: Lexham Press, 2018.

National Centers for Environmental Information. "Wildfires—Annual 2017." Online https://www.ncdc.noaa.gov/sotc/fire/201713 (downloaded January 16, 2018).

Nelson, R. David and Charles Raith II. *Ecumenism: A Guide for the Perplexed*. New York: Bloomsbury T&T Clark, 2017.

Nettleton, Nathan. "Baptist Worship in Ecumenical Perspective." In *Worship Today: Understanding, Practice, Ecumenical Implications*, ed. Thomas F. Best, 72-83. Faith and Order Paper, no. 194; Geneva: WCC Publications, 2004.

Nevin, John Williamson. *Catholic and Reformed: Selected Theological Writings of John Williamson Nevin*. Edited by Charles Yrigoyen Jr. and George H. Bricker. Eugene, OR: Pickwick Publications, 1978.

_____. "The Theology of the New Liturgy." *The Mercersburg Review* 14, no. 1 (1867): 23-45.

Newell, Christopher. "On the Importance of Suffering: The Paradoxes of Disability." In *The Paradox of Disability: Responses to Jean Vanier and L'Arche Communities from Theology and the Sciences*, ed. Hans S. Reinders, 169-79. Grand Rapids, MI: William B. Eerdmans, 2010.

Newman, Barbara J. *Accessible Gospel, Inclusive Worship*. Wyoming, Michigan: CLC Network, 2015.

_____. "Inclusive Worship: Creating a Language and Mutltisensory Options So That All Can Participate." *Review and Expositor* 113, no. 2 (2016): 217-24.

Newsom, Carol A., Sharon H. Ringe, and Jacqueline E. Lapsley, eds. *Women's Bible Commentary*. 3rd ed. Louisville, KY: Westminster John Knox Press, 2012.

Newson, Ryan Andrew. *Inhabiting the World: Identity, Politics, and Theology in Radical Baptist Perspective*. Perspectives on Baptist Identities, no. 1. Macon, GA: Mercer University Press, 2018.

_____. *Radical Friendship: The Politics of Communal Discernment*. Minneapolis: Fortress Press, 2017.

Niebuhr, H. Richard. "The Doctrine of the Trinity and the Unity of the Church." *Theology Today* 3, no. 3 (1946): 371-84.

Nirmal, Arvind P. "Toward a Christian Dalit Theology." In *Frontiers in Asian Christian Theology: Emerging Trends*, ed. R. S. Sugirtharajah, 27-40. Maryknoll, NY: Orbis Books, 1994.

Norris, Kristopher. "Witnessing Whiteness in the Ethics of Hauerwas." *Journal of Religious Ethics* 47, no. 1 (March 2019): 95-124. Online https://doi.org/10.1111/jore.12251 (downloaded February 25, 2019).

Northcott, Michael S. *A Moral Climate: The Ethics of Global Warming*. Maryknoll, NY: Orbis Books, 2009.

Nussbaum, Martha. *Love's Knowledge: Essays on Philosophy and Literature*. New York: Oxford University Press, 1990.

_____. *Upheavals of Thought: The Intelligence of Emotions*. Cambridge: Cambridge University Press, 2001.

Oasis Project, The. *The Oasis Project: Creating Safer Spaces and Providing Interfaith Spiritual Care for Conventions*. Online https://oasis4conventions.wordpress.com/about/ (downloaded December 6, 2017).

O'Brien, Kevin J. *An Ethics of Biodiversity: Christianity, Ecology, and the Variety of Life*. Washington, DC: Georgetown University Press, 2010.

Oddie, Geoffrey. *Imagined Hinduism: British Protestant Missionary Constructions of Hinduism, 1793-1900*. New Delhi: Sage Publications, 2006.

Oden, Amy, ed. *In Her Words: Women's Writings in the History of Christian Thought*. Nashville: Abingdon Press, 1994.

Oden, Thomas C., ed. *Ancient Christian Commentary on Scripture*. Downers Grove, IL: InterVarsity Press, 1998-.

Oduyoye, Mercy Amba. *Introducing African Women's Theology*. Introductions in Feminist Theology, vol. 6. Sheffield, UK: Sheffield Academic Press, 2001.

Orchard, G. H. *A Concise History of the Baptists*. Nashville: Graves, Marks & Rutland, 1855.

Orevillo-Montenegro, Murial. *The Jesus of Asian Women: Women from the Margins*. Maryknoll, NY: Orbis Books, 2006.

Ortiz, Manuel. *The Hispanic Challenge*. Downers Grove, IL: InterVarsity Press, 1993.

Pace, Courtney. "Baptists, Catholicity, and Missing Voices: A Response to Steven Harmon." *Pacific Journal of Baptist Research* 11, no. 2 (November 2016): 16-19.

_____. *Freedom Faith: The Womanist Vision of Prathia Hall*. Athens, GA: University of Georgia Press, 2019.

Page, Hugh R., Jr., Randall C. Bailey, Valerie Bridgeman, Stacy Davis, Cheryl Kirk-Duggan, Madipoane Masenya, Nathaniel Samuel Murrell, and Rodney S. Sadler, Jr., eds. *The Africana Bible: Reading Israel's Scriptures from Africa and the African Diaspora*. Minneapolis: Fortress Press, 2010.

Parker, G. Keith. *Baptists in Europe: History and Confessions of Faith*. Nashville: Broadman Press, 1982.

Parker, Laura. "Hurricane Florence's Rains May Be 50% Worse Due to Climate Change" *National Geographic* (September 13, 2018). Online https://www.nationalgeographic.com/environment/2018/09/hurricane-florence-rain-climate-change-science/ (downloaded September 26, 2018).

Patte, Daniel, ed. *Global Bible Commentary*. Nashville: Abingdon Press, 2006.

Patterson, W. Morgan and Richard V. Pierrard. "Recovery from the War and the Advance to Maturity." Chap. 5 in *Baptists Together in Christ: 1905-2005*, ed. Richard V. Pierrard, 100-27. Falls Church, VA: Baptist World Alliance, 2005.

Payne, Ernest A. "Baptists and the Ecumenical Movement." *Baptist Quarterly* 8: 258-67.

_____. *Free Churchmen, Unrepentant and Repentant*. London: Carey Kingsgate, 1965.

Payne, Ernest A. and Stephen F. Winward, eds. *Orders and Prayers for Church Worship*. 2nd ed. London: Carey Kingsgate Press, 1962.

Pearce, J. Winston. *Come, Let Us Worship*. Nashville: Broadman Press, 1965.

Pelikan, Jaroslav. *Credo: Historical and Theological Guide to Creeds and Confessions of Faith in the Christian Tradition*. New Haven: Yale University Press, 2003.

_____. *The Vindication of Tradition*. New Haven: Yale University Press, 1984.

Pelphrey, Brant. *Love Was His Meaning: The Theology and Mysticism of Julian of Norwich*. Salzburg: Institut Für Anglistik und Amerikanistik Universität Salzburg, 1982.

Phan, Peter C. *Being Religious Interreligiously: Asian Perspectives on Interfaith Dialogue*. Maryknoll, NY: Orbis Books, 2004.

_____. *In Our Own Tongues: Perspectives from Asia on Mission and Inculturation*. Maryknoll, NY: Orbis Books, 2003.

_____, ed. *Christianities in Asia*. Chidester, UK: Wiley-Blackwell, 2010.

Pieris, Aloysius. *An Asian Theology of Liberation*. London: T&T Clark International, 1988.

_____. "Interreligious Dialogue and Theology of Religions: An Asian Paradigm." *Horizons* 20, no. 1 (1993): 106-14.

Pineda-Madrid, Nancy. "Notes Toward a Chicana Feminist Epistemology (and Why It Is Important for Latina Feminist Theologies)." In *A Reader in Latin Feminist Theology: Religion and Justice*, ed. María Pilar Aquino, Daisy L. Machado and Jeanette Rodríguez, 241-66. Austin: University of Texas Press, 2002.

Pius XI. "Encyclical on the Reconstruction of the Social Order (*Quadragesimo Anno*)." May 15, 1931. Online http://w2.vatican.va/content/pius-xi/en/encyclicals/documents/hf_p-xi_enc_19310515_quadragesimo-anno.html (downloaded April 14, 2018).

Pontifical Council for Promoting Christian Unity. *Directory for the Application of Principles and Norms of Ecumenism*. March 25, 1993. Online http://www.vatican.va/roman_curia/pontifical_councils/chrstuni/documents/rc_pc_chrstuni_doc_25031993_principles-and-norms-on-ecumenism_en.html (downloaded February 26, 2019).

Powell, Vavasor. *Spirituall Experiences, of Sundry Beleevers*. London: Robert Ibbitson, 1653.

Prendes, Jorge Cárceres. "Political Radicalization and Popular Pastoral Practices in El Salvador, 1969-1985." In *The Progressive Church in Latin America*, edited by Scott Mainwaring and Alexander Wilde, 103-48. Notre Dame, IN: University of Notre Dame Press, 1989.

Presbyterian Church (USA). *Book of Common Worship*. Louisville: Westminster/John Knox Press, 2018.

Rahner, Karl ed. *Encyclopedia of Theology: The Concise Sacramentum Mundi*. New York: Seabury, 1975.

Randall, Ian M., Toivo Pilli, and Anthony R. Cross, eds. *Baptist Identities: International Studies from the Seventeenth to the Twentieth Century.* Studies in Baptist History and Thought, vol. 19. Milton Keynes, UK: Paternoster, 2006.

Ratzinger, Joseph. "Vi Spiego La Teologia Della Liberazione." *30 Giorni. Mensile internazionale II* (March 1984): 48-55.

Recinos, Harold J. and Hugo Magallanes, eds. *Jesus in the Hispanic Community: Images of Christ from Theology to Popular Religion.* Louisville: Westminster John Knox Press, 2009.

Reichert, Folker. *Das Bild der Welt im Mittelalter.* Darmstadt: Wissenschaftliche Buchgesell-schaft, 2013.

Reid, Barbara E., Marry Ann Beavis, Amy-Jill Levine, Linda M. Maloney, Ahida Calderón Pilar-ski, Sarah Tanzer, and Lauress Wilkins Lawrence, eds. *Wisdom Commentary* [series; volumes individually titled]. Collegeville, MI: Liturgical Press, 2015-.

Reinders, Hans S. *Receiving the Gift of Friendship: Profound Disability, Theological Anthropology, and Ethics.* Grand Rapids, MI.: William B. Eerdmans, 2008.

Reynolds, Thomas E. *Vulnerable Communion: A Theology of Disability and Hospitality.* Grand Rapids, MI: Brazos Press, 2008.

Richter, Klemens. "Liturgical Reform as the Means for Church Renewal." In *The Meaning of the Liturgy,* ed. Angelus Albert Häussling and Philipp Harmoncourt, 119-44. Collegeville, MN: Liturgical Press, 1994.

Riggs, Marcia. *Can I Get A Witness? Prophetic Religious Voices of African American Women. An Anthology.* Maryknoll, NY: Orbis Books, 1997.

Robert, Dana L. *Christian Mission: How Christianity became a World Religion.* Chichester, UK: Wiley-Blackwell, 2009.

Roberts, J. Deotis. "Liberating Theological Education: Can Our Seminaries Be Saved?" *Christian Century* 100, no. 4 (February 2-9, 1983): 98, 113-16.

Roberts-Thomson, Edward. *With Hands Outstretched: Baptists and the Ecumenical Movement.* London: Marshall, Morgan & Scott, 1962.

Rodríguez, Jeanette. *Our Lady of Guadalupe: Faith and Empowerment among Mexican-American Women.* Austin: University of Texas Press, 1994.

Rodríguez, José David and Loida Martell-Otero, eds. *Teología en Conjunto: A Collaborative Hispanic Protestant Theology.* Louisville: Westminster John Knox Press, 1997.

Rothaus Moser, Matthew A. *Love Itself is Understanding: Hans Urs von Balthasar's Theology of the Saints.* Minneapolis: Fortress Press, 2016.

Rudy, Kathy. *Sex and the Church: Gender, Homosexuality, and the Transformation of Christian Ethics.* Boston: Beacon Press, 1997.

Ruether, Rosemary Radford. "The Emergence of Christian Feminist Theology." In *The Cambridge Companion to Feminist Theology,* ed. Susan Frank Parsons, 3-22. New York: Cambridge University Press, 2002.

————. *Women and Redemption: A Theological History.* Minneapolis, MN: Fortress Press, 1998.

Rusch, William G. *Ecumenical Reception: Its Challenge and Opportunity.* Grand Rapids, MI: William B. Eerdmans, 2007.

————. *Reception: An Ecumenical Opportunity.* Philadelphia: Fortress Press, 1988.

Safran, William. "Diaspora in Modern Societies: Myth of Homeland and Return." *Diaspora* 1 (1991): 83–99.

Saiving, Valerie. "The Human Situation: A Feminine View." *The Journal of Religion* 40, no. 2 (1960): 100-12.

Saliers, Don E. *Worship as Theology: A Foretaste of Glory Divine.* Nashville: Abingdon Press, 1994.

_____. *Worship Come to Its Senses.* Nashville: Abingdon Press, 1996.

Samartha, Stanley J. *One Christ Many Religions: Towards a Revised Christology.* Maryknoll, NY: Orbis Books, 1991.

Sanders, Cody J. "Re-Visioning the Care of Souls: The Praxis of Pastoral Care in the Context of LGBTQ Suicide." Ph.D. diss., Brite Divinity School, Texas Christian University, 2015.

_____. *Queer Lessons for Churches on the Straight and Narrow: What All Churches Can Learn from LGBTQ Lives.* Macon, GA: Faithlab, 2013.

Sanneh, Lamin. *Disciples of All Nations: Pillars of World Christianity.* New York: Oxford University Press, 2008.

_____. *Whose Religion is Christianity? The Gospel Beyond the West.* Grand Rapids, MI: Willliam B. Eerdmans, 2003.

Sattler, Michael. "The Schleitheim Articles." In *The Radical Reformation*, ed. Michael G. Baylor, 172–80. Cambridge: Cambridge University Press, 1991.

Schaff, Philip. *The Principle of Protestantism.* Translated by John Williamson Nevin. Chambersburg:, PA: Publication Office of the German Reformed Church, 1845.

Schaff, Philip and David S. Schaff, eds. *The Creeds of Christendom, with a History and Critical Notes.* 6th ed. Grand Rapids, MI: Baker, 2007.

Schelin, Christopher L. "The Contestable Church: southern Baptist Ecclesiology in Conversation with Radical Democracy." Ph.D. diss., Vrije Universiteit, Amsterdam, 2018.

Schipper, Jeremy. *Disability Studies and the Hebrew Bible: Figuring Mephibosheth in the David Story.* New York: T&T Clark, 2006.

Schneider, Paul. "The Oasis Project Origin." *The Oasis Project* (May 8, 2017). Online https://oasis4conventions.wordpress.com/2017/05/08/the-oasis-project-origin/ (downloaded December 12, 2017).

Schreiner, Lothar. "Contextual Theology." In *Encyclopedia of Christianity Online*, ed. Erwin Fahlbusch. Leiden: Brill, 2012. Online http://ezproxy.ptsem.edu:2142/10.1163/2211-2685_eco_C1267 (downloaded January 25, 2019).

Schroeder, Edward H. *Gift and Promise: The Augsburg Confession and the Heart of Christian Theology.* Minneapolis: Fortress Press, 2016.

Schuld, J. Joyce. *Foucault and Augustine: Reconsidering Power and Love.* South Bend, IN: University of Notre Dame Press, 2004.

Schüssler Fiorenza, Elisabeth. *Discipleship of Equals: A Critical Feminist Ekkelsia-logy of Liberation.* New York: Herder & Herder, 1993.

Scott, Clara H. "Open My Eyes, That I May See" (1895). Hymn 395 in *Celebrating Grace Hymnal.* Macon, GA: Celebrating Grace, Inc., 2010.

_____. *The Royal Anthem Book.* Cincinnati: F. W. Helmick, 1882.

_____. *Truth in Song: For the Lovers of Truth Everywhere.* Chicago: Stockholm, 1896.

Second Acts. *Second Acts* (Facebook page). Online https://www.facebook.com/SecondActs/ (downloaded December 6, 2017).

Sefaria Community Translation, trans. "Midrash: Esther Rabbah," *The Sefaria Library.* Online https://www.sefaria.org/Esther_Rabbah.3.13?lang=en&with=all&lang2=en (downloaded November 20, 2018).

Segler, Franklin M. *Christian Worship: Its Theology and Practice.* Nashville: Broadman Press, 1967.

Segovia, Fernando F., ed. *Interpreting Beyond Borders*. Sheffield, UK: Sheffield Academic Press, 2000.

Segovia, Fernando F. and Mary Ann Tolbert, eds. *Reading from This Place: Social Location and Biblical Interpretation in Global Perspective*. 2 vols. Minneapolis: Fortress Press, 1995 and 2000.

Segovia, Fernando F. and R. S. Sugirtharajah, eds. *A Postcolonial Commentary on the New Testament Writings*. London: T.&T. Clark, 2007.

Shakespeare, John Howard, ed. *The Baptist World Congress, London, July 11-19, 1905: Authorised Record of Proceedings*. London: Baptist Union Publication Dept., 1905.

Sharkey, Heather J. *Cultural Conversions: Unexpected Consequences of Christian Missionary Encounters in Middle East, Africa and South Asia*. Syracuse, NY: Syracuse University Press, 2013.

Shaw, Susan M. *God Speaks to Us, Too: Southern Baptist Women on Church, Home, and Society*. Lexington: University of Kentucky Press, 2008.

_____. *Reflective Faith: A Theological Toolbox for Women*. Macon, GA: Smyth & Helwys, 2014.

Shaw, Susan M. and Janet Lee, eds. *Gendered Voices, Feminist Visions: Classic and Contemporary Readings*. 7th ed. New York: Oxford University Press, 2019.

Shenk, Wilbert R. *Enlarging the Story: Perspectives on Writing World Christian History*. Maryknoll, NY: Orbis Books, 2002.

Shenton, Rebecca Horner. "Baptist Agrarians: Rooted in the Soil of Care for the Earth." *American Baptist Quarterly* 35, no. 1 (Spring 2016): 6-21.

_____. "They Were Right: Agrarian Voices of Mennonite CPS Men." In *Rooted and Grounded: Essays on Land and Christian Discipleship*, ed. Ryan D. Harker and Janeen Bertsche Johnson, 229-38. Eugene, OR: Wipf and Stock, 2016.

Shore-Goss, Robert E., Thomas Bohache, Patrick S. Cheng, and Mona West, eds. *Queering Christianity: Finding a Place at the Table for LGBTQI Christians*. Santa Barbara, CA: ABC-CLIO, 2013.

Shurden, Walter B. *The Baptist Identity: Four Fragile Freedoms*. Macon, GA: Smyth & Helwys, 1993.

_____. *Not an Easy Journey: Some Transitions in Baptist Life*. Macon, GA: Mercer University Press, 2005.

_____. "The Problem of Authority in the Southern Baptist Convention." *Review & Expositor* 75, no. 2 (1978): 219-33.

Sloyan, Gerard S. *John*. Interpretation. Louisville, KY: John Knox Press, 1988.

Smith, Andrew Christopher. "Description, Prescription, and the Ecumenical Possibilities of Baptist Identity: Reading Steven Harmon's *Baptist Identity and the Ecumenical Future*." *Pacific Journal of Baptist Research* 11, no. 2 (November 2016): 20-23.

Smith, James K. A. *Desiring the Kingdom: Worship, Worldview, and Cultural Formation. Cultural Liturgies, Vol. 1*. Grand Rapids, MI: Baker Academic, 2009.

Smyth, John. *The Works of John Smyth*. 2 vols. Edited by W. T. Whitley. Cambridge: Cambridge University Press, 1915.

Sobrino, Jon. "Awakening from the Sleep of Inhumanity." *Christian Century* 108, no. 11 (1991): 364-70.

_____. *Christology at the Crossroads: A Latin American Approach*. Translated by John Drury. Maryknoll, NY: Orbis Books, 1978.

_____. "Jesus of Galilee from the Salvadoran Context: Compassion, Hope, and Following the Light of the Cross." *Theological Studies* 70, no. 2 (June 2009): 437-60.

_____. *Jesus the Liberator: A Historical-Theological View*. Translated by Paul Burns and Francis McDonagh. Maryknoll, NY: Orbis Books, 1993.

_____. "Los mártires y la teología de la liberación." *Sal Terrae* (October 1995). Online http://www.servicioskoinonia.org/relat/162.htm (downloaded April 3, 2019).

_____. "Poverty Means Death to the Poor." *Cross Currents* 36, no. 3 (1986): 267-76.

_____. "Systematic Christology: Jesus Christ, the Absolute Mediator of the Reign of God." In *Mysterium Liberationis: Fundamental Concepts of Liberation Theology*, edited by Ignacio Ellacuría and Jon Sobrino, 440-61. Maryknoll, NY: Orbis Books, 1993.

_____. *The True Church and the Poor*. Translated by Matthew J. O'Connell. Maryknoll, NY: Orbis Books, 1984.

Sobrino, Jon and Ignacio Ellacuría. *Companions of Jesus: The Jesuit Martyrs of El Salvador*. Maryknoll, NY: Orbis Books, 1990.

Song, Choan-Seng. *Theology from the Womb of Asia*. Maryknoll, NY: Orbis Books, 1986.

_____. *Tracing the Footsteps of God*. Minneapolis: Fortress Press, 2017.

Southern Baptist Convention. "The Baptist Faith and Message (1963)." Online http://www.sbc.net/bfm2000/bfmcomparison.asp (downloaded January 19, 2018).

_____. "The Baptist Faith and Message (2000)." Online http://www.sbc.net/bfm2000/bfm2000.asp (downloaded November 8, 2017).

_____. "Report of the Baptist Faith and Message Study Committee to the Southern Baptist Convention." Online http://www.sbc.net/bfm2000/preamble.asp (downloaded January 19, 2018).

_____. "Resolution on God the Father." Indianapolis, IN, 199. Online http://www.sbc.net/resolutions/573 (downloaded November 8, 2017).

_____. "Resolution on Ordination and the Role of Women in Ministry." Kansas City, MO, 1984. Online http://www.sbc.net/resolutions/1088/resolution-on-ordination-and-the-role-of-women-in-ministry (downloaded November 8, 2017).

Stamps, R. Lucas and Matthew Y. Emerson. "Liturgy for Low-Church Baptists." *Criswell Theological Review* 14, no. 2 (2017): 71-88.

Stanfield, V. L. *The Christian Worshiping*. Nashville: Convention Press, 1965.

Stanley, Brian. *The Bible and the Flag: Protestant Missions and British Imperialism in the Nineteenth and Twentieth Centuries*. Trowbridge, UK: Apollos, 1990.

_____. "Inculturation: Historical Background, Theological Foundations and Contemporary Questions." *Transformation: An International Journal of Holistic Mission Studies* 24, no. 1 (January 2007): 21-27. Online https://doi.org/10.1177/026537880702400104 (downloaded February 25, 2019).

Stern, Elsie R. "Esther and the Politics of Diaspora." *The Jewish Quarterly Review* 100, no. 1 (Winter 2010): 25–53.

Stevenson, Angus, ed. *Oxford Dictionary of English*. 3rd ed. New York: Oxford University Press, 2010.

Stovell, Beth. "Oned and Grounded in Love: Julian of Norwich and the Johannine God of Love." *Didaskalia* (Summer 2016): 1-28.

Stuart, Elizabeth. "Sacramental Flesh." In *Queer Theology: Rethinking the Western Body*, ed. Gerard Loughlin, 65-75. Malden, MA: Blackwell, 2007.

Sugirtharajah, Rasiah S. *Voices from the Margin: Interpreting the Bible in the Third World*. 25th anniversary ed. Maryknoll, NY: Orbis Books, 2016.

Summerfield, Elizabeth. "Environmental Wicked Problem-Solving: A Case for History." Australian Policy and History (November 13, 2017). Online http://aph.org.au/environmental-wicked-problem-solving-a-case-for-history/ (downloaded March 6, 2018).

Swidler, Leonard. *Dialogue for Interreligious Understanding: Strategies for the Transformation of Culture-Shaping Institutions*. New York: Palgrave MacMillan, 2014.

Swinton, John. "Disability Theology." In *The Cambridge Dictionary of Christian Theology*, ed. Ian A. McFarland, David A. S. Fergusson, Karen Kilby, and Iain R. Torrance, 140-41. London: Cambridge University Press, 2011.

Tan, Jonathan Y. and Anh Q. Tran, eds. *World Christianity: Perspectives and Insights. Essays in Honor of Peter C. Phan*. Maryknoll, NY: Orbis Books, 2016.

Tanner, Allison. "In Formation," Lakeshore Avenue Baptist Church (September 28, 2017), online http://www.labcoakland.org/outreach/september-28-2017-2/ (downloaded December 6, 2017).

Tanner, Kathryn. *Theories of Culture: A New Agenda for Theology*. Minneapolis: Fortress Press, 1997.

Tanner, Norman P., ed. *Decrees of the Ecumenical Councils*. Vol. 2, *Trent to Vatican II*. Washington, DC: Georgetown University Press, 1990.

Taylor, Marion Ann and Agnes Choi, eds. *Handbook of Women Biblical Interpreters: A Historical and Biographical Guide*. Grand Rapids, MI: Baker Academic, 2012.

Taylor, Michael. "Include Them Out?" In *Let Love be Genuine: Mental Handicap and the Church*, ed. Faith Bowers, 46-50. London, UK: The Baptist Union, 1985.

Tertullian. "Apology." In *Ante-Nicene Fathers of the Christian Church*, ed. Alexander Roberts and James Donaldson, 3:17-55. Buffalo, NY: Christian Literature Publishing Co., 1885-96; reprint, Peabody, MA: Hendrickson Publishers, 1994.

Thant, Myint-U. "Myanmar's Resurgent Nationalism Shapes New Political Landscape." *Nikkei Asian Review* (October 05, 2017). Online https://asia.nikkei.com/Viewpoints/Thant-Myint-U/Myanmar-s-resurgent-nationalism-shapes-new-political-landscape (downloaded November 22, 2018).

Thompson, John L. *Reading the Bible with the Dead: What You Can Learn from the History of Exegesis That You Can't from Exegesis Alone*. Grand Rapids, MI: William B. Eerdmans, 2007.

Thompson, Philip E. "Re-envisioning Baptist Identity: Historical, Theological, and Liturgical Analysis." *Perspectives in Religious Studies* 27, no. 3 (Fall 2000): 287-302.

Thurian, Max, ed. *Churches Respond to Baptism, Eucharist and Ministry*. 6 vols. Geneva: World Council of Churches, 1986-88.

Tillard, J. M. R. "Liturgical Reform and Christian Unity." *One in Christ* 19, no. 3 (1983): 227-49.

Toom, Tarmo. "Baptists on Justification: Can We Join the Joint Declaration on the Doctrine of Justification?" *Pro Ecclesia* 13, no. 3 (2004): 289–306.

Tomita, Luiza E., Marcelo Barros, and J. Ma Vigil. *Teologia Latino-Americana Pluralista da Libertação*. São Paulo: Paulinas, 2006.

Townes, Emilie. *Embracing the Spirit: Womanist Perspectives on Hope, Salvation, and Transformation*. Maryknoll, NY: Orbis Books, 1997.

————. *Womanist Ethics and the Cultural Production of Evil*. New York: Palgrave Macmillan, 2006.

Trible, Phyllis. *God and the Rhetoric of Sexuality*. Philadelphia: Fortress Press, 1978.

_____. *Texts of Terror: Literary-Feminist Readings of Biblical Narratives*. Philadelphia: Fortress Press, 1984.

Turvey, Samuel T. et al. "First Human-Caused Extinction of a Cetacean Species?" *Biology Letters* 3, no. 5 (October 22, 2007): 537–40. Online https://doi.org/10.1098/rsbl.2007.0292 (downloaded March 6, 2018).

Underwood, T. L. *Primitivism, Radicalism, and the Lamb's War: The Baptist-Quaker Conflict in Seventeenth-Century England*. Oxford: Oxford University Press, 1997.

United Nations High Commissioner for Refugees. "Rohingya Emergency." August 15, 2018. Online http://www.unhcr.org (downloaded Noember 22, 2018).

United States Conference of Catholic Bishops. *Forming Consciences for Faithful Citizenship: A Call to Political Responsibility from the Catholic Bishops of the United States*. Washington, DC: United States Conference of Catholic Bishops, 2015.

United States Lutheran-Roman Catholic Dialogue. *Justification by Faith: U. S. Lutheran-Roman Catholic Dialogue*. Origins: NC Documentary Service, vol. 13, no. 17. Washington, DC: National Catholic News Service, 1983.

U.S. Department of Homeland Security. "Terrorism Prevention Partnerships." Online https://www.dhs.gov/terrorism-prevention-partnerships (downloaded April 25, 2018).

Vaid, Urvashi. *Virtual Equality: The Mainstreaming of Gay & Lesbian Liberation*. New York: Anchor, 1995.

Vanier, Jean. "What Have People with Learning Disabilities Taught Me?" In *The Paradox of Disability: Responses to Jean Vanier and L'Arche Communities from Theology and the Sciences*, ed. Hans S. Reinders, 19-24. Grand Rapids, MI: William B. Eerdmans, 2010.

Vatican Council II. "Dogmatic Constitution on Divine Revelation *Dei Verbum*." Online http://www.vatican.va/archive/hist_councils/ii_vatican_council/documents/vat-ii_const_19651118_dei-verbum_en.html (downloaded April 14, 2018).

_____. "Pastoral Constitution on Church in the Modern World (*Gaudium Et Spes*)." December 7, 1965. Online http://www.vatican.va/archive/hist_councils/ii_vatican_council/documents/vat-ii_const_19651207_gaudium-et-spes_en.html (downloaded April 3, 2019).

Viefhues-Bailey, Ludger. "Looking Forward to a New Heaven and a New Earth Where American Greatness Dwells: Trumpism's Political Theology." *Political Theology* 18, no. 3 (2017): 194–200.

Vigil, José M., Luiza Tomita, and Marcello Barros, ed. *Along the Many Paths to God*. Interreligious Studies, vol. 1. Berlin: LIT Verlag, 2008.

Vischer, Lukas. "The Convergence Texts on Baptism, Eucharist and Ministry: How Did They Take Shape? What Have They Achieved?" *The Ecumenical Review*, 54, no. 4 (October 2002): 431-54.

Wagoner, Brad J. and E. Ray Clendenen. *Calvinism: A Southern Baptist Dialogue*. Nashville: B&H Publishing Group, 2008.

Waalkes, Scott. *The Fulness of Time in a Flat World: Globalization and the Liturgical Year*. Theopolitical Visions, vol. 6. Eugene, OR: Cascade Books, 2010.

Wagua, Aiban. "Present Consequences of the European Invasion of America." In *The Voice of the Victims*, ed. Leonardo Boff and Virgil Elizondo, 47-56. London: SCM Press, 1991.

Wainwright, Geoffrey. E-mail message to Steven R. Harmon. January 12, 2012.

_____. "Word and Table: Fifty Years of Eucharistic Revisions among English-Speaking Protestant Churches." *Archiv Für Liturgiewissenschaft* 50 (2008): 332-55.

Wainwright, Geoffrey and Paul McPartlan, eds. *The Oxford Handbook of Ecumenical Studies*. Oxford: Oxford University Press, 2018-. Print version in development; individual chapters available online, http://www.oxfordhandbooks.com/view/10.1093/oxfordhb/9780199600847.001.0001/oxfordhb-9780199600847 (downloaded April 6, 2019).

Walker, Alice. *In Search of Our Mother's Garden: Womanist Prose*. New York, NY: Harcourt Brace Jovanovich, 1983.

Walker, Michael J. "Baptist Worship in the Twentieth Century." In *Baptists in the Twentieth Century: Papers Presented at a Summer School July 1982*, ed. Keith W. Clements, 21-30. London: Baptist Historical Society, 1983.

Walls, Andrew F. *The Cross-Cultural Process in Christian History: Studies in the Transmission and Appropriation of Faith*. Maryknoll, NY: Orbis Books, 2002.

————. *Crossing Cultural Frontiers: Studies in the History of World Christianity*. Maryknoll, NY: Orbis Books, 2017.

Walsh, James. *The Revelations of Divine Love of Julian of Norwich*. London: Burns and Oates, 1961.

Ward, Haruko Nawata. *Women Religious Leaders in Japan's Christian Century, 1549–1650*. Burlington, VT: Ashgate, 2009.

Ward, Kevin. "Christianity, Colonialism and Missions." In *The Cambridge History of Christianity*, ed. Hugh McLeod, 71-88. Cambridge: Cambridge University Press, 2006.

Ward, Wayne E. "The Worship of the Church." In *The People of God: Essays on the Believers' Church*, ed. Paul Basden and David Dockery, 63-73. Nashville: Broadman Press, 1991.

Watson, Natalie K. *Introducing Feminist Ecclesiology*. Eugene, OR: Wipf and Stock, 1996.

Watson, Nicholas and Jacqueline Jenkins, eds. *The Writings of Julian of Norwich: A Vision Showed to a Devout Woman and a Revelation of Love*. University Park, PA: Pennsylvania State University Press, 2006.

Weaver, C. Douglas. *In Search of the New Testament Church: The Baptist Story*. Macon, GA: Mercer University Press, 2008.

Webster, John. *Dalit Christians: A History*. New Delhi: ISPCK, 1992.

Werner, Dietrich. "Magna Charta on Ecumenical Formation in Theological Education in the 21st Century—10 Key Convictions." *International Review of Mission* 98, no. 1 (2009): 161-70.

Werntz, Myles. "The Body and the Body of the Church: Coakley, Yoder, and the Imitation of Christ." In *Sarah Coakley and the Future of Systematic Theology*, ed. Janice McRandal, 99-114. Minneapolis: Fortress Press, 2016.

————. "The Revelatory Election for U.S. Churches." *The Baptist Standard* (October 12, 2016). Online https://www.baptiststandard.com/opinion/voices/19598-voices-the-revelatory-election-for-u-s-churches (downloaded February 17, 2017).

West, Traci. *Disruptive Christian Ethics: When Racism and Women's Lives Matter*. Louisville, KY: Westminster John Knox Press, 2006.

Westerfield Tucker, Karen B. "North American Methodism's Engagement with Liturgical Renewal." *Liturgy* 26, no. 4 (October 2011): 57–66.

White, Heather Rachelle. "Proclaiming Liberation: The Historical Roots of LGBT Religious Organizing, 1946-1976." *Nova Religio: The Journal of Alternative and Emergent Religions* 11, no. 4 (2008): 102-19.

White, Vera and Charles Wiley. *New Worshiping Communities: A Theological Exploration*. Louisville, KY: Westminster John Knox Press, 2018.

SOURCES OF LIGHT

Whitsitt, William H. *A Question in Baptist History: Whether the Anabaptists in England Practiced Immersion Before the Year 1641?* (Louisville, KY: C. T. Dearing, 1896.

Whitt, Jason D. "Baptism and Profound Intellectual Disability." *Christian Reflection* 45 (2012): 60-67. Online https://www.baylor.edu/content/services/document.php/188185.pdf (downloaded March 10, 2018).

_____. "In the Image of God: Receiving Children with Special Needs." *Review and Expositor* 113, no. 2 (2016): 205-16.

Wiley, Tatha. *Paul and the Gentile Women: Reframing Galatians.* New York: Continuum, 2005.

Wilfred, Felix, ed. *Oxford Handbook of Christianity in Asia.* New Delhi: Oxford University Press, 2014.

Wilhite, David E. "Baptists, Catholicity, and Visible Unity: A Response to Steven Harmon." *Pacific Journal of Baptist Research* 11, no. 2 (November 2016): 3-11.

Wilken, Robert Louis, ed. *The Church's Bible.* Grand Rapids, MI: William B. Eerdmans, 2005-.

Williams, D. H. *Retrieving the Tradition and Renewing Evangelicalism: A Primer for Suspicious Protestants.* Grand Rapids, MI: William B. Eerdmans, 1999.

Williams, Delores. *Sisters in the Wilderness: The Challenge of Womanist God-Talk.* 20th anniversary ed. Maryknoll, NY: Orbis Books, 2013.

_____. "Womanist Theology: Black Women's Voices." In *Black Theology: A Documentary History, Vol. 2: 1980-1992,* ed. James H. Cone and Gayraud S. Wilmore, 265-72. Maryknoll, NY: Orbis Books, 1993.

_____. "Womanist Theology: Black Women's Voices." In *Feminist Theology from the Third World: A Reader,* ed. Ursula King, 77-87. Eugene, OR: Wipf and Stock, 1994.

Williams, Maurice F. "Structure and Form in Church Worship." *The Baptist Quarterly* 18, no. 7 (July 1960): 293-99.

Williams, Roger. "The Bloudy Tenent of Persecution" (1644). In *The Complete Writings of Roger Williams,* vol. 3, ed. Samuel L. Caldwell. New York: Russell & Russell, 1963.

Williams, Rowan. *The Wound of Knowledge: Christian Spirituality from the New Testament to St. John of the Cross.* London: Darton, Longman, and Todd, 2014.

Wills, Gregory A. *Democratic Religion: Freedom, Authority, and Church Discipline in the Baptist South, 1785–1900.* Oxford: Oxford University Press, 2003.

Wintle, Brian, Havilah Dharamraj, Jesudason Baskar Jeyaraj, Paul Swarup, Jacob Cherian, and Finny Philip, eds. *South Asia Bible Commentary: A One-Volume Commentary on the Whole Bible.* Grand Rapids, MI: Zondervan Academic, 2015.

Winslow, Edward. *Hypocrisie Unmasked: a true relation of the proceedings of the Governor and company of the Massachusetts against Samuel Gorton of Rhode Island.* 1646. Reprint, Providence, RI: Club for Colonial Reprints, 1916.

Winward, Stephen F. *The Reformation of Our Worship.* London/Richmond, VA: The Carey Kingsgate Press/John Knox Press, 1964.

Wirzba, Norman. *Food and Faith: A Theology of Eating.* 2nd Edition. New York: Cambridge University Press, 2019.

_____. *The Paradise of God: Renewing Religion in an Ecological Age.* New York: Oxford University Press, 2007.

Worcester, Thomas. "Chinese Rites Controversy." In *The Cambridge Encyclopedia of the Jesuits,* 165. Cambridge: Cambridge University Press, 2017. Online https://doi.org/10.1017/9781139032780 (downloaded March 25, 2019).

World Council of Churches. *Baptism, Eucharist and Ministry.* Faith and Order Paper no. 111; Geneva: World Council of Churches, 1982. Online https://www.oikoumene.org/en/resources/documents/commissions/faith-and-order/i-unity-the-church-and-its-mission/baptism-eucharist-and-ministry-faith-and-order-paper-no-111-the-lima-text (downloaded April 6, 2019).

————. *The Church: Towards a Common Vision*. Faith and Order Paper no. 214. Geneva: World Council of Churches, 2013. Online https://www.oikoumene.org/en/resources/documents/commissions/faith-and-order/i-unity-the-church-and-its-mission/the-church-towards-a-common-vision (downloaded April 6, 2019).

————. "Church Families: Baptist Churches." Online https://www.oikoumene.org/en/church-families/baptist-churches (downloaded March 13, 2019).

————. *Louisville Consultation on Baptism*. Faith and Order Paper no. 97. Louisville, KY: The Southern Baptist Theological Seminary, 1980. Published as *Review and Expositor* 77, no. 1 (Winter 1980).

————. *The Nature and Purpose of the Church: A Stage on the Way to a Common Statement*. Faith and Order Paper no. 181. Geneva: World Council of Churches Publications, 1998.

————. *One Baptism: Towards Mutual Recognition. A Study Text*. Faith and Order Paper no. 210. Geneva: World Council of Churches, 2011. Online https://www.oikoumene.org/en/resources/publications/one-baptism (downloaded April 6, 2019).

Wright, G. Ernest. *The Old Testament and Theology*. New York: Harper and Row, 1969.

Wright, N. T. *Surprised by Scripture*. New York: HarperOne, 2014.

———— (as Tom Wright). *Matthew for Everyone: Part 2, Chapters 16-28*. London: SPCK, 2002.

Wright, Rebecca, Katie Hunt, and Joshua Berlinger. "Aung San Suu Kyi Breaks Silence on Rohingya, Sparks Storm of Criticism." September 19, 2017. Online https://www.cnn.com/2017/09/18/asia/aung-san-suu-kyi-speech-rohingya/index.html (downloaded November 22, 2018).

Yarnell, Malcolm B. III. "Baptists, Classical Trinitarianism, and the Christian Tradition." In *Baptists and the Christian Tradition: Towards an Evangelical Baptist Catholicity*, ed. Matthew Y. Emerson, Christopher W. Morgan, and R. Lucas Stamps. Nashville: B&H Academic, 2020.

Yeager, D. M. and Stewart Herman. "The Virtue of 'Selling Out': Compromise as a Moral Transaction." *Journal of the Society of Christian Ethics* 37 (2017): 3-24.

Yong, Amos. *The Bible, Disability, and the Church: A New Vision of the People of God*. Grand Rapids, MI: William B. Eerdmans, 2011.

————. *A Theology of Down Syndrome: Reimagining Disability in Late Modernity*. Waco, TX: Baylor University Press, 2007.

————. "Zacchaeus: Short and Un-Seen." *Christian Reflection* 45 (2012): 11-17. Online https://www.baylor.edu/content/services/document.php/188189.pdf (downloaded March 5, 2018).

Zabriskie, Alexander C. *Bishop Brent, Crusader for Christian Unity*. Philadelphia: Westminster Press, 1948.

List of Contributors

Raimundo C. Barreto, Jr. (Ph.D., Princeton Theological Seminary) is Assistant Professor of World Christianity at Princeton Theological Seminary in Princeton, New Jersey. He is an ordained minister affiliated with the American Baptist Churches USA and Aliança de Batistas do Brasil.

Mikael N. Broadway (Ph.D., Duke University) is Associate Professor of Theology and Ethics at Shaw University Divinity School in Raleigh, North Carolina. He is an ordained minister affiliated with the National Baptist Convention, USA and the Lott Carey Baptist Foreign Mission Society.

Amy L. Chilton (Ph.D., Fuller Theological Seminary) is Visiting Assistant Professor of Religion at Wingate University in Wingate, North Carolina and Adjunct Professor of Theology at Fuller Theological Seminary in Pasadena, California. She is an ordained minister in the American Baptist Churches USA.

Jennifer W. Davidson (Ph.D., Graduate Theological Union) is Professor of Theology and Worship at American Baptist Seminary of the West and a member of the core doctoral faculty at the Graduate Theological Union in Berkeley, California.

Noel Leo Erskine (Ph.D., Union Theological Seminary, New York) is Professor of Theology and Ethics at Emory University's Candler School of Theology and Graduate Division of Religion in Atlanta, Georgia. He is an ordained minister in the Jamaica Baptist Union of Churches.

Coleman Fannin (Ph.D., University of Dayton) is Assistant Director of the Honors Program and Adjunct Instructor of Religion at Berry College in Mount Berry, Georgia.

Curtis W. Freeman (Ph.D., Baylor University) is Research Professor of Theology and Baptist Studies and Director of the Baptist House of Studies at Duke Divinity School in Durham, North Carolina. He is an ordained minister affiliated with the Cooperative Baptist Fellowship.

Kate Hanch (Ph.D. candidate, Garrett-Evangelical Theological Seminary) is Adjunct Professor at Central Baptist Theological Seminary in Shawnee, Kansas, and Associate Pastor of Youth and Families at First St. Charles United Methodist Church in St. Charles, Missouri. She is an ordained minister affiliated with the Cooperative Baptist Fellowship.

Steven R. Harmon (Ph.D., Southwestern Baptist Theological Seminary) is Associate Professor of Historical Theology at Gardner-Webb University School of Divinity in Boiling Springs, North Carolina. He is an ordained minister affiliated with the Cooperative Baptist Fellowship.

Derek C. Hatch (Ph.D., University of Dayton) is Associate Professor of Christian Studies at Howard Payne University in Brownwood, Texas.

Stephen R. Holmes (Ph.D., King's College, University of London) is Senior Lecturer in Theology, Principal of St. Mary's College, and Head of School of Divinity at the University of St. Andrews in St. Andrews, Scotland, United Kingdom. He is an ordained minister accredited by the Baptist Union of Scotland.

May May Latt (Ph.D., Lutheran School of Theology at Chicago) is Metadata Analyst for Atla (previously American Theological Library Association), International Student Services Coordinator at Lutheran School of Theology at Chicago in Illinois, Adjunct Professor of Hebrew Bible at Central Baptist Theological Seminary-Wisconsin, and Interim Minister at Myanmar Milwaukee Christian Church affiliated with the American Baptist Churches USA-Wisconsin.

Atola Longkumer (D.Th., Senate of Serampore College [University]) taught Religions and History of Christian Missions at Leonard Theological College, Jabalpur, and South Asian Institute of Advanced Christian Studies in Bangalore, India and currently is the 2018-2019 Mission Scholar at the Overseas Ministries Study Center in New Haven, Connecticut.

Nora O. Lozano (Ph.D., Drew University) is Professor of Theological Studies at Baptist University of the Américas and Executive Director of the Christian Latina Leadership Institute in San Antonio, Texas.

Molly T. Marshall (Ph.D., The Southern Baptist Theological Seminary) is President and Professor of Theology and Spiritual Formation at Central Baptist Theological Seminary in Shawnee, Kansas. She was ordained as a Southern Baptist in 1983 and received privilege of call from the American Baptist Churches USA in 1997.

Courtney Pace (Ph.D., Baylor University) has served as Associate Professor of Church History and Director of Admissions at Memphis Theological Seminary in Memphis, Tennessee. She is an ordained minister affiliated with the Cooperative Baptist Fellowship and The Alliance of Baptists.

Rady Roldán-Figueroa (Th.D., Boston University) is Director of Diversity, Equity, and Inclusion and Associate Professor of the History of Christianity at Boston University School of Theology in Boston, Massachusetts.

Cody J. Sanders (Ph.D., Brite Divinity School, Texas Christian University) is American Baptist Chaplain, Harvard University, Cambridge, Massachusetts and Pastor, Old Cambridge Baptist Church, Cambridge, Massachusetts. He is an ordained minister affiliated with the Alliance of Baptists and the American Baptist Churches USA.

Susan M. Shaw (Ph.D., The Southern Baptist Theological Seminary) is Professor of Women, Gender, and Sexuality Studies at Oregon State University in Corvallis, Oregon. She is an ordained Baptist minister who now makes her church home in the United Church of Christ.

Rebecca Horner Shenton (Ph.D., Fuller Theological Seminary) is Adjunct Professor of Christian Ethics at Gardner-Webb University School of Divinity in Boiling Springs, North Carolina. She is an ordained minister affiliated with the Cooperative Baptist Fellowship.

Philip E. Thompson (Ph.D., Emory University) is Professor of Systematic Theology and Christian Heritage at Sioux Falls Seminary in Sioux Falls, South Dakota. He is an ordained minister in the American Baptist Churches USA.

Myles Werntz (Ph.D., Baylor University) is Associate Professor of Christian Ethics and Practical Theology and T. B. Maston Chair of Christian Ethics at Hardin-Simmons University's Logsdon Seminary in Abilene, Texas.

Jason D. Whitt (Ph.D., Baylor University) is Senior Lecturer in the Honors Program at Baylor University in Waco, Texas. He is an ordained minister affiliated with the Baptist General Convention of Texas.

Khalia J. Williams (Ph.D., Graduate Theological Union), is Assistant Dean of Worship and Music, Assistant Professor in the Practice of Worship, and Co-Director of the Baptist Studies Program at Emory University's Candler School of Theology in Atlanta, Georgia. She is an ordained Baptist minister.

Author and Subject Index

349

United Nations High Commissioner for Refugees, 120, 128n21
United States Conference of Catholic Bishops, 10, 223, 224n16, 229, 284
United States Lutheran-Roman Catholic Dialogue, 284n20
Ursinus, Zacharias, 201
Vaid, Urvashi, 117
Van Doren, Charles, 301n19
Vanier, Jean, 142
Vashti (Queen), 120-131
Vatican Council I, 79, 222-23
Vatican Council II, 10, 16, 18, 82, 151-52, 219, 222, 224, 229, 242-45, 256, 279, 284, 286
Viefhues-Bailey, Ludger, 193n2
Vigil, Jose M., 151n34, 154n46, 157
Vischer, Lukas, 280n8, 286n24
Viswanathan, Gauri, 56n15
Vivian, C. T., 31
Vocation, 111, 163, 165, 167, 207, 243-45, 247n36
Von Bora, Katherine, 77
Von Schurman, Anna Maria, 78
Waalkes, Scott, 254
Wace, Henry, 175n12
Wagoner, Brad J., 233n9
Wagua, Aiban, 147n16
Wainwright, Geoffrey, 281n10
Walker, Alice, 84, 101-03
Walker, Michael J., 259, 261n49
Walls, Andrew F., 62, 145
Walsh, James, 185n12, 185n14, 192
Ward, Haruko Nawata, 55n12
Ward, Kevin, 57n21
Ward, Mary, 78
Ward, Wayne E., 259n46
Watson, Natalie K., 89, 97n34, 98
Watson, Nicholas, 185n16, 187n21, 192
Weaver, C. Douglas, 205
Webster, John, 58n26
Wells, Samuel, 254n7
Werner, Dietrich, 278n3
Werntz, Myles, 11-12, 236n18
Wesley, Susanna, 80
West, Cornel, 234n11
West, Mona, 119, 307
West, Morris, 281n10
West, Traci, 275n13
Westerfield Tucker, Karen B., 257n33
Westminster Confession, 175n6, 202-03
Westminster Larger Catechism, 202
Westminster Shorter Catechism, 202
White supremacy, 27, 64n 4, 66-69, 71, 73-74, 85-87, 275

White, Ellen G., 81
White, Heather Rachelle, 111n5, 11n8, 11n11
White, James F., 260n53
White, Vera, 276
Whiteness, 7, 63-75, 92
Whitley, W. T., 178n22, 181n38
Whitsitt, William H., 178
Whitt, Jason D., 140n25, 141n26
Wicca, 265
Wieman, Henry Nelson, 30
Wild-Wood, Emma, 147n20
Wiley, Tatha, 297n13
Wilfred, Felix, 53n1, 54n6, 55
Wilhite, David E., 2n7
Wilken, Robert Louis, 304n31
Willard, Frances, 80
Williams, D. H., 174n4, 177n20
Williams, Delores S., 84, 86, 93n16, 98, 103-04
Williams, Maurice F., 255n17
Williams, Roger, 72, 250n53, 72, 113, 115, 238
Williams, Rowan, 237n19
Wills, Gregory A., 205
Wilmore, Gayraud D., 32n13, 33n15, 37, 104n10
Winslow, Edward, 5n17, 211n21
Wintle, Brian, 308
Winward, Stephen F., 258n38, 260nn51-52, 260n54
Wirzba, Norman, 161n12, 162-63
Witness, common, 287-88
Wollenstonecraft, Mary, 78
Woman's Auxiliary of the National Baptist Convention, 82
Womanist theology, 2n4, 7, 16, 17n3, 25-26, 32-36, 43, 84, 89, 93, 95, 100-07, 127
Women's Christian Temperance Union, 80
Women's Missionary Union, 69, 82
Women's movement, 35, 60, 88, 94
Women's Political Council, Alabama State College, 31
Worcester, Thomas, 55n12
World Alliance of Reformed Churches, 286
World Christianity, 56, 62, 120-121, 128-131, 145-47, 153, 156-57
World Communion of Reformed Churches. *See* World Alliance of Reformed Churches
World Council of Churches, 5n16, 11n23, 18, 153, 179, 218, 275, 277, 278n3, 279, 280nn7-9, 281n12, 282nn13-14, 283, 284n18, 286, 293n1
World Mennonite Conference, 288
World Methodist Council, 285, 286n25, 289
World Missionary Conference (Edinburgh 1910), 61, 279

Scripture Index

Acts
2:1-41, 293-94, 297
5:29, 198, 204
10:34-35, 297
10:47, 297
15:6-11, 297
20:28, 278

Romans
8:19-23, 8, 158
10:9, 174
12:1-3, 234-36
13:1-2, 196
13:1-4, 203

1 Corinthians
1:18, 135
1:25, 135
1:27, 135
11:1, 252
11:3, 36
12, 140
12:2, 291
12:26, 231
15:58, 169

2 Corinthians
5:17, 36, 232
13:3, 176

Galatians
3:28, 94, 297

Ephesians, 162
4:1-6, 234
5:22-23, 36

Philippians
2:2, 232
2:12, 112
2 Timothy
4:2, 229

James
1:19, 295
2:18, 110
2:18-26, 112

1 Peter
2:14, 200
5:2, 278

1 John
3:1, 109n3
3:23-25, 187

3 John
9-10, 204

Revelation, 162, 241
2:29, 306
12:10, 195